Critical Political Studies
Debates and Dialogues from the Left

A collective picture of modern capitalism suggests that economic prospects, political costs, and implications for human development and freedom under this system are grim indeed. However, the possibility of an alternative viewpoint, and an alternative system, provide grounds for optimism. The authors in *Critical Political Studies* challenge the neoliberal, pro-market ideology that has arisen in the age of the so-called "post-communist" new world order, wrestling with the implications of globalization, democratization, and the politics of radical social change.

Written as a tribute to the remarkable intellectual career of Colin Leys, the debates in this book deal with some of the most pressing problems confronting the majority of citizens in both First World and Third World contexts. Their contributions provide the confidence to pursue new possibilities that permit a more optimistic, if critical, outlook. Topics covered include contemporary debates about globalization and the nation state, African development, prospects for British socialism after Blair, social movements, and current issues in political and social theory.

ABIGAIL B. BAKAN is professor of political studies, Queen's University.
ELEANOR MACDONALD is associate professor of political studies, Queen's University.

Critical Political Studies

Debates and Dialogues from the Left

EDITED BY
ABIGAIL B. BAKAN AND
ELEANOR MACDONALD

McGill-Queen's University Press
Montreal & Kingston · London · Ithaca

Legal deposit second quarter 2002
Bibliothèque nationale du Québec
Pages 11–35, © Colin Leys 2002
Pages 281–318, © Laurie E. Adkin 2002

Printed in Canada on acid-free paper that is 100%
ancient forest free (100% post-consumer recycled),
processed chlorine free, and printed with vegetable-
based, low VOC inks.

McGill-Queen's University Press acknowledges the
financial support of the Government of Canada through
the Book Publishing Industry Development Program
(BPIDP) for its activities. It also acknowledges the
support of the Canada Council for the Arts for its
publishing program.

National Library of Canada Calatoguing in Publication Data

Main entry under title:
    Critical political studies: debates and dialogues from
the left
Essays from a conference held in honour of Colin Leys,
Nov. 1996.
Includes bibliographical references.
ISBN 0-7735-2251-4 (bound).—ISBN 0-7735-2252-2 (pbk.)

    1. World politics—1989– . 2. Economic history—
1990– . 3. Political science—History—20th century.
4. Leys, Colin, 1931– . I. Bakan, Abigail B. (Abigail
Bess), 1954– II. MacDonald, Eleanor, 1959– III. Leys,
Colin, 1931–

JA66.C754 2002   320.9'049   C2001 902707 9

This book was typeset by True to Type in 10/12 Sabon.

Contents

Acknowledgments

The publication of this book is the product of a genuinely collective effort. The original conference that inspired this collection, Critical Political Studies: A Conference in Honour of Colin Leys, took place in November 1996. It relied upon numerous contributions from organizations and individuals, all of which were crucial to its success. Our thanks are extended to the Social Sciences and Humanities Research Council of Canada, Studies in Political Economy, and the following organizations at Queen's University: the Arts and Science Undergraduate Bursary Program, the Campus Bookstore, the Department of Geography, the Department of History, the Department of Political Studies, the Faculty of Arts and Science, the Institute of Women's Studies, the Principal's Office, the School of Graduate Studies and Research, the Program of Studies in National and International Development, and the Visiting Scholars Program. We also want to extend our warmest thanks to Grant Amyot, Susan Anderson, Pauline Bettney, Boris Castell, Karen Dubinsky, Josie de Leon, Ena Dua, Thelma Fernando, Suzanne Fortier, Shirley Fraser, Lynn Freeman, Godwin Friday, Jessie Fyfe, Bernice Gallagher, David Haglund, Roberta Hamilton, David Himbara, John Holmes, A.P. Hurd, Allan Jeeves, Kanga Kalisa, Paritosh Kumar, Eva Lazar, Jayant Lele, Margaret Little, George Lovell, Rianne Mahon, Evelyn McCaugherty, Barb Murphy, Kwasi Ofori-Yeboah, Steve Page, Frank Pearce, Frances Shepherd, Marianne Smith, Robert Stock, Wisdom Tettey, Hilary Wainwright, and Phil Wood.

In the sometimes arduous transition from a conference to a readable publication, the original community spirit that launched this project found new and reinvigorated expression. Our thanks go to Don Akenson, Philip Cercone, and Roger Martin of McGill-Queen's University Press for their ongoing support and encouragement. Thanks also go to Claude Lalumière, Kyla Madden and all of the highly professional editorial and production staff at McGill-Queen's.

For contributing generously to the success of this publication, we would like to thank the following offices at Queen's University: the Office of Research Services, the Department of Political Studies, the Office of the Dean of the Faculty of Arts and Science, the School of Policy Studies, the Department of Geography, the Department of History, and the Advisory Research Committee. We are especially grateful to the following individuals: Sandra Crocker, Steve Page, John Dixon, Keith Banting, John Holmes, Paul Christianson, and Evelyn Peters.

A special word of thanks is owed to Marcus Pistor and Lorie Scheibelhoffer for their expert editorial and administrative assistance. The unending support of Paul Kellogg, Adam McNally, Rachel Kellogg, Marney McDiarmid, and Grace MacDonald ensured that the editors never lost heart as the project progressed to completion.

A final note goes to Colin Leys. Colin allowed us to focus far more attention on his contributions in both scholarship and life than his modest temperament would normally permit. For this – and his energy, inquisitive mind, and trust – we are eternally grateful.

Whatever strengths may surface in this collection are the product of this monumental team effort. Any errors or weaknesses are the responsibility of the editors alone.

Abbreviations

APEC	Asia Pacific Economic Co-operation
CBS	Central Bureau of Statistics
CIDA	Canadian International Development Agency
the City	"The City of London": London's financial district
DFRD	District Focused Rural Development
EU	European Union
FDI	Foreign Direct Investment
FORD	Forum for the Restoration of Democracy
FTA	Free Trade Agreement
FTAA	Free Trade Area of the Americas
GATT	General Agreement on Tariffs and Trade
GDP	Gross Domestic Product
GNP	Gross National Product
GSU	General Services Unit
ILO	International Labour Organization
IMF	International Monetary Fund
IPPG	Inter-Parties Parliamentary Group
KWNS	Keynesian Welfare National State
MAI	Multilateral Agreement on Investment
MNC	Multinational corporation
NAC	National Action Committee on the Status of Women
NAFTA	North American Free Trade Agreement
NGO	Non-governmental Organization
NIE	Newly Industrializing Economy
NSMT	New Social Movement Theory

OECD	Organisation for Economic Co-operation and Development
R & D	Research and Development
SWAPO	South West African Peoples' Organization
TFP	Total Factor Productivity
TNC	Transnational corporations
TUC	Trades Union Congress
UN	United Nations
UNTAG	United Nations Transitional Assistance Group
WTO	World Trade Organization

Biography:
Colin Temple Leys

Colin Leys is one of the world's foremost scholars of African politics, British politics, development theory, and left political thought. He has made significant contributions in all of these fields, having written or edited over fifteen books and penned dozens of articles, reports, and book chapters. His work includes the path-breaking study, *Underdevelopment in Kenya*, published in 1977; the comprehensive analysis of British politics, *Politics in Britain: From Labourism to Thatcherism* (revised for second publication in 1989); and a challenging critique of development politics and theory, *The Rise and Fall of Development Theory*, published in 1996. He has contributed to the *Annual Register*, the *Encyclopaedia Africana*, and *The Listener*. He has been a manuscript co-editor of *Studies in Political Economy* and served on the editorial advisory board of the *Journal of Modern African Studies* and the *Review of African Political Economy*. He has also co-edited *The Socialist Register*, and the *Journal of Commonwealth and Comparative Politics*. His most recent publications are *Namibia's Liberation Struggle*, with John Saul, and *The End of Parliamentary Socialism*, with Leo Panitch (both published in 1997).

Colin Leys began his teaching career at Balliol College in Oxford in 1953 and went on to hold positions as principal of Kivukoni College in Tanganyika, professor and head of the Department of Political Science in Makarere University College in Uganda (1962–65), fellow of the Institute of Development Studies (1967–70), professor and joint head of the Department of Political Theory and Institutions at the University of Sheffield, and professor of Political Studies at Queen's

University in Kingston, Canada until 1997. He has also been visiting fellow and visiting professor at a number of universities including Princeton University (1954–55), the University of Chicago (1964), the University of Nairobi (1969–71), the Université du Québec à Montréal (1989), and the Centre for Development Research in Copenhagen (1989). He is currently professor emeritus at Queen's University in Kingston.

In addition to his academic work, Colin Leys has been an active contributor to educational, political, and economic development. In 1966 he was a member of the Banwell Commission on the Electoral System in Mauritius and played an important role in the development of the University College of Mauritius. He was consultant to the Ndegwa Commission on the Structure and Remuneration of the Civil Service in Kenya in 1970 and 1971. He was also consultant to the United Nations Institute for Namibia in 1983–84 and Observer for the Canadian Council for International Cooperation in Namibia in 1989. He co-founded and coordinated from 1983 to 1987 the Programme of Studies in National and International Development at Queen's University.

In 1996, a conference was held at Queen's University to honour the contributions and scholarship of Colin Leys. Conference delegates included fellow researchers, colleagues, students, and friends. This book, like the conference, is a celebration of his much admired and respected work and, we hope, a part of the continuing tradition of critical political studies that Colin has played such an important role in building.

Critical Political Studies

Introduction
From Colin Leys to Counter-Hegemony: Debates and Dialogues from the Left

ABIGAIL B. BAKAN AND
ELEANOR MACDONALD

As we enter the new millennium, a rising interest in social change and the prospects for the achievement of social justice is capturing the imaginations of intellectual communities and wider social forces in countries around the world. This sentiment was expressed with explosive determination when the World Trade Organization's Millennium Round Meeting was successfully shut down by mass protests in Seattle, Washington, USA, in late November and early December of 1999. Since that time, a new movement for global justice has found its voice. Yet the sentiment that found expression in Seattle did not emerge from nowhere. For months and years prior to the Seattle events, many critical scholars and social activists were involved in developing a challenge to the unbridled rule of global capitalism and its neoliberal agenda. This volume represents one expression of, and hopefully a modest contribution to, such a critical enterprise.

The majority of the articles included in this volume are based on papers originally presented at a conference on Critical Political Studies that took place in November of 1996 at Queen's University, in Kingston, Ontario, Canada. The conference drew together leading intellectuals from North America, Europe, and Africa who collectively are part of a tradition in political studies that is committed to progressive social change.

The conference participants shared a common critical stance: challenging the recognized dominance of neoliberalism and pro-market ideology that had arisen in the age of the so-called "post-communist" new world order. More specifically, the conference was held to honour the contributions of Colin Leys to such a critical tradition on the occasion of his retirement from over twenty years as a professor at Canada's Queen's University. The articles collected in this volume are not, however, typical of a festschrift. Instead, the authors share an engagement in and commitment to the many areas of critical political studies to which Colin Leys has devoted, and continues to devote, scholarly attention.

A shared commitment among the authors, one that links the articles in this volume with the work of Colin Leys, is to increased democratic justice and democratic practice. Colin Leys's work is unique in its simultaneous emphasis on the sharpest critical theoretical clarity and the most detailed empirical focus. The body of scholarship developed by Colin Leys includes a remarkable breadth of expertise over a range of issues and a vast geographic expanse. This combination is, in large measure, why his contributions have inspired scholarship in such a wide variety of academic disciplines, and over so many parts of the world. This broad scope is reflected in the articles in this volume.

While some of the articles address particular contributions by Colin Leys in contemporary contexts – notably the pieces by John Saul (regarding Leys's work on Africa) and Anne Phillips (on his theorization of the political) – others offer original perspectives on the various debates in which Colin Leys has played a central part over the decades. This volume combines widely recognized and established authors with a new generation of critical scholars, many of whom were at one time students of Colin Leys. Contributions span from the First World to the Third World; they move from political economy to social movement theory; and they engage in debates, from the role of social democracy to the politics of amnesty. Central to all of them is a determination to map a road towards an effective alternative to the devastating and destructive impact of globalized capitalism in an age of neoliberalism – whether this is seen in social, economic, ideological, environmental, or theoretical terms. The centrality of the political, however, is a thread of continuity. There is a shared commitment both to understanding the political economy of prevailing powers, and to untangling the ideological hegemonic web that supports them. At the same time, these articles are far from a uniform exegesis of a left "platform." On the contrary, at the heart of this collection is a willingness to engage, head on and without hesitation, in some of the thorniest debates regarding the development of a critical counter-hegemonic project in contemporary conditions.

As with the protests in Seattle, the overriding theme that can be identified to run through this volume is a critical challenge to the politics and praxis of globalization in an age of neoliberalism. To this end, various elements are emphasized by different authors. These elements include the politics and political economy of globalization, strategies for socialism and social change, and the political relevance and impact of theory and ideology. Moreover, the articles combine a varying emphasis on broad issues of theory and politics with specific case studies. Each of these themes is briefly outlined below in the context of the various articles presented in this collection.

One of the most important challenges for the left today is explaining the issue of globalization and the role of the nation-state. Few dispute the importance of international processes in the course of contemporary state and international policy. Indeed, Colin Leys was among the most astute in studying the impact of international imperialism and neo-colonialism in Africa, decades before it was fashionable to do so. However, there is far less unanimity regarding precisely what the nature of the interrelationship between global and national state forces are today.

In his opening article, Colin Leys poses the parameters of this debate. Using Britain as a fulcrum for a wider analytical discussion, Leys notes that the mainstream literature on globalization is "surprisingly unhelpful" in determining what the current global reality is in truth demanding of the state. The adjustments to the role of the nation-state, formerly advocated by the Conservative Party and, currently, by the governing Labour Party cannot clearly be read as responses to globalization. He proceeds to examine the deeper contradictions within the functioning of the state in capitalist society more generally, particularly between the economic concentration of power in capital and the political power of the voting electorate. Identifying Britain as possibly the industrialized country that has gone furthest down the road of marketization, Leys insists that, though there is a marked tendency of globalization to confine national governments to working within the policy parameters approved by the owners of capital, to presume a simple predetermined path along such lines is neither theoretically nor empirically justified.

The issue of the impact of globalization in British politics is continued in the first part of this collection. The articles by Robert Jessop, Leo Panitch, and Alex Callinicos further engage in the debate regarding the wider implications of recent shifts in British politics. Jessop revisits the role of Thatcherism in terms of the issue of internationalization. This article picks up a thread from an earlier debate on the impact of Thatcherism in which both Robert Jessop and Colin Leys were actively engaged through the 1980s. Given the staunchly pro-market bent of Tony Blair's New Labour policies, the implications of the inheritance of Thatcher's Britain continues to be of central relevance. Beyond the issue of the dialectical relationship between the nation-state and globalization, however, this section of the volume also addresses the specific questions posed by social democracy as a strategy for transformation. Leo Panitch maintains that Tony Blair's Labour Party marks a decisive shift in party policy away from the socialist content, or at least from the possibility of socialism, in a social-democratic project. Citing the political vacuum posed by the failures of both the Communist and social democratic parties at the end of the twentieth century, Panitch, with the clarified vision of hindsight, examines in particular the rise and fall of the "new left" strategy of Tony Benn in the 1970s. Alex Callinicos, taking a similar starting point, emphasizes a different aspect of the debate. Callinicos argues that Tony Blair's Labour Party advanced and accelerated ideological currents already developing prior to his leadership. Callinicos stresses the contradictory pressures within the Labour Party and among the British electorate, but sees a distinctive feature in the strained relationship that the Labour Party under Blair may be developing with its formal base in organized labour.

The engaged preoccupation with concrete political strategies for change continues as a thematic strand into the second section of the volume. One of the most unique features of Colin Leys's intellectual life has been his ability to develop internationally acclaimed expertise in both the First and Third Worlds. Moving from the country case study of Britain, arguably the oldest corner of the industrialized world, to the continent of Africa, ravaged by capitalism but reaping few of its purported benefits, John Saul, Bruce Berman, Lauren Dobell, Bonnie Campbell, and Michael Chege wrestle with issues concerning structural adjustment, political change, and the theoretical implications for development and underdevelopment. Central to the study of these African countries is also the question of development strategy and the prospect for an effective anti-imperialist agenda. For these authors, globalization is a familiar theme. Despite a considerable distance from the early dependency/class debates in time and context, the normative challenge of achieving development and democratic practices in an international system that favours profit and market driven multinationals is taken as given.

In a reflective piece on their joint collaboration of over thirty years, John Saul engages with the various self-reflective intellectual transitions of Colin Leys's work on African development; not least in this discussion is Leys's internationally acclaimed contributions to the relationship of class and capital to the "dependency debates." At issue, Saul maintains, is striking a balance between Leys's determination to be boldly realistic, refusing to hide from the harsh realities of capitalist exploitation and its impact on human suffering, while avoiding the risk of falling into a despairing moment of pessimism. The latter Saul refers to as "Afropessimism," a view that negates the potential for local initiative, solidarity, and human agency. Following this general discussion on prospects for African development, are several country case studies where the themes of globalization and state action, or what could be considered the relationship between the international and the national levels, are explored.

In Bruce Berman's careful explication of the contradictions of the development of the state in Kenya over the fifty-year period after 1945, the tragic implications of a failed democratic project in the African context are explored. Drawing on a dialectical synthesis of economic, political, and cultural explanatory criteria, Berman's article acts as one case study in the African tragedy. Bonnie Campbell's exploration of the political aspects of structural adjustment in Côte d'Ivoire acts as another. Campbell exposes the highly interventionist role of multilateral funding agencies, such as the International Monetary Fund (IMF) and the World Bank. These organizations not only demanded internal institutional reform but also control over the process of legitimizing such reform along specifically political lines. Lauren Dobell turns to another type of state experience in Africa, the development agenda for an independent Namibia. However, she similarly examines the domestic impact and options regarding international agencies. To complete this section, Michael Chege offers a powerful contribution to the debate over "race" as a variable in the political economy of Kenya. Taking issue with race- and culture-based arguments in Kenyan political analysis, Chege argues for analyses that focus more on political and economic structures and "social capital" to explain the different material achievements of socio-cultural groups.

In the third part of the collection, ideologies and perspectives for change are examined in the context of political economy, political repression, and social movements in a comparative context. Two pieces that grapple with the big economic picture, one by Manfred Bienefeld and the other by Abigail B. Bakan, open this section of the volume. The former paints a devastating picture of the universally espoused new hegemony of advancing market development policy and development theory over recent decades. Bienefeld challenges the ability of modern development policy to claim the unchallenged hegemonic position it seeks. He attempts to outline some of the most central "imbalances and contradictions" present within the model so celebrated by pro-market international development policy advocates. The article by Abigail B. Bakan specifically focuses on one element of the contemporary international political economy, the global trade arrangements exemplified by the Asia Pacific Economic Co-operation (APEC) group and the Multilateral Agreement on Investment (MAI). Contrary to those who have stood at the graveside of radical theory in the age of the end of history, Bakan maintains that classical Marxism, and the works of Marx himself, are well suited to explaining the politics and policies that have animated the international ruling class in formulating these accords.

Phil Goldman continues to unpack the relevance of ideology, but shifts the framework from political economy to politics. He examines the idea of "amnesty" in a comparative international context. Focusing boldly on the experiential reality of political repression, Goldman explores the intersections of law, justice, and state policy. He does this by weaving together in-depth theoretical problematization with examples that include experiences of victims of the Nazi Holocaust, women in the former Yugoslavia, South African victims of apartheid, prisoners of the junta in Greece, and survivors of torture in Asian and Latin American settings. Goldman grapples with the difficult issues of obtaining justice in the aftermath of profoundly unjust, and painful, circumstances. Moving from a focus on the harsh realities of a system bent on hardship and suffering, the remaining contributions in this section consider strategies to change it, specifically the role of social movements. Laurie Adkin considers the rise and fall of social movement theory, specifically the post-Marxist emphasis on the role of new social actors in the 1980s. Drawing on the cases of the political ecology movements in Canada and France, Adkin argues for an approach to collective action that is neither trapped by moral relativism nor reductionism. She proposes to emphasize a view of collective action for social change that maintains a focus on the relationship between structural conditions and social agency. Marguerite Mendell continues the exploration of social movements in Canada, but examines more specifically the particular links between the labour movement and the activist community in Québec through the 1980s and 1990s. Mendell attempts to unpack the concept of the "social economy" and its relevance for theorizing more broadly the politics and practice of social movements in a period dominated by a neoliberal policy regime.

While all of the articles in this collection are notable for their careful attention to the intersection between analytical clarity and historical reality, it is in the fourth section that several issues specific to contemporary critical theory are explored. The articles by Phillips, Desai, Helvacioglu, and MacDonald serve to develop the growing debate regarding the sufficiency of socialist theory for such contemporary issues as representation, political struggle, ethics, and the status of theory itself. Each is informed especially by the challenge to socialist theory that postmodern theory has represented.

Anne Phillips notes the importance of the "return to the political" and its renewed emphasis on representation and rights as critical to contemporary left dialogue. The struggle for political equality is significant, not least for the possibilities for actual procedural and institutional change that it provokes. Phillips also suggests the need to balance the emphasis on institutional political equality with a broader analysis that includes economic and social as well as political factors. Banu Helvacioglu takes up a similar challenge, that of rethinking the relationship of the individual to social movements and political structures. She focuses on the need for an ethical-political stand that would attend to the specific needs for individual recognition, community solidarity, and the analyses of particular conjunctures. Helvacioglu argues that the modern, liberal resolution of the tension of individual and community was founded in a tempting combination of illusion (of the universality of reason as foundation, for example) and promise (of a future in which this tension would not exist). Postmodernity has rendered these solutions untenable while offering instead an ethics of aporia: the demand to be ethical within an open acknowledgment of the tension and uncertainty of our times. In her article, "Fetishizing Phantoms," Radhika Desai takes harshly to task Chantal Mouffe and others who have found Carl Schmitt's theoretical work useful to their own radical democratic project. Schmitt's anti-rational, anti-liberal theorization of the political, Desai argues, is directly and fundamentally linked to his totalitarian sympathies. Moreover, Desai finds that postmodern theorists are naive in thinking they can adopt aspects of Schmitt's framework while successfully resisting its inherently authoritarian political consequences. In the final article of this section, Eleanor MacDonald explores the theoretical ambivalence of postmodern theory towards its own emergence. A sampling of the works of Jean-Francois Lyotard, Jean Baudrillard, and Jacques Derrida indicates some common themes. These include, for example, an emphasis on technology, which they use to explain the relationship of their theories to their times. Consistently, according to MacDonald, their theories appear to point to the need for theories other than their own to explain, illuminate, and situate their work and its appeal.

One of the themes running through the various pieces in this collection is more difficult to delineate with reference to any specific single article or group of articles. This involves the Gramscian problematic of building a counter-hegemonic force based on maintaining an optimism of the intelligence and a pessimism of the will.[1] The collective picture of modern capitalism presented here is one demanding profound pessimism. The general trajectory of the system, in terms of its economic prospects, its political costs, and the tragedy of its implications for human development and freedom, is grim indeed. However, the prospects for an alternative viewpoint, an alternative system, and for the power of concerted resistance to the status quo, generates grounds for optimism. Various emphases regarding the scope of optimism of the will are presented in the articles that follow. There is certainly no single voice that represents the totality or variety of perspectives. However, the debates that are delineated go to the centre of some of the most pressing problems posed to ensure the most optimistic outcome possible for the majority of citizens who live and work and suffer and struggle in these difficult and challenging times. If these contributions can carry forward the confidence to pursue these issues perhaps a more optimistic, if critical, outlook will find some grounding in reality.

NOTES

1 Gramsci's formulation was, according to his editors and translators, Quinton Hoare and Geoffrey Nowell Smith, drawn from Romain Rolland and made "into something of a programmatic slogan as early as 1919, in the pages of Ordine Nuovo." (Antonio Gramsci, *Selections from the Prison Notebooks,* ed. and trans., Quinton Hoare and Geoffrey Nowell Smith, International Publishers: New York, 1971: 175n75.)

National Politics in a Global Economy: Reflections on the British Experience

COLIN LEYS

It is no longer possible to understand the national politics of any country – except perhaps those of the one remaining superpower – without analysing the impact of global market forces. The economic environment can no longer be treated as a fixed parameter, still less a dependent variable. The influence on a country's domestic policies of external agencies like the World Trade Organization (WTO), or foreign investors in the bond markets, is now as significant in the politics of most Organization for Economic and Cooperative Development (OECD) countries as the influence of the International Monetary Fund (IMF)/World Bank and the Paris Club has always been in the politics of underdeveloped countries. Indeed what used to be the domain of "development theory" often reappears as the domain of "international political economy." In place of "development strategies" we have "national competitiveness strategies"; in place of debates about "national bourgeoisies" versus "compradors," debates about "national champions" versus "footloose corporations."

Britain, which played a leading role in the global deregulation project and where a programme of liberalization and privatization has been carried further than in any other OECD country, is a significant case in point. Any account of British politics since the mid–1980s has to explain, among other things, the transformation of the Conservative Party from a pan-British organization for pragmatically adjusting business interests to those of other classes and groups into a vehicle for a purely English brand of conservative nationalism, social authoritarianism, and dogmatic economic neoliberalism; and the transformation of the Labour Party from a social-democratic political partner of the labour movement (however semi-detached) into an elite-controlled professional machine increasingly oriented to and funded by business and committed to retain the legacy of the previous four Conservative administrations. This legacy involves the reorganization of the BBC and all the social services, including the National Health Service, on "quasi-market" principles; the transformation of the civil service from a coherent patrician apparatus for socio-economic management into a collection of effectively unaccountable market-oriented "executive agencies"; and the emasculation of local democracy by the removal of most local government powers, including effective powers of local taxation – not to mention a severe restriction of trade union rights, a radical redistribution of the tax burden in favour of capital and the highest-paid, a sharp curtailment of civil liberties, and an increase in police powers.

How far, and in what ways, is this phenomenal set of changes in British politics and government – nothing short of a constitutional revolution, pushed through by *force majeure* – linked with or due to the deregulation and globalization of the economy? How far are its current dynamics determined by global market forces? Globalization has been central to the rhetoric of both the neo-conservative leadership of the Conservative Party and the "modernizing" leadership of the Labour Party. Global market forces have been constantly declared to be the "new reality" to which everything must now be adjusted. What is the truth of these claims, and what are the consequences of accepting them? This chapter does not pretend to answer these questions nor can it trace the causal links between globalization and the dramatic reconfiguration of British politics in the 1980s and 1990s. What it does attempt is to explore the no less radical reorientation of political science that is needed if such questions are to be answered.

THE GLOBALIZATION LITERATURE

The mainstream literature on globalization is surprisingly unhelpful. The question posed in most of it is how far globalization has reduced the policy autonomy of national governments, and the results have been signally inconclusive. For some authors, "globalization is largely a myth"[1]; for others, "the nation-state can no longer be held accountable on the very issues which ... affect the daily lives of those it purports to represent ..."[2]

Three reasons for this inconclusiveness stand out. First, in this discourse the focus tends to be on global data, not on the situation in any particular country. Given that the accumulation process is inherently uneven, both geographically and in other ways, and that countries vary so widely in terms of their size, resource mix, capital stock, trading position, and socio-cultural formation, the effects of globalization are bound to vary widely as well. Second, the globalization literature, written mainly by economists and students of international relations, tends to focus on policy, not politics. It asks what economic and social policy options are now open to "governments," which, in this discourse, consist simply of "elites" who represent no particular class or interest but just make choices, in which they show more or less "will," competence, or courage.[3] Suzanne Berger remarks that globalization has opened up new space for "political vision and choice" but that it remains to be seen whose politics will dominate this space. This view is not shared by those who have studied the relative strengths of capital and labour in the lobbying process in Brussels.[4] In short this literature largely ignores the fact that global market forces also have a strong influence on the balance of social forces within countries, and hence on the politics of national responses to globalization.[5]

A third weakness, noted by Robert Wade, is the failure of so much of this debate to focus on what happens *at the margin*. For example, the fact that the low-wage "South" accounts for only 16 per cent of world exports of manufactures does not mean that this is not a powerful force driving down employment and wages in the "North." This can occur through a wide range of *tendencies*, including the defensive shifting of production to lower-wage sites abroad by manufacturers in the North, or the use of cheaper immigrant labour or labour-saving innovations, which result in downward pressure on wages, all reinforced by the threat of unemployment and weakened state of trade unions.[6]

The literature on "convergence" comes closer to the question of how global market forces affect national politics. Here the focus is not just on how far global competition drives governments to adopt similar policies but also on how far it reshapes national institutions and practices (public and private) to make them more like those of other countries. Here too, however, the results are rather inconclusive insofar as the question asked tends to be whether convergence is occurring or not, rather than what kind of politics globalization tends to encourage.[7]

The theorists who have come closest to examining globalization's impact on national politics tend to be those who are interested in establishing regional or global institutions capable of regulating the global market – understandably, since for this to happen there must be appropriate political agents at the national level.[8] What follows has much in common with the thinking of this current in the literature, but with the direction of attention reversed. Instead of asking what political forces can be expected to support the supranational regulation of markets, we ask a prior question: i.e., what effects global market forces are likely to have on domestic political forces.

MODELLING THE MARKET-STATE RELATIONSHIP UNDER GLOBALIZATION

We begin with a traditional political-economy conceptualization of the market/state relationship: the process of accumulation depends on state power to separate labour from the means of production and then to provide security and enforce order and the rights of property. A state form that separates economics from politics makes this possible by making exploitation and inequality seem natural results of free-market transactions. The logic of capitalist accumulation nonetheless tends to destroy the social structure in which the market is embedded. In Polanyi's formulation, the unregulated ("self-regulating") market, by treating land, labour, and money purely as commodities, tends to destroy the environment and the social bonds in which the market is embedded.[9]

The state in capitalist society is correspondingly contradictory. If it is democratic to any significant extent there is a contradiction between the economic power of capital and the political power of voters.[10] If it is not democratic, the distinction between politics and economics is eroded, which tends both to delegitimize exploitation (raising the transaction costs of production) and to distort the operation of market competition (through rent-seeking and monopolies). This contradiction can be expressed as one between the logic of accumulation (driven by a calculus of profitability) and the logic of legitimacy (driven by electoral considerations or some equivalent calculus of coercion/ consent).

So long as capitalist production was confined within the boundaries of states, the two logics interacted in a kind of homeostatic system. When the economic system lost legitimacy because of its social and political costs, this could be periodically remedied by political interventions – the society-preserving side of Polanyi's historical "double movement" (see below). Loss of confidence on the part of capitalists, on the other hand, and hence loss of output growth, employment, consumption, and state revenues, due to state regulation of the market, was responded to by periodic drives to deregulate – at some expense of democracy, where it existed. The mechanisms of adjustment between the two logics could be costly and even violent, or more or less normalized, as in the eras of "social liberalism" and social democracy.[11] The existence of a plurality of states also facilitated the necessary class compromises by permitting these to be based on appeals to nationalism.[12]

Until the 1970s industrial production – as opposed to trade or finance – could still only be carried on to a limited extent outside a few core countries. By the 1970s, however, technological changes, the development of the transnational corporation, and the industrialization of some formerly underdeveloped regions meant that most kinds of production could now be carried on in a much wider range of countries.[13] At the same time, faced with growing balance of payments constraints and declining competitiveness, and the challenge of new left movements responding to the crisis of the post-war Keynesian welfarist/Fordist system, the US government, strongly supported by Britain, effectively enforced a worldwide liberalization of markets, beginning with financial markets.[14] The crucial sanction was the free international movement of capital, achieved by the mid-1980s. A potentially global field of action now existed for all three circuits of capital (commodities, finance, and production).

As a result the mutual adjustment of the two logics no longer operated as before. In relation to any given nation-state, capital now had the option of "exit," not just "voice."[15] The balance of power shifted away from states. The alternative was either regional or global structures exercising the "pooled" sovereign powers of states over globalized capital. But so far all such structures – the EU, the OECD, NAFTA, the WTO, the Bank for International Settlements, and the IMF – have been shaped primarily by and for capital, not by popular forces. Global government – let alone democratic global government – remains a utopian ideal.[16] States continue to confront globalized capital largely on their own. The resulting imbalance is manifested in three main ways: the "discipline of the bond markets," "regulatory arbitrage" by direct corporate investors, and pressures for trade liberalization or protection.[17]

The most fully integrated sector of the global economy is finance: "with instantaneous communication and information flows among the major markets, passive capital and unexploited investment opportunities will not long be kept apart by national borders."[18] In seeking to equalize the risk-discounted rates of return on capital everywhere, capital markets put all national government policies into their equations. The limits imposed depend on investor psychology (for example, at times of loss of confidence in global stability they may move their money home or to the "safest" centres; they are more demanding when neoliberal ideas are in the ascendant, and so on), but government policies are always crucially at issue because they affect the risk that investors may not get the return they have counted on.[19] Each country's whole policy "package" is closely monitored by investment advisors and credit agencies.[20]

This does not mean that national policy packages become identical; on the contrary they may differ very widely, as Hirst and Thompson and other "skeptics" rightly insist; for instance in 1998 the level of government spending – the neoliberals' shibboleth par excellence – varied dramatically, from 30.5 per cent of GDP in the USA to 56.6 per cent in Sweden.[21] There may be a tendency for some elements in the packages to get more similar under the pressure of global market sentiment, as convergence theories suggest; but for the capital markets what always finally matters is each individual package as a whole, the "bottom-line" differences between them being registered in significantly varying interest rates; for example low wages may be offset by low productivity and high political risk (as in many sub-Saharan African countries), high wages and high taxes by high productivity and low political risk (as in Germany). What the markets are ultimately sensitive to is not so much the make-up of each package as the threat of adverse changes in it.[22] At any given time, therefore, most governments can no longer change interest rates to set them below (or the money supply above) what the capital markets approve, or pursue fiscal policies – or indeed any significant social or economic measure – of which the markets disapprove, without the risk of paying a high cost: a falling exchange rate, worsening balance of payments, capital flight, curtailed growth and heightened long-run cost of capital – or even a capital drought.

Foreign direct investment (FDI) exerts only slightly more specific kinds of pressure. Before undertaking any investment, corporate investors look for the most favourable national "regulatory regime" – the country with the lowest corporate taxation, or "the least burdensome environmental constraints, or whose government pursues the most favourable industrial policy, or which offers the most advanced telecommunications facilities or the most attractive tax breaks for R & D activities. *Indeed anything and everything a government does which affects the competitiveness of those firms which must have some latitude in their cross-border locational choices must come under scrutiny.*"[23]

Sol Piciotto, a leading authority on international taxation, goes so far as to say that "the growth of the TNC (transnational corporation) in the characteristic form of an international network of related companies carrying on business in different countries in a more or less integrated way, is to a significant extent attributable to the opportunities it has to take advantage of regulatory differences, or 'regulatory arbitrage.'"[24]

As with the financial markets, the pressure exerted by TNCs is effective at the margin, because states stand to gain by reducing their regulatory requirements below those of other states. Then, once the investment is made, investors not only resist any new measures seen as liable to reduce after-tax profitability but also press for further regulatory changes to match those offered later elsewhere.

FDI pressures are unlike capital-market pressures in being sector-specific, and hence have more readily visible effects. However, because of unemployment, inflows of FDI tend to be seen as a positive gain whose costs (such as weaker workplace or trade union rights, tax concessions and subsidies, reduced environmental protection, etc.) are less apparent (more indirect and diffuse, or more easily delayed and concealed) than the jobs created. The evidence suggests that although FDI is less mobile than financial capital – so that states have, in theory, some leverage over firms with major investments in their countries – it does lead to significant continuing reductions in regulatory regimes.[25] The experience of Canada, Fred Lazar noted in 1996, strongly suggests that "in the absence of international ... rules to ... regulate the activities of companies, global corporations will be able to dictate more aggressively the economic and social agendas for even the largest industrialised countries."[26] Seen from the vantage point of the late 1990s, this prediction would seem to have been vindicated.

The third general effect of global market pressures is trade liberalization. Here the pressure comes from global producers and traders, as well as from governments supporting domestic exporters, but the logic is more complicated. First, as Helleiner points out, trade issues have the opposite "collective action" dynamic from that of capital markets and FDI.[27] A government raising (or keeping) trade barriers – which under WTO rules will mostly be non-tariff barriers – can benefit from "free riding" on other governments' more open trade regimes. Second, individual sectors – often backed by their workforces – want protection in domestic markets, even though they may also want access to markets abroad. So, whereas the tendency of globalized capital markets and FDI is towards further deregulation, the tendency of global trade is more mixed, and apt to veer back towards protection unless this is policed by some supranational agency and sanctioned by the other states. In practice, states get away with a good deal, even under the EU "single market" rules.[28]

Of the three forms of pressure, those of the capital market probably pose the most serious legitimation problem in the long run. They are the most comprehensive and far-reaching, and the least visible. The social costs they impose are dispersed; "financial markets" seem abstract and impersonal (although it should be noted that it has taken a sustained ideological effort to achieve this naturalization of what used to be demonized as the "gnomes of Zurich" – or of Wall Street). They place tight limits on changes in government policy and yet cannot be blamed for doing so without seeming to question market supremacy itself.

All these are indeed only tendencies, but they are tendencies too strong for most medium-sized countries to resist. National-level "demand-side" economic management is now widely seen to be impossible unless it is concerted between the G7 states, but no mechanisms exist to overcome the collective action problem involved in achieving such concertation. The declining contribution to tax revenues by corporations and higher income earners has made taxes more regressive and revenue bases smaller: the average contribution of corporate taxation to the revenues of the OECD countries fell from roughly 11 per cent to 7 per cent from the mid-1970s to the mid-1990s. Virtually all governments have capped social security spending (the income transfers crucial to legitimation) and some have significantly reduced it.[29] Governments increasingly feel themselves limited – apart from trying to maintain non-tariff barriers to imports – to making "supply-side" policy changes aimed at enhancing the value-adding potential of investments (typically investments in education, training, or communications), which ought therefore to be approved by investors. They feel their freedom of action to be greatly reduced, even in regard to many issues that voters might consider "non-economic," and they search for costless measures – including so-called "symbolic" policies – that may gain some electoral credit.

To sum up this discussion: the *tendency* of the globalized economy is to confine national governments to policy courses approved of by the owners of capital. There is no doubt still "a great deal that governments can do" – but increasingly only on condition that it conforms to the interests and values of capital. The scope of national government action may not have greatly changed (sovereignty-pooling excluded), but the forces determining the direction of it undoubtedly have.

THE END OF THE "DOUBLE MOVEMENT"?

Hitherto, theorists of the relation between politics and capitalism have seen the social costs of capitalist accumulation as self-correcting – whether they conceived of the relation as an unstable equilibrium tending towards crisis and overthrow (Marx), a long-term self-adjusting system (Polanyi's double movement), or as a more or less stable equilibrium (liberal democracy and social democracy); and those who insist, non-trivially, that "policy can still shape global forces" must also assume that the accumulation process still tends, in one way or another, to generate a counter-movement that will sooner or later give rise to governments willing and able to impose themselves on market forces again. But history has so far not given much support to those who think like this. Horsman and Marshall, for example, writing in early 1994, thought that governments could still sponsor national welfare programmes, and cited as evidence President Clinton's promise of national health care, and "his high-stakes call for higher taxes and targeted spending on infrastructure" – both of which he was soon forced to abandon.[30] And Robert Boyer's belief, expressed in 1995, that the 1990s would "probably experience a major turning point, from pro-market and conservative strategies towards more solidaristic policies oriented by rejuvenated state intervention in the domains of taxation, welfare, innovation and education," has also been disappointed.[31] What grounds are there, then, for thinking that market forces still tend to generate the social forces necessary for a counter-movement?

Much might seem to depend on whether in the longer run global competition tends to continue to intensify labour (through longer hours and speed-up), increase insecurity (through re-casualization and unemployment), and drive down unskilled workers' incomes (and their "social wage") towards some no longer nationally determined level of subsistence, as has been happening in the countries following the "Anglo-American" model. At some point we might reasonably expect a profound political reaction, but other features of the contemporary accumulation process seem to work against this. The four main factors identified by Marx as tending to mobilize the working class – concentration, homogenization, immiseration, and organization – no longer operate unequivocally to generate resistance to the market in the countries of the North. Let us look briefly at each of these.

First, the initial experience of urban and industrial *concentration* combined a number of different experiences – social dislocation, economic hardship and insecurity, the collective memory of a pre-capitalist order based on social ties and principles of social justice – and the vision of a new (socialist) order to replace it. Today, however, the urbanization of the rural population is largely complete. Many large industrial cities have been contracting, as has average plant size; the share of casual, part-time, and self-employment has risen; homeworking has revived. Both residence and work have thus tended to become less concentrated.

In the nineteenth century workers were *homogenized* in the sense that the pre-capitalist division of labour was broken down and parochial loyalties were displaced. It became possible to construct a new social identity, that of the British or German (etc.) *worker*, with a class consciousness opposed to that of capital. Now, the decline of manual work, the shift from secondary to tertiary industries, and the feminization of the workforce have increased differentiation at work. Housing patterns have tended to become more diverse, weakening the physical and community foundations of class identity. The homogenization that is occurring seems to be primarily in respect of lifestyles and tastes, identifying people with global markets. Such a homogenization works against tendencies for people, as producers, to oppose market forces on the basis of any national or local interest.[32]

A hundred and fifty years ago in western Europe varied and severe forms of *immiseration* were widely experienced: on the one hand the intensification of physical labour through long hours, "speed-ups," and downward pressure on wages; on the other, unemployment and all the other forms of social insecurity. Contemporary immiseration in the North, by contrast, mainly takes the form of the social marginalization of a working class minority through unemployment and homelessness and insecure, casual, and low-paid employment.[33] These are effects of globalization, partly through the competition offered by some 1.2 billion low-paid workers who have been added to the global wage labour force since the mid-1980s – roughly doubling its size – and partly through the accelerated search for profitability by labour-shedding on the part of companies facing intensified competition.[34] Because both forms of immiseration tend to be concentrated in particular sectors of the workforce and particular regions, many of the victims tend to be socially marginalized and to lack electoral leverage.[35] In addition they receive social security support, which however inadequate is increasingly represented as a form of charity on the part of those in work, reducing feelings of solidarity between the waged and non-waged population. So far the unemployed have been a negligible political force. Even those in work but threatened with unemployment have only occasionally generated wider anti-market responses, and electorates have in practice endorsed continual reductions in social security benefits.[36]

The wider implications of rising income inequality might nonetheless be thought likely to provide a long-run basis for anti-market responses. The less states redistribute income, the more unequal its distribution within any given country must become as global competition exerts constant downward pressure on the wage levels of the less skilled. In Britain between 1979 and 1994 income inequality almost doubled.[37]

In the USA real wage fell 20 per cent over the same period; by the mid-1990s there were over three million millionaires and 1.7 million prisoners; the country celebrated the millennium by incarcerating its two millionth prisoner in February 2000. One of the fastest-growing fields of employment was security guards.

Yet in the short run, at least, the chief effect of growing income inequality is to not mobilize a movement for equality but reduce social solidarity. Richard Wilkinson, for example, has argued persuasively that it is the declining sense of social solidarity caused by growing income inequality that is responsible for falling health levels as well as for family breakup, poor educational achievement by children, crime, and suicide in the industrialized countries.[38] He believes that the economic and psycho-social costs of living in an unequal society will lead to the revival of the necessary political "will" to change this,[39] but other responses seem just as likely. For example, what most commentators noted, in the approach to the British 1997 general election after seventeen years of deliberately heightened inequality, was not opposition to this trend but cynicism and political apathy, even on the part of voters dependent on state support.[40] This should not really be surprising, given that "market forces" are seen as allocating resources impersonally, so that, as Wilkinson notes, no-one can be held responsible for the social consequences (and "global" market forces sound even more remote and impersonal).[41] What is clearly involved here is a potent ideological hegemony, still in its prime; to weaken its grip would require the counter-hegemonic efforts of an established party, with access to the mainstream media, determined to show the market to be socially inefficient and anything but impersonal. The absence of such parties is itself a consequence of global market forces. "By the 1990s, socialists and social-democrats throughout Europe were converging upon neo-revisionist positions ... propelled by the contingency of everyday politics and the pressure of electoral considerations."[42]

This brings us, finally, to political *organization*. In the nineteenth century organization was a seemingly natural response to the experience of concentration, homogenization, and immiseration. The weakness of popular political organization today (especially the decline in union density and political influence) reflects the contemporary weakness or ambiguity of these same trends. The vision of an alternative social order inherited from the nineteenth century has also been discredited. The progressive wing of the intelligentsia, displaced by the "market research" strategists from the inner councils of left parties and weakened by the loss of secure state employment, shows few signs of being likely soon to produce a replacement for it. The potential for anti-market politics is also limited by the enormously enhanced role of the mass media, which themselves are increasingly market-driven.[43] Against these negatives must certainly be set the proliferation of non-party social movements, but even after the "battle of Seattle" their potential for making a serious challenge to the power of global market forces remains unclear.

This review of the implications of globalization for the revival of Polanyi's double movement has been very brief and is no doubt open to challenge. The onus, however, is on those who hold, non-trivially, that "policy can shape global forces," to make that challenge, and to suggest what tendencies are likely to generate political forces capable of sustaining such policies – and at the necessary global level, too. Unless such a case can be made, it is hard to resist the conclusion arrived at by Wolfgang Streeck: "Cut off, quasi-constitutionally, from control over the economy, democracy may thus become preoccupied with symbolic politics, or locked into a regressive populism that blames the social dislocations caused by a self-regulating international market on excessive regulatory intervention in national affairs."[44] This is not an unfair summary of the central positions of the right wing of the Republican Party in the USA, the Front Nationale in France, the Freedom Party in Austria, the People's Party in Denmark, and so on.

NATIONAL COMPETITIVENESS STRATEGIES AND "SYMBOLIC POLITICS"

There was plenty of evidence to support Streeck's hypothesis in British politics in the run-up to the 1997 election: on the one hand, the adoption by "New Labour" of "symbolic" policies on such unpromising fields for state action as "parenting," on the other, the crude right-wing and chauvinist populism of the so-called "Euroskeptic" – actually Europhobic – wing of the Conservative Party. An even more general effect of globalization on party politics, however, is the prevalent discourse of "national competitiveness" strategies. The wish to *seem* in control leads governments to represent themselves as managers of national "teams" competing with appropriate "strategies" in the "global marketplace."

These strategies, which are largely ideological representations of existing institutions and practices that individual governments can in fact alter very little, fall into two broad categories, individual-based and group-based. The former see competitiveness as arising from the capital and skills possessed by the country's economically active *individuals* – the "market-based," "Anglo-American," or "Hong Kong" (etc.) model; the latter understands it as arising from many kinds of *co-operation*, organized through institutions – the "institution-rich," "Nippo-Rhineland," "social-cohesion" model.[45]

Market-based strategies are easier to espouse insofar as they assign a very limited role to government. According to these strategies, governments serve their countries' interests best if they simply protect the freedom of individual citizens to compete in global markets, allowing them to deploy their entrepreneurial talents and acquired skills and assets. Paradoxically, this kind of strategy is often legitimized by appeals to nationalist sentiment, even though what it involves is a maximal surrender of national autonomy to global market forces. This is possible thanks to what Streeck aptly calls a "democracy illusion" (by analogy with Keynes's "money illusion") on the part of voters[46]; the social costs of giving away political autonomy through economic liberalization are blamed not on market forces but on alleged external obstacles to their effective operation (including, of course, "Brussels").

"Social-cohesion" strategies are harder to sustain since social cohesion can only be maintained by defending the institutions that support it ("generous" social security systems, egalitarian fiscal systems, "stakeholder" systems of corporate governance, and anti-takeover laws, etc.) – institutions targeted for contraction or abolition by the deregulatory thrust of global market forces. It remains to be seen how far "social-cohesion" strategies will be sustained in countries like Sweden or Germany where the cultural commitment to social-cohesion institutions is longest-established.[47] In countries where such an institutional framework would have to be introduced, such as Britain, the difficulties look so great that it seems very doubtful if this could come about through "normal" electoral politics. The resistance of capital would be fierce, the cultural obstacles would be intractable and, since the economic pay-offs are long-term, any party championing the introduction of a social-cohesion package could not count on being rewarded for it electorally. It was significant that the modernizing leadership of "New Labour" in Britain, after momentarily flirting with the idea of a real social-cohesion strategy under the rubric of "stakeholding," abandoned it as its real political implications began to be questioned by capital.[48] The result was a reversion to market-based policies wrapped in social-cohesion rhetoric, such as have increasingly been adopted by former social-democratic parties everywhere.[49] With the honourable exception of France's Lionel Jospin, Europe's social-democratic leaders endorsed the distinctly vapid discourse of the "Third Way," adopted by the British Prime Minister Tony Blair to try to lend an air of social-democratic principle to his accommodation with neoliberalism.[50] It is hard to disagree with Gary Teeple's conclusion that for the moment "we have arrived at the end of the period of independent national politics, and the neoliberal agenda is so far the only agenda taking us into the era of the global economy."[51]

GLOBALIZATION AND
NATIONAL POLITICS IN BRITAIN

The constraints imposed on national government policy-making feed back, most immediately and influentially, into the thinking and strategies of party leaders. This accounts not just for the switch to symbolic politics, regressive populism, and national competitiveness ideologies but also for drastic changes in party organization. The realization that national-level Keynesianism was no longer viable played an important part in leading the Labour Party's "modernizers" to "reposition" it as a born-again "party of business," facing the "new reality" of global markets. To do this meant disempowering both the party's left-wing activists and the leaders of the trade unions affiliated to the party, which were still supplying most of its funding. By 1997 they had succeeded; power had been effectively concentrated in the hands of the leader and a small group of senior colleagues and their professional political staffs[52]; and with the party's huge parliamentary majority after the election in May of that year the process was pushed steadily forward until nothing effectively remained of the party's former cumbrous but real institutions of internal democracy and its famous "broad church" of ideas.

It could be said, of course, that the modernizers were responding primarily to four successive election defeats (1979, 1983, 1987, and 1992), which seemed to turn mainly on domestic issues, and only secondarily to the implications of globalization. But the two were intimately connected; as Teeple puts it, "Neoliberal [domestic] policies ... represent the political requirements of capital internationalized, highly centralized and global in perspective."[53] The electorate's reluctance to vote for Labour from the late 1980s onwards, when public opinion was already flowing quite strongly against the Conservatives' continuing neoliberal programme, cannot be explained in terms of Conservative propaganda alone; there was a common-sense understanding that the economic changes that the Conservatives had promoted were now a global fact of life that had to be lived with, and that Labour had not yet adapted to doing so. "New Labour's" eventual acceptance of these changes, therefore, was at one and the same time an accommodation to both electoral and global economic realities.

The spectacular triumph of this approach in the election of May 1997, in which Labour won two-thirds of the seats with 44 per cent of the votes cast, owed much to the vagaries of the British electoral system[54]; but it owed even more, perhaps, to the division within the Conservative ranks over Europe. The neoliberal Euroskeptics in the Conservative Party, in their opposition to any further integration, including monetary union, undoubtedly had various motivations, from hostility to the Christian-Democratic/Social-Democratic mainstream in the European Parliament to – in some cases – simple xenophobia. In bringing the party to the brink of disaster they demonstrated all too clearly that a party closely tied to capital in a globalized economy faces a painful difficulty: capital's interests are increasingly supranational, but votes remain national. Many large companies were increasingly alarmed; corporate contributions to the party's funds declined, forcing it to seek funding increasingly from overseas capital looking for present or future favours (a large part of the Conservatives' estimated £12-15 million election budget in 1997 was believed to have been raised abroad, especially in Hong Kong)[55] – a practice that the incoming Labour Government promised to ban.

Even the issue of parliamentary corruption ("sleaze"), which also played a prominent role in the Conservatives' collapse (especially the so-called "cash for questions" scandal, in which a number of Conservative MPs were found to have accepted, or even solicited, substantial payments to use their influence with Ministers or in Parliament on behalf of business interests), had global origins.[56] It reflected the culture of greed ("an enterprise culture") encouraged by the "national competitiveness" discourse of Mrs Thatcher in the 1980s; but the drastic increase in income inequality of these years, which was strongly influenced by global competition in corporate boardrooms, posed real problems for MPs whose sources of income outside Parliament did not keep pace with those in the private sector. Not just CEOs – and the egregious young foreign exchange dealers who set new standards of conspicuous consumption with their huge salaries and bigger bonuses in the American-driven "Big Bang" deregulation of the City of London's financial services sector in 1986 – but many people in "middle management" were now paid two or three times as much as an MP. Aspirations changed. In his diary for 24 December 1987, the former Conservative Minister of State Alan Clark commented ironically on the 1980s cult of self-enrichment and conspicuous consumption by bewailing his inability to afford servants with "only" £700,000 in his "Crazy-High-Interest" bank account and concluded: "I'm bust, virtually."[57] The temptation was great for less fortunate and less talented Conservative MPs – or any MP with social ambitions – to try to make politics pay; and it will be apt to remain so as long as MPs' salaries remain pegged at a mere 200 per cent or so of average national incomes – another problem of democratic legitimacy posed by globalization.

In the aftermath of the election it thus became apparent that the party's failure to police the attitudes of its candidates and MPs on this issue and the decay of its local associations (whose members had become seriously out of touch with public opinion) had been disastrous weaknesses.[58] The Conservative Party now needed a "modernization" quite as radical, in its way, as Labour's, covering its policies, its bases of financial and electoral support, and its organization. Its new leader William Hague, who replaced John Major in 1997, set about this process, creating new institutions to link the membership to the party leadership, giving them a substantial share in the election of the leader, and aiming to increase the membership to a million by 2000.[59] By the end of the 1990s divisions over Europe, and Labour's occupation of so much traditional Conservative policy, continued to paralyse the party, which in September 1999 had only 25 per cent support in the opinion polls, compared to Labour's 52 per cent.[60]

THE ANALYTIC CHALLENGE

Limitations of space make it impractical to try to analyze here the parallel connections between global economic forces and the other changes in British politics outlined earlier in this chapter.[61] By this point it should be clear, however, that the real analytic challenge posed by globalization has hardly begun to be confronted. At every point the analysis leads away from the relatively simple logic of the altered relationship between national economic forces and states or governments to the complex dynamics of the mutual interaction of global market forces with national, economic, and social structures, the resulting interplay of cultures and ideologies, and their political effects.

The neoliberal project, which was aimed primarily at "rolling back" the social-democratic state and social-democratic social policy, and disposing of the threat they posed to the independence of capital at the end of its golden age, resulted this time in a global economy in which "self-regulating" market forces are constantly destabilizing national social and political structures. The old Marxian concept of a self-reproducing "social formation" is put in question; so is the old liberal concept of democracy. It is necessary finally to dispense with models of democracy inherited from nineteenth century liberal utopian thought, constructed around the concepts of sovereignty, mandate, ministerial responsibility, and the rest – models already collapsing under the weight of the qualifications needed to keep them even nominally serviceable – and construct sufficiently sophisticated new models of "actually existing liberal democracies": i.e., national politics as they actually operate under the ceaseless pressures of forces whose momentum derives from sources external to the political system. A Kuhnian "paradigm shift" is overdue.

New models will have to start out from the fact that significant areas of collective life have been shifting – through privatization and through the marketization of more and more branches of the state – from the domain of politics to that of markets (with a corresponding contraction of democracy, unequal purchasing power replacing equal voting power). These new models will have to consider that at some point this shift can indeed make government "a pale auxiliary of the market system."[62]

Perhaps no other industrial country has yet gone as far down this road as Britain, but many have been travelling along it – and the process has a tendency to gather momentum. Consumerist ideology gradually becomes pervasive, increasing the appeal of individual choice and of maximizing real personal disposable income, and so leading to "tax aversion" on the part of voters, and thus to still further contractions of state activity. As the reach and autonomy of national government contract, popular identification with the ideals and institutions of collective consumption is further eroded. There is a "domino" effect. The conception of social services and security as a universal right is replaced by the idea that they are forms of public charity for the disadvantaged. Once it is accepted that trains are best run for profit, why not nursing homes, and if nursing homes, why not hospitals? The logic is essentially the same. It is made to feel more and more natural by people's daily experience of life as both workers and consumers, which in turn makes it easier for governments to ignore and even stigmatize the victims; before long it is accepted that supporting the unemployed, single mothers, or even the aged, in such a way as to enable them to continue to function as full members of society, is "unaffordable."

With fewer and fewer areas of life ring fenced from market determination, however, and with markets themselves increasingly global in scope, the reshaping of the social base on which politics rests tends to become increasingly unpredictable and rapid. Industries arise and disappear within generations. Cultural patterns are equally swiftly transformed, especially through international migration, MNC-driven taste homogenization, and accelerating technological change in the media (which is also driven by the global competition of multinational corporations). Party politics become less and less predicated on fixed economic interests or social identities, at the same time that parties in office are less and less able to influence the forces that are shaping these identities. The new breed of political strategists who undertake to steer parties to electoral victory by discovering the political "products" currently most desired by the voters, and the "images" most likely to sell them, are a logical outcome of this situation.[63] What these new political strategists have grasped practically, political science is still far from adequately grasping theoretically.

NOTES

I am specially grateful to Alan Zuege for invaluable help, both intellectual and technical, in revising this chapter.

1 Paul Hirst, "Is Globalization a Threat to the State? Ten Key Questions and Some Unexpected Answers," paper presented to the Sovereignty Seminar, Birkbeck College, 19 February 1997: 23.
2 Matthew Horsman and Andrew Marshall, *After the Nation State: Citizens, Tribalism and the New World Disorder*, London: HarperCollins, 1995: 217.
3 E.g., Paul Hirst and Grahame Thompson, *Globalization in Question: The International Economy and the Possibilities of Governance*. Cambridge: Polity Press, 1996: 17; and Hirst, "Is Globalization a Threat?" 21.
4 Suzanne Berger, "Introduction," in Suzanne Berger and Ronald Dore (eds), *National Diversity and Global Capitalism*, Ithaca: Cornell University Press, 1996: 25; but cf. S. Mazey and J. Richardson, *Lobbying in the EEC*, London: Oxford University Press, 1993; and J Greenwood and K. Ronit, "Interest Groups in the EEC," *West European Politics*, vol. 17, no. 1, January 1994.
5 Among the exceptions see especially Vivien A. Schmidt, "The New World Order, Incorporated: The Rise of Business and the Decline of the Nation-State," in *What Future for the State: Daedalus*, vol. 124, no. 2, Spring 1995: 75–106, which particularly stresses the loss of "deliberative democracy" at the national level. A recent critical recapitulation of the issues from a political economy perspective that helps to restore intellectual coherence to the debate is Hugo Radice, "Taking Globalization Seriously," in Leo Panitch and Colin Leys (eds), *Global Capitalism Versus Democracy: Socialist Register 1999*, London: Merlin Press, 1999: 1–28.
6 Robert Wade, "Globalization and Its Limits: Reports of the Death of the National Economy Are Greatly Exaggerated," in Berger and Dore, *National Diversity*, 68, 76–7.
7 See for instance the diverse positions of the contributors summarized in Berger and Dore, *National Diversity*, 11. The convergence literature has, however, produced valuable case studies and attempts to systematize the forms and scope of the various kinds of pressure towards convergence: see, e.g., Ronald Dore, "World Markets and Institutional Uniformity," in Geraint Parry (ed.), *Politics in an Interdependent World*, Cambridge, Cambridge University Press, 1994: 52–65; and Robert Boyer, "The Con-

vergence Hypothesis Revisited: Globalization but Still the Century of Nations?" in Berger and Dore, *National Diversity*, 48–9. A good summary of the limitations of all convergence theses is J. Rogers Hollingsworth and Wolfgang Streeck, "Countries and Sectors," in Hollingsworth, Philippe C. Schmitter and Streeck (eds), *Governing Capitalist Economies*, New York and Oxford: Oxford University Press, 1994: 284–8.

8 See especially Susan Strange, "The Limits of Politics," *Government and Opposition*, vol. 30, no. 3, Summer 1995: 291–311; Strange, "Global Government and Global Opposition," in Geraint Parry (ed.), *Politics in an Interdependent World*, London: Edward Elgar, 1994: 20–33; Wolfgang Streeck, "Public Power Beyond the Nation-State: The Case of the European Community," in Robert Boyer and Daniel Drache (eds), *States Against Markets: The Limits of Globalization*, London: Routledge, 1996: 299–315; and Eric Helleiner, "Post-Globalization: Is the Financial Liberalization Trend Likely to Be Reversed?" ibid., 193–210, especially 205–6.

9 Karl Polanyi, *The Great Transformation*, New York: Rinehart, 1957.

10 "The classes whose social slavery the constitution is to perpetuate, proletariat, peasants, petty-bourgeoisie, it puts in possession of political power through universal suffrage. And from the class whose old social power it sanctions, the bourgeoisie, it withdraws the political guarantees of this power ..." Marx, "The Class Struggles in France," in Marx and Engels, *Collected Works, Vol. X*, London: Lawrence and Wishart, 1978: 79.

11 Cf. Adam Przeworski, *Capitalism and Social Democracy*, Cambridge: Cambridge University Press, 1985.

12 Joachim Hirsch, "Nation-state, international regulation and the question of democracy," *Review of International Political Economy*, vol. 2, no. 2, Spring 1995: 267–84.

13 Peter Dicken, *Global Shift*, London: Chapman, second edition 1992.

14 Eric Helleiner, *States and the Re-emergence of Global Finance*, Ithaca and London: Cornell University Press, 1994; and Philip G. Cerny (ed.), *Finance and World Markets: Markets, Regimes and States in the Post-Hegemonic Era*, Aldershot: Edward Elgar, 1993.

15 Even fixed capital, while relatively immobile, was becoming less so and formed a declining component of the total capital structure even in manufacturing (Wade, "Globalization and its Limits," 85–7).

16 On global politics and institutions see, e.g., David Held et al., *Global Transformations; Politics, Economics and Culture*, Stanford: Stanford University Press, 1999: 49–86. On the EU see Bernard Moss, "Is the European Union Politically Neutral? The Free Market Agenda," in Bernard Moss and Jonathan Michie, (eds), *The Single European Currency in National Perspective: A Community in Crisis?*, London: MacMillan, 1998: 141–67. Some optimists imagine that a new world order introduced by "enlightened elites" will establish a system of regulation in the

global "public interest" at the global level (see The Group of Lisbon, *Limits to Competition*, Cambridge, MA, and London, England: MIT Press, 1995: 121 ff.), but more realistic writers envisage only such global developments as will reduce the risks to capital. The Multilateral Agreement on Investment, prepared by the staff of the OECD, was a good example; it would in effect have permanently barred any state from independently increasing its regulation of capital.

17 The following section, looking successively at capital markets, FDI, and trade liberalization/protection, follows the pattern of Vincent Cable's lucid discussion in "The Diminished Nation State: A Study in the Loss of Economic Power," *What Future For the State?* (op. cit.), 23–53; he also speculates about the kind of politics that will characterize the state in the global economy (national competitiveness strategies, identity politics, and defensive nationalism).

18 Ben Steil, "Competition, Integration and Regulation in EC Capital Markets," in Vincent Cable and David Henderson (eds), *Trade Blocs? The Future of Regional Integration*, London: Royal Institute of International Affairs, 1994: 155. "Globalization skeptics" point to the persisting differences in national interest rates, and the high correlation between domestic savings and investment rates, to suggest that even capital markets are not a significant global market force. People who operate on these markets tend to speak a different language, however. In 1990 Theodore Levitt wrote, for instance, that "a change of ten basis points in the price of a bond causes an instant and massive shift of money from London to Tokyo. The system has a profound impact on companies throughout the world." He went on to argue that, even in Japan, traditionally high debt-to-equity ratios of companies had already been driven down by the availability of higher interest rates in overseas markets (Theodore Levitt, "The Globalization of Markets," in H. Vernon-Wortzel and Lawrence H. Wortzel (eds), *Global Strategic Management*, New York: Wiley, second edition 1990: 317)."

19 The risk is not that of losing their money through default or unrest: "firms simply do not get involved in countries, or even regions, that they perceive to be risky" in any general sense (Stephen J. Kobrin, "Political Risk: A Review and Reconsideration," in Wortzel and Wortzel, *Global Strategic Management*, 188). What portfolio investors worry about is inflation eroding the value of their loans, which dictates that national governments make themselves open to sanctions for ensuring that this does not happen: see Gerald Epstein and Herbert Gintis, "International Capital Markets and National Economic Policy," *Review of International Political Economy*, vol. 2, no. 4, Autumn 1995: 693–718; and Gerald Epstein, "International Capital Mobility and the Scope for National Economic Management," in Boyer and Drache, *States Against Markets*, 211–24.

20 Timothy J. Sinclair, "Passing Judgement: Credit Rating Processes as Regulatory Mechanisms of Governance in the Emerging World Order," *Review of International Political Economy,* 1994: 133.

21 OECD *Economic Outlook 66,* Paris: OECD, 1999: 220.

22 Michael Wallerstein and Adam Przeworski, "Capital Taxation with Open Borders," *Review of International Political Economy,* vol. 2, no. 3, Summer 1995: 425–45.

23 John H. Dunning, *Globalization: The Challenge of National Economic Regimes,* Twenty-Fourth Geary Lecture, Economic and Social Research Institute, Dublin, 1993: 14–15 (italics added).

24 Sol Piciotto, "Transfer Pricing and the Antinomies of Corporate Regulation," in Joseph McCahery, Sol Piciotto and Colin Scott (eds), *Corporate Control and Accountability,* Oxford: Clarendon Press, 1993: 381. See also Yves Dezalay, "Professional Competition and the Social Construction of Transnational Regulatory Expertise," ibid., 203–15, for a convincing account of the scale of legal resources that regulatory arbitrage consumes.

25 In many sectors the increasing rate of technological change and the declining role of materials in total value added has significantly reduced the costs of moving fixed capital, which further increases corporations' regulatory leverage. According to the *Economist,* out of eighty-two major changes made in the FDI laws in thirty-four countries in 1991, eighty "lightened the regulatory burden" (cited in Wade, "Globalization and Its Limits," 72, although Wade cautions against placing too much reliance on such "facts").

26 Fred Lazar, "Corporate Strategies in Global Markets," in Boyer and Drache, *States Against Markets,* 293.

27 Helleiner, *States and the Reemergence of Global Finance,* 197.

28 According to Tsoukalis, *The New European Economy,* 139–47, "the jury is still out" on the result of the politics of harmonization or deregulation (to create a single market) vs regulation (to protect domestic markets) within the EU. For some case studies that show the real-world obstacles to regulatory competition within the EU, see Jeanne-Mey Sun and Jacques Pelmans, "Regulatory Competition in the Single Market," *Journal Of Common Market Studies,* vol. 33, no. 1, March 1995: 67–89.

29 Canada's drastic curtailment of unemployment insurance coverage and benefits is a notable example. Most of the large Federal budget surplus in 2000, which was largely devoted to tax cuts for corporations and middle and upper income earners, was accounted for by the surplus in the Employment Insurance fund achieved by this means.

30 *After the Nation State,* 232.

31 "Globalization and Internationalization," 110.

32 Juliet Schor, "Beyond Work and Spend," paper presented to the seminar

on "European Left Alternatives to Neoliberalism," Amsterdam, February 1997.

33 In the EU in 1997 an average of 12.2 per cent of the workforce was in temporary employment. In the UK in the same year 108,000 people were officially homeless. *Social Trends 29*, London: Office of National Statistics, 1999: 76 and 211.

34 Wade, "Globalization and Its Limits," 72.

35 In effect the disjunction between immiseration and "social power" that Arrighi noted as a feature of the global workforce at the end of the 1980s has begun to be reproduced within the countries of the North; see Giovanni Arrighi, "Marxist Century, American Century: The Making and Remaking of the World Labour Movement," *New Left Review*, no. 179, 1990: 29–63.

36 It is sobering to contrast the British miners' strike against pit closures in 1984-85, which aroused widespread public sympathy but was comprehensively defeated (and the mining industry set on a path to elimination by early in the next century), with the German miners' strike of March 1997, which demanded only a slower pace of closure.

37 The disposable incomes of the richest 20 per cent rose from 3.75 times those of the poorest 20 per cent to 5.75 times over this period. *Economic Trends 1996*, London: HMSO, 1996.

38 Richard Wilkinson, *Unhealthy Societies: The Afflictions of Inequality*, London: Routledge, 1996: 152–72.

39 Ibid., 222–3.

40 In March 1997 a *Guardian* journalist wrote, after spending some days in Northampton, a marginal seat, that "it is hard to find anyone at all under 30 who has thought about voting ... The media talk of almost nothing but the election. The majority of people in Northampton appear to understand almost nothing about it." This applied even to people wholly dependent on social security, one of whom declared "the government means nothing to me." The author commented: "The crude, tribal inheritance of a party allegiance is gone; all that is left to inform voters is stray prejudice and a right-wing press." Decca Aitkenhead, "Election? What Election?" *Guardian*, 10 March 1997. Personal impressions suggest that similar findings would be obtained anywhere in England outside the party heartlands where older voters, at least, still had "tribal" party allegiances.

41 Wilkinson, *Unhealthy Societies*, 143.

42 Donald Sassoon, *A Hundred Years of Socialism*, London: I.B. Tauris: 754. One may dissent from Sassoon's judgement that "they could not do otherwise" – but that is a different debate.

43 The pace of change in the global media industry means that textbooks tend to understate the true impact of global market forces on politics. See however Brian McNair, *News and News Journalism in the UK*,

London: Routledge 1994, and the annual editions of the *Guardian Media Guide*.

44 Streeck, "Public Power," 314.

45 For early formulations of these models see Michel Albert, *Capitalism Against Capitalism*, London: Whurr Publishers, 1993; and Lester Thurow, *Head to Head: The Coming Economic Battle Among Japan, Europe and America*, London: Nicholas Brealey, 1993.

46 Streeck, "Public Power," 311–12: " ... electorates are liable to fall victim to a 'democracy illusion' comparable to Keynes's 'money illusion': that by exercising their political rights of citizenship they can get purchase on their economic fate"; whereas in reality they have already been persuaded to surrender this through economic liberalization – and furthermore when, in Europe, the alleged enemy, "Brussels," is in principle their one potential instrument for recovering it.

47 On Sweden see Stuart Wilks, "Class Compromise and the International Economy: The Rise and Fall of Swedish Social Democracy," *Capital and Class* 58, 1996: 89–111; on Germany see Brigitte Mahnkopf, "Between the Devil and the Deep Blue Sea: The German Model Under the Pressure of Globalization," in Leo Panitch and Colin Leys (eds), *Global Capitalism Versus Democracy: Socialist Register 1999*, Rendlesham, Suffolk: Merlin Press, 1999: 142–77.

48 Will Hutton's *The State We're In*, London: Vintage, second edition 1996, provoked a major debate on this issue; for an early comment see C. Leys, "A Radical Agenda for Britain," *New Left Review,* no. 212, July–August 1995: 3–13. See also Hutton's sequel, *The State To Come*, London: Vintage, 1997.

49 For western Europe see Donald Sassoon, *One Hundred Years of Socialism*, London: I.B. Tauris, 1996: chapter 24, "The New Revisionism."

50 For a definitive review see Alan Zuege, "The Chimera of the Third Way," in Leo Panitch and Colin Leys (eds), *Necessary and Unnecessary Utopias: Socialist Register 2000*, London: Merlin Press, 1999: 87–114. For Blair's version, see *The Third Way: New Politics for a New Century*, London: Fabian Society, 1998. Anthony Giddens tried to give the idea some intellectual coherence in *The Third Way: The Renewal of Social Democracy*, Cambridge: Polity Press, 1998; but Zuege (108) cites the *Economist's* "glib but fairly accurate" description of the whole idea: "Trying to pin down an exact meaning is like wrestling with an inflatable man. If you get a grip on one limb, all the hot air rushes to another."

51 Gary Teeple, *Globalization and the End of Social Reform*, New Jersey and Toronto; Humanities Press and Garamond Press, 1995: 145 and 147.

52 In addition to numerous party policy documents and speeches, a convenient guide to the modernizers' thinking is Peter Mandelson and Roger Liddle, *The Blair Revolution: Can New Labour Deliver?*, London: Faber

and Faber, 1996: chapters 3–4. For an account of the changes in Labour's policy and organization see Leo Panitch and Colin Leys, *The End of Parliamentary Socialism: From New Left to New Labour, Second Edition*, London: Verso, 2001: chapters 10, 11, and 13.

53 Teeple, *Globalization and the Decline of Social Reform*, 75.

54 Including, however, significant amounts of tactical voting by both Labour and Liberal-Democratic voters in seats where the others' candidate had the only realistic chance of defeating the Conservatives; voters had finally learned the lesson taught by four successive elections in which Conservatives had gained power through the division of the opposition vote.

55 *Guardian*, 9 May 1997.

56 The "sleaze" issue dominated the first weeks of the 1997 election campaign and was kept alive throughout by the highly publicized election campaign against Neil Hamilton, MP for Tatton, the Conservatives' third-safest seat. Hamilton had taken "cash for questions"; the Labour and Liberal-Democratic candidates withdrew in favour of an independent anti-corruption candidate, the journalist Martin Bell, who took the seat from Hamilton with a huge majority. On the general issue see Martin Linton, *Money and Votes*, London: IPPR, 1994; Judith Cook, *The Sleaze File*, London: Bloomsbury, 1995; and David Leigh and Ed Vulliamy, *Sleaze: The Corruption of Parliament*, London: Fourth Estate, 1997.

57 Alan Clark, *Diaries*, London: Phoenix, 1994: 186–7.

58 Paul Whiteley and Patrick Seyd thought that Conservative Party membership was quite likely well below the official figure of 250,000 in 1997 and on present trends would fall to 100,000 by the year 2000, since half the membership was over 66 years old and only five per cent were under 35 (*Guardian*, 9 May 1997).

59 "Reforming the Tory Party: Highlights of William Hague's 'blueprint for change,'" http://ourworld.compuserve.com/homepages/ccfhub/PARTYREFM.HTM.

60 *Times*/MORI poll, September 1999.

61 A more extensive and intensive analysis is attempted in my *Market-Driven Politics*, London: Verso, 2001.

62 Peter Self, *Government by the Market? The Politics of Public Choice*, Boulder, Colorado: Westview Press, 1993: 63.

63 In April 1998 Peter Mandelson, then Minister Without Portfolio in the Labour Government, and the party's chief electoral strategist, told the Institute of Directors in London that in the 1997 election "it had been the job of New Labour's architects to translate their understanding of the customer into offerings he or she was willing to pay for ... And then, and only then, to convey to potential customers the attributes of that offering through all the different components that make up a successful brand – product positioning, packaging, advertising and communications. Politics

is no different" (*Guardian*, 30 April 1988). The problem with Peter Mandelson is that one cannot be sure he is joking. In May 1997 he told a
meeting in Germany that "ballot boxes and Parliaments were elitist
relics," and that people wanted to be more "involved in government"
through "the far superior instruments of plebiscites, focus groups and the
internet ... It may be that the era of pure representative democracy is
slowly coming to an end." The Germans were not amused (Nick Cohen,
"New Labour ... In Focus, on Message, Out of Control," *Observer*, 28
November 1999).

PART ONE

From Thatcher to Blair: British Politics at the Turn of the Millennium

Introduction

For centuries, British politics has been at the centre of international debates. The articles in part 1 of this collection consider the impact of politics in Britain over the recent turn of the millennium, focusing on the years of transition from Margaret Thatcher's ultra-conservative Tory rule to Tony Blair's pro-market Labour government.

In this section the authors grapple with such issues as the implications of the decline of the Keynesian welfare national state, the relevance of Antonio Gramsci's theory of hegemony to conditions of late capitalism, the rise and fall of the Labour left, and the potential long-term impact of Tony Blair's embrace of market mechanisms. While such arguments will be of particular interest to area specialists, these debates have far reaching implications for the broader field of critical political studies.

In his article, "Revisiting Thatcherism and Its Political Economy: Hegemonic Projects, Accumulation Strategies, and the Question of Internationalization," Robert D. Jessop picks up a thread from a previous exchange with Colin Leys. Jessop seeks to clarify and focus their points of disagreement regarding the relationship between Thatcher's economic and political aims. He focuses his argument by unpacking Antonio Gramsci's theory of hegemony. He insists that, though the theory is useful, its framework is flawed. Jessop further explores the relative weight of possibility of national economic reform in an "after-Fordist" era.

The two remaining articles in this section consider the impact of the government that successfully ousted the Tories: the British Labour

Party government under the leadership of Tony Blair. Leo Panitch, in his article "Rethinking the Labour Party's Transition from Socialism to Capitalism," looks at Tony Blair's arrival on the scene with a wide lens. Panitch starts with a sober assessment of the global dominance of capitalism at a time when both the Communist parties and those committed to a social-democratic platform "have ended the century as historic failures." The specific issue that Panitch attempts to untangle in this essay is the crisis of social democracy. In a detailed consideration of the rise and fall of Tony Benn's left alternative, Panitch concludes that the "defeat of the project of the Labour new left eventually brought the Labour Party to Blair."

Alex Callinicos places the Blair project under the microscope in his article, "Tony Blair and the British Left." Without underestimating the historic victory and acknowledging the celebratory atmosphere that saw the defeat of eighteen years of Tory rule with the 1 May 1997 election, Callinicos's attack on Blair from the left is unforgiving. Callinicos examines in detail the ideological roots of Blair's embrace of capitalist market principles, and how the abandonment of Labour's long-standing commitment to social ownership of the economy was constructed in the name of party "modernization." Callinicos cautions, however, against leaving the analysis at this level. He sees the Labour Party as incorporating contradictory internal pressures.

These articles in combination represent an impressive, reflective, knowledgeable and important contribution to our understanding of British politics. They also illuminate the interaction of state and society in the contemporary world system.

Revisiting Thatcherism and Its Political Economy: Hegemonic Projects, Accumulation Strategies, and the Question of Internationalization

ROBERT D. JESSOP

I am pleased to participate in this festschrift on Colin Leys and his work. Colin Leys and I have long shared interests in postwar British politics and Thatcherism, as exemplified by his critique, in *New Left Review,* of a monograph on *Thatcherism* that I co-authored.[1] Amidst some characteristically generous comments on our book, Colin offered three main criticisms. First, in emphasizing the political economy of Thatcherism, we neglected its hegemonic moments. We thereby understated how far its success was politico-ideological rather than economic. Second, our political economy was one-sidedly concerned with more domestic aspects of the background, overall project, and policies of Thatcherism and had therefore ignored its central international dimensions.[2] Third, taken together, these errors supposedly led us to propose an economic and political strategy that was profoundly mistaken – especially in its purported assumption that the basic task facing any British government is to create a *national* economy able to support rising living standards.

It might appear improper to use this occasion to revive a dying, if not long extinguished, dispute. There are two good counter-arguments for doing so. Politically, in addition to the continued dominance in Britain of the Thatcherite legacy (including its broad acceptance by "New Labour"), Thatcherism has strong parallels in Ontario and elsewhere in Canada. In this sense, the political stakes are still very current. And, theoretically, the intensification of globalization as process and project makes questions of political economy, hegemony, and left strategy even more pressing. It is changing the context and issues of left politics and needs more serious consideration than it often receives in current "newspeak" and "professortalk."[3] Thus, rather than return to earlier debates, I will attempt to update them. More specifically, I will try to reproblematize the familiar concept of hegemony, rethematize the changing nature of internationalization, and refocus the discussion of left strategies. I thereby offer a partial critique of my own work as well as others' accounts of Thatcherism. This is to operate in the same spirit as Colin himself – who, as John Saul reminds us, never shies away from justified self-criticism (see article by John Saul, this volume).

ONCE AGAIN ON HEGEMONY

Leys criticized our monograph for treating Thatcherism as "a failed economic project, rather than a successful political one."[4] Among its political achievements he listed: resolving the 1970s impasse in capital-labour relations by removing labour's veto, restoring the security of capitalist rule while retaining a parliamentary framework, and dissolving the common sense and social imaginary associated with the postwar settlement.[5] We shared this view. Our first article stressed that, while it had not exactly succeeded economically, Thatcherism had already been a political success. Indeed, our own account of political successes offered much the same evidence.[6] We also discussed Thatcherism's impact on "the politics of support, the recasting of the institutional forms of political domination, and the recomposition of the power bloc."[7]

Since we clearly agreed on the importance of hegemony and the more specific political achievements of Thatcherism, any disagreement should presumably be traced to our respective explanations for these achievements. There appear to be two key differences: how to read Gramsci on hegemony and how far Gramsci's work needs to be supplemented by post-Marxist discourse analysis. Colin has long advocated a Gramscian approach, as *Politics in Britain* demonstrates so well. In addition, in his critique of our own work, he appeared to flirt, albeit briefly, with a discourse-analytical account of the basic conditions for securing hegemony. Our own view was that Gramsci's analyses of hegemony were generally brilliant but flawed[8] and that these flaws were compounded in post-Marxist discourse-analytical appropriations of his work.[9]

Chief among the flaws in Gramsci's work on hegemony is that he focused mainly on the politics and ideology of class *leadership* and therefore neglected the *structural determinations* of hegemony. This matters because political and ideological domination is often inscribed within the state apparatus and the manner of its structural coupling to the economy and civil society. Counter-hegemonic forces are thereby handicapped in mobilizing support and carrying through counter-hegemonic policies should they gain formal control over the state. Moreover, although Gramsci stressed that hegemony always requires a "decisive economic nucleus," he never adequately defined this crucial relationship. This is surely important where economic failure is allegedly combined with political success! Conversely, if one does adopt Gramscian concepts for analysing hegemony, one should note four further distinctions in Gramsci's writings that might help one avoid flawed culturalist analyses. He contrasted hegemonic projects that are "organic ideologies" with "arbitrary, rationalistic, and willed" projects; distinguished hegemonic leadership from direct domination; proposed a continuum running from "force, fraud, and corruption" through "passive revolution" to an integral, expansive hegemony; and noted the need to move from the "economic-corporate" phase of a revolution to its "ethico-political" stage.[10] Each of these four distinctions has real utility in discerning the limits to any proposed hegemonic project.

Stuart Hall claimed that, while Thatcherism had a hegemonic project, it never actually achieved *hegemony*: at most it could be said to have been dominant. This raises the question of how Thatcherism achieved dominance without securing active popular consent. An alternative explanation would refer to the overall strategic capacities of the leading forces. Thus Colin preferred another argument from Hall: hegemony consists in the capacity to lead the key sectors, win the strategic engagements, and stay in front when challenged.[11] I believe this definition is too broad. These capacities could also be due to sheer economic, political, or ideological dominance. Contributing factors here could include serious disorganization of the resistance to Thatcherism, basic institutional obstacles to such resistance (not all of them located in the politico-ideological realm), strategic errors on the part of the left in an otherwise favourable conjuncture.[12] Rather than explore such alternatives, however, Leys argued, at least in his discourse-analytical turn, that Thatcherism's success in shifting the balance of forces to the right was due to its successful articulation of a new common sense.[13] He explained this through the power of Thatcherite discourse – its ability to redefine the social imaginary – and grounded this power primarily in ideological factors.

One should not mistake the reality of the crisis of hegemony that created the conditions for the rise of Thatcherism for the success of the alternative hegemonic project proposed by the Thatcherite social movement. For, while the Thatcherites certainly succeeded in blaming the crisis of the Keynesian welfare national state (hereafter KWNS) on the labour movement and unnecessary state intervention, they failed to define (let alone win massive support for) a new social imaginary during the dying years of the Wilson-Callaghan government. Moreover, once in office, their fragile hold over the social imaginary was clear in the government's growing unpopularity. Indeed, their survival was not so much due to hegemonic leadership as to sheer dominance in the state system. Even after the Falklands War, political success was due more to a well-timed boom and the opposition's disarray than to their still incomplete hegemony. The inability of other parties to defeat the Conservatives certainly helped the latter to become the dominant force on the political scene – it does not mean that Thatcherism ever really became hegemonic. That Thatcherism "has no serious rival" (to cite one of Colin's indicators of hegemony) tells us nothing in itself about hegemony; it could just as easily indicate Thatcherite dominance over the mass media or reflect opposition party splits due to a pre-existing crisis in the postwar settlement (with which Labour was still very closely identified).

Turning to specific instances of Thatcherite success, can one really argue that the government's defeat of the miners' strike through prior strategic stockpiling of coal, increased oil burning, police action, open manipulation of the social security system, financing and promoting a yellow union, and behind-the-scenes control over Coal Board negotiations was chiefly due to Thatcherism's ability to "address the fears, the anxieties, the lost identities, of a people"? Could Thatcherism abolish the Greater London Council (GLC) six metropolitan councils because of its ability to "address our collective fantasies"? Exactly how much did reorganization of education, the health service, community care, and other sectors of the welfare state – which typically occurred through prolonged cash starvation followed by a selective release of additional funds on condition that new market-oriented activities be undertaken – really owe to the power to win the "struggle for ideas"? And exactly what specific form of hegemonic "social imaginary," an idiom that Thatcher supposedly made her own, led her to introduce the poll tax with such resounding effects in "the battle for hearts and minds"? Did growing disquiet among businessmen about Thatcher's (and subsequently Major's) stance on Europe stem just from their unwillingness to share her particular vision of "Britain as an imagined country"? Did growing cynicism in the right-wing broadsheets and the business press in 1989–91 about the priority given to electoral calculations in the government's plan to enter the Exchange Rate Mechanism indicate a certain weariness with Thatcherite posturing rather than political leadership? Did the unremitting assault on the independence of the mass media, the autonomy of local government, or the free flow of information between state and people, represent nothing but an aberration that was in fact unnecessary since Thatcherism had won the hearts and minds of the people? Or was it a response to failure to establish an expansive hegemony, which, according to Gramsci, is quite consistent with a pluralistic political system?

Even where the Thatcherite hegemonic project does seem relevant, one must always distinguish between the production and reception of discourse. Some ideological elements are hard to rearticulate, some individuals and forces are more receptive than others to specific ideological appeals and political mobilization, and, once persuaded, some remain committed, and others are volatile.[14] Thus Bea Campbell noted how Thatcherite attempts to mobilize support around women's issues and identities failed.[15] And Thatcher recognized similar problems when, following a marked loss of support in the 1987 general election in declining urban areas, she remarked that "we must do something about those inner cities."

In practice, of course, Colin's own work on Thatcherism has adopted a more nuanced account of the conditions making for Thatcherite political success. He certainly does not reduce it to a question of hegemony interpreted purely from a discourse-analytical viewpoint. Thus, in discussing Thatcherite attempts to "change attitudes," he lists tactics as varied as deliberate non-intervention in major industrial disputes, redistributing the tax burden in favour of skilled workers and the middle classes, selling council houses, assisting and celebrating small firms, and political repression.[16] This list emphasizes the allocative and/or coercive powers of the state rather than the "social imaginary" and the reconstitution of identities. It highlights the critical roles played by "'direct domination' or command exercised through the State and 'juridical government'"[17] as well as the "fraud-corruption"[18] involved in promoting popular capitalism. In like vein, he attributes industrial capital's failure to resist Thatcherite economic policies not to Thatcherite hegemony but to a crisis of political representation.[19]

If Thatcherism was ever to have become hegemonic, more than an "arbitrary, rationalistic, and willed" hegemonic project was required. Our own book did suggest three key conditions for hegemony to be consolidated: a successful economic strategy, an effective reorganization of the state, and success in pursuing its project of popular capitalism.[20] It was largely in its restructuring of the state (a domain largely under its own direct control) that these conditions were advanced furthest. In a later article,[21] we assessed the reversibility of Thatcherism's legacy by dealing with its differential

inscription in a variety of material practices rather than limiting ourselves to issues of hegemony. Thus we referred to not only the fran-
tic Thatcherite efforts to legitimate yet again the "two nations"
effects of earlier policies but also the attempt to "move beyond the
economic-corporate stage of revolution to an ethico-political stage
in which 'all the superstructures must be developed if one is not to
risk the dissolution of the state.'"[22] In citing Gramsci here we wanted to emphasize that hegemony involves much more than uttering a
populist discourse – it also involves major changes in the state and
its articulation with civil society, the recomposition of micro-powers,
and the building of a new power bloc and a new social basis for the
state.

Addressing such questions is especially important given the different stages through which Thatcherism passed. Colin recognized this
too. His own account of Thatcherism periodized it in ways similar
to our own work and he employed similar arguments about its initial rise, its difficulties during the first years of office, and its subsequent consolidation.[23] It is dangerous to generalize across different
stages because they are typically linked to shifts in the weight of the
politics of support and politics of power, of short-term conjunctural
factors as opposed to institutional consolidation, of economic-corporate and ethico-political struggles, etc.[24] This neglect of the key
differences between the rise of Thatcherism and its institutional consolidation is one reason why we criticized Stuart Hall's over-extend-
ed analysis of hegemony. Recognition of the difference is one reason
why I admire Colin Leys extended analyses of Thatcherism in power,
but it also explains why I reject his critique of our monograph for
neglecting the discursive successes of the Thatcher regime. Even if
the articulation of a hegemonic project (or, at least, a redefinition of
common sense) did play a key role in the rise of Thatcherism, any
subsequent consolidation would involve "force, fraud, and corruption," direct domination, and passive revolution as well as attempts
to extend any hegemony and promote active consent. It follows that,
if a Labour Government under Blair is elected on the basis of a
modernized party and a new politico-ideological project that accepts
much of the Thatcher-Major legacy,[25] its eventual success will necessarily depend not just on hegemonic appeals but also on its capacity
both to restructure the state apparatus and to reverse the much
reinforced structural bias in the economy towards the City, the
South-East, and private consumption. For it is these latter factors as
much as any residual hegemonic appeal of Thatcherism that will hinder the formulation and implementation of a new social-democratic
project.

NEOLIBERALISM AND GLOBAL CAPITALISM

Our book on *Thatcherism* did tend to neglect the international dimensions of postwar political economy and its Thatcherite denouement. Here Colin's critique was justified. But our primary focus lay elsewhere. Other work had strongly emphasized the international character of British capitalism,[26] and had also noted how the international division of labour between the three core capitalist economies affected Thatcherism's neoliberal accumulation strategy.[27] *Thatcherism* itself noted that no other major capitalist economy revealed such marked internationalization in its leading sectors as Britain. The resulting "disintegration of the UK economy as a nationally integrated economic space" meant there was no significant bloc of domestic UK capital that could provide the economic, political, and social basis for a national strategy. The market-led recovery favoured by the Thatcher regime would further reinforce British de-industrialization and balkanize Britain's industrial core among sectors tied into the circuits of American, Japanese, German, and UK multinational capital.[28] Indeed we suggested that Thatcherism might well be promoting a worldwide post-Fordist age by entrenching a rentier British economy, with a secondary industrial role in the world economy and a low wage, low-tech service sector at home. This might consolidate the dominance of the City's *financial* interests and multinational capital at home and abroad but also posed strategic dilemmas in economic and political terms. In particular, it suggested the Conservatives would find it hard to balance the international orientation of the key growth sectors in the economy and the political requirements of a national politics of support.[29] Growing disputes over Europe and the rise of little Englandism in the Tory Party under Thatcher and Major are indicators of this problem.

Concern with internationalization in the form indicated by our own comments and Colin's critique has since been superseded by concern with globalization. For all the problems with this concept, it does mark a major shift in economic and political structures, forces, and strategies. These have changed significantly since the heyday of Atlantic Fordism. The latter involved the primacy of the national economy and national state as parameters of economic and political action. This was reflected in several key features of the postwar settlement in Britain and elsewhere in Western Europe.[30] Among different scales of formal political organization, the sovereign state was primary. Local authorities served as relays for national economic and social politics; and key supranational institutions were inter*governmental* as well as *inter*national and operated under US hegemony to promote co-operation among national states. Likewise, among various scales of economic organization, the national economy was adjudged dominant for state action, was defined and measured in terms of national aggregates, and was managed primarily through state targeting of variations in these aggregates. In short, the main focus of state economic strategies and economic regulation was a relatively closed national economy, with local or regional economies being regarded as territorial sub-units of the national economy (with cross-regional differences regarded as unimportant) and with the international economy largely taking the form of financial and trade flows among different national economies. In social policy terms, the primary object of welfare and social reproduction policies was the resident national population and its various constituent households and individual citizens. Indeed, many social policies were also premised on the predominance of stable two-parent families in which men received a "family wage" and could expect lifetime employment. In this context, the primary axes of conflict in postwar politics included the debate over the appropriate balance of market and state in the "mixed economy."

The process of internationalization gradually undermined these parameters of postwar politics, however, undermining the national economy as the obvious object of economic management – let alone as something to be managed primarily through macro-level demand-side management and infrastructural policies. The growth of new social movements in response to the crises of Fordism and the KWNS also contributed to their delegitimation – making it harder to maintain the postwar settlement, its tripartite balance of forces organized around the dominance of producer group interests, and its commitment to "big is beautiful" in economic and social affairs. The decline of the traditional nuclear family form and the "family wage" also aggravated the crisis in the KWNS. These factors (among others) are crucial reference points for attempts to develop an alternative left strategy.

This said, internationalization is an inadequate concept for interpreting the key changes in British political economy. So is globalization.[31] Neither takes full account of the current complexities of economic and political scale. For, while certain trends towards globalization are discernible (without thereby making it a causal process in its own right), they are often closely linked to processes on other scales. These processes typically involve complex and tangled causal hierarchies and eccentric "nestings" rather than a simple, unilinear, bottom-up, or top-down movement. Thus global economic integration may be promoted through structural trends and explicit strategies on less inclusive spatial scales and be sutured through global cities and regional gateways that are extroverted rather than anchored in, and oriented to, particular national economies. Moreover, since the national economy is no longer so taken for granted, sub-national regions, cities, and local economic spaces as well as supranational blocs are now pursuing quite varied strategies to secure a favourable place in the changing international division of labour. But less inclusive scales of economic and political organization also serve as sites of major counter-tendencies and resistance to globalization. This is evident in phenomena such as localism, "tribalism," cross-border regionalism, forms of interregional co-operation that by-pass the national state, and so forth.

What passes nowadays as "economic globalization" hardly ever involves full structural integration and strategic coordination across the globe even at the level of transnational firms or banks. It includes: (a) internationalization of national economic spaces through penetration (inward flows) and extroversion (outward flows); (b) growth of more "local internationalization" through the development of economic ties between local and regional authorities in different national economies; (c) extension and deepening of multinationalization as MNCs move from limited economic activities abroad to more comprehensive and worldwide strategies, sometimes extending to so-called "global localization" in and through which firms pursue a global strategy based on exploiting local differences; and (d) the emergence of globalization proper through the introduction and acceptance of global norms and standards, the development of globally integrated markets together with globally oriented strategies, and rootless firms with no evident national operational base. All these processes contribute to the further integration and coordination of capitalism. But they do so in a dispersed, fragmented, and partial manner. This reinforces tendencies to uneven development by reordering differences and complementarities on various scales as the basis for competitive advantages.

Nonetheless, in spite (perhaps because) of their misleading quality, discourses about globalization are often deployed to naturalize and/or legitimate certain kinds of economic, political, and social policies. The range of such policies varies widely. Some sense of this can be inferred from the market-led globalization favoured by the World Bank, the horizontal "global governance" favoured by proponents (especially NGOS) of international regimes, and plans for more top-down interstatal government. In addition, much of what passes as globalization is actually conducted at the level of three supranational growth poles and thereby excludes significant areas of the globe. Major economic structures and strategies are also proliferating on other scales. Indeed this is an important feature of the current situation compared with Atlantic Fordism. Whereas the latter involved the dominance of the national level, no level has become dominant in the after-Fordist period. No spatial scale (whether global or not) now provides the predominant level around which the remaining levels (however many and however identified) are organized in order to produce structured economic coherence. Instead there is considerable "unstructured complexity" as different economic scales are structurally consolidated and/or become so many competing objects of economic management, governance, or regulation.

The current dialectic of globalization/regionalization is linked to four major trends in the organization of political economy with consequences for economic and political strategy. First, there has been a relative *de-nationalization of the state* (or "hollowing out") through the transfer of state powers upwards to supranational authorities, downwards to local and regional states, and sideways through translocal linkages across national borders. Second, there is a tendential *de-statization of political regimes*. This is reflected in a relative shift from government to governance on various territorial scales and across various functional domains as official state apparatuses share power with partnerships involving governmental, para-governmental, and non-governmental organizations. Although this typically involves a loss of decisional and operational autonomy by state apparatuses (at whatever level), it may also enhance their capacity to project state power and achieve state objectives by mobilizing knowledge and power resources from influential non-governmental partners or stakeholders. Third, there is a further *internationalization of policy regimes*. There is greater strategic significance of the international context of domestic state action, expansion of the circle of key players in domestic policy-making to include a wide range of foreign (or at least "interiorized") actors, and extension of the state's field of action for domestic purposes to include an extensive range of extraterritorial or transnational factors and processes. Fourth, there is a *recommodification of economic and social policy*. National states' prime objects of economic and social intervention are no longer managing the domestic performance of the "national economy" and securing "social inclusion" based on national citizenship. They now consist in the economy's overall "international competitiveness" and subordination of social policy to the demands of labour market flexibility and control of the "social wage" as an international cost of production.

These shifts are necessary starting points for an alternative left strategy. In identifying them, I have no wish to naturalize them. Each of them contains positive as well as negative elements; and each is linked to counter-trends that also have ambivalent implications for a progressive strategy. Thus the "hollowing out" of the national state creates a space for local and regional strategies as well as transnational co-operation. The rise of governance creates space for partnerships, the "third sector," and self-management on different scales. The internationalization of policy regimes could be used to pursue human rights, fair trade, and environmental policies as well as to entrench the interests of capital. Moreover, owing to the continuing role of the "national state" as the key site for addressing social cohesion, for articulating different scales of government and governance, and for managing how the nation is inserted into the international arena, there is also scope for developing a coherent "national-popular" program for supporting local, regional, and transnational initiatives both symbolically and materially.

THE LEFT ALTERNATIVE

This brings us directly to questions of left strategy. My work on Thatcherism cautioned against a one-sided emphasis on long-term ideological preconditions for left hegemony at the cost of developing a feasible medium-term economic and political program. For such one-sidedness could lead to deep pessimism ("battening down the hatches") and/or long-term utopian calls for building an "alternative vision." Both responses would have led to purely defensive, short-term, and uncoordinated resistance to Thatcherism and neglect of the need for a coherent, positive, medium-term economic and political strategy.[32] Yet Leys followed a criticism of our account of "the *medium-term* priorities of any incoming governments" with a call to admit "the enormity of the *long-run* ideological task: the construction of a new 'social imaginary.'"[33] It was because we recognized the enormity of this task – defined in our first analysis of Thatcherism as a *necessary* but *insufficient* condition of left socialist hegemony – that we also addressed the short- and medium-term problems confronting the left.

This is the context for Leys's charge that we assumed "the task confronting governments in Britain today is one of creating a national economy capable of supporting rising living standards for the masses."[34] Presumably this meant that we wanted to restore the KWNS in a relatively closed national economy. But it is clear that there can be no return to the postwar Atlantic Fordist status quo ante. Nor could any so-called "national economy" today (even a quasi-Continental one such as the American economy) compete in all areas of manufacturing against all-comers on a global scale. On the contrary, our view at the time was that the key to national economic success – hence to the high wages and high employment we wanted to see – was the competitive positioning of key sectors or firms within the changing international division of labour. This required neither Thatcherite abandonment of the economy to arbitrary world markets nor determined pursuit of national autarky. It required action to promote an ensemble of internationally competitive sectors or firms – the kind of strategy pursued by small, open economies in Atlantic Fordism, and one we believed appropriate to larger economies in the after-Fordist period.

I have since related this strategy to the shift from the KWNS to the Schumpeterian workfare postnational regime.[35] Although often condemned for appearing to legitimate the neoliberal critique of Keynesian welfarism and, even worse, neoliberal attempts to dismantle the full employment welfare state, this analysis aimed both to show the difficulties of returning to the KWNS and to demonstrate that neoliberals erred in claiming that "there is no alternative" to their own strategy. In distinguishing neoliberal, neo-corporatist, and neo-statist variants of the Schumpeterian workfare concern with innovation, structural competitiveness, labour market flexibility, and the contribution of the social wage to international costs of production, I wanted to emphasize the potential economic, political, and moral superiority of the neo-corporatist and neo-statist variants. It is in this sense, perhaps, that Colin's critique was justified. For my earlier work did tend to assume that the national economy and national state would be the primary foci of a reinvigorated social-democratic project; and it also restricted the alternatives to reinvigorated forms of liberalism, corporatism, and statism. I thereby ignored the problems of "social democracy in one country" in its new guise as the strategy of "progressive competitiveness" and also neglected the potential contribution of more communitarian and/or environmentalist approaches to an alternative left strategy.[36]

This suggests that there is still much to be done in rethinking a social-democratic strategy in an after-Fordist era. The crises of Atlantic Fordism and the KWNS are only part of the transformation of the economic and political conjuncture. Also crucial are the denationalization of the state, the de-statization of politics, and the internationalization of policy regimes. Together these have fundamentally reconstituted the terrain for economic and political struggles even before we begin to address the question of hegemony or left strategy, but they have not reduced the role of the national state as the focal point for hegemonic struggles or as a key site for supporting more local, regional, trans-local, or international struggles and strategies. Thus, although questions of national-popular hegemony are still pertinent, they must be addressed in the light of new constraints.

CONTEXTUALIZING THE DEBATE YET AGAIN

In a final, conciliatory statement about the debate with Stuart Hall on the politics of hegemony, I noted that our disagreement was partly due to differences in our respective vantage points. Hall was initially concerned with the rise of Thatcherism as a social movement; we were preoccupied with Thatcher's survival despite mounting opposition. For Hall, ideological success was paramount because Thatcherism did not yet command that "direct domination" that comes from control of the state and, therefore, could only promise but not yet deliver material rewards. We were more concerned with the years in office – for many of which Thatcherism's appeal to "hearts and minds" was somewhat limited. Hall was more concerned with Thatcherism's success in the war of position against the postwar settlement, we were more worried about the decisional autonomy and dominance of Thatcher governments. In stressing these different reference points, I hoped to historicize and relativize the debate and show our appreciation of Hall's pioneering work. Colin's work stands in the same fine tradition but, as befits a political scientist, it has also extended to more fine-grained analysis of the state and political economy.

The analysis of Thatcherism matters above all to those who want to challenge its legacies. If its success was mainly due to the conquest of hearts and minds, then the main task will clearly be to win the battle for socialist ideas through developing a new "social imaginary." I still believe Thatcherism's ideological success was actually less important than its ability to consolidate institutional power through control of a centralized state and to modify the structural balance of power in state/economy/society relations. Its economic project later faltered under the combined weight of the internal contradictions of the neoliberal accumulation strategy and the growing primacy of party political calculation in government policy. Thatcherism also acquired a stale, grey visage under Major and was challenged by a post-Thatcherite "New Labour" that benefited from internal divisions in the Thatcher regime and economic and social disgruntlement among voters. Since "New Labour" has still failed to come up with a big "new idea" (the "stakeholding society" was the most recent short-lived attempt), let alone build an alternative vision, its capacity to move beyond Thatcherism is clearly limited. It will be even more limited if no concerted effort is made to dismantle Thatcherism's institutional legacies in the state system (in its broadest sense) and to tackle the economic and social consequences of an excessively internationalized and extroverted British economy. In this sense what is at stake today is not so much a question of hegemony qua class leadership but the structural inscription of class dominance in the economic and political system. To dismantle this will certainly require an alternative vision, but it will also require an interconnected set of specific economic, political, and social programs adapted to the realities of after-Fordism.

NOTES

1 Bob Jessop, Kevin Bonnett, Simon Bromley, and Tom Ling, *Thatcherism: a Tale of Two Nations.* Cambridge: Polity, 1988; Colin Leys, "Still a Question of Hegemony," *New Left Review*, no. 181, 1990: 119–28.

2 Leys was criticized in the same year for the same error. Reviewing *Politics in Britain*, Newsinger complained that he "completely neglects the international dimension ... A domestic focus consequently leads to the British state being seen as primarily concerned with welfare, economic management, and ideological containment, as being concerned with *hegemony*." John Newsinger, "Review of Colin Leys, *Politics in Britain*," *Capital and Class*, no. 40, 1990: 190 (italics mine).

3 I owe this term for the discourse of the more academic among the chattering classes to Blake Pearce, the youngest participant in the conference, "Critical Political Studies: A Conference in Honour of Colin Leys," Kingston, Ontario, 1996.

4 Leys, "Still a Question of Hegemony," 120.

5 Ibid., 123–4.

6 Jessop et al., *Thatcherism*, 76–9, 83–5, 91.

7 Ibid., 85–92.

8 Cf. Bob Jessop, *The Capitalist State*, Oxford: Martin Robertson, 1982.

9 Cf. Jessop et al., *Thatcherism*; Bob Jessop, *State Theory*, Cambridge: Polity, 1990.

10 Antonio Gramsci, *Selections from the Prison Notebooks*, London: Lawrence & Wishart, 1971: 12, 57–9, 80n, 94–5, 151, 160, 376–7, 404.

11 Leys, "Still a Question of Hegemony," 114.

12 Jessop et al., *Thatcherism*, 115.

13 Leys, "Still a Question of Hegemony," 110; cf. Stuart Hall and Martin Jacques, "Introduction," in idem (eds), *New Times*, London: Lawrence & Wishart, 1989.

14 Jessop et al., *Thatcherism*, 46.

15 Bea Campbell, *The Iron Ladies. Why Do Women Vote Tory?*, London: Virago Press, 1987.

16 Colin Leys, *Politics in Britain: From Labourism to Thatcherism*, London: Verso, 1989: 10.

17 Gramsci, *Selections from the Prison Notebooks*, 12.

18 Ibid., 80n.

19 Colin Leys, "Thatcherism and British Manufacturing: a Question of Hegemony," *New Left Review*, no. 151, 1985: 5–25.

20 Jessop et al., *Thatcherism*.

21 Bob Jessop, Kevin Bonnett, and Simon Bromley, "Farewell to Thatcherism? Neo-liberalism and New Times," *New Left Review*, no. 179, 1990: 81–202.

22 Ibid., 96, citing Gramsci, *Selections from the Prison Notebooks*, 404.

23 See Leys, *Politics in Britain: From Labourism to Thatcherism*.

24 Cf. Jessop et al., *Thatcherism*, 20.

25 Cf. Colin Leys, "The British Labour Party's Transition from Socialism to Capitalism," *The Socialist Register 1996*, 7–32.

26 Bob Jessop, "The Transformation of the State in Postwar Britain," in Richard Scase (ed.), *The State in Western Europe*, London: Croom Helm, 1980: 23–93.

27 Bob Jessop, "The Mid-Life Crisis of Thatcherism," *New Socialist*, March 1986.

28 Jessop et al., *Thatcherism*, 132ff, 158, 165ff, 172–3; and Jessop et al., "Farewell to Thatcherism?" 88.

29 Cf. Jessop et al., *Thatcherism*, 172.

30 References to support the following arguments are not included due to space limitations. For details see Bob Jessop, "Narrating the Future of the National Economy and the National State," in George Steinmetz (ed.), *State/Culture*, Ithaca: Cornell University Press, 1997.

31 Cf. Paul Q. Hirst and Graham Thompson, "Globalization and the Future of the Nation-State," *Economy and Society*, vol. 24, no. 3, 1995: 408–42. Although based on a forced, ideal-typical distinction between international and global economies, Hirst and Thompson's work is useful in deconstructing many myths surrounding globalization.

32 Jessop et al., *Thatcherism*, 96.

33 Leys, "Still a Question of Hegemony," 128.

34 Ibid., 119.

35 Bob Jessop, "Towards a Schumpeterian Workfare State," *Studies in Political Economy*, no. 40, 1993: 7–40.

36 See Greg Albo,"'Competitive Austerity' and the Impasse of Capitalist Employment Policy," *Socialist Register 1994,* 144–70; and Leo Panitch, "Globalization and the State," *The Socialist Register 1994,* 60–93.

Rethinking the Labour Party's Transition from Socialism to Capitalism

LEO PANITCH

In what sense can we speak of a "transition *from* socialism" under Tony Blair?[1] After all, the Labour Party was never predominantly or unproblematically socialist. What Blair symbolizes is a social democracy that has rid itself of all socialist pretence and, more important, of all socialist possibility; that is, it represents a party that revels in its defeat of those elements within its ranks that sought to revive socialist strategies and prospects in our era. It presents this triumph over socialism as the necessary condition of its electoral success. Blair's success will likely be taken as a model by other social-democratic parties. The story we have to tell has relevance elsewhere, in other words. *De te fabula narratur*.

It is necessary to begin by putting Blair's Labour Party in context. Capitalism stands astride the whole globe in our time, yet for the first time in well over a century there are no significant socialist movements to challenge it. The working class parties, both Communist and social democratic, that played such a large role in the politics of the twentieth century have ended the century as historic failures. With the perspective of the whole century now behind us we can see that, as regards the dramatic collapse of Communism, three compounded failures sum up the history of those parties that were founded on the success of the Bolsheviks in bringing about the first socialist revolution. This triptych begins with the failure to achieve the international revolution after 1917; it is followed by the failure of "socialism in one country"; it ends with the failure of Gorbachev's attempt to turn the ruling

Communist parties into social-democratic ones and the Communist regimes into Swedish-style mixed economies and welfare states.

But what about social democracy? The parties that go under this name are still very much around and the failure of Communism appears to have confirmed the strategic orientation of the social-democratic parties. Nevertheless, with the perspective of the whole century now behind us, we can see that a series of compounded failures also sum up the history of social democracy. The failure of social-democratic internationalism in the famous collapse of the Second International in the face of World War One is followed by the failure of gradualism: the frustration of the expectation that cumulative reforms within each nation-state would add up to a process of peacefully transcending capitalism in each country. This in turn is followed by the subsequent failure of reformism. It proved impossible to gradually reform capitalism out of existence, and the triumph of neoliberal globalization has made it impossible to hold onto the most significant social-democratic modifications of capitalism, such as full employment, public ownership, the mixed economy, and the welfare state. We actually arrive, at the end of the century, at a new social-democratic internationalism – but it now has nothing to do with socialism. Forced by capitalist globalization to abandon the Keynesian "corporatism in each country" that defined social-democratic practice after 1945, the kind of regional integration of the EU-type and export-oriented strategies of "progressive competitiveness" that social-democratic parties have embraced in the 1990s involves a full accommodation – ideological as well as strategic – to working within the framework of global capitalism.

This full accommodation to capitalism is what really is meant by today's social-democratic buzzword, "modernization." As Donald Sassoon puts it in his monumental history of the western European left in the twentieth century: "To give up the ambition of abolishing capitalism ... is not much of a strategy. Modernization as a slogan sounds appealing, but it has done so for over a hundred years. No party of the Left in post-war Europe (and hardly any party of the right) has ever been against modernization. One suspects the watchword, devoid as it is of any practical content, is used purely symbolically: to be for modernization means to be for progress without abolishing capitalism."[2]

Despite this insight, Sassoon's 700-page book, it should be noted, amounts to an endorsement of social democracy's trajectory. It is Sassoon's position that Gramsci, for all his perspicacity in recognizing the inapplicability of the insurrectionary strategy in the West, was nevertheless wrong in his conception of the party as a counter-hegemonic force. In envisaging as its role the creation of an alternate state, Gramsci was setting the working class party an impossible task. The lesson Sassoon wants to teach from his study of a century of socialism is that working class well-being is dependent on capitalist prosperity; that no other type of party than ones that practice the art of accommodating to what makes capitalism prosper is possible; that there can be no viable, let alone historically progressive, alternative to neoliberalism except one that also accommodates to the globalization of our era.

A great deal rides on this sort of reflection on the fate of socialism at the end of the twentieth century. We understand what is possible in the future in light of how we understand the determinations of the past. To accept Sassoon's view is to ascribe to the naturalization of globalization. Not very long ago, social-democratic intellectuals liked to insist that "politics matters." They argued that strong social-democratic movements in certain European welfare states proved that full employment policies could still be successfully practised in the 1980s.[3] This version of "politics matters" has been proven incorrect to the extent that even Sweden has succumbed to mass unemployment over the succeeding decade. Politics *does* matter – but when it comes to the effects of social democracy in our time, it has mattered most in terms of determining how we got to the end of the twentieth century with no alternative to global capitalism in sight.

We need to pay particular attention to the role that social-democratic parties have played in closing off new socialist possibilities at the crucial turning points that marked the demise of the post-war Keynesian order and its replacement by global neoliberalism. As productivity growth faltered in the late 1960s, and international competition intensified, the post-war compromise between capital and labour began to break down. Governments began shifting the burden of taxation from capital to labour in order to sustain after-tax profits, while labour began to seek compensation through higher wages and improved social services. This led to a crisis in social-democratic Keynesian regimes everywhere. The effect of this crisis was to give rise to a new left within many social-democratic parties. It was influenced by extraparliamentary and counter-hegemonic tendencies of the late 1960s, which understood that if the reforms of the post-war era could not be used as a basis for now issuing a fundamental challenge to the capitalist nature of the economy, those reforms would be now subject to challenge and reversal by capital itself.

This was everywhere resisted by the leadership of the social-democratic parties. The "Waffle's" challenge to the NDP in Canada before it was expelled in 1972 was an early example. In Germany, the Jusos

(Young Socialists) were similarly stifled in their attempt to link the party with extraparliamentary activity – and this eventually contributed strongly to the emergence of the German Greens. In the Dutch Labour Party in the early 1970s a new left called for greater control by activists over the process of candidate selection and for limits on the power of the party leadership to compromise on the party's declared policies when in office. In Sweden the LO's Meidner Plan for democratizing the whole economy through "wage-earners' funds," was first delayed, then gutted, by the SAP through the course of the 1970s and into the early 1980s. Most progress appeared to be made within France's Socialist Party, the PSF, which by the end of the 1970s was poised to achieve a stunning electoral victory under a leader, François Mitterand, who insisted that his project had "nothing in common with the corrupt compromises of a Schmidt or a Callaghan."[4] In spite of the rhetoric of making a radical break with the "errors of the past," the PSF, after it came to power in 1981, quickly reverted to conventional social-democratic politics both in its relations with the state and in its internal organization.

Among all of these attempts to transcend the limits of social democracy, the most determined and creative was perhaps the one advanced by a new left that had emerged in the Labour Party by the early 1970s and showed the greatest staying power until its defeat a full decade later. It seemed to recognize earlier than most, as its leading spokesman Tony Benn put it in 1970, "a new philosophy of government now emerging everywhere on the right ... promising [the new citizen] greater freedom from government, just as big business is to be promised lower taxes and less intervention." This would allow big business "to control the new citizen at the very same time as the Government reduces its protections for him."[5] This Labour new left also saw quite clearly at this time that the internationalization of capital, in the form of the multinational corporation, was posing the greatest new challenge to the post-war settlement. It was in this context that it made the case for going well beyond Keynesian demand management by bringing the financial system into the public domain as well as micro intervention in industrial investment through statutory planning agreements with major firms.

These policies were not necessarily more radical than others being advanced on the social-democratic left at the time. What really made the Labour new left important was its understanding that the policies advanced under its alternative economic strategy would have little effect on the party leadership without a fundamental transformation in the mode of political representation itself. Labour had successfully inserted itself into what Marx derided as the political form wherein universal suffrage amounted to "deciding once in three to six years which member of the ruling class was to misrepresent the people in Parliament."[6] The Labour Party had a base in the working class and its leaders were motivated by a vague commitment to the idea of alternative social order, but overriding all else – and devaluing it – was its strong and unwavering belief in parliamentarist politics. In practice this meant adopting not only the trappings of a certain aristocratic embrace within the gentleman's club that is Westminster but also accepting the notion that democracy is no more than a contest between competing parliamentary teams that treat the extraparliamentary party and its activists as either nuisances or servants, and the citizens as passive actors, except for the occasional act of voting.

Labour's inability to manage the crisis of British capitalism, already so evident in the 1960s, long before the collapse of the "golden age" elsewhere, had brought the contradiction between a vague commitment to socialism and a strong commitment to parliamentarism starkly to the fore and this explained in good part the vitality and influence of the British new left in the 1960s. The failure to nurture the extraparliamentary party as a counter-hegemonic community became a clear liability in the face of a crisis of hegemony of the kind that eventually gave rise to Thatcherism in Britain. A new left within the Labour Party developed in the 1970s, spearheaded by young activists who worked in local community development projects and who understood, as Gramsci had, the need for conceiving their party as an alternate state.

The struggle the Labour new left undertook for transforming the party (and through it the state) entailed the following six central strategic considerations:

1. The unaccountability of the party leadership – and especially of the parliamentary elite – to the extraparliamentary party had to be challenged by instituting new mechanisms of securing the accountability of members of parliament and the national executive to local party activists and to delegates to the annual party conference; this initiative was led by the Campaign for Labour Party Democracy through its fight for the reselection of MPs and the election of the party leader not just by the parliamentary caucus but by the whole party conference; this attempt to secure accountability challenged both the aristocratic traces embedded in Burkean conceptions of parliamentarism and the democratic centralist traces embedded in what Michels called "the iron law of oligarchy" in mass working class parties;
2. Challenging the party's narrowly electoralist orientation to politics; as Benn put it in 1971: "Political leaders often seem to be

telling us two things: first – 'There is nothing you have to do except vote for us'; and second – 'If you do vote for us, we can solve all your problems.' Both of these statements are absolutely and demonstrably false ... The people must be helped to understand that they will make little progress unless they are more politically self-reliant and are prepared to organize with others to achieve what they want"[7];

3. The struggle for the accountability of parliamentarians and the rejection of electoralism took the form of organizing party members as a force for change in the party; it was recognized, moreover, that this would have to involve further institutional reforms to ensure that members did not remain atomized, passive, and deferential vis-à-vis party leaders; and it also required attempting to politicize the trade unions (such as through the establishment of party branches in the workplace) to the same end;

4. Ultimately the point of organizing the members was to turn the extraparliamentary party into a force for change beyond the party, to turn the energy of the party activists outwards; this would involve linking the party to popular struggles in the community through the redefinition of its political role as one of organizing, education, mobilization, and coordination;

5. This was still all designed to get a Labour Government elected, but with the understanding that the main role of the party and its leadership, even when in government, remained that of an educator and mobilizer of the forces for radical change; the role of political leader was, as Benn put it, "to give way to the forces he has encouraged and mobilised by a process of education and persuasion. *Legislation is thus the last process in a campaign for change*"[8];

6. At the same time, however, this whole approach also meant explicitly calling the bluff of those many adherents of the new left that had opted for a return to revolutionary strategies and building new parties of a Leninist type; the Labour new left (with a few notable "entryist" exceptions, like the Militant Tendency) took the view that there was no-one seriously planning a revolution in Britain, despite much Trotskyist rhetoric, nor could an insurrection in the Bolshevik form any longer be conceived in the advanced capitalist world.

Against the backdrop of the abandonment of Keynesianism and the inauguration of monetarism under the 1974–79 Labour Government, the new left in the party gained in strength. But the Labour Party proved very resistant to change. The protracted battle that ensued through the 1970s and early 1980s to attempt to change the party along the lines advanced by the new left contrasted sharply with the quick success the new right scored in winning over the Conservative Party in the mid-1970s. The result was that the forces represented by Thatcher were able to turn their energies outwards to the broader population with the resources of the unified party behind them, while the energies of the Labour new left were consumed in challenging the tenacious hold that centre-right social democrats had over the parliamentary party and its leadership. The latter were able and willing to use their close ties to the media to engage in a vicious campaign of denigration against their opponents inside the party ("the loony left"). They increasingly won allies among the timid and confused (but nevertheless tenaciously parliamentarist) old stalwarts of the Bevanite left in the party (epitomized by Michael Foot) once it became clear that the main concern of the new left was the mode of representation rather than just advancing left-wing policies.

The very legitimacy of any argument to the left of centre came into question in Britain amidst incessant vilification of the Labour new left not only by Thatcher and the media but by the most "respectable" leaders of the Labour Party itself. Increasingly the enormity and high risk of the task in which the Labour new left was engaged began to make itself clear. The protracted battle left the party divided while Thatcher conducted her *blitzkrieg* against the welfare state and the unions. In this context, the growing awareness that divided parties can't win elections slowly but surely began to traumatize those who were initially sympathetic to the new left project.

Among the left-wing union leadership, in particular, there was a desire to be done with the intraparty debate over the meaning of democracy. They continued to sponsor radical socialist resolutions at party conferences but drew back from making the party leadership accountable for not even campaigning for, let alone not introducing, such policies. They began to fear that the battle for democracy and accountability in the party was spilling too far over into their own organizations. Their concern that the unions not be blamed in the media for undermining parliamentary sovereignty (and their readiness to accept from party leaders pledges that they would really adhere to governing in a corporatist partnership with the union leaders "next time") trumped the commitment some of the union leaders had once shown to the intensive political education of their members in the wake of the crisis of social democracy and the rise of the new right.

Intellectual grounds for this were provided by the widely read "Euro-Communist" magazine *Marxism Today*. Its influence had initially been based in good part on Stuart Hall's brilliantly insightful essays directly linking the popularity of Thatcherism to the limitations of social democracy. Among these, the most serious were the "deeply undemocratic character" of the institutions of the labour movement and the tendency to treat ordinary people as passive "clients of a state over which [they] have no real ... control." Although Hall had a clear premonition that attempts to address these limitations might prove too traumatic to be successful, his analysis could only be read as encouraging the Labour new left in its attempt to change the party: "The question of the nature, procedures, organizational structures and conceptions of new forms of political representation, of a more broadly mass and democratic character" was not a matter to be attended to "after the immediate struggle was over" but had to be "what the 'immediate struggle' is about."[9]

But *Marxism Today* changed its tune in face of the actual trauma that the attempt to change the Labour Party did in fact produce on the British left. In this respect, the leading Communist historian Eric Hobsbawm's interventions were influential in providing the intellectual underpinning for the position Neil Kinnock adopted against the Labour new left.[10] On the basis of an acute analysis of declining proletarian culture, Hobsbawm called for the broadest political unity to oppose Thatcherism while, like Kinnock (and Michael Foot before him), remaining silent about the issues raised in the debate on intraparty democracy and policy, as well as about the role played by the centre-right in the course of it. A second current within *Marxism Today*, closer to that of Stuart Hall himself, adopted the approach of suggesting that a Kinnock leadership would be open to Greater London Council-style "social movement" political activism and would distance itself from the old Labourist class politics. But this was an illusion. The parliamentary leadership actively disliked – and feared being embarrassed in the eyes of the press by – black and feminist activists as much as or even more than they disliked the "while male" socialist activists in the constituency parties.

Marxism Today helped to create a climate that undermined the kind of enthusiasm that supporters of the Labour new left had once had (and which *Marxism Today* had once encouraged) for intraparty democracy and for the Alternative Economic Strategy. The trouble was that the kind of thinking *Marxism Today* represented was incapable of producing (any more than Hobsbawm could with his more sober "popular front" line) any *other* kind of socialist strategy. As Donald Sassoon, who still sees "the iconoclasm" of *Marxism Today* as having been "indispensable," admits: "once the ground was cleared of old-fashioned leftism, the journal and its followers remained unable to go beyond it ... In the manner of modern gurus they noted a trend (post-Fordism, flexible specialization or charity events for Third World Countries), called it progress, and projected it into the future. By the time the journal folded in the 1990s, it had nothing left to say."[11]

Tactical and strategic weaknesses and divisions within the Labour new left contributed heavily to its defeat. But factored into the equation must also be the political timidity of the left union leadership as well as political particularism of the new social movements, which never themselves succeeded in uniting to found a lasting new politics "beyond the fragments." Nor, as our discussion of Marxism Today suggests, should we let socialist intellectuals off the hook. From having been a fount of creativity through the 1960s and 1970s the British intellectual left became increasingly politically confused and anodyne in the face of Thatcherism. Today, their commitment to democratic reform is centered around devolution and the promotion of proportional representation – both of which, however necessary, avoid the deeper problems of representation brought to the fore by the Labour new left. Their commitment to internationalism, reflected above all in their enthusiasm for the European Union, also avoids most of the key issues of class power that attend economic and monetary integration amidst globalization.

The defeat of the project of the Labour new left eventually brought the Labour Party to Blair. The sense in which he represents a transition *from* socialism rests on the destruction of the potential represented by that new left for authoring a politics *beyond* social democracy. It is in this sense that we can justifiably say of social-democratic experience in the 1980s and 1990s that it proves that *politics matters*. Unfortunately, this is so *not* in the sense of social democracy being able to sustain full employment and welfare state policies; rather it is so in the sense of social-democratic parties having effectively closed off the possibility of socialist renewal that developed within their ranks.

Of course, social democracy is only part of the problem for the left, although it is hardly a minor one given the space it has occupied, and still does. While it has not been my goal to take this up on this occasion, it must be said that no less a problem has been the failure of the Marxist left to adequately address the question of organization, as was noted by both Gramsci and Lukacs in their time. This problem still remains. Yet the struggle continues. As the left gropes its way beyond the historic failures of social democracy and Communism and begins to build new types of political institutions in the decades to come, it may well be that the concerns of the Labour new left regarding the nature of political organization will prove instructive. This is what Colin Leys likes to call their "communication with the future": "They have not won their political battles; they have not carried their main points, they have not stopped their adversaries' advance; but they have told silently upon the mind of the country, they have prepared currents of feeling which sap their adversaries' position when it seems gained, they have kept up their communication with the future." [12]

NOTES

1   The title of this essay is taken from Colin Leys's lead essay in the 1996 *Socialist Register*, and what I have to say draws on the work that Colin and I have done together for our book on the Labour Party – a book that tries to put what Tony Blair represents in historical perspective. See Colin Leys, "The British Labour Party's Transition from Socialism to Capitalism," *The Socialist Register 1996*, London: Merlin Press, 1996; and Leo Panitch and Colin Leys, *The End of Parliamentary Socialism: From New Left to New Labour*, London: Verso, 1997.

2   Donald Sassoon, *One Hundred Years of Socialism: The West European Left in the Twentieth Century*, London: I.B. Tauris, 1996: 58-9.

3   See G. Therborn, *Why Some Peoples Are More Unemployed Than Others*. London: Verso, 1986. For an earlier usage, see F.G. Castles and R.D. McKinley, "Does Politics Matter? An Analysis of the Public Welfare Commitment of Advanced Capitalist States," *European Journal of Political Research*, no. 7, 1979.

4   Quoted in R.W. Johnson, *The Long March of the French Left*, New York: Macmillan, 1981: 159.

5   Tony Benn, *The New Politics: A Socialist Reconnaissance; Fabian Tract*, no. 402, September 1970: 12.

6   "The Civil War in France: Address of the General Council," in Marx, *The First International and After*, D. Fernbach, ed., Vintage, 1974: 210.

7   *Speeches by Tony Benn*, Nottingham, Spokesman, 1974: 277-8.

8   Ibid.

9   Stuart Hall, "The Great Moving Right Show," *Marxism Today*, January 1979; see also, "Thatcherism – A New Stage," *Marxism Today*, February 1980.

10 Hobsbawm's interventions in this period are collected in his *Politics for a Rational Left: Political Writing 1977-88*, London: Roultledge, 1989.

11 Donald Sassoon, *One Hundred Years of Socialism*, 692.

12 Matthew Arnold, cited in Fred Inglis, "The Figures of Dissent," *New Left Review*, no. 215, January/February 1996: 82.

Tony Blair and the British Left

ALEX CALLINICOS

The British general election of 1 May 1997 may be one of the great watersheds in modern electoral politics. An estimated 3.2 million voters who had backed John Major's Conservative Government in April 1992 now abandoned the Tories.[1] They helped to produce a landslide victory for the Labour Party under Tony Blair, whose majority of 179 seats was even greater than the majority won by the historic Attlee government in 1945. The Tories were reduced to their smallest number of seats since another great landslide, the Liberal victory of 1906. The eighteen years in which Britain had been a testing ground for the policies of the free-market right were over.

But what did the new Blair government portend? The scale of the Labour victory and the sheer exhilaration of seeing long-standing Tory ministers evicted from office and replaced by Labour politicians long condemned to opposition created an atmosphere close to euphoria. Skilful presentation helped reinforce a sense of rapid change. Yet Labour's victory had been preceded by careful efforts to reconstruct or "modernize" the party. Blair's "New Labour" abandoned its long-standing commitment to social ownership of the economy and eschewed any promises of substantial social and economic change.

This stance continued to shape Labour's approach during the general election itself. The party pursued a highly defensive campaign, seeking to further narrow its policy differences with the Tories and to illustrate its new-found conservatism. This approach reflected political conviction as well as tactical caution, as this anecdote, told by a journalist close the Blair camp, *Financial Times* columnist Philip Stephens, illustrates: "Early on in the campaign, I was foolhardy enough to ask Mr Blair if there might be some small role for wealth redistribution in the politics of the centre left. It would have been safer to venture he regularly beat his wife."[2]

THE RISE AND FALL OF STAKEHOLDER CAPITALISM

The development of New Labour policy in opposition provides some indications of the likely course the government would follow. The history of the idea of stakeholder capitalism, briefly endorsed by Blair in a speech in Singapore in January 1996, is thus highly symptomatic. The significance of the concept of stakeholding lies in the manner in which it seemed to offer a resolution of the main dilemma of right-wing social democracy.[3] Essentially, this current based itself after the Second World War on the economics of John Maynard Keynes. The two classic works of post-war "revisionism," Tony Crosland's *The Future of Socialism* and John Strachey's *Contemporary Capitalism* argued that Keynesian demand-management made it possible for the state to secure economic growth, full employment, and rising living standards without there being any need to expropriate capital. From the fruits of growth would come the resources needed to eliminate absolute poverty and to reduce social inequality. The revisionists claimed still to be socialists, in the sense that they were committed to the objective of social equality, but they renounced the traditional methods of the left – class struggle and nationalization – as means for attaining this goal.

Keynesian social democracy flourished during the long boom of the 1950s and 1960s. The faltering and then collapse of that boom in the late 1960s and early 1970s, and a return to class confrontation not just in Britain but throughout the advanced capitalist world threw the social-democratic right into crisis. British politics briefly polarized between the revived classical liberalism of Margaret Thatcher and the more radical reformism of Tony Benn.[4] The Tory electoral triumphs and the defeats suffered by the miners and other groups of workers during the 1980s helped to drive Labour back to the right. Intellectually, traditional social democracy was in tatters. Given the apparent failure of Keynesian economics, what plausible strategic vision could Labour now offer?

Under Blair two ideological trends already under way before he became leader accelerated. First, and negatively, the belief – central to Keynesian social democracy – that the nation-state can manage and regulate capitalism so as to avoid significant market fluctuations was definitively abandoned. As Blair put it in his 1995 Mais lecture: "We must recognize that the UK is situated in the middle of an active global market for capital – a market which is less subject to regulation today than for several decades. An expansionary fiscal or monetary policy that is at odds with other economies in Europe will not be sustained for very long. To that extent the room for manoeuvre of any government in Britain is already heavily circumscribed."[5] Globalization, as it has become fashionable to call it, had thus killed off national economic management. Where did this leave any party committed to reforming capitalism, however modestly? It is here that we come to the second ideological development. The concept of stakeholder capitalism was used to provide Labour with the strategic vision so desperately needed after the collapse of Keynesian social democracy.[6]

One important source for the concept is provided by the French economist and businessman Michel Albert. His book *Capitalism against Capitalism* (1991) is to some extent a response to Francis Fukuyama's famous thesis that the collapse of Stalinism marked the end of history in the sense that liberal capitalism no longer faced any rivals capable of offering it a systemic challenge. Fukuyama is wrong, Albert contends, because history will continue as the conflict is now not between rival social systems but between different models of capitalism:

With the collapse of communism, it is as if a veil has been suddenly lifted from our eyes. Capitalism, we can now see, has two faces, two personalities. The neo-American model is based on individual success and short-term financial gain; the Rhine model, of German pedigree but with strong Japanese connections, emphasize collective success, consensus and long-term concerns. In the last decade or so, it is this Rhine model – unheralded, unsung and lacking even nominal identity papers – that has shown itself to be the more efficient of the two, as well as the more equitable.[7]

The contrast Albert drew between Anglo-American and Rhine capitalism was seized on by intellectuals associated with the Labour right. Of these probably the most important were the journalist Will Hutton, columnist on the *Guardian* and now editor of the *Observer*, and the academic David Marquand, ex-Labour MP and founder of the breakaway Social Democratic Party, but welcomed back into the fold under Blair.[8] It provided them with both the basis of a critique of Tory Britain and an alternative to Thatcher's and Major's policies.

The *locus classicus* of both is provided by Hutton's celebrated bestseller *The State We're In* (1995). Here he damns Tory policies for reinforcing the long-term tendency of British capitalism, under the domination of the City, to pursue short-term speculative investment.

Any reform of the British economy and state must be in the direction of "stakeholder, social capitalism," taking as its model the possession by continental European, Japanese, and even American societies of "strong institutions that allow their firms to enjoy some of the gains from co-operation as well as from competition" and which "are created and legitimized by some broad notion of public or national purpose." The organized working class, shunned and excluded under the Tories, would find their place in these institutions as, like their German counterparts, "social partners in the management of capitalism."[9]

What Albert claims to be one of the lessons of Rhine capitalism, that "top economic performance can be wedded to social solidarity through the social market economy," had obvious attractions to social democrats eager to offer reforms without confronting capitalism.[10] Thus in their "Dos and Don'ts for Social Democrats," James Cornford and Patricia Hewitt tell their readers: "Decide what kind of capitalist you are ... Social democrats have to do more that recognize market failure when they see it: they have to advance an alternative conception of how market economies should work ... The Left must construct markets which work by raising standards, not by driving them downwards."[11]

There are three major difficulties with the idea of stakeholder capitalism. The first is that it seems to be in contradiction with the other ideological shift under Blair – the rejection of any Keynesian strategy of using the power of the nation-state to manage the economy. Actually existing stakeholder capitalisms, such as Germany and Japan, have relied on a high level of state intervention in the economy.

In his Mais lecture, Blair committed Labour to "the control of inflation through a tough macro-economic policy framework" – in other words, he accepted the Thatcherite argument that the priority of government policy is to reduce inflation to a minimum, primarily by controlling public spending. UBS chief economist Bill Martin comments: "Brown, Blair and his economic adviser Derek Scott have chewed, swallowed and digested the central-bankerly proposition that stability is the key to improved economic performance; so much so that Labour's growth strategy comprises little else."[12] It is interesting that Hutton, whose most important intellectual contribution has been to revive Keynes's stress on the pervasive uncertainty endemic in capitalist economies, should have criticized Blair's Mais lecture for its "underlying assumption that capitalism works best if left to its own devices."[13] Hutton has also vigorously attacked the closely related "myth of globalization" – the idea, in other words, heavily relied on by Blair and Brown, that the internationalization of capital makes national reforms impossible.[14]

The second difficulty with stakeholder capitalism is really a concrete example of the contradiction just discussed. Quite simply, actually existing stakeholder capitalism is in a lot of trouble. Japan is just beginning to recover from its worst slump since the 1930s, brought on by a frenzy of rather Anglo-Saxon speculation in securities and real estate in the late 1980s, the so-called "bubble economy." Germany meanwhile has experienced extreme cyclical instability over the past few years – the reunification boom at the beginning of the 1990s, slump in 1993–94, a brief recovery in 1995, and then back again to recession. These problems have helped provoke intense debate, in which large sections of German capital have begun to press for drastic reductions in the welfare spending and in the other benefits workers enjoy in order to enhance competitiveness and profitability.[15]

If the proposed restructuring of "Rhine capitalism" is successful, the result will be an economy in certain respects closer to the Anglo-American model than it has been in the past. Thus, the conservative government of Helmut Kohl introduced legislation to allow publicly quoted companies to buy back up to 10 per cent of their capital and reward executives with stock options. These are moves that the *Financial Times* claims "will help promote the idea of shareholder value in Germany," and thus introduce more of precisely the kind of Anglo-American "short-termism" derided by Hutton and Marquand.[16]

Both the difficulties outlined above point to the same fundamental reality. Stakeholder capitalism in Germany and Japan is just as much a variant of the capitalist mode of production as its Anglo-American counterpart. It is based on the same social and economic inequalities reflecting the exploitation of the working class. It is subject to the same tendencies towards crisis that arise from the nature of capitalism as a system driven by competitive accumulation. The trends described above for German capitalism, under the pressures of international competition, to take on some of the characteristics of the more speculative Anglo-American model indicate that the present crisis is one of capitalism as a system rather than of one particular version of that system.[17]

These two problems – the contradiction between state intervention and "globalization" and the problems facing the German and Japanese economies – concern the general question of whether or not stakeholding capitalism really is an attractive objective for the left. The third, however, follows from the former while pertaining specifically to its attractions to Blair and his co-thinkers. As envisaged by Hutton and Marquand at least, the shift to stakeholder capitalism would require considerable institutional changes. These would be of two kinds.

First of all, constitutional reform. Hutton and Marquand subscribe to the interpretation of British history perhaps most influentially developed by Perry Anderson and Tom Nairn, but also defended by Colin Leys, according to which Britain has never achieved a modern capitalist state. The relative decline of British capitalism is, in large part, a consequence of its political domination by a patrician oligarchy closely integrated with the City of London, itself a set of financial institutions characterized by their lack of involvement in industrial investment.[18] Thus Hutton argues that "the semi-modern nature of the British state is a fundamental cause of Britain's economic and social problems." Reforming British capitalism therefore requires reforming "the semi-feudal state" that presides over it through the kind of measures advocated by Charter 88: the introduction of a written constitution, proportional representation, and the like.[19] Secondly, achieving stakeholding capitalism means overhauling British company law. Hutton, for example, argues for "initiatives in corporate governance" to "break the self-perpetuating oligarchy of most British firms ... This could be negotiated initially as a voluntary code, but ultimately it would have to [be] backed by legislation."[20]

Introducing PR and reforming "corporate governance" are hardly the stuff of revolution. But, as Colin Leys noted in a perceptive review of The State We're In, "Hutton's analysis is more profound and disturbing than 'New Labour's', and his project – in spite of its frankly 'bourgeois' character – much more radical."[21] However much it is based on a questionable interpretation of British history and fails to identify the real source of our problems, the Hutton-Marquand vision of stakeholding capitalism requires for its implementation a confrontation with entrenched capitalist interests in the shape of the City and its allies in the Treasury and company boardrooms. But no sooner had Blair pronounced the words "stakeholder economy" in Singapore in January 1996 than he and his spin-doctors sought to disavow any radical implications it might have. They were particularly eager to dissociate Blair's conception from the detailed proposals for institutional change that Hutton had spelt out in his book.[22]

Peter Mandelson, one of Blair's closest collaborators, and Roger Liddle, another returnee from the SDP, in their book The Blair Revolution argue that a New Labour Government "must do whatever it can to promote a stakeholder culture in industry and the City." They consider the idea of legislation to make company directors "take into account the full range of interests of those with a stake in a company," but object: "The danger in any such step is that it would weaken the external discipline that the threat of take-over puts on companies to be efficient and profitable. In other words, it could protect the sleepy at the expense of the thrusting and go-ahead."[23]

Six months after Blair's Singapore speech the *Financial Times* reported under the headline "Labour Softens on Stakeholding" that a Labour draft industrial policy document "fails to live up to the pre-publicity" since it contained "few specific reforms." Alasdair Darling, Labour's City spokesperson, told the paper: "There is a limit to how many of Britain's corporate ills can be resolved by legislation. What you are trying to do is change people's behaviour and attitudes."[24]

The *Financial Times*, hardly a stronghold of "Old Labour" thinking, seemed taken aback by the extent of this retreat:

Perhaps most damning is the way that Conservative party officials admit to being surprised by Labour's decision to try to neutralize the stakeholder issue. They had been concerned that Labour would portray City fund managers as the "union barons of the 1990s" and attack the government for failing to stop their excesses ... Labour insiders do not deny that it wants to neutralize the stakeholder debate rather than make a virtue of it. The decision stems from the Conservative party's effective campaign representing stakeholding as a return to the corporatism of the 1970s.

"They are clearly scared rigid of the Tory line and as a result they have bottled what could be an imaginative set of policies," one Labour official said.[25]

BACK TO LAISSEZ-FAIRE

The retreat from stakeholder capitalism reflected more than timidity and caution on New Labour's part. It was also a matter of the positive preferences of Blair and his closest allies; thus Blair on a number of occasions – for example, during a visit to New York in April 1996 – went out of his way to reassure business audiences that his promise to sign up to the Social Chapter of the Maastricht Treaty would not threaten Britain's "flexible" labour markets or raise social costs. In July 1996 he wrote to 10,000 business executives to assure them that a Labour Government would "insist that any measures adopted under the Social Chapter promote fairness, not inflexibility. It will not be used to import foreign social security systems or ways of organizing the board-room."[26]

This move represented the effective abandonment of the principal basis on which the British labour movement had come to overwhelmingly support the European Community in the late 1980s: the belief that Brussels could act as a bastion to help protect British workers from the Tory drive to increase "flexibility" and cut welfare spending. As so often, it was left to Peter Mandelson to make explicit the grounds on which Blair took this stance – the more or less unqualified endorsement of market capitalism and of the inequalities that unavoidably accompany it. Writing with Roger Liddle, Mandelson declares: "New Labour's belief in the dynamic market economy involves recognition that substantial personal incentives and rewards are necessary in order to encourage risk-taking and entrepreneurialism. Profit is not a dirty word – profits are accepted as the motor of private enterprise."[27] Mandelson was even more explicit in a newspaper article he wrote in April 1996 after completing a tour of the Far East paid for by Barclays Bank in order that he might "meet many of its Asian corporate customers to talk about trade and investment under a Labour government." The piece is an extraordinarily crude and unqualified celebration of private enterprise and profit-making. Thus Mandelson defends the East Asian boom economies from the charge that they are "based on sweatshop labour producing cheap, bargain-basement goods, with huge profits and vast wealth for a few being earned through exploitation of the many."[28]

"Of course," he declares, "profits are very substantial and there are some very rich entrepreneurs, but what's wrong with that?" Mandelson pays lip service to the idea of stakeholder capitalism when, for example, he praises the "conscious attempt by governments such as those in Japan, Korea and Singapore to give their workforce a stake in the country's economic success." At the same time he highlights among the "lessons of Asia-Pacific ... an unambiguous commitment to backing entrepreneurial flair – and its rewards – and rejecting the corporatist notion that, by sitting around a table with an agenda of business problems, national representatives of 'both sides' of industry can somehow find the solutions."

Social bargaining between government, big business, and trade-union leaders is, of course, a central feature of the Rhine model championed by Hutton and Marquand. Mandelson underlines his rejection of this model by sympathetically quoting a Korean executive's complaint about "the high costs of the social security system in Germany." He continues: "Tony Blair was right in his recent New York speech to rule out the introduction of similar German costs for Britain, an issue, it should be noted, which is quite separate from the social chapter." In effect Mandelson selects for praise in the East Asian variant of stakeholder capitalism not those aspects stressed by Hutton – the alleged importance of social co-operation in achieving economic efficiency – but rather the unbridled pursuit of profit.

No wonder, then, that one Labour frontbench spokesman on industry, Kim Howells, should appeal to the party: "Brothers and sisters, embrace competition!" Howells, a former member of the Communist Party, denounced the idea of state intervention in the economy and valorized the cult of entrepreneurs like the billionaire founder of Microsoft: "The success of Bill Gates and the crises at IBM and Apple were not determined by Washington's efforts at second-guessing trends in the personal computer markets."[29] New Labour thinking, at least when practised by the like of Howells, increasingly resembled unabashed celebrations of Victorian laissez-faire such as Samuel Smiles's *Self Help*.

A more nuanced version of the same strategic conception was defended by the group of Blairite intellectuals associated with the think-tank *Demos*. Its director, Geoff Mulgan (appointed a Downing Street adviser in May 1997), and the journalist Charles Leadbeater attacked stakeholding: "For all their virtues of the past, the German and Japanese economies are not models for the British economy of the future. That future is likely to lie with smaller companies in services or high technology, and with a far more fluid and fast-moving economy."[30] Hutton and the economist John Kay accurately dismissed this as an "attempt to construct 'capitalism with a human face.'"[31]

Against this background, Gordon Brown's announcement in January 1997 that Labour in office would not raise existing income-tax rates during the next parliament and would observe the extremely tight spending targets laid down by the Major government for 1997–99 appears less as a tactical manoeuvre to defuse Tory attacks on Labour's traditional "tax-and-spend" policies and more as a reflection of deep-seated convictions. This impression was further reinforced when, within days of taking office, Brown announced that he was giving the Bank of England operational independence by allowing it to set the level of interest rates. This proposal, first mooted by Nigel Lawson, Thatcher's most ideologically neoliberal Chancellor, as a way of insulating the market from democratic control, was now implemented by a Labour Government. And when a more traditional reformist coalition under Lionel Jospin won the French legislative elections on 1 June 1997, Blair responded by presenting himself as the champion of flexible labour markets and deregulation in the European Union. Even the *Observer*, "the Paper for the New Era," concluded after two months of the new government: "The Tories are out of office, but in power."[32]

"Decide what kind of capitalist you are," James Cornford and Patricia Hewitt advise social democrats. Tony Blair and his co-thinkers have decided: they have opted for what looks suspiciously like the bad old Anglo-American free-enterprise model championed by Thatcher and Reagan.

MORAL AUTHORITARIANISM AND
HESITANT DEMOCRATIZATION

To economic conservatism was matched an increasingly ugly tone of moral authoritarianism. Blair had first made a public impact when, as shadow home secretary, he effectively took over the New Right's case on law and order. "Family values" became a dominant theme of New Labour propaganda. Images of vacuously grinning (and all-white) families shone from the party's publicity material. The few specific proposals Blair and his cronies were prepared to make were often directed at families. And, should families prove to be dysfunctional, Blair's future home secretary, Jack Straw, was there on cue to invoke the power of the state to coerce and punish. One of Labour's five specific election promises was "fast-track punishment for persistent young offenders."

The ideological basis for New Labour's moral authoritarianism was spelled out by Blair in his 1995 *Spectator*/Allied Dunbar lecture. "Duty is the cornerstone of a decent society," he argued. It followed that "[t]he rights we receive should reflect the duties we owe."[33] The priority thus given to duties over rights justified the Labour front bench's increasingly casual attitude towards civil liberties and its efforts to outflank the Tories on law and order issues – for example Straw's initial failure to oppose the outgoing government's 1997 Police Bill despite the arbitrary powers of search and seizure it gave the police.

New Labour's combination of economic and social conservatism antagonized many of Blair's natural supporters in the liberal middle class. Thus Shirley Williams, former Labour cabinet minister, founder of the breakaway SDP, and now a Liberal Democrat peeress, declared during the election: "I have a profound disquiet that, especially on law and order and on redistribution, they have taken up positions in the campaign that in practice will be very difficult to change in power."[34]

Counter-balancing such concerns, however, was the enthusiasm that Labour's commitment to constitutional reform generated among centre-left intellectuals. As we have seen, political change was a crucial plank in the Hutton-Marquand project of stakeholder capitalism. Writing just before the general election, Hutton acknowledged the "risk ... that New Labour will remain imprisoned by the ideas it has learned to ape, and will govern too much within the parameters laid down by its predecessors." But he went on to praise "Labour's commitment to constitutional change, the most serious package advocated by any political party since before the First World War," as "a dramatically radical statement."[35]

Hutton's *Observer* accordingly welcomed the political reforms outlined in the new government's first Queen's Speech on 14 May: "The politics of constitutional reform has so long lived in the abstract realm of workshops, pamphlets, books, speeches and dashed hopes that the centre-left this weekend is pinching itself as it comes to terms with the fact that its dreams are turning into practical reality ... The great fear of the chattering classes – that Tony Blair once safe inside Downing Street would betray the cause of decentralization and reform – has proved comprehensively false."[36] Yet Blair's key commitments on constitutional reform – a referendum on proportional representation, devolution in Scotland and Wales, the abolition of the voting rights of hereditary peers – were inherited from his predecessor John Smith, an eminently Old Labour figure. Blair himself did not conceal his personal opposition to proportional representation, though he still promised to hold a referendum on electoral reform.[37] Mandelson and Liddle were similarly unenthusiastic about institutional change, declaring: "we do not believe that constitutional reform offers the panacea that is sometimes claimed." They go on to argue: "The reform agenda must spring from the voters' concerns and not follow the master plan of constitutional theorists or be dictated by the interests of the chattering classes."[38]

In June 1996 Blair caused an uproar in the Scottish Labour Party by insisting that a referendum be held not simply to establish whether or not the Scottish people desired their own parliament but also whether it should have tax-raising powers – a concession to the Tory campaign against "the Tartan tax" that devolution would supposedly produce. During the election campaign Blair played down devolution, comparing a Scottish parliament to an English parish council. The priority given to the issue in the Labour's first legislative program reflected less a positive enthusiasm for constitutional reform than a desire to get two complex bills out of the way quickly. The sticky issues of House of Lords reform and PR were deferred and could easily become casualties of the vicissitudes of government.

If anything, the most immediate impression of the new government was not of freshly released democratic impulses but of the centralization of executive power. The *Financial Times* commented after Blair's first two weeks in office: "Mr Blair has adopted many of the control mechanisms of Lady Thatcher. He has created others." With the help of his chief of staff, Jonathan Powell, and of Mandelson, appointed minister without portfolio responsible for policy coordination, Blair sought to monitor and control the activities of his ministers. The ethos of the new government was expressed in its threat to have any Welsh Labour MPs who opposed devolution deselected. "Mr Mandelson last Sunday appeared to reinvent the job description of Labour MPs. Their prime duty, he said, was to promote the manifesto. Independent thinking is permitted, but independence is limited to the parameters of the creed. Says one minister: 'Our leader believes in consensus, but not compromise.'"[39]

BREAKING WITH THE UNIONS

These developments pose more sharply than ever the question inherent in Blair's "Project" from the start: to what extent does it represent a radical break with Labour tradition? Blairite boosters stress its novelty – a claim implicit in the very name "New Labour." But others are justifiably more skeptical. Thus David Coates argues:

Of course, New Labour likes to *present* itself as qualitatively different from Old Labour, and it is true that the internal story of the Labour Party since 1983 has been one of a retreat from Bennite radicalism, from the Alternative Economic Strategy and from nuclear disarmament. But the degree of retreat (which *is* marked, and which is indeed the basis of New Labour's claim to be new) actually tells us more about the degree of leftward shift that occurred between 1979 and 1983 than it does about the novelty of New Labour. In many ways New Labour is working its way back to the Party's conventional understanding of how to trigger economic growth through the construction of a close and collaborative relationship with the owners of private capital.[40]

Coates is right to highlight the continuities in respect of *policy* between New and Old Labour. The similarities between Gordon Brown's self-image as an "Iron Chancellor" and Philip Snowden, Ramsay Mac-Donald's disastrously orthodox Chancellor of the Exchequer in 1924 and 1929–31, have often been noted. And it was, of course, Denis Healey's tenure as Chancellor in the 1974–79 Labour Government that marked the decisive break in post-war British economic policy, away from Keynesian interventionism and into a monetarist framework that gave priority to reducing public expenditure.[41]

Nevertheless, there is one crucial respect in which the Blairite project does mark a break with the past, namely its now unconcealed intention to scrap the Labour Party's link with the trade unions. According to Philip Stephens, writing nearly two years before Labour took office, Blair's calculations were based on the rapid

growth in party membership since he was elected leader in July
1994: "In its leader's mind this means a new party, one made in his
own social democrat image. The new members are his power base ...
And every addition reinforces the irrelevance of the trade unions.
No, Mr Blair is not strong enough yet to deny the union leaders their
annual outing to party conferences. Yes, if he wins the election, there
is little future for the present institutional link between party and
unions. Remember the Social Democratic party's gang of four? Well,
think of Mr Blair as the gang of one."[42] These intentions came out
into the open at the conference of the Trades Union Congress (TUC)
in September 1996. The furore created by proposals that suggested
that a Labour Government, far from repealing Tory anti-union legislation, would further restrict workers' ability to organize and go
on strike was intensified when Stephen Byers, a junior spokesperson
close to Blair, leaked a scenario under which such a government
would use the pretext of a public sector strike to hold a membership
ballot on breaking the union link. To cap it all, the week ended with
Kim Howells' call for Labour to stop using even the word "socialism." Blair refused to repudiate Byers or Howells and lamented "the
division in radical politics at the end of the last century and
the beginning of this century, between Liberals and the Labour
Party."[43]

It is doubtful whether Blair and his advisers had worked out a
detailed strategy for actually breaking the union link. The introduction
of state funding of political parties, canvassed in New Labour circles as
a device for reducing the party's massive dependence on the unions'
financial support and thus for making a break feasible, would be a
complex and lengthy process. Nevertheless, the practicability of such a
step was less important than the fact that Blair desired to take it. When
the SDP broke away from Labour in 1981, one of its main complaints
concerned the party's alliance with the trade unions. The Labour Party
now has a leader who accepts this critique, and indeed who apparently believes that the formation of the party he now heads was a
mistake.[44]

The New Labour *Weltanschauung* is thus evident. It includes what
Nic Cohen calls "a visceral dislike of trade unionists and, in the words
of one member of the Shadow Cabinet, a 'positive hostility' towards
union leaders which no electoral calculation can explain."[45] Underlying this is an acceptance of many of the ideas – if not the philosophical terminology – that became fashionable in the 1980s under the
brand name of postmodernism: the *Demos* camarilla in particular is in
many ways the intellectual and political heir of *Marxism Today*, one of
the chief British popularizers of postmodernism.[46]

Blair's ideologically committed supporters were a comparatively narrow coterie, disdainful and uncomprehending of the labour movement and its traditions. One journalist recently observed of one Blairite groupuscule, Labour 2000: "They had that visionary, slightly deranged look that will be familiar to anyone who ever experienced university branches of the ultra-Tory Monday Club in its triumphalist heyday of the 1980s."[47] Their social roots do not seem deep: intellectually they are united by a shared incomprehension of social forces, indeed by the denial that large-scale social forces, especially social classes, exist at all.

The dominant assumption in such circles is that we now live in a world that somehow combines the characteristics of a globalized, competitive capitalism with an absence of large structures, class antagonisms, and collective identities. Consequently individuals can and should shape their own destinies – hence Blair's announcement at the 1996 party conference of a new "Age of Achievement." Inasmuch as Labour remains a class party, it plainly is, on this analysis, obsolete. The logical terminus of Blair's "Project" is thus a party like Bill Clinton's New Democrats, that employs mildly progressive rhetoric, but cultivates close links with big capital. Such a party is ready – in supporting market capitalism, undermining the welfare state, and practising moral authoritarianism – to match the Republicans' reactionary measure for reactionary measure.

Realizing *this* objective does imply a radical break with the entire Labourist tradition. The Labour Party has been what Marxists, following Lenin, have called a capitalist workers' party. It has based itself on the organized working class but has sought to pursue that class's aspirations for change exclusively by parliamentary means and to contain the conflict between labour and capital within the framework of the existing mode of production.[48] The Blairite "Project" means, we now see, cutting Labour loose from its social anchorage in the organized working class and floating free to allow the party (perhaps under a new name) to compete with the Conservatives to represent the interests of capital, no longer embarrassed by intemperate union demands.

This is a recipe for profound internal conflict. It is conceivable that, in the right circumstances, Blair could win a majority in a membership ballot formally to break the union link, but the constitutional representation of the trade unions in Labour is in some respects symbolic of something much deeper. The reality of the Labour-union link is a nexus of social and political relationships that, at a local level, bind together Labour councillors, ward and constituency activists, full-time union officials, convenors, shop stewards, union branch secretaries, school governors, and others in a complex set of alliances.

Tearing this up would be an enormous task. It would certainly bring Blair into conflict with many on his own front bench. The new foreign secretary, Robin Cook, took great care tacitly to project himself as leader-in-waiting of a left opposition. Thus in April 1996, a week after Blair had assured New York business leaders that Labour was now a party of the centre, Cook told the Scottish TUC that "Labour must speak for the poor." He argued that "[t]he relationship between the Labour Party and the unions is not a marriage of convenience. It is a recognition of our common commitment to collective action." Labour and the unions, he said, shared two "core values," community and equality – the former a familiar Blairite theme, the latter a concept missing from the New Labour vocabulary.[49] Moreover, Deputy Prime Minister John Prescott derived his position from his role as mediator between New and Old Labour. Shearing off the unions would deprive him of his *raison d'être*. It is hard therefore to see the powerful centre-left wing of the Labour Government quietly acquiescing in a break with the unions.

Blair and his immediate coterie were aware that they might not have as easy a ride in office as they have had in opposition. This was no doubt a major consideration behind proposals drafted in 1996–97 to tighten up party discipline, weed out "below standard or disloyal" back-benchers, and encourage constituency parties to select candidates from a nationally vetted list, and behind plans to greatly reduce the role of the annual conference and the National Executive Committee. Such plans were symptomatic of an authoritarian style of party management that went well beyond anything attempted by Hugh Gaitskell in the 1950s or Neil Kinnock in the 1980s. The influx of new members into the party encouraged Blair to adopt a plebiscitary approach to leadership, in which U-turns are announced without consultation and then ratified by an atomized membership through postal ballots.[50] Though most of Blair's first cabinet was solidly Old Labour, a sprinkling of junior ministers in key positions – for example, Frank Field with the crucial responsibility for "Welfare Reform," and Stephen Byers in Education – suggested the existence of an alternative network of power bypassing the cabinet and centered on Blair and Mandelson in Downing Street.

Undoubtedly the scale of Labour's election victory would, in the short term at least, hugely strengthen Blair's hand. A prime minister with a 179-seat majority normally enjoys enormous authority within both government and party. Nevertheless, it would be a mistake to believe that the landslide of 1 May 1997 represented a simple endorse-

Table 1.   1997 general election, % (change on 1992 in brackets)

	Conservative	Labour	Liberal Democrat
Professional & managerial	42 (–11)	31 (+8)	21 (0)
Routine white-collar	26 (–22)	47 (+19)	19 (–1)
Skilled manual	25 (–15)	54 (+15)	14 (–4)
Other manual	21 (–8)	61 (+9)	13 (0)

Source: *Sunday Times*, 4 May 1997 (based on 1992 ITN/Harris exit poll & 1997 BBC/NOP exit poll)

ment of Blair's policies, transformation of Labour's social base, or the conquest of "Middle England" that Blair and Mandelson proclaimed it to be. It was, in fact, a huge switch of routine white-collar and skilled manual workers from the Tories to Labour, rather than a successful courtship of the affluent professional middle class that placed Blair in 10 Downing Street (see table).

The 1997 general election is best understood as a rebellion against the Tories and their policies by large numbers of wage-earners many of whom had not previously voted Labour. If the opinion polls are to be trusted, this rebellion began in the autumn of 1992, long before Blair became Labour leader. Black Wednesday – 16 September 1992, when the pound was swept out of the Exchange Rate Mechanism of the European Monetary System – marked the effective collapse of the Major government. It came to symbolize for millions their betrayal by a party that only a few months earlier had been re-elected on promises of economic recovery but that had offered them in practice continued recession, more closures, redundancies, and dispossessions.

Immediately after the 1997 election, Samuel Brittan, the *Financial Times*'s lugubrious neoliberal columnist, pointed to the consistent evidence provided by the British Social Attitudes Surveys that a large majority of the voters supported higher social spending and redistributive taxation. He accordingly sought to comfort disgruntled free-marketeers with the thought that under Blair "UK capitalism will be far more unconstrained than the electorate really desires."[51]

These considerations suggest that a Blair government that pursues the same economic and social policies as its Conservative predecessors is likely to find itself clashing with the expectations of many of those who elected it. Thus the scale of Labour's triumph – the sense of its being a seismic upheaval, a rejection not merely of the Tories but of the values they represented – is likely to be, in the long run, less a source of strength for the government, than a factor productive of constraints and conflicts.

BLAIR'S CHALLENGE

No-one can seriously entertain the proposition that a Blair government will bring about a significant transformation of British society. Even Martin Jacques, a leading *Demos* luminary, and Stuart Hall, both architects of the old *Marxism Today* project, recently acknowledged this. Writing during the election, they dismissed Blair as "a weak leader, constantly bending to powerful private interests (Murdoch, *Daily Mail*, private schools, the City, the business community), unprepared to criticize any entrenched group outside Labour's own ranks, unwilling to define a political vision of his own," who would form "a crypto-Conservative administration."[52]

Blair's significance is nevertheless undeniable, empty though his program may be, and reactionary though his personal views undoubtedly are. The long agony of Labourism in opposition finally brought into the party leadership and now into 10 Downing Street a man who essentially believes that the entire reformist tradition in Britain is a failure. Yet Blair's attack on the reformist tradition from the right and the disarray of the defenders of Old Labourism can open the way to a challenge from the left. The failure of Labourism is undeniable. Successive Labour governments proved unable to transform capitalism. Even the achievements of the post-war Attlee administration are now being eroded. And the labour movement under its current leadership has not offered an effective defence of the British working class against the Tory onslaught of the past two decades. Blair concludes from this experience that there is no alternative to embracing unbridled market capitalism. But this offers nothing to the mass of those who voted Labour on 1 May 1997.

Could the political space thus vacated be filled by a robustly socialist party that can begin to offer a genuine response to the ills of the age? Answering this question requires careful consideration of the program and strategy such a party would develop. And here an important choice needs to be confronted. Colin Leys posed the alternatives in some reflections on the causes of and possible remedies for Britain's economic decline. Among the latter he included a "counter-hegemonic project" allying the labour movement with fractions of manufacturing capital to overturn City dominance and achieve industrial revival on the basis of "strategic planning by a national state." Leys noted that "such a counter-hegemonic strategy of the Left must also be capable of securing the requisite advances in national productivity in a world of competing corporate and national capitalisms – or have an alternative international policy which offers a credible alternative to that world."[53]

It is fair to say that the principal thrust of reformist thinking in Britain over the past twenty-five years has been along the lines of such a "counter-hegemonic project." The Alternative Economic Strategy developed by the Bennite left in the 1970s sought to use the power of the state not to abolish private capital but to control and direct it along lines that would at once enhance economic competitiveness and reduce social inequality. Will Hutton's conception of stakeholder capitalism is both a considerably less interventionist and, in some ways, a more intellectually powerful version of the same idea. Leys's own discussion of *The State We're In* treats it as a "Gramscian," "hegemonic" attempt to construct "a broad coalition of forces" under Labour leadership.[54] Hutton himself envisages Blair leading "a progressive political coalition" comparable to those headed by Asquith and Attlee.[55]

Even Hutton's proposals for rehabilitating British capitalism have, as we have seen, proved too radical for Blair and his co-thinkers. This reflects, no doubt, their own politics. But there are deeper questions raised by the retreat of the Labour leadership from stakeholding. These partly concern the doubts expressed above about the concept of stakeholding capitalism itself and the interpretation of British history in which it is embedded, but they also relate to the fundamental political problem of *agency*.[56]

Whatever one's precise views about the internal structure of British capitalism, it is plain that Hutton's program requires a substantial transformation of that structure. Any attempt to achieve this would involve confronting an extremely powerful constellation of interests entrenched in the British state and economy. It is hard to see how the reformers could succeed without mobilizing the power of organized labour behind them. Such a mobilization would in turn be likely both to scare away many of the "progressive" capitalists whom Leys and Hutton consider potential supporters of their "counter-hegemonic project" and to provoke an extremely negative response in the financial markets in the familiar forms of capital flight, currency collapse, etc.

In other words, any real attempt to reform the British political economy would be likely to precipitate a profound social and political crisis. The signs that Britain was entering the very early stages of such a crisis in 1974–75 led the Wilson-Callaghan government and its allies among the trade-union leaders decisively to turn course towards what proved to be Thatcherite policies. From their own perspective, Blair and his allies are therefore right to shun stakeholding, since it leads along a path that they are sure is a dead end. Equally, those eager to see real change must confront the limits imposed on even "bourgeois" reforms by the national structure of class power and its entanglement with the international circuits of capital. Overcoming these limits would require exploring the other option to which Leys alluded – that of developing "a credible alternative" to "a world of competing corporate and national capitalisms."

NOTES

1 *Observer*, 18 May 1997.
2 *Financial Times* (hereinafter *FT*), 9 April 1997. For more background on, and analysis of the Labour Party under Tony Blair, see A. Callinicos, *Against the Third Way*, Cambridge: Polity, 2001; and C. Leys, "The British Labour Party's Transition from Socialism to Capitalism," in L. Panitch (ed.), *The Socialist Register 1996*, London: Merlin Press, 1996. Andy McSmith's collection of journalistic portraits, *Faces of Labour*, London: Verso, 1996 offers many insights into the nature of New Labour. An earlier version of parts of this paper has appeared in A. Callinicos, "Betrayal and Discontent: Labour under Blair," *International Socialism*, no. 72, 1996.
3 See C. Harman, "From Bernstein to Blair," *International Socialism*, no. 67, 1995.
4 For an analysis of this process from a revisionist standpoint, see D. Marquand, *The Unprincipled Society*, London: J. Cape, 1988: chapters 1–3.
5 *FT*, 23 May 1995.
6 See, for a useful critical survey, N. Thompson, "Supply-Side Socialism: The Political Economy of New Labour," *New Left Review*, no. 216, 1996.
7 M. Albert, *Capitalism against Capitalism*, London: Whurr, 1993: 18–19.
8 The intellectual climate on the new Labour right is well conveyed in the papers (including contributions by Hutton and Marquand) collected together in D. Miliband, ed., *Reinventing the Left*, Cambridge, MA: Polity Press, 1994. Hutton calls Marquand's *The Unprincipled Society* "one of the inspirations behind the concept" of stakeholder capitalism in "Raising the Stakes," *Guardian*, 17 January 1996.
9 W. Hutton, *The State We're In*, London: Vintage, 1995: 258, 297, 316.
10 Albert, *Capitalism*, 211.
11 J. Cornford and P. Hewitt, "Dos and Don'ts for Social Democrats," in Miliband (ed.), *Reinventing*, 252.
12 B. Martin, "So Steady They're Standing Still," *New Statesman*, 19 July 1996.
13 W. Hutton, "By George, This is Not What Labour Needs," *Guardian*, 29 May 1995.

14 W. Hutton, "Myth That Sets The World to Right," *Guardian*, 12 June 1995. More systematic critiques are provided by P. Hirst and J. Thompson, *Globalization in Question*, Cambridge, 1996; and C. Harman, "Globalization," *International Socialism*, no. 73, 1996.

15 See A. Callinicos, "Crisis and Class Struggle in Europe Today," *International Socialism*, no. 63, 1994.

16 *FT*, 16 July 1996.

17 See also C. Harman, "Where Is Capitalism Going?" *International Socialism*, no. 58, 1993, and *Economics of the Madhouse*, London: Bookmarks, 1995: 94–9.

18 See esp. P. Anderson, "Origins of the Present Crisis" and "The Figures of Descent," both reprinted in *English Questions*, London: Verso, 1992. Colin Leys's version of the same analysis is to be found in *Politics in Britain*, London: University of Toronto Press, 1983, especially part IV. Among the many criticisms of this interpretation of British history, see A. Callinicos, "Exception or Symptom? The British Crisis and the World System," *New Left Review*, no. 169, 1988; and C. Barker and D. Nicholls (eds), *The Development of British Capitalist Society*, Manchester, 1988.

19 Hutton, *State We're In*, xi-xii, 323. Hutton's interpretation of British history is scattered throughout his book, but see especially chapters 5 and 11. Marquand offers a more systematic historical account: see *Unprincipled Society*, especially chapters 5–7.

20 W. Hutton, "Time for Labour to Put Some Spine into Its Stakeholding Idea," *Guardian*, 22 January 1996; see also D. Marquand, "Elusive Visions," ibid., 24 June 1996.

21 C. Leys, "A Radical Agenda for Britain," *New Left Review*, no. 212, 1995: 12.

22 See Thompson, "Supply-Side Socialism," 38.

23 P. Mandelson and R. Liddle, *The Blair Revolution*, London: Faber and Faber, 1996: 87–8.

24 *FT*, 26 June 1996.

25 Ibid., 26 June 1996.

26 Ibid., 16 July 1996.

27 Mandelson and Liddle, *Blair Revolution*, 22.

28 *FT*, 23 April 1996.

29 K. Howells, "Industrial Policy," *New Statesman*, 7 June 1996.

30 C. Leadbeater and G. Mulgan, "Stakeholding: Nice Idea, Shame about the Reality," *Observer*, 6 October 1996.

31 W. Hutton and J. Kay, "Only Working Together Will Save the Economy," *Observer*, 13 October 1996.

32 *Observer*, 22 June 1997.

33 T. Blair, "The Conservative Party Seems Neither to Understand Nor to Act Upon the Concept of Duty," *Spectator*, 25 March 1995.

34 J. Lloyd, "A Fortnight to Go," *New Statesman*, 18 April 1997.

35 W. Hutton, *The State to Come,* London: Vintage, 1997: 105, 108.

36 *Observer*, 18 May 1997.

37 T. Blair, Interview, *New Statesman*, 5 July 1996.

38 Mandelson and Liddle, *Blair Revolution*, 209–10.

39 *FT*, 17 May 1997.

40 D. Coates, "Labour Governments: Old Constraints and New Parameters," *New Left Review*, no. 219, 1996: 67.

41 See Callinicos, *New Labour*, 15–24.

42 *FT*, 21 July 1995.

43 T. Blair, "My Radical Task," *Observer*, 15 September 1996. Blair went on to make the extraordinary claim that "[t]he TUC was created when some trade unions disapproved of the unions forming the Labour Party and wanted their own Labour Party." Such ignorance – the TUC was formed in 1868, the Labour Representation Committee in 1900 – is remarkable in a politician who was, for a while, shadow employment secretary.

44 The original draft of Mandelson and Liddle's *The Blair Revolution* was apparently considerably more sympathetic to the SDP critique of Labourism than the published version: McSmith, *Faces*, 285–91.

45 *Observer*, 28 July 1996.

46 See Leys, "Labour Party's Transition," 21–6.

47 A. McElvoy, "What A Load of Winkers!" *Spectator*, 5 October 1996.

48 See T. Cliff and D. Gluckstein, *The Labour Party – A Marxist History,* London: Bookmarks, 1996 (new edition).

49 *FT*, 18 April 1996.

50. The progressive centralization of power in the leader's hands under Kinnock and Blair is one of the main themes of Leys's "Labour Party's Transition."

51 *FT*, 3 May 1997.

52 M. Jacques and S. Hall, "Blair: the Greatest Tory since Thatcher?" *Observer*, 13 April 1997. Elsewhere Jacques was even more scathing, calling Blair "a minor public schoolboy" who "never kicks against privilege": R. Taylor, "Chattering against Mr Blair," *Spectator*, 19 April 1997.

53 C. Leys, "The Formation of British Capital," *New Left Review*, no. 160, 1986: 120.

54 C. Leys, "Radical Agenda," 10; see generally ibid., 9–13.

55 Hutton, *State to Come*, 110.

56 I owe this formulation to David Howell.

PART TWO

Politics in Africa: Trajectories, Transitions, and Contradictions

Introduction

Part two shifts the focus to a region that has reaped few benefits from its long-standing integration with global capitalism. Looking at politics in Africa, this section considers a region that has been a focal point for Colin Leys's contribution to critical scholarship and, also, that has been at the centre of debates regarding underdevelopment theory since the 1960s. The essays in this section will be highly informative for those who are regional specialists, and no less engaging for those interested in the theoretical problematic of the uneven impact of the global market.

John S. Saul introduces this section with, "Afropessimism/optimism: The Antinomies of Colin Leys." This is an exploration of Colin Leys's extensive body of scholarship on the "African tragedy." From his studies of Rhodesia (now Zimbabwe) to Kenya to Namibia and beyond, Saul identifies in Leys's work an emphasis on empirical precision combined with theoretical rigour and self-reflection. More centrally, Saul stresses Leys's dual occupation: an "intellectual grappling with the nature of the globalization process and its impact on Africa," and a deeply engaged empathy regarding African outcomes. This renders a scholarship "not to be easily cowed morally by the globalization process." The central issue for Saul concerns the prospects for capitalist development and for a socialist alternative to that development, both in the African reality and in the work of Colin Leys. It is through this lens that Saul poses the problematic of "Afropessimism/optimism" within a nuanced and challenging framework.

Following this general reflection on development prospects in Africa, the four remaining articles in this section address particular case studies, all arguably moments in the African tragedy. Bruce J. Berman, in his article "Caught in the Contradictions: The State in Kenya, 1945–2000," traces the recent evolution of Kenyan politics. Beginning with an assessment of the "Kenya debate" of the early 1980s, Berman argues that the recent period of economic stagnation and political disorder in this country have revealed the limitations of both the Marxist and dependency sides of the controversy. Berman proceeds to trace the development of the Kenyan state and politics over a fifty year period with these factors at the forefront. Berman concludes with a sober assessment of Kenyan politics since the 1990s. He maintains that the limitations of political leadership have led to a situation where "the process of democratization has repeatedly become a hollow facade as the powerful forces of ethnicity and patronage" have been reasserted.

In the next article in this section, Lauren Dobell moves to consider an African nation in a recent post-colonial setting, where the impact of the degree of independence – rather than its relative absence – is the focus of discussion. In her "Constructing a Development Agenda for Namibia," Dobell explores the implications of this country's specific history under South African occupation and the distinct political features of the new state. The governing SWAPO (South West African Peoples' Organization) party was forged and gained experience through the course of the liberation struggle. Dobell maintains that "once installed in an independent government," SWAPO's leadership appears too eager to access sources of overseas trade, aid, and development assistance while domestic and regional sources remain overlooked. Beginning with a careful assessment of the particularities of SWAPO's successes, Dobell than considers the place of Namibia in the more general context of African, and Third World, development issues. From this purview, the Namibia focus allows for a more general discussion of state and civil society relationships.

In "Political Dimensions of the Adjustment Experience of Côte d'Ivoire," Bonnie Campbell takes aim at the effects of structural adjustment policies and the multilateral funding agencies that have insisted on their implementation. The analysis presented by Campbell identifies the interaction of domestic political and economic conditions with the demands of Bretton Woods institutions such as the International Monetary Fund and the World Bank. Campbell identifies a "key problem" through her "political rereading of the Ivorian experience."

In the final article in this section, Michael Chege takes the state and civil society problematic back to Kenya. In "Introducing Race As a

Variable into the Political Economy of Kenya Debate: An Incendiary Idea," Chege revisits the thorny issue of the role of indigenous capitalism in economic transformation in light of recent literature and events. In a polemical article stylistically well within the tradition of critical political studies, Chege challenges arguments that emphasize cultural and racial characteristics as determinate of degrees of success in Kenyan capitalist development. Chege takes issue with the view that it is the Indo-Pakistani sector of the Kenyan capitalist class, seen to have been neglected in previous accounts, that has driven efficiency and a competitive edge. Chege's objections are on the grounds of methodology, substance, empirical data, and the claims of Kenyan exceptionalism. Moreover, he cautions readers about the implications of such a view.

These articles indicate starkly that the issues of globalization and political economy, particularly in the Third World, are of more than academic interest. At stake are matters of human survival. The intensity with which these articles are presented is reflective of the authors' commitment to social transformation, even in the face of overwhelmingly difficult circumstances. Readers will no doubt benefit from the sober reflection and thoughtful insights presented in this section on politics in Africa.

Afropessimism/optimism: The Antinomies of Colin Leys[1]

JOHN S. SAUL

It is at least fifteen years since the literature began to be full of references of an African "crisis." Today it seems more appropriate to use another word, not just because "crisis" has been so overworked in so many contexts, but because Africa is not in fact balanced on a knife between recovery and collapse: it is a tragedy that is already far advanced. Millions of people have already died from hunger, disease and violence, and millions more face Hobbesian existences in conditions of accelerating environmental and social degradation: famines, chronic malnutrition, the collapse of health services, the erosion of education, reappearing endemic and epidemic diseases, AIDS, endemic criminal violence, civil wars, genocide – the capitalism-induced barbarism of which Rosa Luxemburg warned. These are the facts of the African tragedy: the issue is not whether they will happen, but whether they can be prevented from getting worse, and gradually brought to an end.[2]

An exploration of Colin Leys's body of work on Africa – including, not least, his most recent reflections on "the African tragedy" as viewed in the context of current trends towards an ever more unregulated and extreme process of capitalist "globalization" – provides a particularly appropriate point of entry into a discussion and evaluation of the post-colonial trajectory of Sub-Saharan Africa. For one thing, his writing has served as a kind of first-hand witness to that process, beginning with his study of the Rhodesian political scene in the mid-50s, through his outpouring of highly regarded, empirically driven writings on East Africa in the 1960s and 1970s (and, of course, on Namibia in the 1980s and 90s), to his more general reflections on the state of the continent in recent years.[3] Even more important, perhaps, is the fact that this body of work has been informed by a singularly impressive and unyielding effort to "get it right," a commitment that has marked him as the very best kind of social scientist. For Colin Leys has seen the stakes, in both analytical and human terms, as being simply too high to allow him to do otherwise: indeed, the high seriousness exemplified in the epigraph quoted at the outset of this essay captures this aspect of his intellectual project entirely accurately. If this, in turn, has led him to craft, over the years, an almost agonizingly self-reflexive intellectual project, one that finds him constantly doubling back on his earlier writings, questioning premises, re-examining the data, even contradicting himself from time to time, then so be it. Was it Emerson who once said that "consistency is the hobgoblin of petty minds"? Colin Leys's career gives new resonance to that phrase. And, as I will seek to show in this essay, our own understanding of Africa is very much richer for the intellectual travails his unsettled muse and troubled conscience has, in consequence, subjected us to.

First things first: In my view the great strength of Leys's work is the continuing centrality of a "political economy" sensibility in his work as a professional political scientist. This is not now so very fashionable a trait in the profession as it once was. And of course, as I have written elsewhere, there are perfectly good reasons for taking more purely political considerations seriously: "the need to discipline abusive authority; the need to create fresh space for individual and collective self-expression; the need to institutionalize the possible means of reconciling communal (ethnic and racial) differences and of reviving and refocusing some more positive sense of national purpose."[4] Can Leys's work be criticized for occasionally collapsing politics into political economy? Recalling my own experience of working closely with him in investigating the workings of Namibia's liberation movement, SWAPO, and thus witnessing, at close hand, the kind of fine-grained analysis of (relatively) self-contained political processes that Leys is capable of, I'm not so sure. True, some important variables – gender, for example, and ethnicity – may be less effectively canvassed in his work than others, as his critics sometimes charge.[5] Nonetheless, in so much of what passes for political analysis these days, the underlying economic factors that frame politics are taken for granted, commonsensically assumed to be either profoundly rational or merely inevitable or both.[6] Political science as neoliberal ideology is too often the result. In contrast, the kind of tension between political considerations narrowly defined and political economy more broadly defined that stands at the centre of Leys's work on Africa is, as we will see, essential to a critical understanding of the continent and its prospects.

Nor has Leys been inclined to apologize for the materialist bent to his discussion of development that such a foregrounding of political economy might suggest. In a postmodern world where the term "development" is deemed particularly redolent of all the dangers the adoption of "grand narratives" is said to imply, Leys stresses – with his eyes wide open – the centrality of the fact of poverty of Africa and the continent's weakness in terms of the development of its productive forces, whatever else may also be deemed to be important. In consequence he chooses "to adopt a conceptual framework which as far as possible embraces the interests of those who are exploited and oppressed in the third world and tries to disclose 'the necessity and at the same time the conditions of transforming industry as well as the social structure' through which their poverty and subordination are perpetuated."[7]

Leys's move towards foregrounding political economy in his intellectual endeavours itself has a history, with his early work actually evidencing rather little of this emphasis. His studies of Central Africa, written from his Oxford base after a year of fieldwork in Rhodesia and finding first fruit in his book, *European Politics in Southern Rhodesia*,[8] are careful and insightful, but firmly grounded in the deeply empiricist tradition so central to the mainstream British political science of the time. Of course, there is also, already, a linking of this work to a compassionate concern about the human outcomes of political processes in Africa. Leys's anti-colonial politics were also evidenced in a second book from this early period, *A New Deal for Central Africa*.[9] A similar blend of empirical rigour and humane concern marks his valuable, if rather neglected, short study of Acholi, *Politicians and Politics*,[10] the most impressive product of his first East Africa sojourn.[11]

When Leys now began to look for a more solid theoretical grounding for his work, it was, in his state of relative theoretical innocence, to American-based behaviouralism and to modernization theory that he turned for guidance. The University of East Africa (of which Makerere College formed a part) was, after all, a prime target of American political scientists,[12] seeking to advance the claims of such approaches on the ground. Similarly, stirrings were also in the air at Sussex where Leys next moved (1965–68), with a development studies community very self-conscious about distancing itself from the presumed stuffiness of "the institutional and historical tradition of British political science." This "theoretical moment," in turn, found prime expression in *Politics and Change in Developing Countries* (a volume he edited), especially in his introduction. There one finds paeans of praise for various "formulae for speculative thinking about politics" said to have sprung from the likes of Talcott Parsons and, more generally, from "the great strength of American sociology." And one also finds the bold assertion that field work thus "theoretically-inspired" [*sic*] has "established the study of politics on an independent footing," producing such an "impressive accumulation of scientific knowledge" that "we have possibly learned more about politics from studies of underdeveloped countries than from studies of developed ones in recent years."[13] Leys's own substantive contribution to the volume is a rather abstract, self-consciously "behavioural," exercise in model-building, claiming to elucidate the inner workings of Tanzania's planning process.

In the end, however, Leys proved to be too alert to both the concrete realities of African politics and to their broader human import to find a comfortable home either at Sussex or within the confines of American behaviouralism-cum-modernization theory. Soon enough he was on the move, back to Kenya (where he taught from 1969 to 1971), and, increasingly, onto the terrain of a *Marxisant* political economy perspective on African politics that he was henceforth never really to abandon. His move to Nairobi was propitiously timed: a wave of radicalization was beginning to wash through African Studies in the late 1960s, not least in East Africa. This was a radicalization that gave expression, in continental terms, to what had come to be thought of, more globally, as "dependency theory." And it was with reference to these intellectual trends (he identifies his new touchstone as being, quite specifically, "the work of 'underdevelopment' and 'dependency' theorists"[14]) that Leys framed his next book. And this is the one for which he is perhaps best known in Africanist circles, *Underdevelopment in Kenya*. A careful analysis of post-colonial Kenya, it presents both the weaknesses of the country's economic project and the vagaries of its politics in the most uncompromising of terms. "The underdevelopment which begins with colonialism (if not before) and continues under neo-colonialism implies limits to growth and a growing polarization of classes as the exploitation of the masses become more apparent ... Perhaps the most [academic] studies can do is to try not to obscure the structures of exploitation and oppression which underdevelopment produces, and which in turn sustain it."[15] Interestingly, this book has won accolades from even those not particularly enamoured of dependency theory, including high praise from such pillars of the American African Studies establishment as David Apter and Carl Rosberg. Thus, in the historical account of "Changing African Perspectives," which introduces their recent state-of-the-art collection of essays on *Political Development and the New Realism in Sub-Saharan Africa*, they write that, once upon a time, radical approaches "not only drastically altered many of the assumptions on which the modernization paradigm was based but opened up a range of entirely different questions about social formations, perhaps the outstanding example being Colin Leys' discussion of the contradictions of neocolonialism."[16] This kind of recognition from such an unlikely source speaks to the high quality of the book, of course. But one may suspect that other factors are involved, not least the rapidity with which Leys himself was to beat a retreat from both the book and from the allegiance to dependency theory that seemed to frame its argument. Leys, in subsequent writing, was to give two reasons for this intellectual move. The first was his fear that the preoccupation with "dependency" tended to blur the very real possibility of development – capitalist development – in Africa, a possibility that, subsequent to writing his book, he felt he had begun to discern with fresh eyes in Kenya itself. We will return to a discussion of this point shortly. It is a second reason for his defection from dependency theory that bears emphasizing here.

Unlike many his peers who, throughout this period and in the light of our negative reading of the then current capitalist moment in Africa, continued to look (perhaps a bit too uncritically) to socialist alternatives as providing some kind of antidote, Leys remained profoundly skeptical as to the possibility of mounting any such project. The notion of socialism in Africa, he was soon to suggest, was not even a "serious question." Since dependency theory could only ground its critique of capitalism in Africa by implying the existence of just such an alternative, the weaknesses of that theory itself were bound to be profound. Indeed, in an essay commissioned by Apter and Rosberg for their aforementioned volume, Leys is to be seen stating quite explicitly that "Dependencistas tend to assume an historical path which is not plausibly shown to exist even in theory, let alone one which existing organized social forces appear capable of implementing."[17] But this merely repeats a theme that he had already articulated even more explicitly much earlier: "The most important shortcoming of dependency theory is that it implies that there is an alternative, and preferable, kind of development of which the dependent economies are capable, but which their dependency prevents them from achieving – when this alternative does not in fact exist as an available historical option," not least, he suggests, if that "implied suppressed alternative is a socialist path of development." For in this case it would be necessary to show the social and political forces capable of carrying through such a strategy, and that it could reasonably be expected to be superior. In most African countries this would be difficult to say the least. There has to be something wrong with a conceptualization that insists that the world should be other than it can be.[18]

As Leys argues in another closely related essay, "Several illusions that tended to haunt the debate about dependency have been destroyed, such as the dream of an alternative socialist development path waiting to be taken (if only a 'genuinely radical' African leadership would take it)." Time to focus instead on what Leys apparently does allow to be "a serious question," viz: "in any given country, what are the obstacles confronting a sustainable process of development of the forces of production under capitalist relations of production and how do the historically given characteristics of the country's internal capitalist class bear on the possibilities of overcoming these obstacles?"[19]

Of course, Leys is polite enough in these essays to grant some marks for effort to socialists in Africa. There are positive lessons to be learned, he says.

The accomplishments of African socialism are not, on the whole, to be measured in terms of growth rates. They are primarily social and political, above all in having posed the question of the form within which development is to occur, in having made it comprehensible to ordinary people that they do have collective historical choices which they may try to exercise if they will. The achievement of the Tanzanians and the Ghanaians in this respect is epochal. One can also say that the accomplishments of actually existing African socialism lie partly in its failures; to paraphrase Marx, what succumbed in these failures was not African socialism, but the "persons, illusions, conceptions, projects, from which the idea of socialism in Africa was not free, from which it could be freed... only by a series of defeats."[20]

Yet, despite the vigour of this statement, one will search his writings of the period in vain for any very precise statement as to what such lessons could possibly be. For the fact is that, as we have shown, he has not left much scope in his emerging argument for seeing such efforts as anything but singularly unpromising. Not surprisingly, then, Leys himself hurries on: it is not "socialism" but the range of possibilities on offer on the terrain of a (perhaps unavoidably) capitalist Africa that are to preoccupy him in many of his writings about Africa through the 1980s and into the 1990s.[21]

Launching this latest phase of Leys's intellectual odyssey was a celebrated article he published in *The Socialist Register* in 1978, entitled "Capital Accumulation, Class Formation and Dependency – The Significance of the Kenyan Case." Here he took the remarkable step of virtually disavowing the book on Kenya that he had published to great acclaim only four years earlier. The reason: his sense, mentioned above, that the possibility of capitalist development could not be written out of the African/Kenyan equation as easily as he, in the underdevelopment/dependency theory phase of his work, had been inclined to do. Profoundly influenced by the work of researchers like Michael Cowen and Nicola Swainson on the ground in Kenya, he is now prepared to see real seeds of capitalist growth/development in "the emergence of the African bourgeoisie" that he had missed before.[22] More generally, he concludes, "capitalist production relations may be considerably extended in a periphery social formation, and the progressive forces may be considerably expanded within and through them, for reasons having primarily to do with the configuration of class forces preceding and during the colonial period: and that the limits of such development cannot be determined from the sort of general considerations advanced by underdevelopment and dependency theory."[23] Leys is quick to situate his new turn on firmly Marxist terrain, of course: the Marx of inexorable capitalist expansion (and, only after that, the possibility of socialist achievement). And he is also hot in pursuit of the African bourgeoisie. Indeed, "in the absence of any practicable alternative to capitalist development ... it becomes very important to understand what determines the relative strengths and weaknesses of each underdeveloped country's internal or domestic capitalist class."[24]

And yet even as he articulates this new project Leys, characteristically, is soon probing its weaknesses, and this on two levels. First, despite his continuing preoccupation with the nature and strength of Africa's fledgling bourgeoisie, he begins to qualify that premise significantly. As fanciful now as was any socialist possibility is the fantasy of a smooth and socially benign alternative path of "genuinely independent" or "progressive" national capitalist development – dreams or fantasies against which researchers often implicitly contrasted the corrupt, socially dislocating, ugly and immiserating experience of "actually existing" capitalist development.

No, he had probably posed the question wrongly.

By now it is easy to see that the existence of an internal capitalist class, even a relatively nationalist and efficient one, is not a sufficient condition for capitalist growth; in some circumstances perhaps it might not even be a necessary condition. Similarly with the state: whether or not it is in general more responsive to the domestic capitalist class than to foreign capital is a priori not conclusive for the prospects for capitalist development. The whole question was wrongly posed in these terms. What needed to be asked was what were the chief issues affecting the prospects for capitalist growth, and what dynamic forces were at work that would most likely determine how these issues would be resolved.[25]

Secondly, and even more significantly, Leys begins to rethink the prospects for capitalist economic growth and development in Africa on any terms, i.e., as driven either by a "national capitalist class" or by "foreign capital," or by some combination of the two. True, Leys had never been a true believer in capitalism's power for universal transformation, after the manner, for example, of Bill Warren and those Manfred Bienefeld has labeled the "Chicago Marxists." He was saying merely that capitalism had more growth/development potential, at least in certain settings, than either he or many of its other *dependencista* critics has allowed. In any case, according to Leys, capitalism was the only plausible game in town. But even having jettisoned the socialist option, Leys is not prepared to abandon his critical faculties in the face of contradictions of capitalism in Africa that he cannot ignore. Not for him is the kind of escape hatch offered by a Jeffrey Alexander when the latter writes in, of all places, the *New Left Review*:

It is impossible even for already committed intellectuals to ignore the fact that we are witnessing the death of a major alternative not only in social thought but in society itself. In the foreseeable future, it is unlikely that either citizens or elites will try to structure their primary allocative systems in non-market ways. For their part, social scientists will be far less likely to think of anti-market "socialist societies" as counterfactual alternatives with which to explain their own. They will be less likely to explain economic stratification by implicitly comparing it with an egalitarian distribution produced by publicly rather than privately held property, a "plausible world" that inevitably seems to suggest that economic inequality is produced by the existence of private property itself ... Similarly, it will become much more difficult to speak about the emptiness of formal democracy, or to explain its limitations by pointing merely to the existence of a dominant economic class, for these explanations, too, require counterfactuals of a traditionally "socialist" kind. In brief, it will be much less easy to explain contemporary social problems by pointing to the capitalist nature of the societies of which they are a part.[26]

It is to Leys's credit that he finds himself in the 1990s forced to articulate a critique that states, more strongly than he has since the early 1970s, that Africa's most important "social problems" are, precisely, to be explained "by pointing to the capitalist nature of the societies of which they are a part."[27]

There are two aspects to this development, exemplifying once again the simultaneous interplay of both intellectual curiosity and humane concern in driving Leys's work forward. Intellectually, his work is marked by a sharpened focus on the intensified imperatives of capitalist-driven globalization. "Our leaders," he says, "are directing a process of the self-destruction of our societies in the name of an [irrational] utopia ... This utopia is the idea of a world-wide market in which the people of the world relate to each other as individuals and only as individuals; 'globalization' is the process of trying to reach this ideal ... [I]n the name of this idea a critical decision has been made to accept capital's freedom to move across national boundaries."[28] And as Leys's understanding of this process grows, any residual confidence he has in the prospect of a developmental capitalism for Africa begins to wane. Thus, cumulatively, it is a pretty grim picture he feels forced to paint:

It would be much easier for Africa to industrialize if average industrial productivity worldwide had remained at the level it was at 150 years ago. As a result, African populations are becoming increasingly marginal to global production ... What all this means is that the political problem confronting any African capitalist class, even if it can find solutions to the complex technical and economic problems involved in expanding capitalist production, often seems close to insoluble ... These sombre reflections are not intended to imply that capitalist development is nowhere possible in Africa ... But in studying the capacity of Africa's dominant classes to play their distinctive role in African development, we must face realistically the difficulties they confront in the shape of world capitalism as it actually exists and not as it existed fifty or a hundred years ago ... The internal contradictions in any given individual country today may seem more acute, and the external environment of late twentieth century capitalism, dominated by the International Monetary Fund (IMF) and policed by the USA, may seem more hostile, than was the case one or two hundred years ago for any of today's industrial countries.[29]

Despite such insights, Leys shows no signs of recasting himself as a born-again dependency theorist. For him, there is no self-conscious reassertion of that theory, unlike Manfred Bienefeld, who not so long ago wrote (convincingly, I think) that:

Both those on the right and the left would do well to remember that the present African crisis was most clearly foreseen by those looking at Africa from a dependency perspective in the 1960s. After all it was their contention that a continuation of a "neo-colonial" pattern of development would lead to disaster because it would produce a highly import and skill dependent economic structure that would depend critically on external markets and external investors and decision makers; that dependence would eventually become disastrous in its implications because the long term prospects for Africa's terms of trade were almost certainly poor; moreover, that dependence would be further reinforced because it would also create within African countries a degree of social and political polarization that would lay the foundations for an increasingly repressive response once those contradictions became critical. Finally, that view was also very clear as to the fact that this entire edifice was essentially constructed on the back of the peasantry who would have to pay for it eventually. This describes exactly the present circumstances of Africa.[30]

But Leys's own most recent accounts of why Africa finds itself in its present predicament do seem to re-echo many of these themes of the underdevelopment theory that he once left behind. As he concludes his magisterial recent survey of the history of development theory: "If, as I fear, it seems that not much scope for change exists – especially for small, severely underdeveloped countries – without a radical subordination of capital to democratic control, development theory will have to be about this, and agents capable of undertaking it."[31]

If this theory does indeed reveal Africa to be just too weak in capitalist terms to stand up for itself vis-à-vis global capitalism, what then? Certainly, the negative implications of this possibility/probability are something Leys is very willing to explore. In a number of his recent writings he sets out powerfully his conviction that the globally induced "death of society" that market fetishization – carried out so often in Africa in the name of "Structural Adjustment" – promotes is particularly costly for that continent: "The result has not been a market-based social and economic recovery based on individuals and their initiatives in the marketplace. It has been, instead, an ethnic based regression, as people have been pushed back into reliance on traditional social bonds for survival. And in some cases it has resulted in social and economic catastrophe, aggravated by the legacy of three decades of superpower-sponsored militarization."[32] Leys reverts here, as he often does in his writings, to Karl Polanyi's observations about the dangers of allowing "the market mechanism to be sole director of the fate of human beings," noting that "Polanyi's statement about what taking the utopian doctrine of the market literally would mean, was meant as a warning of a dystopia: it was something that had only ever been imposed on colonial peoples when [as he wrote] 'unimaginable suffering [had] ensued.'" Leys asks: "What would he think of a world that, thirty years after decolonization is imposing it on those same peoples again?"[33]

Earlier we mentioned two keys to Leys's current position, one being, as we have just seen, his intellectual grappling with the nature of the globalization process and its impact on Africa. Yet such is the strength of his "humane concern" regarding African outcomes that he is not to be easily cowed morally by the globalization process. After all "development theory cannot be content with merely showing why nothing can be done."[34] Not for Leys, then, the kind of passive, morally neutered acceptance of the right-wing logic of globalization that has come to haunt so much of the academic left – as exemplified, for example, in the crack-pot "realism" of Hirst and Thompson's own recent, widely read reflections on the process:

Such institutional arrangements and strategies can assure some minimal level of international economic governance, at least to the benefit of the major advanced industrial nations. Such governance cannot alter the extreme inequalities between those nations and the rest, in terms of trade and investment, income and wealth. Unfortunately, that is not really the problem raised by the concept of globalization. The issue is not whether the world's economy is governable towards ambitious goals like promoting social justice, equality between countries and greater democratic control for the bulk of the world's people, but whether it is governable at all.[35]

To this we can usefully contrast the tone and substance of Leys's own project as captured in our epigraph – evoking as it does the grimly human dimensions of what he terms "Africa's tragedy" – to epitomize this point. There is also, however, by way of more positive affirmation, his refusal to assert "that questioning the moral and political implications of capitalist development is pointless, or that alternative paths of development are not worth seeking. On the contrary ... such questions seem more urgent than ever."[36]

Nor will he accept any of the soft answers to such questions that are available in some of the recent literature. As demonstrated in his *New Left Review* article, Leys is not prepared, so long as Africans are mired in tragedy, to allow Jean-François Bayart to bask in the postmodern comfort of a mere affirmation of local "authenticity" or to allow Basil Davidson to substitute some fuzzy form of feel-good ethnic-identity politics for the "curse" that the latter now claims the nation-state to be in Africa. As regards that very "nation-state," for example, Leys affirms: "Negatively, and in no polemical spirit, I would say that the African state, for all its record of abuse, remains a potential line of defense for Africans against the depredations of the world economic and political system: part of the solution, if there is one, not necessarily part of the problem, as the drive by the IMF and the World Bank to weaken the African state in the name of market efficiency implicitly acknowledges. The problem in Africa, to repeat, is not the state but the weakness of the social formations on which the state rests."[37] Moreover, as he now contemplates the probable failure of capitalist development to reproduce itself in much, if not most, of Africa, Leys is even prepared to hint at, amongst other possible outcomes, the revalidation of a socialist impulse. As he writes, the continuing failure of capitalism with its accompanying "marginalization and social distress may lead either to recolonization (via successive forms of aid programmes, including military aid, for example) or to various kinds of anti-capitalist reactions – fundamentalist or nativist, perhaps, or some new forms of socialism – whose contours cannot as yet even be imagined."[38] Given his long-standing skepticism regarding the real possibilities open to any socialist attempt, this is a mixed message, of course. But when, speaking more generally, Leys states that "what I am confident of is that any society that is not in a position to resubordinate the market will be destroyed by it," we sense movement on this front. Especially when he adds that "what we can and must do is prepare the ground for a new social project ["a unified hegemonic project" he later adds] in which the social surplus is used to serve society, not destroy it."[39]

There remains, of course, the denouement to his crucial "Africa's tragedy" article, one that many will find all too unresolved. Running down a litany of things – debt relief, adjustment of terms of trade, more positive forms of resource transfer, and the like – that might reasonably and compassionately be done on the global level to ease Africa's way forward, Leys concludes that "the problem with these ideas is that they have no attraction for those who currently own Africa's debt, buy Africa's exports or arrange official capital-assistance flows. Such ideas could come to seem rational only in a world that was in the process of rejecting the currently predominant ideology of the market. While this world must come, it is not yet in sight, and meantime the African tragedy will unfold."[40]

"While this world must come." But why must it come? Is this merely a statement of faith on Leys's part or is it prolegomenon to a fresh strategic vision? Too much the former perhaps, for, in the absence of any sustained discussion of strategy (in *The Rise and Fall of Development Theory*, for example), there are indeed times when Leys's world view, as it has developed over time, can seem dangerously close to that articulated in Przeworski's celebrated dictum: "Capitalism is irrational; socialism is unfeasible; in the real world people starve – the conclusions we have reached are not encouraging."[41] Hence the possible charge arises that Leys is reinforcing rather than subverting the sort of continental mood that has been identified in some of the recent literature on Africa as one of "Afro-pessimism." Yet the fact remains that, when all is said and done, Leys is deadly serious about the need to struggle against any too pessimistic a conclusion, while Przeworski, by contrast, seems merely jaded, world-weary, defeated.

Perhaps Leys has not said enough about what sites of struggle, and what socio-political agents, bear most promise for the struggle to

create the new world he has in mind. Colin Leys is explicit in his
modesty: "We – I at any rate – cannot foresee how [the crisis of neo-
liberalism] will be resolved, by what combination of social forces."[42]
Perhaps, as some have charged, his recent writings emphasize too
one-sidedly the absolute necessity to contest neoliberalism at the
global level, while underestimating (or, at the very least, not articulating clearly) the promise of local or national level assertions and/or
the possible interplay between struggles pitched at these various levels. Nonetheless, the fact that his Africa-related writings keep forcing us back to such questions – questions of site, of agency and of
struggle, of mode of production, and of modalities of human better-
ment – keep forcing us, in short, to engage with Africa at the same
high level of scientific and moral concern that has never failed to
mark his own work, is, finally, what defines such writings' unshak-
able importance.

Two reflections are relevant in this regard; the first in the form of a
reply to a critique of his views about globalization, as expressed in the
SAR article cited above, from Jonathan Barker. Barker is concerned
that Leys, in his preoccupation with globalization and the need to
confront its very globalness, has underestimated the range and significance of local resistances occurring on the ground, in Africa and
elsewhere. He also worries about the possible dangers of hierarchy
and authoritarianism inherent in the kind of "unified hegemonic
project" of opposition that Leys says he has in mind.

In his response, Leys does express concern about the possible roman-
ticization of grassroots struggles he senses in Barker's formulations.
Leys reiterates, too, his sense of the danger of understating the malignant impact of "transnational market relations" on "local solidarities." Indeed, "if conditions become too extreme," such solidarities
may merely become "last resort defences against disaster, based on ethnicity" or worse, as "transnational market relations" drive "African
societies towards forms of social disintegration – Liberia, Somalia,
Angola, Mozambique, Rwanda, Sierra Leone, Zaire – not seen since
King Leopold's Congo." Most important in his response, however, is
further evidence that the political economist in Leys has by no means
submerged his political sensibilities. He knows that building a counter-
hegemonic project "cannot be based on some new 'totalizing' doctrine
on the lines of historical communism (or neo-liberalism)" and must
instead be profoundly democratic: "Looked at in one way it will necessarily be a multiplicity of projects, in different sectors, nations and
regions, the aspirations of different groups, movements and peoples."
But Leys also knows that "unless these unite to confront the political
and economic power of the transnationals and the states that back

them, they will ultimately fail." What is required, in short, are "nation-wide movements and/or parties capable of exercising state power, and making it felt in supra-national institutions."[43]

The second reflection, on the ideological terms in which such a revived left politics would have to be cast, arrives from Scandinavia, in the form of a pithy paper prepared by Leys on the subject of "Development Theory and Africa's Future" for an April 1997 conference in Uppsala. It is well worth taking note of this piece in light of what has been argued above, not least for what it shows of Leys's ability to sustain the kind of "creative inconsistency" that has been so much a part of his fertile and committed presence, over the decades, within African Studies. For he concludes:

This last consideration brings us back to theory by raising the question of ideology. For radical change there must be a radical vision, and a credible theory of how it is to be achieved; and this doctrine must in turn be articulated with ordinary people's moral and religious beliefs and feelings. Neither of the twentieth century's two most widely influential radical ideologies – the Leninist version of Marxism, or radical Islam – will serve. Formulating a new philosophy of development and articulating its practices is a huge and urgent task facing African theorists and activists.

In this ideological and theoretical effort the issue of production will have to be faced again. Global capitalism is not about to develop most of sub-Saharan Africa, so some sort of socialist relations of production have to be constructed instead. We know from bitter experience how difficult this is. Working out ways to socialize what can be administered, and to leave the rest to market relations – not necessarily capitalist market relations – while at the same time keeping markets subordinate to wider, democratically-determined goals, is going to be an acid test of African development theory's capacity to help.[44]

Socialism? Earlier, we had momentarily aligned Leys, in his apparent "Afro-pessimism," with the jaded "realism" of an Adam Przeworski. A better guide, perhaps, to the antinomies of Colin Leys is to be found in a formulation of Roger Murray, a distinguished Africanist of Leys's generation. Many years ago Murray wrote of the need for radical advance in Africa, noting that "the historically necessary should not be confounded with the historically possible."[45] Yet, slowly but surely and by the most agonizing of routes, Leys seems finally to have worked his way through – and beyond – the wisdom of Murray's formulation. Does one not hear him now saying – to Jonathan Barker, again at Uppsala, and against the grain of some of his earlier formulations – that the historically necessary must in fact be made the historically possible? If this is indeed the case, it may well be that it is in these recent (guardedly) "Afro-optimistic" arguments that one sees the most formidable of all the challenges Leys's lifelong project as Africanist has thrown forward to other Africanists, and to Africans.

Permit me one other observation on that project.[46] We must, of course, hope that Colin Leys has not said his final word on matters African. But if this challenge from Uppsala were indeed to stand as some kind of summing up of his wisdom on such issues, it bears reiterating that his has been a position won the hard way. For he has demonstrated time and again that the subjects with which he is engaging are just too important to allow him to fall back comfortably on mere formulae, or on the kind of glib and unyielding affirmations that too often pass for wisdom and insight in leftist circles. I set out on this intellectual biography of Colin Leys by evoking Emerson on the virtues of inconsistency. Perhaps I may be permitted – in not too grandiose a manner, I trust – to conclude by quoting Montaigne on much the same issue:

I cannot keep my subject still ... I may presently change, not only by chance but also by intention. This is a record of variable and changeable occurrences, and irresolute and, when it so befalls, contradictory ideas: whether I am different myself, or whether I take hold of my subjects in different circumstances or aspects. So, all in all, I may indeed contradict myself now and then; but truth, as Demades said, I do not contradict. If my mind could gain a firm footing, I would not make essays, I would make decisions; but it is always in apprenticeship and on trial.[47]

My sense: it is precisely because Colin Leys, in his intellectual journey through Africa, has been similarly willing to contradict himself, but not "truth," or the imperatives of its pursuit, to reveal his "apprenticeship" and to put his own ideas "on trial," that we have learned so much from him about that continent.

NOTES

1 The present chapter is closely based on my presentation at the conference "Critical Political Studies: A Conference in Honour of Colin Leys" (Kingston, Ontario, 1996) held to mark the occasion of Colin Leys's retirement from Queen's University. Most of the other papers then presented sought to honour Colin Leys less by engaging with his own work than by attempting to advance knowledge in one of the many fields touched by that work over the years – and to do so, as far as possible, with the same spirit of high intelligence and deep commitment that has

for so long marked Colin Leys's own intellectual endeavours. In taking as the subject of my presentation the present crisis in Africa and the stark challenges that confront the African continent as we approach the new century, I hoped to do no less. But I permitted myself to give the exercise one additional twist, seeking not merely to craft my observations on this subject matter in the spirit of Colin Leys's important corpus of writings on Africa but to do so through a critical discussion of those writings themselves.

I choose to do so not merely or even primarily in a spirit of appropriate celebration. True, that would be reason enough. My own acquaintance, and ultimately close friendship, with Colin Leys goes back over thirty years and he has taught me a very great deal. Indeed, I feel that much the most rewarding intellectual experience of my own scholarly career was the opportunity I had to work closely with him, and to learn so very much from him, during our joint project on the Namibian liberation struggle that produced, among other things, our book *Namibia's Liberation Struggle: The Two-Edged Sword* (London: James Currey, 1995). Thus I was not really joking when I told workshop participants that insofar as I would be reflecting critically on Colin Leys's work in my paper I would be doing so in the spirit that Edmund Burke – of all people to quote in the context of honouring Professor Leys – recommended as best defining the mood in which we should approach any criticism or alteration of the prevailing British political institutions of his time: I would approach Colin Leys's work, in Burke's words (more or less), "as one would approach the wounds of one's father: with trembling awe and humble solicitude!"

Colin Leys may have retired from Queen's University and from the vocation of formal teaching. It will come as no surprise to those who know him, however, that he is very far from having retired from the scientific fray, from the class struggle, or indeed (and despite his threats to do so in favour of his work on Britain and on broader global patterns) from the field of African Studies.

2 This statement introduces the concluding chapter, "Development Theory and the African Tragedy," in Colin Leys, *The Rise and Fall of Development Theory*, London: James Currey, 1996: 188 [hereinafter *The Rise and Fall*]. Closely related themes were also adduced in Leys's widely read article, "Confronting the African Tragedy," in *New Left Review*, no. 204, March–April, 1994.

3 Many of these latter materials having been brought together in his 1996 volume, *The Rise and Fall*.

4 I have discussed in more general terms the tension, creative and otherwise, between the "political economy" and "political science" approaches in two linked articles on "Liberalism vs. Popular Democracy" in recent

issues of *Review of African Political Economy* (ROAPE), nos. 72 and 73, 1997, from which (pp. 73 and 351) this characterization of relevant political concerns is quoted.

5 See, for example, Crawford Young, "Evolving Modes of Consciousness and Ideology: Nationalism and Ethnicity," in David Apter and Carl G. Rosberg, *Political Development and the New Realism in Sub-Saharan Africa*, Charlottesville: University Press of Virginia, 1994: 72–3, for a critique of Leys's approach to ethnicity in some of his work.

6 For a particularly distressing example of where the political science of Africa has come to position itself in this regard, at least in the United States, see David Apter and Carl G. Rosberg, "Changing African Perspectives," ibid., 40.

7 Colin Leys, *Underdevelopment in Kenya*, Los Angeles and Berkeley: University of California Press, 1975: xi; the internal quotation is from Marx and Engels, *The German Ideology*.

8 Colin Leys, *European Politics in Southern Rhodesia*, Oxford: Clarendon Press, 1959.

9 Colin Leys and Cranford Pratt (eds), *A New Deal in Central Africa*, New York: Frederick Praeger, 1960.

10 Colin Leys, *Politicians and Politics: An Essay on Politics in Acholi, Uganda 1962–5*, Nairobi: East African Publishing House, 1967.

11 This was at Kivukoni College in Dar es Salaam, 1960–62, and then at Makerere College in Uganda, 1962–65.

12 Note that it was led by James S. Coleman and sponsored by the Rockefeller Foundation.

13 The quotations in this paragraph are drawn from Leys's own "Introduction" to Colin Leys (ed.), *Politics and Change in Developing Countries*, Cambridge: Cambridge University Press, 1969: 1–12.

14 Leys, *Underdevelopment in Kenya*, xiii.

15 Ibid., 271, 275.

16 David Apter and Carl G. Rosberg, "Changing African Perspectives."

17 Colin Leys, "Learning from the Kenya Case," in Apter and Rosberg, *Political Development and the New Realism in Sub-Saharan Africa*, 226, and republished as chapter 8 in *The Rise and Fall*, 150.

18 From Leys's essay, "African Economic Development in Theory and Practice," reprinted as chapter 5 in Leys, *The Rise and Fall*, 113–14. The essay was originally published in *Daedalus*, vol. 111, no. 2, Spring, 1982.

19 Colin Leys, "African Capitalists and Development," reprinted as chapter 8 in *The Rise and Fall*, 177–8. This chapter was originally published in Bruce J. Berman and Colin Leys (eds), *African Capitalists in African Development*, Boulder: Lynne Rienner, 1994.

20 Colin Leys, "African Economic Development in Theory and Practice," in *The Rise and Fall*, 131.

21 See, in particular, the three essays "African Economic Development in Theory and Practice," "Learning from the Kenya Case," and "African Capitalists and Development," all previously cited and which have become chapters 5, 7, and 8, respectively, in *The Rise and Fall*.

22 Colin Leys, "Capital Accumulation, Class Formation and Dependency – The Significance of the Kenyan Case," in Ralph Miliband and John Savile (eds), *The Socialist Register 1978*, London: Merlin, 1978: 251.

23 Leys, ibid., 261. A more theoretical pendant to this Kenya article which also serves to mark Leys's move away from "'underdevelopment' and 'dependency' theory (UDT)" is his "Underdevelopment and Dependency: Critical Notes," first published in the *Journal of Contemporary Asia*, vol. 7, no. 1, 1977, and reprinted as chapter 2 in *The Rise and Fall*; here he takes as his point of critical departure the premise that "UDT is no longer serviceable and must be transcended," 45.

24 Leys, "African Capitalists and Development" in *The Rise and Fall*, 164.

25 Leys, "Learning from the Kenya Debate" in *The Rise and Fall*, 153. Note, however, that Leys, in the very next sentence, moves to qualify his qualifications: "It seems perverse to suppose that the prospects for capitalist development are not affected in any way by the size and nature of the domestic capitalist class; there was a rational kernel in the emphasis laid out in my 1978 article, even if the reasons were unclear ... What cannot be imported or purchased are the cohesion, organization, leadership and political skills needed to secure the hegemony of the accumulating and above all the productive class, so that state policy serves the needs of capitalist production."

26 Jeffrey C. Alexander, "Modern, Anti, Post and Neo," in *New Left Review*, no. 210, March-April, 1995: 65.

27 Leys, "Learning from the Kenya Debate," in *The Rise and Fall*.

28 Leys, "The World, Society and the Individual," *Southern Africa Report* (*SAR*), vol. 11, no. 3, April, 1996: 17.

29 Leys, *The Rise and Fall*, 184ff and 151.

30 Manfred Bienefeld, "Dependency Theory and the Political Economy of Africa's Crisis," *ROAPE*, no. 43, 1988: 85–6.

31 Leys, "The Rise and Fall of Development Theory," being the central, title essay to Leys's book of the same name *The Rise and Fall*, 44.

32 Leys, "The World, Society and the Individual," 19. As he argues the point further in *The Rise and Fall*, 44, current trends "suggest to me that unless the global economic and political forces bearing on Africa radically alter, much if not most of the continent is doomed to further decline, material and moral degradation and suffering."

33 Ibid., "The World, Society and the Individual," 19.

34 Leys, *The Rise and Fall*, 191. As Leys expands on the point, "for all its shortcomings the great merit of development theory has always consisted

in being committed to the idea that we can and should try to change the world not just contemplate it – which means, in practice, being willing to abstract from the detail, to identify structures and causal relationships and to propose ways of modifying them," 196.

35 Paul Hirst and Grahame Thompson, *Globalisation in Question*, London: Polity Press, 1996: 189.

36 Leys, "African Capitalists and Development," in *The Rise and Fall*, 178.

37 Leys, "Confronting the African Tragedy," 46.

38 Leys, "African Capitalists and Development," in *The Rise and Fall*, 187.

39 Leys, "The World, Society and the Individual," 19–20.

40 Leys, "Confronting the African Tragedy," 46.

41 Adam Przeworski, *Democracy and the Market*, Cambridge: Cambridge University Press, 1991: 122.

42 Leys, "The World, Society and the Individual," 20. Compare his equally honest admission at the end of "Confronting the African Tragedy" as to what are the practical implications of his way of understanding the "African tragedy": "I confess I don't know," he writes, 46.

43 The quotations in this paragraph are drawn from "Colin Leys Replies" in *SAR*, vol. 12, no. 4, September 1997: 22–3. He is responding to Jonathan Barker, "Debating Globalisation: Critique of Colin Leys," in the same issue, 20–2.

44 Colin Leys, "Development Theory and Africa's Future," unpublished paper presented to a conference to honour Lars Rudebeck at Uppsala, Sweden, in April, 1997.

45 Roger Murray, "Second Thoughts on Ghana," *New Left Review*, no. 42, March-April, 1967: 39.

46 This is an observation appropriate, finally, to the occasion of a festschrift.

47 Michel de Montaigne, *The Complete Essays of Montaigne*, Stanford: Stanford University Press, 1958: 610–11.

Caught in the Contradictions: The State in Kenya, 1945–2000

BRUCE J. BERMAN

INTRODUCTION

During the "Kenya debate" of the early 1980s, proponents on both the Marxist and dependency sides of the issue generally assumed the existence in Kenya of a dominant and effective state, capable of acting to ensure the conditions of accumulation, whether by international capital or the indigenous bourgeoisie.[1] Focused on evidence from the Kenyatta years (1963–78) of generally robust economic growth and relative political stability, neither side of the debate was capable of effectively dealing with the changed circumstances of the 1980s and 1990s, when increasing economic stagnation, growing political disorder, and increasing evidence of decay of the state apparatus muddied the country's reputation as one of Africa's economic and political "successes." In retrospect, the debate was driven too much by deterministic theoretical assumptions on both sides, and too little by detailed reading of the empirical evidence. In particular, the instrumental capability of the Kenyan state was substantially overestimated and its relationship to indigenous society largely neglected.[2] Preoccupied with arguing the conditions for national industrialization at the periphery of the capitalist world system, the proponents in the debate paid scant attention to the continuity of the predominantly agrarian character of the political economy of Kenya, the continuing power of the colonial state apparatus of control and its linkages to rural society, the development of ethnicity and its relationship to class formation, and the salience of ethnically defined patronage politics in Kenyan institutions and culture.

By the second half of the 1980s, concern over an increasingly troubled Kenya shifted to more mainstream political scientists debating the issues of civil society and democratization as both state repression and political opposition to the Kenya government grew. The external "aid community" of Western powers and international agencies became involved in intensifying pressures for economic and political "reforms" to restore the conditions of capitalist development.[3] Although recent writings on Kenyan politics show concern for the importance of the institutional structures of state and economy in Kenya,[4] there is a similar misunderstanding of the contradictory legacy of colonialism in the post-colonial state and how it can explain important aspects of the country's economic and political crises.

This essay will sketch a perspective on the development of the state and politics in Kenya over the past half-century, beginning with the contradictory establishment within the colonial state of an apparatus of rural control anchored in ethnically defined patron/client networks along with sophisticated state and parastatal agencies of capitalist growth and economic management. We trace the further development of the state in the post-colonial period, starting with the relatively favourable economic conditions of the Kenyatta years. These conditions permitted the further growth and reasonably effective functioning of the state apparatus of economic management and development and the pervasive spread via agencies of the state of the networks of patronage politics, under the domination of the Kikuyu and their allies. We will then examine how worsening economic conditions and the attempt by the Moi regime after 1978 to affect a drastic ethnic shift in control of the state and access to its diverse resources brought a significant deterioration of the state and the rising internal opposition and external pressure for political reform and democratization. We conclude with a critical review of the Kenya state and the process of democratization after the restoration of multi-party politics in 1992.

CONTRADICTORY FOUNDATIONS OF THE COLONIAL STATE

An uneasy combination of the peasant-based colonies of West Africa and the settler societies of Southern Africa, the distinctive contradictions of the political economy of colonial Kenya were reproduced in its state structures.[5] Throughout the colonial era the state authorities struggled to balance the conflicting demands of maintaining stable political control and providing the conditions for the development of capitalist relations of property, labour, and commodity production on settler estates, African peasant farms, and, later, in urban commerce and industry. The contradiction between control and accumulation was expressed in the ambivalence of the colonial authorities, especially in the countryside, towards pressing the full development of agrarian capitalism with the consequent disruption of indigenous societies and threat to political order.[6] They presided, instead, over a desultory and often fragmentary capitalist transformation of African societies that repeatedly halted when pressures for the production of commodities and the extraction of labour for settler estates provoked African resistance. Administrators often also attempted to resuscitate what they believed were "traditional" institutions in order to maintain the order and integrity of "tribal" society. Nevertheless, the frequent coercive interventions of the colonial state into African societies to collect tax, register and recruit labour, and control commodity production and marketing required reliance on an extensive grassroots network of African agents and collaborators.

In Kenya, few of these local collaborators had any indigenous precedent for their authority; they were overwhelmingly chiefs and headmen directly appointed by the provincial administration, rapidly joined by police, interpreters, clerks, other lower-level officials, and a local petty bourgeois intelligentsia of teachers, clergy, and traders. As the colonial state forged its links with indigenous society, its local collaborators appear to have increasingly overlapped with members of locally dominant sub-clans and lineages. Rather than being the egalitarian tribal communities of anthropological myth, the largely stateless societies of pre-colonial Kenya contained significant internal differences of wealth and power, both between individuals and corporate kin groups, and connected rich and poor by diverse forms of clientage. To be rich and powerful meant the use of material wealth to build and maintain extensive networks of kin and clients.[7] The colonial state was thus, at its lowest level, articulated with indigenous societies by incorporation of the latter's structures of wealth and power, by selecting its agents either from powerful patrons and their families or from "new men" who used their relationship with the state to build their own clientelistic networks of wealth and power. Poorly paid by the state, these agents often pressed hard on the local populace to extract taxes and labour and to accumulate resources to maintain their own networks of support and control. The provincial administration often ignored such "corruption" – unless it provoked local disorder – and encouraged its African agents to take advantage of new opportunities for enrichment through cash cropping, business ventures, and education that opened more highly paid employment for children and other kin. The fundamental state/society linkage was thus based on the mutual dependence of the colonial state and local strongmen who controlled access to land, labour, and the benefits of modernity and development through extensive patron/client networks. Hierarchies of personal rule in rural districts and locations were linked to the wide discretion of the provincial administration to adjust colonial domination to the pattern of local social forces.

Beneath this apparatus of collaboration and control, African societies in Kenya were disrupted in varying degrees by moral and material crises stemming from the differential impact of capitalist relations of production, wage labour and migrancy, and the alienation or threat of loss of control over land and people. The increasing social differentiation and disparities of wealth and poverty that marked the beginnings of class formation were accompanied by heightened conflicts over the meaning of custom, the distribution of wealth and power, and the definition of civil order.[8] In moral economies of clientage and reciprocity colonial change produced clashes over social rules and identities, particularly the mutual obligations of rich and poor, as people struggled either to take advantage of new opportunities or to protect themselves against disruption and loss. In this process the African agents of the state, along with the first generation of educated *athomi* (literally "readers"), stood in the vanguard of accumulators and at the heart of indigenous politics.[9] Ethnicity became the fundamental idiom of this process, encapsulating the new forms of class cleavage and conflict in contests over the redefinition of indigenous custom and identity. In a striking dialectic of assimilation and differentiation, the exacerbation of ethnicity had internal and external dimensions. Internally, moral ethnicity represented the outcome of the internal crises over the boundaries of community, ties of custom and moral economy. Externally, political tribalism expressed the growing competition between ethnic communities, often encouraged by the colonial state, for access to the wider material benefits of development. Within administrative subdivisions that the colonial state strived to define as ethnically homogeneous units, patron/client networks were ethnically defined; ethnic identity became a primary means of claiming access to land and other material resources.

Parallel to the growth of ethnic patronage networks in African rural societies, a more "modern" state apparatus of capitalist development and regulation emerged, operating at first largely in the urban areas and in the "White Highlands" districts of settler estate production. Spurred initially by the serious weakness of the settler economy, the state developed a remarkably effective apparatus of labour recruitment and regulation, joined during the Depression and the Second World War by parastatal agencies of credit, production, and market-

ing. After 1945 a rapidly growing and increasingly complex and pro-
fessionalized state apparatus pursued a more systematic commitment
to growth, spurred by an essentially Keynesian vision of economic
development. A formal system of functional ministries emerged by the
early 1950s, with those of Finance, Agriculture, Labour, and Commerce and Industry playing crucial roles in shaping the colony's development, while new parastatal agencies were created to attract investment and promote industry. As the political balance began to shift
against the settler community, senior officials of the colonial state,
conscious of Kenya becoming a "developing nation," moved to cut
the props of the settler economy, open the colony to international
investment, and incorporate Africans more fully into the rapidly
growing "modern" economy.[10]

The central contradiction in the colonial state was between the
ostensibly disinterested professional rationality of the managerial
technocratic apparatus of capitalist development and the ethnically
focused personalized authority of the patronage apparatus in the
rural periphery. Initially isolated by the racial compartmentalization
of colonial society in Kenya, the two spheres of state development
were increasingly brought together during the 1950s by a combination of rapid economic growth and political crisis. Increasing social
differentiation and internal cleavages in African societies, especially
among the Kikuyu, along with a visibly widening gap between the
rapid economic growth experienced by the European and Asian
immigrant communities and the relative stagnation in the African
rural districts and deteriorating conditions for Africans in urban centres underlay the Emergency of 1952-59.[11] Parallel to the efforts to
sustain investment and growth in the colony's economy, particularly
in the emerging manufacturing sector, the provincial administration
in the countryside was significantly reinforced. The patronage system
expanded both to reward the Kikuyu loyalists (mostly the official
agents of the regime and the wealthier members of the community
and their clients) for their support in suppressing the Mau Mau and
to prevent other African communities from joining the uprising.
Material benefits included an extensive agrarian development program to bring Africans more direct benefits of economic growth
through wider involvement in cash-crop production and land consolidation and registration schemes providing freehold titles. The focus
of these programs was on smallholder peasant production, rather
than promoting capitalist development, and included in the last years
of colonialism efforts to absorb the landless, a palpable threat to
political order, in smallholder settlement schemes on former settler
estates. More elite-focused efforts by both the state and internation-

al capital assisted the development of African business and transferred the more viable settler estates to African owners as intact units
of commercial production.[12]

After the complete ban on African political activity imposed by the
colonial state at the beginning of the Emergency, district level organizations or parties were permitted in 1957. This encouraged the consolidation of a politics focused around major local patrons and their
ethnic constituencies, largely ensuring, once colony-wide "national"
organizations were again permitted in 1960, that the two "nationalist"
parties that emerged, KANU and KADU, were loosely structured coalitions of ethnic factions led by major political figures sitting atop their
own networks of clients. The fundamental cleavage between them was
based on several smaller ethnic communities' fear of the Kikuyu-Luo
alliance in KANU. The independence constitution attempted to accom-
modate these fears with a federal state structure (*majimboism*) of
regional governments and assemblies, with a federal parliament in
Nairobi. With KANU in control at the centre and KADU in the Rift Valley region, conflict focused in the years immediately before and after
independence (1962–64) on the land issue, particularly the disposition
of the former settler estates in the Rift Valley Province between the
Kalenjin and Luhya on its western borders and landless Kikuyu peasants, many of them former squatters on European farms, who could
not be accommodated within the densely populated Kikuyu districts to
the east. The confrontation was defused by adroit political manoeu-
vring by Jomo Kenyatta and the leadership of KANU that exploited
internal splits in KADU between the Luhya and Kalenjin leadership,
buying them off with former settler estates, while the bulk of the land
in the Rift Valley went to high-density settlement schemes for landless
Kikuyu. KADU MPs began to cross the floor of the parliament to join
KANU. Within a year of independence both KADU and the *majimbo* constitution were no more, and a unitary, defacto one-party, state was
restored.[13]

THE KENYATTA STATE:
PATRONAGE AND CAPITALIST ACCUMULATION

The passage from the colonial to the post-colonial state brought its
contradictory elements into closer and ultimately more disruptive
conjuncture. The shift of control of the state into the hands of a KANU
government under Jomo Kenyatta, and the rapid Africanization of
the bureaucracy, brought the extension of the ethnic patronage networks throughout the state apparatus, including the cabinet room
and the president's office. At the same time, the regime grounded its

legitimacy in the incorporation of local rural patrons and their clientage into those networks.[14] This meant that the high politics of elite competition was focused on the political tribalism of ethnic rivalry and, linked via the tracks of clientelism to the deep politics of moral ethnicity, also on the contest over the reciprocal relations of elites and masses. The essential linkages between state and society in Kenya ran through the conflicting ethnic networks of personal power from Kenyatta and the political magnates in Nairobi into the furthest reaches of the countryside.

Kenyatta and his hegemonic faction of senior Kikuyu ministers, many of them drawn from powerful Kiambu families, whose dominant positions reached back through colonial chieftaincies to pre-colonial society, managed the loose KANU alliance of "big men" and their ethnic factions through a combination of co-optation, arbitration and coercion, allowing considerable autonomy of local networks at the periphery, and also promoting competition among them for portions of patronage just sufficient to sustain the coalition. Playing his long-established role as *muigwithania* (the reconciler),[15] Kenyatta nonetheless relied heavily on the provincial administration as the central arm of state control, following the elimination of the *majimbo* federal structures.[16] Ultimate control in the countryside remained in the hands of the provincial and district commissioners, not the politicians or KANU (which was little more than an institutional shell). At one point, three of the six PCs were related to Kenyatta. Even KANU MPs and local politicians needed the administration's permission to address public meetings. Other organizations and political figures, mobilizing support on a transethnic and/or class basis, proved harder to contain within the system of patronage networks and drew more coercive reactions from the state. The trade union movement was brought under state control and efforts were made to replace independent labour leaders with compliant clients of the regime. The transethnic urban appeal of Tom Mboya, Kenyatta's most brilliant minister and the populist radicalism of the Kenya People's Union and, later, the flamboyant former Mau Mau detainee, Josiah Kariuki, were dealt with through a combination of assassination and repression. Oginga Odinga's break with Kenyatta and departure from KANU for the KPU took the Luo out of the ruling coalition and cost them dearly in access to patronage and development resources.[17]

The pervasive spread of the networks of patrons and clients through the structures of the state not only blurred the boundaries between political and administrative institutions, politicians, and bureaucrats, rigorously maintained under the colonial state but also those between the public and private sectors.[18] This led to the appropriation of public resources for private gain and distribution to clients, and also to the use of public office to gain privileged access to private sector rents and profits. The 1971 Ndegwa Commission on the Civil Service legitimated the holding of private business assets by officials, bringing the bureaucracy fully into the circuits of the patronage structures. Meanwhile, a substantial portion of the political elite, including the "big men" of the major ethnic communities, became important land owners in their home districts and often in the former settler districts of the Rift Valley as well, which served to tie further together state and rural localities and the interaction of high and deep politics.[19] The Africanization of the state made dominant a political rationality that undermined the economic management of capitalist development by the central agencies of the state and the parastatal apparatus of public corporations, bringing a decline of both professional competence and public accountability.

The deterioration of the state apparatus was obscured through the Kenyatta years by several conjunctural factors that permitted the apparently benign coexistence of ethnic patronage politics and state-managed capitalist development. First, the Africanization of the state apparatus, the settler agrarian economy, and, with increasing political pressure, significant sectors of Asian-owned commercial enterprise gave the Kenyatta regime an extraordinary range of jobs, land, and other economic assets to distribute through the patronage networks and sustain its ethnic alliance. Second, the accommodation of key interests was further enhanced by strong, broad-based economic growth both in agriculture, including peasant smallholder production, and in manufacturing that lasted from independence through the end of the 1970s.[20] Third, the combination of patronage politics and a managerial state was helped by the fact that the Kikuyu, the dominant ethnic group in KANU, were favourably positioned to quickly assume a preponderant position in both the state and the economy. Kikuyu politicians, civil servants, and businessmen formed a powerful, although far from internally harmonious, web of patronage networks that facilitated the use of state resources and support for movement into the private sector. Kikuyu dominance was visible in the expanded parastatal sector that combined both the promotion of growth and the distribution of patronage in management of the Africanization of the economy. The performance of public corporations varied widely from excellent to abysmal: the Agricultural Finance Corporation, which financed the transfer of large land holdings to the political elite, was the most flagrantly politically manipulated; while the development finance institutions that focused on manufacturing and the public utilities and infrastructure corporations performed relatively well through the 1970s.[21]

It must be noted, however, that the industrial sector, particularly in manufacturing, remained dominated by international corporations and firms owned by local Asians, many of whom moved from commerce to manufacturing with alacrity and remained the most vibrant sector of the indigenous bourgeoisie, despite their lack of political support and often tense relations with the African government. African presence in manufacturing, with inexperienced part-time managers distracted by political and other business interests, survived largely because of political favours and support from state agencies, a fact that was not clearly visible until these props were removed in the 1980s and many of these predominantly Kikuyu-owned firms quickly collapsed.[22] Nevertheless, this political dependence reveals the extent to which the state remained both the largest employer and principal source of wealth for Africans in Kenya, fostering capitalist enterprise through protective controls and ethnically biased preferential access to loans, licenses, contracts, etc. Even in the countryside, the accumulation of wealth and the growing gap between rich and poor was largely based on differential access to patronage, state resources, and non-agricultural income, rather than on investment in commercial agriculture.[23]

The resources of the state were also deployed to manage the central contradiction between accumulation and legitimation in the face of the growing disparities of wealth and rising levels of unemployment and poverty that were clearly visible within a decade after independence. Whatever their ethnic group, most Kenyans had little if any direct access to powerful patrons and their resources. Families survived through a combination of occasional wage labour, often including periods of urban residence, and limited cash-crop income from often minuscule farms. The survival of the mass of middle peasants was helped by government policy that focused on the development of smallholder production, rather than pressing the further expansion of capitalist agriculture that would have led to growing proletarianization. Rural development was actually pursued as a solution to growing unemployment.[24] State-funded development programs and infrastructure projects also constituted visible public benefits, as well as resources for patronage distribution, that displayed the ability of the local elites to deliver on the implicit moral contracts between rich and poor within different ethnic communities. The growing inequality of wealth was also partially offset by the ubiquitous Kenyan phenomenon of *harambee* – self-help development projects, especially for schools and health facilities, that continued the colonial programs of community development and were visibly manipulated by politicians and other wealthy members of the dominant class, up to and including the president himself. The public pledges of substantial contributions to harambees, usually at the official public meetings known as *barazas* were a form of "pork barrel clientelism" that appeared to tax the rich and provide a degree of public patronage and accountability.[25] The barazas themselves were the principal public occasions for the meeting of elites and masses that linked high and deep politics in confrontations reproducing the authoritarian paternalism of the colonial state and also providing opportunities for the vociferous expression of both sycophantic support and derisive opposition.[26]

THE MOI STATE: ETHNIC POWER SHIFT AND DETERIORATION

The death of Kenyatta and the constitutional succession to power of Daniel arap Moi, despite the opposition of some senior Kikuyu politicians, brought important changes in Kenyan politics and society marked by economic decline, deterioration of the state apparatus, growing ethnic conflict, and intensifying opposition to the regime. The conditions that made possible the coexistence during the Kenyatta years of patronage politics and the state apparatus of economic management and growth largely disappeared and the contradictions between them began to corrode the country's political institutions and processes. Although there was a substantial power shift to Moi's Kalenjin and their ethnic allies from Kenyatta's Kikuyu, the changed circumstances made a stable consolidation of power more difficult and led to increasing dependence on external aid and financing, as well as to growing external pressures for political and economic reforms.

Moi grounded his power, as did Kenyatta, on the provincial administration and state agencies of coercion, where he moved to end Kikuyu hegemony and replace it with senior Kalenjin appointees, especially after the failed coup attempt by the air force in August 1982.[27] In addition, however, he revitalized KANU, virtually moribund under Kenyatta, and built it into an effective instrument of political control and personal rule.[28] Ironically, the original ethnic alliance in the party was replaced with that of the long-dead KADU. With control of the state and party, the Moi regime rapidly shifted the distribution of state resources, development funds, jobs, and educational opportunities away from the Kikuyu and their allies towards the Kalenjin-led coalition. At the centre, Moi's inner circle attempted to advance Kalenjin capital at the expense of Kikuyu interests and oust the latter from dominant positions in the statist economy. In the countryside, meanwhile, Moi attempted to command direct loyalty as "father of the nation" and legitimate his regime by being the principal dispenser of patronage and by using barazas personally to distribute support for extravagant harambee projects. From 1983 the District Focused Rural Development (DFRD) policy, under the guise of decentralizing state development activities, brought development allocations under increased central control.[29] Moi attempted to blunt Kikuyu resistance and maintain a degree of support by appointing and later excluding major Kikuyu politicians from senior positions in the regime, including the vice-presidency, and by creating his own network of Kikuyu clients from factions excluded during the Kenyatta years.[30]

This attempt at a major shift in the ethnic coalition controlling the state took place, however, within the far less favourable national and international economic context of the 1980s, which was characterized by slower growth of the economy and declining fiscal resources for the state, making maintenance of the patronage networks increasingly difficult and seriously corroding the state apparatus of economic management and development. The levels of corruption and incompetence in state agencies increased markedly during the 1980s. The Moi regime was marked by increasing pillaging of state funds by officials and a growing inability to provide essential services for business. Both politicians and officials were increasingly predatory in their relations with local capital, moving from the graft of the Kenyatta regime, which traded access to state resources for payoffs and interests in businesses, to direct seizure of control of firms or to make quick profits at the expense of local businesses.[31] The most striking deterioration of performance came in the parastatal sector of public corporations as the regime manipulated them to support its ethnopolitical agenda of "regional redistribution." The performance and financial conditions of many parastatals, particularly undercapitalized new corporations started by the regime after 1978, deteriorated markedly during the 1980s. The most spectacular failures were in the agricultural sector, where there was a dramatic polarization in performance between the seven successful and the nine unsuccessful firms, with the Kenya Meat Commission, the National Cereals Production Board, and two of the four sugar refiners incurring huge losses.[32] At the same time, efforts to promote African capital were thwarted by major failures of African banking and manufacturing companies between 1985-90 and the closing by the government in April 1993 of twelve "political banks" under pressure from the international donor community to end corruption and mismanagement.[33] Finally, international investment also declined significantly from the late 1970s, spurred by the collapse of the East African Common Market and increasing political instability, with substantial divestment mostly by sale to local Asian companies, which continued to be the most dynamic sector of the economy, despite the lack of state support.

In agriculture, the regime's ethnic bias showed most clearly. While government policy continued to favour smallholder production, there was a distinct shift of the distribution of state resources from the principal producers of export crops, the predominantly Kikuyu tea and coffee farmers, towards the mostly Kalenjin grain producers in the Rift Valley. A major focus of the Moi regime's ethnic shift, inefficient, but politically well-connected, wheat producers were paid 140 per cent of the world price. This policy was behind the severe losses of the NCPB and involved high costs in foreign exchange along with the exploitation of the more efficient coffee and tea producers to support it. In 1985 the government also replaced the Kenya Farmers Association, the principal national interest and service organization for farmers (although seen as Kikuyu-dominated) with a more docile state-controlled organization, the Kenya Grain Growers Cooperative Union.[34]

The combination of declining rates of economic growth, deteriorating terms of trade and balance of payments problems with growing corruption, political constraints on tax collection and the disappearance of effective controls on public expenditure caught up with the state in growing budgetary deficits and a general crisis of public finance, which required increasing dependence on loans and grants from the international donor community.[35] Consequently, the state resources to sustain the patronage networks of Kenyan politics declined and the ability of the regime to manage the contradictions between accumulation and legitimation deteriorated steadily. With far fewer resources at hand and facing the resistance of Kikuyu officials and businessmen entrenched by the Kenyatta regime, Moi and his circle simply did not have the same success in promoting the Kalenjin. Moreover, the increasing insecurities of life led to a growing competitive scramble for patronage resources that accentuated ethnic competition, fuelled conflict between patrons and clients, and divided extended families.[36] The harambees became sources of popular disillusionment with the regime as promised projects failed to materialize while ordinary citizens were forced by state and party officials to make contributions. For all of the diverse ethnic components of the Moi regime's patchwork coalition, the increasing uncertainties of patronage politics undermined their ability to meet the moral contract of "development" with their communities and exposed the shallowness of their clients' loyalties.

THE KENYAN STATE AND THE STRUGGLE
FOR DEMOCRATIZATION SINCE 1992

Several important consequences flow directly from the salience of ethnically based patron/client relations in Kenyan politics.[37] First, it has thwarted the development of a unified, pan-ethnic dominant class capable of effectively employing the state in pursuit of a coherent project of national development. Intra-class conflict between feuding ethnic factions seriously hobbles the Kenyan bourgeoisie. Second, as in much of the rest of Africa, it has generated a largely non-ideological and crudely materialistic "politics of the belly" of shallow loyalties linked to the flow of material benefits, and largely lacking effective mobilization and organization towards collective goals or interests. Instead, ethnic elites derive a tenuous legitimacy through an implicit social contract with their communities, the outcome itself of the internal contests of moral ethnicity. A distinctly authoritarian paternalism is accepted in return for the provision of the material benefits of "development."[38] Third, while during the colonial period patronage politics was largely contained in rural districts by the provincial administration as part of a strategy of fragmenting and isolating African political activity, after independence patron/client networks spread throughout the state apparatus. These networks turned agency after agency into a hollow carapace in which the ideology and practices of disinterested professional expertise were replaced by the competitive squabbles of ethnic factions for the private appropriation of public resources. Fourth, in consequence, the ability of the Kenyan state, and especially its parastatal sector, to act as agent for the development and management of capitalist modernity has steadily deteriorated.

These factors of ethnic conflict and political and economic decline have generated an extended crisis that has now lasted more than a decade. Recurrent waves of opposition and pressure for reform have engaged the bitter and intransigent resistance of the regime. By the late 1980s Kenyan politics was marked by a dialectic of increasingly open expressions of opposition and escalating repression by the government, including widespread rioting in Nairobi in 1990 and arrests and assassination of opposition leaders. While the regime functioned in an atmosphere of growing sycophancy and fear, by the early 1990s opposition was centered in the trade unions, the press, women's organizations, and, in particular, professional associations and churches, which represented transethnic bases of affiliation and interest in Kenyan society. These were led by an urban middle-class and professional elite that was strongly influenced by Western ideas of liberal democracy and articulated a politics of more principled opposition. At the same time, most of the emerging opposition leaders, even in the churches, were drawn from the communities, notably the Luo and Kikuyu, which had been most negatively affected by the regime's ethnic biases. Many of them also had held senior government positions before falling out with Moi and his circle. By the end of 1991 internal opposition was powerfully reinforced by intense external pressures for political reform from the international donors on which the government depended for aid, which was suspended pending the legitimation of opposition parties and the conduct of multi-party elections in 1992.

The first phase of the struggle for reform and democratization of the state in Kenya, 1990–92, involved only the restoration of multi-party politics and the formal end of the single party state. No fundamental agreements were reached between the regime and the opposition parties on the rules of the political game.[39] Instead, KANU insured its victory by relying heavily on the partisan bias of the state apparatus, including an iniquitous electoral system favoring small rural constituencies and state controlled media, as well as judicious rigging of key swing constituencies and promotion of factionalism among the opposition.[40] The authoritarian backbone of the state, the provincial administration, invoked a complex of repressive colonial laws from the Emergency in the 1950s, to constantly harass opposition parties and candidates, prohibit their public meetings, prevent collection of funds, and limit their access to rural constituencies.[41] Meanwhile, from December 1991, a government-sponsored campaign of ethnic violence descended upon the Kikuyu farmers whose settlement in the Rift Valley had been a key issue in the decolonization process thirty years before, and the regime's supporters called for the expulsion of all non-Kalenjin from the Rift Valley and restoration of the *majimbo* federal system. Moi, with the coldest cynicism, repeatedly blamed the outbreaks of violence on the opposition.

In the wake of its election victory, the regime moved to get the flow of aid restored, but rejected the conditions demanded by the donors. However, a growing economic crisis and further revelations of financial scandals eventually forced acceptance of IMF/World Banks conditions that included promises of civil service reform and privatization of the parastatal sector. In November 1993 the international and bilateral donors agreed to a resumption of some US$850 million in aid, including $170 million in "quick disbursing" funds that covered immediate budget shortfalls.[42] At the same time, the regime deployed its control of the patronage and coercive resources of the state to blunt the threat of multi-partyism and public accountability, as well as weaken and isolate the opposition. It "maintained the pressure on opposition MPs, employing the district administration to obstruct their rallies and recalling loans from state financial institutions, whilst offering monetary inducements to those who can be persuaded to defect."[43] The result was a decline in the number of opposition members in the parliament from eighty-eight to seventy-six by June 1997 through defections to the ruling party and KANU victories in by-elections.

The second phase of the democratic struggle began with the revival of opposition activity in the lead up to the 1997 election. Human rights abuses by the police and provincial administration continued unabated through harassment, detention, threats against opposition politicians, human rights organizations, civic associations and journalists, and further attacks on Kikuyu in Rift Valley Province by gangs covertly armed and encouraged by the regime.[44] After a brief recovery of growth, the Kenyan economy slipped back into stagnation, with the living standards of most Kenyans declining and the proportion of the population living below the official poverty line climbing to 50 per cent.[45] Despite promises to donors, corruption continued without significant restraint, reaching new levels of frenzied looting of public resources. With traditional patronage sources in increasingly short supply, the attention of the regime's kleptocrats turned to land grabbing – the illegal appropriation and private distribution of both urban and rural public lands – which generated growing public anger and frequent resistance.[46]

The central focus of opposition by 1997 was a coalition of party and civil society groups organized in the National Convention Assembly and its National Convention Executive Council. These produced powerful pressures for removal of legal restrictions on freedom of assembly and political expression, as well as for fundamental constitutional changes. Widespread public demonstrations in favour of reforms on 7–8 July, however, were violently repressed by the police. Later that month, ethnic violence spread to the Coast province in riots directed against Luo and Kikuyu "outsiders."[47] International anger over the regime's violence and continued inaction against corruption led to a second suspension of aid by the international financial institutions. Under increasing pressure, Moi moved with characteristic suppleness to co-opt the opposition by calling for an Inter-Parties Parliamentary Group (IPPG) of KANU and opposition MPs to discuss and propose reforms. As opposition parties moved to join the IPPG, a clear split opened between the most of the party politicians and the leaders of the civic associations.[48] The professional politicians, men like Kenneth Matiba, Mwai Kibaki, Martin Shikuku, and Raila Odinga (the dominant Luo political figure after the death of his father in 1994), represented the continuing dominance of the politics of ethnicity and patronage and its patriarchal, patronizing, and elitist political culture. For them, opposition politics is primarily a means of removing Moi and his circle and regaining access to the state and its resources. In contrast, the leaders of the civic and professional associations -including Paul Muite, Peter Anyang Nyong'o, Richard Leakey, Charity Ngilu, and Gibson Kamau Kuria – sought more fundamental procedural reforms that would implement effective institutions of liberal democracy.

The late parliamentary passage of a package of reforms in October 1997 curbing the states powers of repression, but leaving the powers of the presidency and other fundamental issues untouched, made little difference in the outcome of the election. The weakly organized opposition parties were even more fragmented by ethnic cleavages and the personal rivalries and ambitions of their leaders. The electoral system, revised by the KANU-controlled Electoral Commission in 1996, was even more iniquitous, allowing KANU to pile up seats in gerrymandered constituencies with small numbers of voters, while the major opposition parties wasted their support in huge majorities in constituencies with very large number of voters.[49] The chaotically mismanaged election, full of glaring irregularities and rigging that made the early days of 1998 fraught with opposition threats of rejecting the result, returned Moi to the presidency with a slightly increased popular vote of 40 per cent, but a significantly reduced KANU majority of only four in the parliament.

The third phase of the struggle since early 1998 has focused on constitutional reform, human rights, and an increasingly intense confrontation over corruption. The crucial issue has been the institutional locus of the reform process, namely either a popular "people's" constitutional body dominated by the civic reform organizations behind the NCEC or one contained within the parliament through the IPPG under the control of MPs from KANU and other parties. By the end of 1998, the NCEC had been marginalized through the Constitution of Kenya Review (Amendment Bill), which created a constitutional review commission, the majority of whose members would be appointed by the president.[50] Exactly what groups or interests would be represented and the precise manner of their appointment remained issues of contention into 2000. At the same time, in the face of increasing internal anger and external pressure from donors fixated on the issue, the regime took further, albeit grudging, initiatives against corruption. Simeon Nyachae, a leading KANU moderate, was appointed minister of finance and promised both a war on corruption and an austerity program to repair the government's finances.[51] Nonetheless, ferocious internal struggles in KANU led to Nyachae's apparent demotion to a less important portfolio in a cabinet shuffle in May 1999, and his subsequent resignation and return to the back benches as leader of a small band of KANU dissidents. Aid from international donors remained suspended, however, until serious action was taken against corruption. This led to the surprise appointment in July of opposition MP Richard Leakey of the Safina Party to be cabinet secretary and head of the civil service, with a public mandate to pursue a vigorous war against corruption and develop an economic recovery program. By early 2000, MPs in the key parliamentary investment committee were demanding of Leakey and other senior officials when the promised dismissals and indictments of corrupt officials up to the most senior levels and repossession of looted public resources would take place.[52] An attempt to eliminate some 6,000 assistant chiefs, a crucial link between the provincial administration and rural ethnic power networks and primary agents of grassroots control, was quickly overruled by Moi, suggesting continuing intense resistance to reform within the regime.[53]

It is not clear what the outcome of this lengthy struggle might be. Internal conflicts in KANU over the presidential succession when Moi departs in 2002 may give the opposition its best opportunity yet for an electoral victory. For both the internal opposition and external interests, however, constitutional reforms and restoration of the probity and competence of the state are imperative for advancing the development of liberal democracy, reviving the conditions of capitalist accumulation and extending the integration of Kenya into the world economy.

While reaching these goals requires a broad transethnic and transclass coalition capable not only of electoral victory but also of driving the process of institutional reform, the ethnic and patronage logic that continues to dominate Kenyan politics makes the achievement of such an alliance problematic. Class remains imbedded in the folds of ethnicity, where confrontations take place over the reciprocal obligations of rich and poor and clientelism reaches across class cleavages. At the elite level, class has shaped the distinct ideological limits of the opposition parties, whose leadership represent factions of the same class with little interest in the issues relating to the poverty and insecurity of the mass of the population. Moreover, opposition political discourse has become increasingly centered on the personalities of the leaders, less and less on issues and hardly at all on the parties themselves. The educated urban leadership of the civic, professional, and religious associations has vigorously promoted a narrowly procedural democratization with little if any program of development beyond the neoliberal policies and market reforms pressed by the external donor community. They have only sporadically succeeded in mobilizing support from the urban poor or the now substantial middle class and have had little success in reaching rural society. Kenya's weakly organized and deeply divided business community has played little direct role in the reform struggle. Instead, the process of democratization has repeatedly become a hollow facade as the powerful forces of ethnicity and patronage have reasserted the crude materialism of Kenyan "politics as usual."

NOTES

1 The major contributions to the debate are discussed in Colin Leys's retrospective essay "Learning from the Kenya Debate," *The Rise and Fall of Development Theory,* London: James Currey, 1996.

2 David Himbara, *Kenyan Capitalists, the State, and Development,* Boulder and London: Lynne Rienner, 1994: 18–21.

3 See the critical discussion in Frank Holmquist, Frederick Weaver, and Michael Ford, "The Structural Development of Kenya's Political Economy," *African Studies Review,* vol. 37, no. 1, April 1994.

4 Most strikingly in the work of the "new institutionalists" like Robert Bates, *Beyond the Miracle of the Market,* Cambridge: Cambridge University Press, 1989; and Jean Ensminger, *Making a Market,* Cambridge: Cambridge University Press, 1992.

5 The next paragraphs are adapted from Bruce Berman, *Control and Crisis in Colonial Kenya,* London: James Currey, 1990: chapters 3 and 5.

6 See also Michael Chege, "The Political Economy of Agrarian Change in Central Kenya," in Michael Schatzberg, *The Political Economy of Kenya,* New York: Praeger, 1987; and M. P. Cowen and R.W. Shenton, *Doctrines of Development,* New York and London: Routledge, 1996: 334–9.

7 Chege, "The Political Economy," 98-9; Bates, *Beyond the Miracle,* 14–17; Angelique Haugerud, *The Culture of Politics in Modern Kenya,* Cambridge: Cambridge University Press, 1995: 112–17.

8 This paragraph is based on John Lonsdale, "The Moral Economy of Mau Mau," in Bruce Berman and John Lonsdale, *Unhappy Valley, Book Two: Violence and Ethnicity,* London: James Currey, 1992.

9 Haugerud, *The Culture of Politics,* 133–6; Chege, "The Political Economy," 98-9; Bates, *Beyond the Miracle,* 30–9.

10 Berman, *Control and Crisis,* chapters 6 and 9; Himbara, *Kenyan Capitalists,* 8–11, 22–5, 103–11.

11 David Throup. *Economic and Social Origins of Mau Mau*, London: James Currey, 1987.

12 Berman, *Control and Crisis*, chapter 8; Cowen and Shenton, *Doctrines of Development*, 298-9, 340-7; Himbara, *Kenyan Capitalists*, 75-84.

13 Bates, *Beyond the Miracle*, 47-63.

14 David Throup. "The Construction and Destruction of the Kenyatta State," in Schatzberg, *The Political Economy of Kenya*, 33-4; Holmquist et al., "The Structural Development of Kenya's Political Economy," 80-1.

15 Muigwithania was Kenyatta's nickname from the early days of his political career with the Kikuyu Central Association in the late 1920s and derived from the journal of that title that he edited in 1928-29. For its significance see Bruce Berman and John Lonsdale, "The Labours of Muigwithania: Jomo Kenyatta as Author, 1928-1945," *Research in African Literatures*, vol. 29, no. 1, 1998: 16-42.

16 Control of the provincial administration was given to Peter Mbiyu Koinange, minister of state in the office of the president, Kenyatta's brother-in-law, close friend, and the son of the late Senior Chief Koinange Mbiyu of Kiambu. On the management of patronage politics and the use of the provincial administration see Karuti Kanyinga, "Ethnicity, Patronage and Class in a Local Arena: 'High' and 'Low' Politics in Kiambu, Kenya, 1982-92," in Peter Gibbon, ed., *The New Local Politics in East Africa*, Stockholm: Scandinavian African Institute, 1994: 98-9; Joel Barkan, "Divergence and Convergence in Kenya and Tanzania: Pressure for Reform," in Barkan, ed., *Beyond Capitalism vs. Socialism in Kenya and Tanzania*, Boulder: Lynne Rienner, 1994: 5, 16-17; Holmquist et al., "The Structural Development," 78-9, 88-9; Goran Hyden, "Party, State and Civil Society: Control vs Openness," in Barkan, *Beyond Capitalism vs. Socialism*, 80-1.

17 Richard Sandbrook, *Proletarians and African Capitalism: the Kenyan Case, 1960-72*, Cambridge: Cambridge University Press, 1975: 123-43; Throup, "The Construction and Destruction," 80-2; Bates, *Beyond the Miracle*, 63-70. Cowen and Shenton argue persuasively for the essentially social-democratic character of Mboya's project of capitalist development (*Doctrines of Development*, 319-21, 324-5), a project that clashed with the logic of the patronage apparatus.

18 Haugerud, *The Culture of Politics*, 94-6; Benno Ndulu and Francis Mwega, "Economic Adjustment Policies," in Barkan, *Beyond Capitalism vs. Socialism*, 104-5.

19 Haugerud, *The Culture of Politics*, 39-41; Michael Lofchie, "The Politics of Agricultural Policy," in Barkan, *Beyond Capitalism vs. Socialism*, 150-2, 156-7.

20 Holmquist et al., "The Structural Development," 76–7, 80–3; Himbara, *Kenyan Capitalists,* 13–4, 59–65; Lofchie, "The Politics of Agricultural Policy," 129–32, 152–3; Ndulu, "Economic Adjustment Policies," 102–3, 108–9.

21 Barbara Grosh, *Public Enterprise in Kenya: What Works, What Doesn't and Why,* Boulder: Lynne Rienner, 1991: 76–88, 116–19, 151–2.

22 Himbara, *Kenyan Capitalists,* chapters 2–3.

23 Haugerud, *The Culture of Politics,* 145–7, 189–91.

24 Chege, "The Political Economy," 93–7, 102–9; Haugerud, *The Culture of Politics,* 184–8; Cowen and Shenton, *Doctrines of Development,* 303–7.

25 Holmquist et al., "The Structural Development," 88–9; Cowen and Shenton, *Doctrines of Development,* 311–17; Kanyinga, "Ethnicity, Patronage and Class in a Local Arena," 96–7.

26 Haugerud, *The Culture of Politics,* chapter 3.

27 The replacement of Kikuyu with Kalenjin included the Special Branch and CID of the police and the feared paramilitary General Services Unit (GSU). Holmquist et al., "The Structural Development," 92–5; Throup, "The Construction and Destruction," 65–7.

28 Jennifer Widner, *The Rise of a Party State in Kenya: From Harambee to Nyayo,* Berkeley: University of California Press, 1992.

29 The most dramatic instances of the reduction of Kikuyu power in the economy was the replacement of Kenyatta's son-in-law Udi Gecaga by Mark arap Too as chairman of Lonrho (Kenya) and the eventual banning of GEMA (Gikuyu, Embu and Meru Association), the key organization of major businessmen among the Kikuyu and their ethnic cousins (Throup, "The Construction and Destruction," 61–2; Himbara, *Kenyan Capitalists,* 93–5). On Moi's use of patronage and barazas see Kanyinga, "Ethnicity, Patronage and Class," 106–7; and Haugerud, *The Culture of Politics,* 81–6. Although often described as a decentralization, the DFRD was more accurately described as a deconcentration of officials and activities to increase the state presence in the countryside, and actually increased state control over development allocations (Kanyinga, "Ethnicity, Patronage and Class," 96–7) .

30 Throup, "The Construction and Destruction," 52–3, 68–70; Kanyinga, "Ethnicity, Patronage and Class," 98–9, 104–5.

31 Himbara, *Kenyan Capitalists,* 120–33.

32 Grosh, *Public Enterprise in Kenya,* 28–40, 55–75, 153–70.

33 Himbara, *Kenyan Capitalists,* 88–91.

34 Holmquist et al, "The Structural Development," 92–3; Chege, "The Political Economy," 114–16; Lofchie, "The Politics of Agricultural Policy," 157–64.

35 Ndulu and Mwega, "Economic Adjustment Policies," 110–11.

36 Holmquist et al., "The Structural Development," 90–1, 94–5; Throup, "The Construction and Destruction," 71–3; Haugerud, *The Culture of Politics*, 33–43.

37 These points are developed more fully in Bruce Berman, "Ethnicity, Patronage and the African State: the Politics of Uncivil Nationalism," *African Affairs*, vol. 97, no. 388, July 1998.

38 Ibid., 71–81; Bates, *Beyond the Miracle*, 91–2; Jean-Francois Bayart, *The State in Africa: The Politics of the Belly*, London: Longman, 1993: especially chapter 9.

39 John W. Harbeson, "Political Crisis and Renewal in Kenya – Prospects for Democratic Consolidation," *Africa Today*, vol. 45, no. 2, 1998: 164–6.

40 The conduct of the 1992 election and the basis of the KANU victory are masterfully analysed in David Throup and Charles Hornsby, *Multi-Party Politics in Kenya*, Oxford: James Currey, 1998: 3–5, 435–55, 526–7.

41 Stephen Ndegwa, "The Incomplete Transition: The Constitutional and Electoral Context in Kenya," *Africa Today*, vol. 45, no. 2, 1998: 198–202.

42 Throup and Hornsby, *Multi-Party Politics in Kenya*, 560–5.

43 Ibid., 533–6, 568–9.

44 Amnesty International, *AI Report 1999: Kenya*, Africa Regional Country Index.

45 Roger Southall, "Reforming the State? Kleptocracy & the Political Transition in Kenya," *Review of African Political Economy*, no. 79, 1999: 95.

46 Jacqueline Klopp, "Pilfering the Public: the Problem of Land Grabbing in Contemporary Kenya," *Africa Today*, forthcoming, Spring 2000.

47 Harbeson, "Political Crisis and Renewal," 171–2.

48 Ndegwa, "The Incomplete Transition," 194–7, 208–9; Frank Holmquist and Michael Ford, "Kenyan Politics: Towards a Second Transition?" *Africa Today*, vol. 45, no. 2, 1998: 236–7.

49 For example, KANU won ninety-five seats with an average of 14,138 votes, while the Forum for the Restoration of Democracy (FORD) – Kenya won thirty-one seats with and average of 35,152 votes and the Democratic Party won twenty-three seats with an average of 43,779 votes (Ndegwa, "The Incomplete Transition," 206–8).

50 Southall, "Reforming the State?" 100–5. Efforts to fight corruption were repeatedly thwarted when the government stepped in to terminate charges against several senior officials brought by the appropriately acronymed Kenya Anti-Corruption Authority (*Daily Nation on the Web*, 26 July 1998).

51 Ibid., 95–8. With only a few exceptions, pressure from external international and bilateral donors regarding human rights and democratization

diminished significantly after the 1997 election as trade and economic concerns have monopolized their attention (see Human Rights Watch, *Kenya: Human Rights Developments,* New York, 1999; and Harbeson, "Political Crisis and Renewal," 174–5).

52 *East African Standard* (online edition), 23 March 2000.

53 The elimination of the assistant chiefs was announced by the permanent secretary in the office of the president and rescinded by Moi two days later (see the *Daily Nation on the Web,* 14 and 16 March 2000).

Constructing a Development Agenda for Namibia[1]

LAUREN DOBELL

In early 1996, a new species of joke was all the rage among the well-groomed young urbanites populating Windhoek's trendy hangouts. The following is illustrative of the genre: "Two cows were perched in a tree playing cards. One of the cows, obviously exasperated, suddenly flung down her cards, climbed down from the tree and stormed away. Just then an egg flew by. 'Say egg,' said the remaining cow, 'wouldn't you like to play cards with me?' 'Not now,' the egg replied, 'I must go comb my hair.'" It is possible to read too much into such a surreal brand of humour. Still, taken as an expression of "radio troit-toir," given voice by the cynical sophisticates who frequent the hotspots where such jokes were popular, it suggests some parallels with the politics of the day. What makes the jokes funny, of course, is the unlikeliness of the rifts (two cows falling out over a game of cards), alliances (the abandoned cow making overtures to a flying egg), and priorities (the egg rejecting the cow's invitation, implausibly preferring to comb its hair). What makes contemporary politics in Namibia fascinating, if at times equally opaque, is just that – the seeming improbability of existing alliances, the unexpectedness of certain rifts, the occasionally baffling expression of development priorities, and the enigmatic channels, formal and informal, through which they are determined.

What spoils any joke, of course, is too literal an interpretation: "A hirsute flying egg?" "Cows can't climb trees!" Similarly, to seek to unpack and explain political behaviour is to strip policy-making of all mystery and to render it dull. But with both jokes and politics – at the risk of straining the analogy – bafflement is a symptom of exclusion, whether from the laughter or from the process. The less transparent the humour (or the system), the less accessible and democratic it is.

In contrast to the telling of jokes, when writing about politics, it is customary to anticipate the punchline. This paper is concerned with the moulding of development policy during the first years of independence in Namibia. It argues, in essence, that Namibia's specific history under South African occupation and SWAPO's distinctive experience and practice as a liberation movement had important, if ambiguous, consequences for the pursuit of development and the consolidation of democracy following independence. Notably, it proposes that the survival strategies adopted over the course of the Namibian liberation struggle served to render SWAPO's leaders, once installed in an independent government, particularly open to and perhaps insufficiently skeptical of overseas sources of trade and aid, technical assistance, and generic development blueprints promulgated by visiting development experts. At the same time, regional opportunities for trade, local sources of investment, and the priorities and potential contributions of its own domestic constituencies are routinely overlooked in the framing of specific development policies and the construction of a comprehensive development agenda for postcolonial Namibia.

Having first sketched the historical basis for the SWAPO[2] government's "extraverted" bent, the paper then explores the possibility that a disproportionately powerful "development industry" in Namibia – its size, political heft, and striking uniformity of outlook consequences, in large measure, of the timing and political contours of the transition to independence – may unwittingly serve as a potentially anti-democratic force in three distinct ways. First, it provides a separate source of support and legitimation for the ruling party, which during the liberation struggle established ties to a wide range of international development organizations and donor agencies. These ties were reinforced by SWAPO's command of the language and discourse of development and, since 1990, its control of the state apparatus. Second, while enjoying on the whole a mutually supportive relationship with the Namibian state, the development industry simultaneously "hijacks" many of the state's developmental functions – arrogating important aspects of public decision-making to the private realm and thereby both limiting public participation and debate over political issues and undermining the government's accountability to its electorate. This double-edged impact illustrates an essential paradox of much development assistance, in which the professedly anti-statist philosophies of the donors are at odds with their actual prescriptions, which in turn seem at odds with many ostensible development goals, even their own.[3] Finally, in a country where the institutions of civil society have historically been weak, it appears that the presence and activities of powerful, well-funded and internationally staffed bilateral and multilateral donor agencies may act to hinder the emergence – or at least seriously limit the capacity – of those indigenous non-state structures upon which the successful consolidation of new democracies is widely thought to rely. These claims will be examined following a brief review of some salient characteristics of the liberation struggle.

THE SECRET OF SWAPO'S SUCCESS

Namibia's peculiar circumstances as a "Mandate C" territory, entrusted by the League of Nations to the not-so-gentle care of the South African administration following World War I, dictated from the outset that its emerging nationalist movement adopt a strategy of "extraversion," as Bayart[4] would call it, in pursuing the twin objectives of liberation from a particularly oppressive brand of colonial rule and self-government for Namibia's people.[5] From the mid-1940s onwards, emulating the example of the indomitable and indefatigable Herero Chief Hosea Kutako, Namibia's anti-colonial forces focused their attentions on petitioning the United Nations, successor to the defunct League of Nations, in their efforts to secure recognition for their demands. The efforts of a coalition galvanized by the Herero Chiefs' Council (HCC), assisted by an English-born Anglican minister acting as their courier and appointed representative, kept the campaign of a tiny, scattered population alive at the UN for more than a decade – and against formidable odds – before the emergence of self-consciously nationalist movements in Namibia.[6] It is a fascinating period in Namibia's independence struggle and one insufficiently credited, in the nationalist history especially, for its pivotal role in shaping, for good or ill, the subsequent direction of the struggle.[7] For thirteen years before the formation of SWAPO, the case of South West Africa was heard annually before the United Nations Trusteeship Commission.[8] By thus addressing themselves to the multilateral body as the perceived best means of redressing the gross asymmetry of power between the territory and its occupying power and by demanding recognition of their plight as an international responsibility, the territory's first petitioners were responsible for turning the nationalist struggle's focus outwards even before its inception. Following in the HCC's wake, SWAPO's leaders inherited and sustained the first petitioners' focus on the UN. This remained for three decades the fulcrum of the movement's international campaign for Namibian independence.[9]

Initially conceived as the Ovamboland People's Congress, and concerned primarily with ameliorating the working and living conditions of contract labourers from northern Namibia, by 1960 SWAPO had evolved into one of two movements claiming a national base and espousing a nationalist program. In contrast to its rival, SWANU,[10] a grouping with its roots in student politics and a largely Herero base among teachers, social workers, and clerical staff, SWAPO's leaders proved both philosophically better disposed and practically better suited to the requirements of a struggle that was to be fought primarily on diplomatic (in contrast to populist or military) terrain. What might initially have been perceived as weaknesses, in particular the movement's lack of an ideological core (which led to some early unflattering comparisons with SWANU),[11] were transformed into strengths. This was accomplished by the exigencies of waging a struggle in which pragmatism was the overriding *modus operandi*. All other considerations were subordinated to the quest for independence. While undoubtedly dictated in significant part by historical circumstance, it was a choice that entailed considerable sacrifices.[12]

SWAPO's pursuit of an internationalist strategy, combined with South Africa's draconian crackdown (in the late 1960s) on the internal leadership of the emerging nationalist movement, shifted control over decision-making to a small band in exile and permanently ensured the political ascendency of the exiled leadership over SWAPO's hamstrung internal wing. This core group would retain a firm grip on power as thousands more Namibians joined them outside, although it resorted to ever more authoritarian measures to suppress perceived critics and competitors within the movement.[13] In this they were not deterred by the governments of the host countries – initially Tanzania, later Zambia and Angola – which generally observed a policy of laissez-faire (blended with an "intra-presidentialist" acknowledgement of the existing hierarchies of governments-in-waiting) towards the liberation movements camped on their soil. The undemanding nature of its external support, too, gave the SWAPO leadership almost unfettered latitude in conducting its own internal affairs.[14] Sufficient aid was available on SWAPO's oft-iterated edict of "no strings attached" that onerous conditionalities need not be accepted.[15]

Reinventing its appeals for support as necessary, SWAPO competed successfully against SWANU for recognition in international forums. SWAPO achieved, by the mid-1970s, recognition from the UN General Assembly as "the sole and authentic representative of the

Namibian people (1976)," a title accorded to SWAPO by the Organization for African unity in 1964, together with exclusive access to the resources attached to such recognition. Membership or observer status in a number of specialized UN agencies was secured, so too a place in the Non-Aligned Movement and quasi-diplomatic positions in countries and multilateral bodies spanning five continents. Meanwhile, the impact of the oppressive measures used by the South African administration to thwart domestic attempts at community organization and its effective exclusion (until the late 1980s) of international development organizations were reinforced by SWAPO's own neglect of internal mobilization. Assistance was withheld from any community-based initiatives that it feared might either threaten its political predominance internally or somehow interfere with its manoeuvres abroad. This is not to downplay the significant role of the Council of Churches of Namibia (CCN), which occupied, on behalf of the nationalist movement, the small political space created after 1980. The CCN was active in both establishing and channelling external funds to some local development projects and approved civic organizations. The relationship between the CCN and community-based activists was complex. The evidence suggests that the CCN may have done more in the end to contain than to encourage manifestations of independent association and organization of interests that would have formed the basis for the emergence of a vibrant civil society following independence.[16]

In sum, it was SWAPO's diplomatic corps's exceptional skill at keeping pace with the vagaries and shifting topography of regional and international Cold War politics, while successfully wooing support from non-aligned sources of solidarity aid, that won for the movement a virtual monopoly of the resources – diplomatic, military, material, moral, and humanitarian – made available to the Namibian struggle. To observe further that these were years of opportunity for SWAPO's leaders does not deny their stamina and determination, nor does it callously overlook the immense human toll of the thirty years' war on Namibians in exile as well as at home. It does, however, recognize that the struggle also presented a privileged stratum within the movement with important opportunities for the personal accumulation of wealth and education, of cultural referents and international networks, and of myriad languages and ideological discourses. In effect, SWAPO's leadership acquired the assets of a dominant class while still in exile by virtue of its access to the resources of extraversion and effective seizing of the "international opportunity." These same skills were to prove indispensable in consolidating its political hegemony following independence.

Adopting the diplomatic option in waging the struggle against South Africa, instead of one based primarily on internal mobilization, required a high degree of centralization within the movement. It enabled the leadership to quickly follow the shifting political tides.[17] This made ideological scruples unaffordable, and debate inadmissible. It ensured, instead, that the leadership's thinking about Namibia would come to reflect predominantly the movement's multilateral reliance on external support. SWAPO's fluency in the political idioms of its diverse allies entailed the sacrifice of a coherent vision for post-independence reconstruction and development, grounded in Namibian realities. It must be remembered that the problem was compounded by travel and other restrictions imposed by the South African state, which ensured that there was little outside access to Namibian news or reliable data – a handicap reflected in the policy-oriented studies churned out by the Lusaka-based United Nations Institute for Namibia (UNIN). Much of SWAPO's top leadership, returning to Namibia in 1989 – and subsequently installed in cabinet portfolios – were setting foot in their own country for the first time in twenty to thirty years.[18] That they were naturally more familiar with well-trodden paths connecting the airports of Belgrade, Sofia, Moscow, East Berlin, Havana, Frankfurt, Stockholm, London, and New York than conditions in the Namibian countryside or the townships is of fundamental importance in understanding political dynamics in post-colonial Namibia.

The overdetermined circumstances of the transition to independence itself – the outcome of a bargaining process designed and presided over by Western negotiators, implemented during the collapse of Communism (the inaugural election, held from 7–11 November 1989, literally took place as the Berlin Wall fell), and overseen by a United Nations Transitional Assistance Group (UNTAG) in the face of South African obstructionism – did not allow any quiet reflection about the shape of things to come.[19] In some respects the timing and circumstances of the transition undoubtedly favoured a peaceful and orderly transfer of power and the inauguration of formal democratic political structures along outlines originally stipulated by a Western Contact Group comprising the US, Britain, France, Germany, and Canada.[20] At the same time, however, these significantly undermined the potential for fundamental socio-economic transformation in Namibia.[21] The effect of the transition was to endow independent Namibia with the neoliberal outlines necessary for a smooth insertion into the global capitalist economy, rather than the tools to construct a more egalitarian social order. In the first years following independence, attempts to challenge the inequities of the prevailing order foundered repeatedly against constitutional provisions protecting private property from expropriation and civil servants belonging to the previous administration from dismissal.[22] The mantra of "national reconciliation," while a valuable mechanism for smoothing the reciprocal assimilation of Namibia's elite, served in practice to legitimate the socio-economic status quo. Further, it facilitated the rapid consolidation of a dominant class incorporating the existing economic elite and the new political elite.

This very cursory discussion locates in Namibia's specific experience of struggle the origins of some features of SWAPO as a government and of Namibian society that would serve to reinforce, rather than mitigate, the potentially anti-democratic effects of foreign interventions in Namibia, whether through aid or trade. These are, on the one hand, SWAPO leaders' deeply ingrained pattern of reliance on an extensive network of external allies and longstanding habits of non-accountability to domestic forces and, on the other, the weakness of Namibian civil society and the absence of a tradition of political opposition, criticism, or debate within an overall context of widespread poverty and extreme inequities in the distribution of wealth and resources. The remainder of the paper examines the relevance of these traits to the development policy process in Namibia during SWAPO's first term in office, using the Swedish assistance program as an example of a bilateral aid relationship.

THE DEVELOPMENT APPARATUS

Two questions underlie much contemporary writing about Africa, and indeed about much of the world (the economic crisis bedevilling the Asian tigers will undoubtedly inject new life into some old debates). The first concerns whether and how democratic practices can be introduced and consolidated in the wake of dismantled non-democratic or authoritarian regimes. The second concerns the means of achieving development, however this desirable objective is conceived. These questions in turn inform myriad debates about the respective roles of the state, civil society, and an international "development apparatus" in pursuing these ends.

What the "development apparatus" is up to in Namibia does not appear to differ very dramatically, for the most part, from what it is up to in the rest of Africa and elsewhere.[23] Namibia's small population, recent independence, and stark social polarization offers an exceptional opportunity to examine these relationships in the process of formation. It presents a means to follow the struggles and negotiations among state structures, elements within civil society, and agents of the development apparatus in the construction of a comprehensive development agenda for a new nation and to observe the identification of social priorities, the setting of economic goals, the imposition of the preferred solutions of powerful interests, and the marginalization of weaker ones.

In discussing the processes and channels through which decisions about development are arrived at, precision about what is meant by "state" and "civil society" is obviously desirable. For present purposes, however, a cursory word about the "development apparatus" must suffice. The term represents a collective label used, often pejoratively, and with some variations in nomenclature – the unrestrained Graham Hancock replaces it with "development incorporated," while the oft-cited James Ferguson places the quotation marks around "development" to underline his skepticism about its actual function.[24] It usually encompasses the multilateral financial institutions (the World Bank and IMF), the UN and its specialized arms, bilateral agencies such as USAID and CIDA, and often, though not always, the big-budget international NGOs such as CARE. These are frequently lumped together, not without some justification, as adherents of a common market-liberal meta-ideology, whose prescriptions, if not always their rhetoric, appear to conceive of development primarily in terms of a rapid transition to a modern capitalist economy, and not in terms of the alleviation of poverty and the empowerment of people. Such generalizations must be reproduced with caution. The key contentions of the recent cornucopia of literature concerned with the nature of the beast are cursorily summarized below.

The development apparatus occupies an ambiguous role in what has generally been treated as a complex but essentially two-way relationship between the constructs of state and civil society.[25] Its insertion into both the organizational and ideological structures of the state influences both state's "powering" and "puzzling" functions.[26] It may be regarded as increasing the state's autonomy and capacity vis-à-vis civil society, while at the same time limiting its freedom of action by importing and imposing "forms of knowing" and standardized or blueprint models of what the state can and should do to develop the nation. In the general theory of "etatization" advanced by Dutkiewicz, Shenton, and Williams,[27] the development apparatus is seen as simultaneously contributing to, legitimating, and benefiting from the steady expansion of state power, while James Ferguson has focused on the "depoliticizing" effects of state interventions.[28] In one significant respect the contention is the same: that the state and the development apparatus together act to reduce the space for associational life and democratic participation in, and opposition to, state functions.

Obviously the "development apparatus," however defined, cannot so easily be treated as a monolith, or as uniform in its effects. It may act both to reinforce state structures and to limit the state's autonomy. Similarly elements within the development industry may be helping to strengthen elements within civil society, to redistribute resources, and to decentralize state power, while at the same time the overall effect may be to rob domestic non-state organizations of their functions, to limit political participation, and to centralize and expand state power. And of course none of this may reflect – certainly not in any straight-forward way – the actual or stated intentions of the donor agencies or development organizations in question. As Ferguson has neatly put it, to understand the way in which intentional plans interact with struc-tures on the ground, it is necessary to recognize that they may be "intelligible, not only as unforseen effects of an intended intervention but also as the unlikely instruments of an unplotted strategy."[29] What effect, then, does donor involvement actually have on the shaping of a development agenda for Namibia?

GETTING SET

The pragmatism that was SWAPO's most marked characteristic in its dealings with potential allies throughout the years of nationalist strug-gle was very much in evidence during its first months in office. It is essential to recognize that the facility with which it appeared to accom-modate into its official discourse the orthodoxies of global capitalism was a product of strategic choice, and not of helpless capitulation to the circumstances imposed on the neophyte government of a small developing country. The ability to position themselves to attract the greatest possible share of available external resources, while alienating no potential allies, was not only a skill derived from decades of lobby-ing for support in exile, it was also a lesson SWAPO's leaders had gleaned over the years from the harsh experiences of African neigh-bours' abortive experiments with socialism: that defiance of capitalist doctrines exacts a punishing toll. Coming to independence as the Cold War receded only streamlined the task. In contrast to the multiple idioms and languages with which SWAPO had previously engaged diverse allies, a single discourse – encompassing a respect for democ-ratic freedoms and an adherence to the pillars of multi-party democra-cy, an emphasis on the importance of the private sector as the engine for economic growth, and enthusiasm for creating an enabling envi-ronment for foreign investors – would suffice for most potential sources of aid and trade. Subsidiary statements of intent to address the need for poverty alleviation, access to social services, environmental protections, affirmative action and gender awareness would alienate none and capture the rest.

Within three months of independence, these elements were encapsulated in the Namibian submission to an international Donors' Conference convened by the United Nations in New York. The gist of the submission was captured in a "General Policy Statement" that recognized the need for "a strong and democratic state" to "initiate growth and development," but acknowledged the pre-eminent role of "a dynamic private sector and well-functioning markets" as "engines of income generation and safeguards against stagnation."[30] The necessary ingredients of an economic regime conducive to local and foreign investment were laid out in a separate "Policy Recommendations for Private Sector Development," while a "Provisional Investment Programme" listed development projects under four priority sectors: agricultural and rural development, education and training, health, and housing. It was hardly surprising that there was a remarkable confluence between the assistance donors most willing to volunteer and the specific projects submitted to the donors' conference, between the conditionalities generally imposed by the World Bank and IMF in structural adjustment programs and the new government's undertakings with respect to private sector development, and between UN "devspeak" and the tenor of the general policy statement. The World Bank, the UNDP, and core donors had crafted key parts of the submission and addressed it to themselves, to be delivered by a Namibian government delegation led by the president of the new republic.[31]

With its submission to the Donors' Conference, the world's youngest nation had cemented its integration into the world capitalist economy on the latter's neoliberal terms. Not surprisingly, under the circumstances, the documents submitted to the donors' conference were well received. Namibia's aims were commended as "realistic," and its prospects for economic growth and development deemed "promising." Repatriated following the conference, the same documents became the basis for the National Planning Commission's "Transitional National Development Plan" for Namibia,[32] which was intended to provide the government with a development agenda for its first term in office. In the first years of independence, the Namibian government's bilateral relations with individual states and donors evinced the same pattern of tactical acquiescence to the priorities and conditionalities imposed by its partners. These in turn supplied the new government with backing not limited to technical assistance and budgetary support.

THE SWEDISH CONNECTION[33]

As an example of an aid relationship with Namibia, the "Swedish Connection" seems an obvious choice to illustrate several important themes in the interaction of a representative of the "development apparatus" with both state structures and Namibian civil society. Sweden was among the first countries to establish an official presence in independent Namibia. Its generous material aid during the first five years of Nambian independence was exceeded by German and American support, yet its public profile and apparent influence surpassed that of any other donor organization. This needs explaining.

Engagingly candid, widely read, and prone, under cross-examination, to charming existential crises about their function, the staff attached to the Swedish embassy and the Swedish International Development Authority (SIDA) worried about their impact on Namibian civil society, the lack of progress on the poverty front, and, increasingly (especially in the wake of any ostentatious spending by the president or his cabinet), about the fungibility of budgetary assistance. Collectively perhaps the most reflective members of the donor community, Sweden's representatives were nonetheless satisfied that their role in Namibia was very constructive on the whole. They viewed their exceptional access to government leaders and considerable influence over the shaping of many state institutions and much public policy as a natural by-product of a longstanding and supportive relationship with the leadership of the ruling party. In this they were largely correct; nonetheless, the history of Swedish involvement in independent Namibia suggests some troubling implications for the role of donors more generally.

From 1990–95 the Swedish connection, in essence, boiled down to two people – its first ambassador to Namibia, Sten Rylander, and his wife, Berit. Between them, they had not only very largely determined the nature and extent of Swedish aid to SWAPO as a liberation movement for twenty years before independence[34] but, through their official posts and personal access, continued to wield considerable influence over post-colonial Namibia. During the 1970s, Sten worked for the Southern Africa division of Sweden's foreign affairs ministry, charged with managing aid to the region's liberation movements. In the mid-1980s, he was named ambassador to Angola, where Berit was already placed as SIDA's program officer, responsible for liberation movements with Angolan bases. Here they developed especially close ties to SWAPO personnel in Luanda, who shared little of what they knew or suspected was taking place in the movements' camps in southern Angola.[35] In 1990 Sten was posted to Namibia, a job he had lobbied for, while Berit was hired into the newly established National Planning Commission as coordinator of all donor programs. In these various capacities they had, *inter alia*, made possible the June 1988 Stockholm conference at which SWAPO officials had first advanced their notion of national reconciliation to a number of prominent liberal members of Namibia's white community, supplied considerable assistance to SWAPO in producing its draft constitution (the basis for the Namibian constitution), and introduced SWAPO's President Nujoma to Eric Carlsson, who served as an advisor to the president until shortly after independence, at which time he was appointed governor of the Bank of Namibia. It was during Carlsson's tenure that Namibia's own currency was introduced.[36] Based on a country support program that Berit had, from 1988–90, a considerable role in designing, Sweden also provided substantial "targeted budgetary support" in the areas of transportation, education, and health and extensive financial and technical assistance under the rubric of a public administration program encompassing the Bank of Namibia, the Central Statistics Office, the National Planning Commission, and the Auditor-General's Office.[37]

Widely acknowledged by Windhoek diplomats as exceptionally accessible hosts (though local constituents found them somewhat less so), high-ranking SWAPO officials were nevertheless especially open to deputations from the Swedish Embassy. On the less easily penetrable social level, too, the Rylanders maintained close ties with a number of SWAPO leaders, including some who had lived for years in Sweden[38] and others with whom they had first become close in Luanda. Those cabinet members with whom they had the most contact on a professional level commended the Swedes' understanding of SWAPO's development priorities and flexible administration of aid.[39] Although personal ties – and the deliberate amenability of the Swedish assistance program – facilitated bilateral agreements, the Swedish embassy also found itself hampered by them. Three years into SWAPO's first term, it grew sufficiently troubled by the government's inaction on a number of corruption cases, including some related to an emergency drought relief program, to speak up. When the purchase of a new presidential jet was announced, the Swedish Ambassador led a delegation of Nordic governments in discreetly appealing to the SWAPO executive for less conspicuous consumption and prompt action on instances of corruption in the civil service and among parliamentarians. The well-intentioned plea resulted in an immediate cooling of relations, which, while not dramatic to observers, served as a sharp reminder that SWAPO preferred its allies' assistance, as in days of old, to come with "no strings attached." That, as during its days as a liberation movement, SWAPO had a wide range of potential partners to choose from, enabled the government to assert its independence from any single source of assistance when any partnership threatened to impose onerous conditions for its continued support.

More worrying to the Swedes, in terms of Namibia's long-term development prospects, was the lack of progress, during SWAPO's first term, on two other fronts: public service reform and poverty alleviation. With respect to the first, SIDA launched a Public Sector Analysis, completed in 1994. It concluded that the wage bill of the public service, which, since independence, had grown by more than 20,000 people to 66,000 and consumed approximately 50% of GDP, urgently needed to be rationalized and reduced:

This new structure is permeating society and proposing new and additional functions for itself ... [E]xpansion is easy because civil society places large demands for services and reforms on the apparatus, at the same time as the formal structures of civil society are in most places weak ... The fact that [the state] is present there [in all sectors] means that no-one else is entitled to do various important things, even if the state is not managing to deliver. In this way the state can actually block community-driven development instead of promoting it.[40]

While, to the acknowledged frustration of the authors, the Public Sector Analysis appeared to be interminably glued – in its embargoed state – to the prime minister's desk, a SIDA-sponsored "Namibia Poverty Profile" was in progress. Released in 1995, shortly after the Namibian electorate returned SWAPO to office for a second term with a substantially increased majority, the report warned that, five years after independence, poverty remained "a major economic and social problem" and was "not receiving the priority attention that it urgently needs." Among the findings it relayed was that:

government has not provided sufficient leadership and coordination to date in terms of anti-poverty strategies and policies. The consequence has been a failure to prioritise poverty reduction, and a policy vacuum which has allowed certain donors to set the agenda instead of government. It was also widely felt that government has avoided taking the really "tough" decisions, for example on land reform,[41] that could have the biggest impact in terms of poverty reduction.

Bilateral and multilateral donors have focused much of their attention to Namibia (perhaps too much) on institutional development – supporting government ministries and infrastructure projects – rather than channelling assistance to the poor through community-based organisations and NGOS ... NGOS are perhaps more effective in terms of working directly with the poor at the local level.[42]

To address poverty reduction successfully, the report's authors concluded, it was necessary to ensure a "decentralisation of decision-making power away from Windhoek." At the same time, however, they recommended "the immediate establishment of an inter-sectoral Poverty Commission within government."[43]

By the end of SWAPO's first term in office, its bilateral aid partner of longest standing, and one of Namibia's most important donors, was evincing both concern about the new government's priorities and self-recrimination for its unintentional and unwitting complicity, as part of the donor community, in perpetuating a policy vacuum within government. At the same time, by providing some much-needed services in several sectors themselves, they were perhaps both protecting SWAPO from criticism by its constituents for non-delivery and depriving non-government organizations of the opportunity to do it themselves by channelling funds through and logistical support to them instead. It recognized the contradiction inherent in the policy of channelling its assistance through government structures; too much assistance both concealed a lack of capacity and was a disincentive to self-reliance, but assistance to central institutions was especially needed if these were to provide the government with the capacity for coherent development planning. However, Swedish aid seemed to have difficulty breaking from a tradition of solidarity with SWAPO's leadership. It was with these longstanding friends whom they mixed socially and professionally. SWAPO leaders shared Swedish referents and sometimes the language, some had attended Swedish universities. At a minimum, they spoke both fluent English (increasingly the *lingua franca* of development), and fluent "devs-peak," skills not shared by many community activists outside Namibia's urban centres.

Despite SIDA's genuine concern about the conspicuous weakness of Namibian civil society in theory, in practice it appeared to be compensating for, rather than directly addressing the weakness of non-government and community-based organisations. This was apparent not only with respect to the delivery of services but in terms of lobbying the government on behalf of its constituents for more attention to issues of social justice and criticizing, however *sotto voce*, its excesses. These were all dilemmas for Swedish donor policy, as a senior embassy official noted:

I personally think that it's rather dangerous for statal organisations like ourselves, who represent governments, to get too involved in NGO activities, but there is always the problem of what some governments want to call the transmission belt, as it were, between bureaucrats in their offices and communities in the field ... So some people would like to see NGOs as transmission belts in that process – and often if you give them money they become transmission belts, but maybe their legitimacy is such that they are not transmission belts ... I don't know – that's an aid and development dilemma that I don't think any agencies cope with very well. There's a lot of talk about participation and all that, but there has rarely been any clear success on that happening. I would prefer, in fact, that one had a state that was able to negotiate and work through and if necessary finance NGO activities, so the donors didn't actually get thrown directly on top of the NGOs ...

Still, it's because of a number of particular factors, maybe, that the Swedish connection [in Namibia tends] to start behaving like the NGOs in society – when the government says things the critical voice comes from the Embassy instead of from the NGOs – I don't know, that's not good either, but we try to keep a dialogue going on the basis of what we think would be good for the majority of Namibians in the long run.[44]

If the best of donors increasingly lacked conviction, others remained full of passionate intensity. While Sweden's representatives in Namibia brooded about their statist bias, USAID's flagship READ (Reaching out with Education to Adults in Development) program was illustrating many of the dangers of redirecting donor attention to civil society. In its administration of an ostentatious, multi-million dollar "capacity-building" and "empowering" exercise for Namibian NGOs, USAID appeared to substitute active manipulation for neglect in an ultimately disempowering exercise. These and many other stories are, unfortunately, grist for another mill. For reasons of space, Sweden must here bear the burden of evidence for observations intended to have a more general application. Its merit, as a lonely case study, is that if Sweden, as perhaps the best and best-intentioned of donors, unintentionally contributes to a process in which both democratic participation in setting a development agenda and the achievement of development goals are compromised, then the problem must be addressed as a structural one.

CONCLUSION

SWAPO's apprenticeship as a "government in waiting" during the long years of its liberation struggle, and the circumstances of its transition, enabled post-colonial Namibia to insert itself exceptionally smoothly into the global capitalist economy. It also prepared SWAPO leaders to assess rapidly their degree of freedom to manoeuvre within the new constraints imposed, and position themselves to benefit from the new opportunities presented, at independence. Indeed few governments illustrate so well as Namibia's, Bayart's declaration that, "Far from being the victims of their very real vulnerability, African governments exploit, occasionally skilfully, the resources of a dependence which is, it cannot ever be sufficiently stressed, astutely fabricated as much as predetermined. Both on their political stage and within the world system, they pursue their own objectives, within the margins of failure and success that the implementation of any strategy entails."[45]

SWAPO's pursuit of political hegemony within the contours of an independent Namibia, it has been argued above, was facilitated, however unwittingly, by the constituent parts of a development apparatus, which, in contradiction to both their stated (and often actual) intentions, appear to contribute to, rather than help to mitigate, a situation in which the opportunity for democratic participation in development agenda-setting and the prospects for greater social equity are perhaps more limited than they need be, even in the context of global neoliberalism.

NOTES

1 As an MA student, I was one of several contributors to a study, conceived in 1990 by Colin Leys and John Saul, of the impact on Nambian civil society of thirty years of war. This paper draws on subsequent research undertaken for a doctoral dissertation that will aspire to the fine balance of critical analysis, fairness and, ultimately, optimism that are – as always in his work – the hallmarks of Colin Leys's writing on Namibia.

2 The South West Africa People's Organization was known by its acronym SWAPO until independence, shortly after which it adopted "Swapo" as a proper name. Throughout this text, for consistency, I have used "SWAPO."

3 See, for example, Frances Stewart et al., *Alternative Development Strategies in SubSaharan Africa,* London: MacMillan Press, 1992; Robert Cassen et al., *Does Aid Work?* Oxford: Clarendon Press, 1986; S. Commins, *African Development Choices and the World Bank: Hard Questions and Costly Choices,* Boulder: Lynne Rienner, 1988.

4 Jean-Francois Bayart, *The State in Africa: The Politics of the Belly*, New York: Longman, 1993.

5 Despite appearances, Namibia wasn't, strictly speaking, a South African colony. The terms of the "c"-class mandate – i.e., concerned with the least developed of Germany's former colonies – did not confer sovereign powers over Namibia but merely administrative responsibility for the territory. Ruth First, *South West Africa*, Penguin, 1963, provides an excellent account of Namibia's colonial history to 1962.

6 The recruitment of Reverend Michael Scott by the Herero Chief Hosea Kutako – one of the strangest stories in a history peppered by remarkable contingencies – is recounted in Freda Troup, *In Face of Fear*, London: Faber and Faber, 1950. The Africa Bureau Papers, a large and valuable repository of primary documents collected mainly by Michael Scott (including the text of the petitions and transcribed oral histories of the Herero and Nama peoples) are held at Rhodes House, Oxford.

7 This period is the subject of another paper by the author, "The Secret of Swapo's Success: The Pursuit of Hegemony in Namibian Liberation Politics, 1946–1966," forthcoming.

8 The name "Namibia" was only officially adopted by the United Nations in 1968, not long after it became common usage among nationalists.

9 swapo's diplomatic campaign for Namibian independence is examined in Lauren Dobell, *Diplomacy by All Means: Campaigning for Namibia, 1960–1991*, Basel: Schlettwein Publishing, 1998.

10 The South West Africa National Union.

11 At the time she was writing *South West Africa*, Ruth First was among those informed observers expressing more confidence in swanu's ability to represent the nationalist aspirations of Namibians. Personal correspondence contained in the Amy Thornton collection at the University of Cape Town archives indicates that Brian Bunting, the editor of the Cape Town-based *New Age*, was another.

12 The costs – ideological, societal, humanitarian – are examined in the contributions to Colin Leys and John Saul (eds), *Namibia's Liberation Struggle: The Two-edged Sword*, London: James Currey, 1995.

13 The issue of swapo "detainees" imprisoned or killed as alleged South African spies during the 1970s and 1980s is the subject of Siegfried Groth, *Namibia – The Wall of Silence*, Wuppertal: Peter Hammer Verlag, 1995. See also Colin Leys and John Saul, "Liberation without Democracy? The Swapo Crisis of 1976," *Journal of Southern African Studies*, vol. 20, no. 1, 1994, and Lauren Dobell, "Silence in Context: Truth and/or Reconciliation in Namibia," *JSAS*, vol. 23, no. 2, 1997.

14 See Dobell, *Diplomacy by All Means*, chapter 2, for a discussion of the sources, nature and motivations of SWAPO's material, military, moral, and diplomatic support.

15 The terms of the substantial annual grant to SWAPO by the World Council of Churches were illustrative of the unconcerned stance of major donors: "Grants are made without control of the manner in which they are spent and are intended as an expression of commitment to the cause of economic, social and political justice." *Times*, 22 September 1981, cited in Dobell, "New Lamps for Old: The Evolution of Swapo's Philosophy of Development," MA thesis, Queen's University, 1992: 70.

16 Philip Steenkamp, "The Churches," in Leys and Saul (eds), *Namibia's Liberation Struggle*: *A Two-Edged Sword*. See also Sue Brown, "Assessment of Popular Participation in the Formulation and Implementation of Development Policies and Programmes: A Case Study of Namibia," Windhoek: Namibian Economic Policy Research Unit (NEPRU) Working Paper no. 20, November 1992.

17 Paul Trewhela argues convincingly, if perhaps too forcefully, that it was no accident, for example, that the first widespread detentions within the movement coincided with the complex negotiations arising from the attempt to broker a "detente" deal in Southern Africa in the mid-1970s. See "The Kissinger/Vorster/Kaunda Deténte: Genesis of the SWAPO Spy-drama," *Searchlight South Africa*, vol. 2, no. 1 and vol. 2, no. 2, 1990.

18 President Sam Nujoma left the country in 1960; of his first cabinet, dominated by members of the former leadership in exile, Hifikepunye Pohamba, Peter Mueshihange Theo-Ben Gurirab, Libertine Amathila, Hage Geingob, Hidipo Hamutenya, Richard Kapelwa, Nicky Iyambo, Mose Tjitendero (Speaker), Ngarikutuke Tjiriange, Nahas Angula, Ben Amathila and Helmut Angula had all left Namibia by 1966. Minister of Youth and Sport Penny Ithana was the sole cabinet member from exile who left during the mass exodus of 1974.

19 David Lush, *Last Steps to Uhuru*, Windhoek: New Namibia Books, 1993; and Lionel Cliffe et al., *The Transition to Independence in Namibia*, Boulder: Lynne Rienner, 1994, provide two useful overviews of the transition period, from a journalist and a team of UK-based academics, respectively.

20 UNSCR Resolution 435 (September 1978) and "Principles Concerning the Constituent Assembly and the Constitution for an Independent Namibia," 12 July 1982.

21 Guillermo O'Donnell and Philippe Schmitter, in a four-volume study (edited with Lawrence Whitehead), *Transitions from Authoritarian Rule: Tentative Conclusions about Uncertain Democracies*, Baltimore and Lon-

don: Johns Hopkins University Press, 1986, elegantly summarize the explanations given for this common trajectory.

22 The wage bill for the unwieldy and expensive civil service inherited from the South African administration, whose apartheid policies, as in South Africa, required an extensive bureaucracy, estimated at 43,000 people at independence, was already daunting. By 1995, the ranks of the public service had swelled to more than 60,000, accounting for more than half of government expenditure, according to the"Report of the Wage and Salary Commission," submitted to the Nambian Parliament in 1995. A confidential four-volume "Public Sector Analysis," undertaken by the Swedish International Development Authority and the Namibian Economic Policy Research Unit in 1994 gives even higher estimates.

23 For a spectrum of perspectives, albeit weighted towards the cynical, see D. Abernathy, "The Influence of Aid Agencies on African Development," in Carter Centre, *Beyond Autocracy in Africa*, vol. 1, no. 4, 1989; J. Clark, *Democratizing Development: The Role of Voluntary Organizations*, London: Earthscan, 1991; Matt Bivens, "Aboard the Gravy Train," *Harper's Magazine*, August 1997; Graham Hancock, *Lords of Poverty*, London: Mandarin, 1989; and, of course, James Ferguson, *The Anti-politics Machine: "Development", Depoliticization and Bureaucratic Power in Lesotho*, Cambridge: CUP, 1990.

24 Hancock, ibid.; Ferguson, ibid.

25 For example, John Harbeson, Donald Rothchild and Naomi Chazan (eds), *Civil Society and the State in Africa*, Boulder: Lynne Rienner, 1994; John Keane (ed.), *Civil Society and the State*, London: Verso Press, 1988; Joel Migdal, *Strong Societies and Weak States: State-Society Relations and State Capabilities in the Third World*, Princeton: PUP, 1988; and Michael Bratton and Nicholas van de Walle, *Democratic Experiments in Africa*, Cambridge: CUP, 1997.

26 The terms are Hugh Heclo's. See *Modern Social Politics in Britain and Sweden*, New Haven: Yale University Press, 1974; see also Philip Abrams, "Notes on the Difficulty of Studying the State," *Journal of Historical Sociology*, vol. 1, no. 1, March 1988.

27 Piotr Dutkiewicz and Gavin Williams. "All the King's Horses and All the King's Men Couldn't Put Humpty Dumpty Together Again," *IDS Bulletin*, vol. 18, no. 3, 1988; Piotr Dutkiewicz, and Robert Shenton, "Crisis in Africa: Étatization and the Logic of Diminished Reproduction," *ROAPE*, no. 37, 1986.

28 Ibid.

29 Ferguson, *The Anti-Politics Machine*.

30 Republic of Namibia, "The Reconstruction and Development of Namibia: a General Policy Statement," Windhoek, May 1990;

presented to the United Nations Donors' Pledging Conference, 21 June 1990: 5.

31 The "Policy Recommendations for Private Sector Development," as well as the four priority sectors for development assistance were drawn directly from the World Bank's "Preliminary Economic Review" of Namibia, dated 11 May 1990. The "General Policy Statement" was drafted by a working group headed by three UNDP economists, while individual countries contributed their proposals for assistance to the "Priority Project Profiles." Interview with the director-general of the National Planning Commission, Dr. Zedekiah Ngavirue, 11 September 1991. Jan Isaksen and Richard Moorsom, "Comments on papers prepared for the donor pledging conference," Windhoek, June 1990 (later released as NEPRU working paper no. 5) take no issue with the source of the documents or their overall direction, but point out some oddities and inconsistencies in the data in recommending ways in which the documents might form the basis of a Transitional National Development Plan for Namibia (TNDP). Four months later the World Bank released a detailed internal report entitled "Namibia: Poverty Alleviation with Sustainable Growth," Report no. 9510–NAM, 29 October 1991, which listed the government's key economic challenges as "reactivating growth, restraining and redirecting public expenditures, reducing poverty and creating employment." These development objectives, and many of the reports' observations and recommendations, were subsequently reproduced in the TNDP.

32 In the event, the final draft of the TNDP was not completed until late 1994, some months before its mandate expired, making way for the first National Development Plan for 1995–2000. A polished draft of the NDP1 was available to select decision-makers by August 1995.

33 The following is drawn from chapter 3 of my dissertation: "Trading Aid or Aiding Trade: The Swedish and Malaysian Connections."

34 In 1975 Sweden set a precedent of government to government aid to SWAPO. Other Nordic governments followed suit.

35 SWAPO "detainees" incarcerated as alleged South African spies during the mid-late 1980s were mainly kept in Lubango. See John Saul and Colin Leys, "SWAPO: The Politics of Exile," in Leys and Saul (eds), *Namibia's Liberation Struggle*. Nico Basson and Ben Motinga (eds), *Call Them Spies,* Windhoek and Johannesburg: African Communications Press, 1989, is a useful collection of primary and secondary documents related to the "spy drama," if read with careful attention to the sources.

36 After an open competition, Swedish and Norwegian mints won the tenders for the design and production of the new banknotes and coins, respectively. As per conventional practice, the Governor's signature graces every bill.

37 Interviews with the author: Sten Rylander, 1 March 1995; Sten and Berit Rylander, 3 February 1995; Eric Carlsson, 2 March 1995; Ingrid Loftstrom-Berg (Counsellor, Development Cooperation, Embassy of Sweden), 16 March 1995, 4 and 15 March 1996; Anton Johnston (Chief Economist, Embassy of Sweden), 26 and 31 January and 16 March 1995; Prime Minister Ingvar Carlsson, 23 February 1995; Ambassador Ulla Strom, 11 March 1996. Nordiska Afrikainstitutet, "Namibia and External Resources: The Case of Swedish Development Assistance," research report no. 96, provides details of the Swedish aid program from 1990–93. See also SIDA, "Swedish Development Cooperation with Namibia," Windhoek: 1992, 1995.

38 Among top government officials who had lived for years in Sweden were Ministers Ben Amathila (SWAPO's official representative to Scandinavia based in Sweden for most of the 1970s) and Libertine Appolus-Amadhila (director-general of the National Planning Commission), Dr Zed Ngavirue, and Dr Kaire Mbuende (Namibia's representative to SADC).

39 Ministers Hifikipunye Pohamba, Ben Amathila, Nahas Angula, Nicky Iyambo; interviews with the author.

40 National Planning Commission, SIDA and NEPRU, *Public Sector Analysis, Namibia*, no. 1, July 1994: 5.

41 For an overview of the land issue by one of Namibia's foremost authorities on the subject, see Wolfgang Werner, "Land Reform in Namibia: The First Seven Years," Basel: BAB working paper no. 5, 1997, in which he argues that investment in basic social services and subsidising employment in urban centres would benefit far more people than spending vast sums of money, as proposed, on land purchases and redistribution and an ambitious resettlement plan. In a chapter entitled "Gambling with Land and Landed with Gambling," my D.Phil. dissertation contrasts the government's approach to legislation concerning the land question, ostensibly the most "burning development issue" facing Namibia, and legislation affecting the construction and operation of casinos in Namibia.

42 Stephen Devereux et al, "Namibia Poverty Profile: A Report Prepared for SIDA," Windhoek: Social Sciences Division, Multi-Disciplinary Research Centre, University of Namibia, February 1995.

43 Ibid., iv.

44 Anton Johnston, speaking in his personal capacity, interview with the author, 26 January 1995.

45 Bayart, ibid., 25.

Political Dimensions of the Adjustment Experience of Côte d'Ivoire

BONNIE CAMPBELL

There was a certain degree of incredulity in October 1995 when former President Konan Bédié decided that in order to win that year's elections convincingly he would be attributed an inflated 95 per cent majority. His victory had, in any case, left nothing to chance: the electoral code had been modified to exclude the only realistic opponent. Even his most loyal supporters within the French Government must have been somewhat embarrassed by this disregard for appearances. Had he had the opportunity, he would most probably have attempted a similar score in the October 2000 election, where once again he had disqualified his principal rival, former Prime Minister Alassane Ouattara, on the ground of supposed "non-Ivoirité," but the military putsch of 24 December 1999 was to change his plans radically, to chase him from power and from the country.

The important issues facing Côte d'Ivoire for the years to come do not merely concern the rotation of political leaders and elites. Among the key questions is whether the terms of the economic and institutional reforms proposed by the Bretton Woods institutions as the counterpart to much needed external funding, in interaction with the internal dynamics of Ivorian politics, will permit the country to move beyond the past – particularly the selective and highly unequal modes of social and political regulation[1] that have characterized the post-independence period and adjustment experience and had brought the country to the brink of violent civil strife by the end of the 1990s – and renew the basis for more equitable and sustainable social, economic, and political compromises.

Côte d'Ivoire has always been a rich terrain for students of political economy. In the case of the 1995 elections, as with the circumstances of Bédié's downfall in 1999, the explanation of what might appear to be essentially "political" phenomena, leads us to much broader questions, notably the manner in which the Ivorian economic growth and structural adjustment experience have been conceptualized.

From a "miracle" model of economic growth during the 1960s and 1970s, the country then served, until the middle of the 1980s, as an example of successful adjustment for multilateral funding institutions. By the early 1990s, as the World Bank's 1994 *Adjustment in Africa: Reforms, Results and the Road Ahead* illustrates, Côte d'Ivoire had become the object of criticism and the example of what should not be done.[2]

However, the orientation of the policies implemented in Côte d'Ivoire had not fundamentally changed since the beginning of the adjustment experience in 1980 and during its various stages to the end of the 1990s. If the policies have not been modified, then what can explain the passage of Côte d'Ivoire from the position of model student to that of such a poor one, from an example of political stability to a state rocked by a *coup d'état*?

Our objective will not be to review the nature of prescribed policies and their implementation and consequences but rather to underline the wealth of the existing literature on this subject. To cite one example, F.R. Mahieu has described, against the backdrop of failure, four generations of adjustment policies: standard adjustment (1980–87), the social dimensions approach (1987–91), the national approach to programs, (the beginning of the 1990s), and finally monetary stabilization (reinforced by the January 1994 devaluation).[3]

This paper intends to suggest the importance of undertaking a rereading of the Ivorian adjustment experience, of doing so from a political stance not only with the object of understanding the "disappointing" results, as international institutions refer to them, but, more broadly, in order to explore the complex links between the adjustment strategies that seek a particular form of integration of the country into the world market and the prolonging of particular modes of political and social regulation over the last two decades. The hypothesis that will be developed is the following: The Ivorian adjustment experience has always has been an eminently political process in that it has shaped and continues to condition the choice of development strategies and the means by which these are to be achieved in the domestic sphere; it also shapes and conditions the place the country occupies on the world market and ultimately, through these strategies, the possibility of prolonging or renewing particular modes of social and political regulation.

During the first two decades of adjustment, there appears to have been a correspondence between, on one hand, the type of measures proposed and the conditions under which they were introduced and, on the other, the capacity of those in power to short-circuit these measures and, consequently, to reproduce existing modes of political management. This would explain the success of the strategies for maintaining the power of the dominant alliances until the 1999 *coup d'état* – in spite of the persistence of a mode of redistribution of economic resources that appeared rather incompatible with the objectives of economic renewal and financial reform, and also in spite of the announcement of the broadening of the political arena as of 1990.

Over time, however, the insistence on the part of multilateral financial institutions for furthering the liberalization of certain strongholds of the former Bédié ruling faction – notably the circuits of selective redistribution provided by such institutions as the Caisse de Stabilisation et de Soutien des Prix des Produits Agricoles (the country's key marketing board) – represented an increasingly direct challenge to previous modes of social and political regulation. The growing constraints imposed by the Bretton Woods institutions on those in power were undoubtedly important factors in the contextualization of the "derive autoritaire" and of the growing repression in Côte d'Ivoire that led to the military uprising in December 1999. The issue at hand since then is whether external and internal constraints will allow a successful transition not only in terms of opening new political space but more fundamentally an in-depth renewal of the modes of social and political regulation.

The object of this study is to present certain elements for a political rereading of the adjustment experience of Côte d'Ivoire and to review questions raised by recent studies that propose such a reading and by the strategies of institutional reform put forward as a solution to the political dimensions of adjustment. This chapter, divided into three parts, retraces the Ivorian adjustment experience[4]:

1 standard adjustment (1980–87);
2 the social dimensions of adjustment (end of the 1980s);
3 the "national" approach to the adjustment program, the reconceptualization of the state, and institutional reform (from the beginning of the 1990s).

STANDARD ADJUSTMENT (1980–87)

During the first stage of adjustment – the "standard" stage according to Mahieu – Côte d'Ivoire was presented as a model student. The macroeconomic indices on which this type of evaluation was premised reveal the objectives and performance criteria of the reforms at that time. Attention focused above all on consolidating the deficit of the public sector and reducing the deficit of the current account. The positive results obtained up until 1985 may be explained by an important reduction of the overall public sector deficit, accompanied by increasing transfers from stabilization operations. Concerning the former, Mahieu notes: "This improvement was due to a very brutal deflation of the public and parapublic sectors as of 1981: dissolution of public enterprises, transformation of the status of public entities, serious reduction of the salaries of those concerned, compression of personnel. Spectacular measures were taken concerning recurrent expenditures: the termination of administrative leases, a reduction of the number of scholarships and of technical assistance, the introduction of user fees to cover health expenses. On the other hand, the state attempted to pay back its arrears to the private sector."[5]

The precariousness of the initial results did not take long to reveal itself. As of 1987, export receipts collapsed due to the situation on international markets; the balance of payments was once again negative; the results (necessarily positive) of the commercial account were insufficient to compensate for the net negative transfers, especially the haemorrhaging of the capital account. Consequently, the balance of payments deficit rocketed from 50 billion CFA francs in 1987 to a record level of 700 billion in 1989.[6]

Of particular interest here are the consequences of this first stage on the patterns of internal redistribution of resources, and on the integration of the country into the world market and the more general implications for the conduct of political affairs.

According to Mahieu, during the first stage of adjustment, real GNP decreased on average 4 per cent annually, which provoked over the same period a cumulated decrease of GDP per person of 21.6 per cent. During the 1981–88 period, internal demand decreased by 19 per cent. The consequences of this were to be unequally shared. Underlining the extent to which little attention has been paid to the social impact of adjustment and the resulting survival strategies, Duruflé summarized the costs of Ivorian deflationist adjustment as follows: "between 1980 and 1985, total investment fell to almost half in constant francs and public investment by 70 per cent; consumption per capita decreased by over 30 per cent, as did employment in the modern sector."[7]

As Mahieu and others have pointed out, the impact of adjustment on employment was to be particularly severe: "Unemployment affected the young in particular : estimated at 36 per cent for men and 26 per cent for women ... The closure of nationalised industries led to 10,000 redundancies (Kouadio Bénié, 1989). The slump in the private sector, between 1980 and 1985, in turn, led to the issue of more than 1,000 personnel reduction notices affecting more than 30,000 people. Unfortunately, the deflationary phase was not followed by even the slightest expansion and the official unemployment rate remained at 15 per cent. However, official unemployment led to a strong increase in employment in the informal economy, estimated at about more than 10 per cent per year since 1981."[8] Beyond these social costs, the re-establishment of certain accounting aggregates was to prove fragile and limited.

As elsewhere in Africa, priority during this period had been given to opening up the economy, aligning internal prices with international prices, and, especially with the third structural adjustment program in 1986, attempting to encourage export producing agro-business indus tries. What followed, however, was a gutting of world markets as a result of commercial liberalization (with the end of the international agreements and of the financing of buffer stocks), combined with the fact that other Asian and African countries (Ghana and Cameroon) were following the same policies. As a result, Mahieu writes, "After the 1988/1989 round of payments, none of the partners in the coffee and cocoa industries could be paid. The Caisse de Stabilisation's cash flow crisis (a deficit of 290 billion FCFA) spread to planters, industrialists, bankers. The Bank and the IMF made the halving of the price paid to coffee and cocoa producers a pre-condition for negotiating any agreement, just a few months after they had strongly recommended an increase in the price paid to producers!"[9] The political dimensions of this first phase of "standard" adjustment are numerous and can be illustrated by the following examples :

1 the setting of official development objectives and the means by which these were to be achieved were increasingly determined by external agents;
2 the direct intervention by these agents into the decision-making process, for example, in the setting of price levels for producers and consumers and in approving or removing subsidies;
3 the redefining of the role to be played by the public and parapublic sectors and of their respective sizes;
4 the introduction of new political measures and controls as a counterpart to increasingly restrictive social and economic conditions.

Most fundamentally, however, during this same period, the overall orientation of the first three adjustment programs, which gave priority to private enterprise and privileged the opening up of borders and dismantling of protection and the re-establishment of macroeconomic and financial equilibrium though the compression of demand, was to prove in large measure compatible with the prolonging of the essentially "political" mode of economic management of the country's resources throughout the post-independence period. The general orientation of the conditionalities introduced with the first three structural adjustment programs was not only relatively compatible with the overall liberal orientation of the country but it served also to legitimize the reshaping of certain alliances in power to the detriment of others. More specifically, there occurred a curbing of certain dominant groups and a reshaping of the political class, notably with the far-reaching reforms of the public enterprises, as well as important modifications in the relations between the new dominant alliances and other sectors of society.

It is this process and the contradictions that accompanied it that gave rise to the introduction of the second phase – known as the "social dimensions" – of adjustment as of the end of the 1980s. Before describing this period, it is worth underlining that during the "standard" phase, on the domestic front, President Houphouet Boigny's self-styled past mode of political regulation remained largely intact at least in part because of the availability of increasing transfers from coffee and cocoa stabilization operations up until 1985. Externally, the demonstration of Côte d'Ivoire's "success" was important in itself in order to legitimate, even if in a purely symbolic fashion, the considerable power of decision that the multilateral financial institutions had achieved during the 1980s on the destiny of this country and the large majority of the countries of Africa.

THE "SOCIAL DIMENSIONS" OF ADJUSTMENT (END OF THE 1980s)

In World Bank projects, the "social dimensions" approach appeared in 1987. In this initiative, Côte d'Ivoire occupied a position of privilege both because of the country's important statistical system and because of its status as a "model pupil" in the area of structural adjustment. There exist in this regard, a number of detailed studies on the survey methodologies[10] and certain social consequences of adjustment.[11] The severity of the resulting poverty in Côte d'Ivoire leaves little doubt and is now well documented. For example, a 1996 World Bank study suggests that the share of the population living in poverty had increased by 16 per cent over the three years 1985–88.[12] Of interest to us here are the political dimensions of the social consequences of adjustment and the methodologies adopted by various analysts in order to take account of them. It seems paradoxical, however, that, as the multilateral lending institutions intervened more and more deeply into the social fabric of the country, notably through the social dimensions of adjustment, the analyses on which their interventions were based seemed less and less able to take into account the constraints, disequilibrium, and specificity of the country.

Without entering into detail, it is worth mentioning that the approaches adopted by more recent studies that evaluate Côte d'Ivoire's adjustment experience (World Bank 1988,1990,1992,1996), the social dimensions of adjustment (World Bank 1990, OECD 1992), and the political feasibility of adjustment (OECD 1994) privilege points of entry, methodologies, and conjunctural explanations of the origins of Côte d'Ivoire's disequilibrium that represent a significant loss of ground when compared to the analytical depth and explanatory capacity of the analysis published for the World Bank in 1978 on the Ivorian growth experience[13] and other previous studies. Because of their approaches, these more recent studies fail to grasp the importance of the structural characteristics specific to the Ivorian experience. Notably, they fail to consider the costs and constraints that resulted from the particular pattern of internal and external allocation and redistribution of resources that accompanied this particular growth model.

To illustrate this point, attention may be drawn to the treatment of the origins of the crisis in various documents, notably those of the World Bank (1988 and 1992) and the 1994 OECD study. According to the 1988 World Bank study, "The cocoa and coffee boom of 1975–77 destabilised Côte d'Ivoire's economy."[14] The 1992 study suggests: "The crisis in Côte d'Ivoire was caused by a favourable external shock."[15] Similarly, the approach taken by the authors of the 1994 OECD study also privileged an explanation in terms of conjunctural external shocks .[16]

The ideological and political role of this type of interpretation merits special attention. Concerning its ideological dimension, Professor H. Memel-Fôté notes, "the origin of the economic crisis is not to be found merely in the down slide of the prices of primary agricultural products. It is to be found as well in the model of development chosen, in the essentially political mode of economic management, in the specific form of governance that was put in place."[17]

Politically, the absence of discussion of internal costs and internal constraints (for example with regard to foreign factors: expatriates, capital, techniques, etc.), elements that were considered of key importance in the 1978 World Bank study, leads to a rereading of the Ivorian experience and to the identification of certain alternate internal social groups generally believed to have benefited from positions of privilege: "Hence, this country threw itself with a certain zealousness into a program of stabilization and adjustment which attacked a good number of embedded interests. The most spectacular opposition to these reforms was to come from those who had for a long time been the privileged of the régime – that is the students and their teachers."[18]

This rereading of the Ivorian experience, notably the selectivity and omissions that characterize such an interpretation, suggests a political design seeking to discredit certain sectors of society (as has happened elsewhere when similar attempts focused on doctors, civil servants, and other professional groups). Social groups identified as those often benefiting from a position of relative social and economic privilege were the object of criticism that clearly sought to delegitimize them by presenting their demands as corporatist (and therefore selfish). These groups were and are also often the most articulate and most structured "porte-parole" of the opposition to the manner in which the adjustment process is carried out and of the consequences of this process in terms of the redistribution of resources and the possibilities of social reform. The above suggests the importance of undertaking a political reading not only of the limits of the Ivorian model but also of the analyses that have been carried out concerning the social dimensions and political feasibility of adjustment in this country.

The authors of the Côte d'Ivoire section of the OECD study *Ajustement et équité dans les pays en développement*[19] note a net impoverishment in urban areas and conclude that the country should have adjusted *before* the crisis. Why this did not happen is not fully developed. The explanation provided – that the county had hoped that there would be a reversal in the terms of trade (thus helping the efforts to reimburse the debt) – can hardly be considered complete. The reason for this lacuna is surely related to the methodology adopted by this study. It consisted of proceeding with a series of experiments on reduced theoretical (calculable general equilibrium) models of the economies studied.[20] By adopting a broader perspective, it may be shown, however, that the timing of the implementation of adjustment policies and the unfolding of this process are inextricably linked not only to the structural and economic characteristics of the country but also to the existing modes of political regulation.

If Côte d'Ivoire had not adjusted earlier, it is at least in part because of internal constraints – notably strong resistance from the former modes of political regulation, which were the counterparts of the Ivorian growth model. The constraints or limits of the model were already apparent during the second decade of independence and recognized, as noted above, by the study prepared for the World Bank and published in 1978. Interestingly, it would seem that throughout the adjustment process, although the country's political leadership was faced with little margin of manoeuvre, it was nonetheless able to use the process to its political advantage. However, the political dimensions of the country's adjustment experience have received little analytical attention.

The existence not only of economic but also of tight political constraints have conditioned the adjustment experience from the beginning – most notably, the manner in which the question of equity has been treated and is likely to be treated in the future. If the hypothesis of the prolonging of a specific mode of political regulation based on selective redistribution is correct, it would contribute not only to explaining in a more satisfactory manner the "lateness" of Ivorian adjustment but also certain characteristics specific to the processes all too often described as distortions, dysfunctionnings, or pathologies. The selectivity with which austerity reforms were introduced over the first fifteen years of adjustment provides good examples: certain key places in the complex circuits of Ivorian public finances (Caisse de Stabilisation, Caisse Nationale de Prévoyance Sociale, Caisse de Péréquation, etc.) were left unbudgeted; note also the "non-transparency" (to use L. Demery's term in his 1994 study of Côte d'Ivoire for the World Bank) of the thirty or so privatizations of public enterprises between 1987 and 1989.[21] On the circumvention of the measures ostensibly introduced to reduce the role of the public sector, Richard Crook comments:

As Fauré and Contamin have so persuasively argued ... there was in fact a convenient coincidence between the need to reduce the scope of state patronage and a political agenda aimed at redistributing the opportunities which remained whilst renewing presidential power. This did not mean that the President was slavishly following a World Bank agenda; on the contrary, as a close analysis of the fate of the reforms during the 1980's shows, the President in fact spent the decade evading or circumventing the logic of the structural adjustment programmes ... Many of the parastatals which were supposed to be abolished under the restructuring programme in fact survived through reintegration into the public service as EPN (Établissements publics nationaux).[22]

These examples underline the importance of internal constraints as well as the possibility of sidestepping certain reforms during the 1980s.

Consequently, they help explain the prolonging of a particular mode of political regulation. Rather than being of secondary importance, these aspects are central characteristics of the Ivorian adjustment experience and revealing of its eminently political nature. More generally, they point to the fact that a preoccupation with the redistributive consequences of adjustment or "equity" implying a redefinition of the pattern of resource allocation cannot be treated as distinct from an analysis of the current mode of political regulation. In terms of methodology, this implies that the political dimensions of adjustment must be placed at the centre, rather than at the margin or as a post-facto explanation of failure, in the analysis of the process of adjustment and equity.

THE "NATIONAL APPROACH" TO ADJUSTMENT, THE RECONCEPTUALIZATION OF THE STATE, AND INSTITUTIONAL REFORM (THE 1990S)

At the beginning of the 1990s, the preoccupation of the World Bank, the IMF, and bilateral funding institutions with the "internalization" of adjustment and their renewed interest in "governance" and "capacity building" came at a precise juncture. The conditionalities accompanying adjustment, which had become increasingly heavy and multiform, were recognized as politically and technically unmanageable. Policies of state shrinkage and state withdrawal had also shown their limitations. Consequently, concerned with the political dimensions and feasibility of adjustment, these institutions recognized the need to reassert control over the process of adjustment and the strategic elements to do so. Renewed control over the process of adjustment was to be achieved by a two-fold approach : (1) putting forward a national approach to adjustment programs and (2) redefining the role of technical assistance.

1 With the failure of the "exogenous" Ivorian adjustment programs, the proposed solution was a plan conceived by nationals themselves, more specifically by technicians formerly employed in the Bretton Woods Institutions. It is in this context, as F.R. Mahieu has described, that the prime minister at the time, A.D. Ouattara, and his economic advisor, J.C. Brou, both formerly of the IMF, drew up a medium term national economic plan for 1991-95 within the new framework of a national approach to adjustment programs. While the overall orientation of the Medium Term Economic Programme (1991–95) did not differ markedly from past orientations (re-establishment of economic and financial equilibrium, reform of the

financial sector, improvement of competitiveness, development of human resources) it was introduced in a context characterized by new issues. As has been shown by Mahieu, this national plan drawn up by the government in collaboration with international support and agencies was in fact a regrouping or assembling of the sectorial plans wanted by the various agencies (the World Bank, the UNDP, the ILO, the EDF, etc.). Consequently, "The power strategy on this plan, in the name of a national approach becomes even more important."[23]

2 Simultaneously, and in parallel fashion, there occurred an explicit redefinition within international co-operation agencies of the relations between donors and governments. To this end, the key vehicle "technical assistance" was to be reoriented – better managed, with renewed emphasis being placed specifically on institutional reforms and capacity building, in order to guarantee the success of the adjustment programs. In this regard, Elliot Berg recommended that, "More technical co-operation resources should be allocated to the achievement of these approaches to state shrinkage."[24]

The Ivorian national program was introduced within this context: the repositioning of foreign lending organizations. This ensured that these organizations would not have to depend on the conditionalities of the past to secure the introduction of the measures they favoured. As B. Losch noted, "The objectives of the external reformers included the abandoning of the system of administered prices and producer prices, the total liberalization of internal commerce and exporting – with the 'reduction' and, subsequently, the opening up of the fortress Caistab – and the introduction of the principle of 'no leakage' of the 'filières,' as a means to prevent any 'run-away' of resources towards other sectors and interest groups."[25]

Losch has documented the slowness with which negotiations and decisions proceeded and, further, a tendency for losing ground. By the early 1990s, the co-operative system had not gained access to the export of major crops, leaving intact the former circuits of internal and external marketing at the root of the past redistributive patterns (allocation of margins and prebends through the complex interaction of permits and the releasing of contracts to export); in addition, the devaluation of the CFA franc in January 1994 tended in itself to reinforce former redistributive practices. "The doubling in local currency of the value of exports, multiplied by the recovery of export prices, provided the state apparatus with strong arguments in its negotiations with international financial organizations. This situation opens the way for those concerned to take up again, without need to be concerned with appearances, past redistributive practices that the former conjuncture had seriously obstructed."[26]

As the same author suggested, this situation was, however, only one of remission vis-à-vis an increasingly marked trend in favour of the "rules" of international commerce towards free trade. It illustrates nonetheless the extent to which the ruling class succeeded up to that time, and in fact throughout the 1990s, in consolidating its power through the use of the state apparatus in order to better control the strategic coffee and cocoa sectors.[27] This "remission" also played a role in the presidential election of 22 October 1995. According to well informed sources, funds from the Caisse were used to finance a large part of the campaign of interim President and former President of the National Assembly Konan Bédié, who came to power after Houphou-et Boigny's death was announced in December 1993. While this was the last time such procedures were to be followed by Bédié, they are illustrative of the persistence of a "culture politique" more reminiscent of the past, than of a signal of political liberalization. They also bring us to the institution at the heart of what has been called the "complexe ivorien" – the Caisse de Stabilisation.[28]

As noted in the previous section, the World Bank had called for better budgetary control of the Caisse for many years. From the time of the country's independence (1960), the Caisse, created by the French colonial administration in the 1950s, played a central role both in establishing producer prices and in acting as the intermediary in the marketing of major export commodities. The fabulous surpluses from the rich coffee and cocoa sectors, which, for the 1975–89 period, generated revenues estimated at over 2,000 billion CFA francs, supplied what had come to be called the former régimes' "caisses noires." It was only as of the 1990s – particularly as of the end of 1995, when a fifteen-million-dollar structural adjustment loan for the agricultural sector was at stake – that increasingly stringent reform of this institution was put forward as a condition for access to funding.[29] By that time, it had become clear that the Bretton Woods institutions would no longer tolerate such a lack of transparency. This lack was considered incompatible with the objectives of the subsequent (1994–97 and 1998–2001) structural adjustment loans. Consequently, after two years of tight negotiations, the "filière café" was finally liberalized in October 1998; and the marketing of cocoa, in August 1999. The Caisse itself was dissolved by a decree on 20 January 1999[30] and replaced by the Nouvelle Caistab. Its role is limited to simply registering contracts and supplying information for the sector.

If the dismantling of the former Caisse succeeds effectively in putting an end to the patterns of selective redistribution that it nurtured, there is no doubt that over time this could change certain historical key characteristics of the Ivorian political economy. However, pressure from different political factions, notably, but not only from those associated with the Bédié régime, to regain control of these valuable circuits of wealth[31] remains. As with other privatizations in Côte d'Ivoire, time will reveal how, in practice, the cards are redistributed as a result of the attempt to reform this strategic sector. In certain ways, to the extent that these measures mark the success of pressures to end the state monopoly of the Caisse and, through privatization, open up the possibility of Ivorian minority control in international holdings, they are reminiscent of the 1946-59 period, which was also one of redefinition and internalization of control over the production and marketing of export crops.

However, the international order of 1999 is not that of 1959. The dilemma for those in power until the overthrow in 1999 was that, if they respected the reforms recommended by the Bretton Woods institutions, they would have been denied precious resources, notably those of the Caisse, which were critical for political regulation; but if they did not respect these reforms, they risked the withdrawal of resources essential to economic recovery. As Losch has written with regard to this period, "It is indeed the constraints of the regulation of political power that prevent the spontaneous emergence of a new compromise."[32]

The apparent impossibility of reconciling these contradictory imperatives and the awareness of this impossibility are quite certainly important elements in explaining why the political leadership of the Bédié régime was so extremely intolerant of any form of opposition – whether it be that of democratic opposition parties, candidates or the press.[33] This intolerance translated into a total unwillingness on the part of the former ruling class (because of its inability) to put forward a new mode of social and political regulation, which would necessarily have entailed a new pattern of redistribution.

Although the intransigence of the Bédié government ushered in its own overthrow, the contradictory imperatives behind that intransigence remained after its fall. Moreover, the legacy of the dilapidation of public funds by the former régime was to make the challenges of transition all the more difficult.

A key dimension in the delicate post-Bédié era is the pivotal role played by the multilateral financial institutions as they exercise pressures for economic and institutional reform. The hegemonic position of these agencies raises a series of unanswered questions concerning their understanding of the nature, depth, and timing of the needed reforms, and how best to bring them about. These questions, in a situation as politically sensitive as that which developed in Côte d'Ivoire after the overthrow of the Bédié régime, merit the closest attention.

As mentioned above, two decades of adjustment have led multilateral funding institutions such as the World Bank to intervene more and more deeply into the social and economic fabric of the societies in which they are present, notably into areas of institutional reforms, with an aim to guarantee the success of their recommendations for economic reform: "Successful implementation of these reforms (structural adjustment) implies a fundamental transformation in the role of the state, not easy in the African context of weak institutions and often intense political opposition."[34] These administrative imperatives have been put forward with increased precision by the World Bank since the end of the 1980s – most explicitly formulated in *Governance and Development* (1992) and *Governance, The World Bank's Experience* (1994) – and have been the object of lively debates (to which only brief reference can be made here).

As made clear in the World Bank's 1994 report on Africa,[35] the Bank had by then already adopted a quite specific conception of the role of the state, namely an instrumentalist one drawn from the functionalist school of thought. Such a notion – put forward so as to conceptualize the state "in general" and in such a way as to be applicable to fifty African economies – does not, however, permit taking into account the historical specificity and internal social and political dynamics of a country such as the Côte d'Ivoire. Similarly, this mode of thought cannot take into consideration the particular origins of structural disequilibriums – nor does it consider the system of redistribution and the social and political regulations intimately linked to these disequilibriums and characteristic of the Ivorian experience.

Beyond its marked cultural and ideological bias and its incapacity to take into account the divers historical experiences that have characterized the state (elements that have been developed eloquently by Mick Moore[36]), the World Bank's conception is very reductionist of the multiple and changing roles that states assume. T. Biersteker has underlined the importance of considering these changing roles. Adjustment policies have affected these roles in very different ways, and this has critically important political consequences for the organization of production within the country and the integration of any particular economy into the world market.[37] In the case of Côte d'Ivoire, for example, reform policies favoured the abandonment of import-substitution policies encouraged by the state and privileged export strategies of primary products in which the country was considered to have a comparative advantage – cotton in the north and central regions and coffee and cocoa in the south. Biersteker's analysis is interesting in that it points out in general terms how an overly simplified view of the state, which fails to take into account its multiple roles, notably during the introduction of structural adjustment policies, neglects important issues, such as the following three:

1 the complexity of relations between the public and private sectors;
2 the danger of undermining the fiscal basis of the state;
3 the risk of undermining the legitimacy of the state itself. [38]

Recent policies and analyses of the World Bank, which have privileged particular growth strategies and proposed a quite specific reconceptualization of the role of the state, raise, in regards to the specific adjustment experience of Côte d'Ivoire, a series of problems with direct political implications, of which the following points may serve as an illustration.

1 The particular conception of the state put forward by the World Bank[39] as the subordinate adjunct to market forces fails to catch the originality of market/state interactions that has characterized the Ivorian economic growth experience historically and the complexity and depth of the interdependence between liberal growth strategies and past selective modes of social and political regulation.
2 Polarizing private and public sectors opened the door to uniform and non-differentiated policies of state "withdrawal" and to a perspective that saw in almost all forms of state intervention a distortion of the market, of efficient price operations, and of private initiatives.
3 By attributing the responsibility for slow growth to poor internal policies,[40] official studies sidestepped the need to consider the interaction between the choice of these policies, international prices, market forces, and the external environment – in spite of the fact that, elsewhere in the volume, regarding Côte d'Ivoire, the 1994 Report underlines, "Real producer export prices fell more than 50 percent between the beginning of the decade and the end."[41]
4 Through its unwavering stance in favour of further opening up the economy and privileging export strategies, the World Bank's approach seemed incapable of incorporating the importance of external constraints or of putting forward recommendations that would make the country less vulnerable vis-à-vis external constraints.

5 Past analyses systematically neglected the internal socio-political dynamics in Côte d'Ivoire that are essential to the analysis of the characteristics specific to the Ivorian experience. Notably, they neglected the links between the interventions of the state, the operation of markets, the patterns of social and political redistribution, and the modes of economic growth. An understanding of these would seem a prerequisite to any strategy to renew economic growth. The absence of consideration of the modes of social and political regulation throughout the adjustment process has made it impossible to grasp the reasons for the disappointing redistributive consequences of adjustment and of social dimensions policies – or to understand the failure of "adjustment and equity" in Côte d'Ivoire.

6 Most fundamentally, past analyses failed to grasp the political constraints of the adjustment process. They failed to take into consideration the implications of prolonging a system of selective social and political redistribution. They ignored the conditions necessary to construct new coalitions – even though such coalitions are indispensable for the success and durability of the reforms that external lenders themselves wish to see implemented.

CONCLUSION

In addition to the political changes that brought down the Bédié régime on 24 December 1999, one of the major key issues now – and in the years ahead – facing Côte d'Ivoire is whether the economic and institutional reforms proposed by the Bretton Woods institutions, in interaction with the internal dynamics of political change, will allow the country to build more equitable and sustainable modes of social and political regulation. After two decades of adjustment, the Bretton Woods Institutions succeeded in formally dismantling certain key sources of selective redistribution, such as the former Caisse, which had been at the heart of the exercise of Ivorian political power since independence. However, various political factions, of which the heirs of the Bédié régime are but one, remain intent on updating former political practices as a means of gaining access to economic resources – if necessary, by increasing degrees of authoritarianism and adopting divisive strategies, whether based on regionalism, religion, ethnicity, or purity of Ivorian "identity." In this context, the impact of the policies of various external actors – whether the former metropolitan power or multilateral financial institutions – becomes of vital importance in shaping the possibilities of updating and redefining past socio-economic and political compromises in Côte d'Ivoire. For example, economic reforms that place overriding emphasis on rectifying fiscal deficits and reimbursing the country's debt in the short term and ignore the need for social spending in vital and sensitive sectors (education, health, the civil service, and the military) may well endanger the transition period and the emergence of new compromises.

Furthermore, the legacy of the adjustment period has been the delegitimization of the state. This is partly because of the nature of the reforms, which selectively retrenched certain state functions. It is also because of the apparent compatibility of the reform process with the perpetuation of parallel modes of accumulation by certain political factions, a pattern that has been accompanied by the highly selective and unequal redistribution of resources. Among other things, therefore, there is a need for renewed state legitimacy; to redress the fiscal basis of the state and to permit public spending, the state must be allowed to carry out such functions as the collection of indirect taxes (on real estate and imports) and to introduce a minimum level of taxation on the potentially very lucrative mining and petroleum sectors.[42] Institutional reforms that are formulated in essentially managerial terms, destined above all to increase "efficiency," as they have been in the past, may well fall short of creating the political conditions necessary for legitimizing the state's capacity to enforce budgetary and fiscal discipline, a precondition for the introduction of more equitable patterns of social redistribution.

In the medium term and critical period of transition, it is much less clear if the measures of austerity and the increased liberalization of the economy – further opening to foreign capital and emphasis on export strategies of primary products – as proposed by the IMF and the World Bank, in the context of current policies of state retrenchment, notably with regard to the state's redistributive role and its capacity to tax and to mediate, will permit the creation of sufficiently large coalitions. These would help avoid destabilizing tendencies and permit the emergence of a new social compromise based on alternative modes of social and political regulation.

A critical political rereading of the Ivorian experience brings us to key problems: the positioning of the various external agents and the question of control over the reform process. These become particularly acute during a period of political transition. If we have learnt one thing from the failure of the conditionalities of the last twenty years, as the long, drawn-out, and financially disastrous experience of attempting to bring the Caisse de Stabilisation under budgetary control illustrates, it is that there cannot be successful reform without a reappropriation of the reform process based on a widely shared internal consensus and a coalition of political forces to support it. However, there cannot be reappropriation if the choice of strategies apt to receive financing is defined in advanced. What guarantee is there, as Biersteker has appropriately asked, that a country proposing policies that seek to redefine a passive integration into the world market and attempting to follow a nationally coherent strategy with the help of a more developmentalist state will also receive financial support?

Concluding with this question illustrates the paradoxical and unresolved nature of current policies and points to the "problème de fond": the impossibility of managing adjustment, institutional, and economic reform from abroad – whether from Paris or Washington. If a new social compromise based on a new mode of social and political regulation is to emerge in Côte d'Ivoire, it is imperative that the debates and the resulting process of policy formulation made possible by the situation of political transition, with regard to important issues such as the restructuring of the state and the objectives sought by policies of economic and social reform, be reappropriated by Côte d'Ivoire itself.

NOTES

I am grateful to Bruno Losch for his very helpful comments on an earlier version of this chapter. Any errors are my own.

1 By "mode of social and political regulation," I refer to the role that the state assumes in a post-colonial rent economy driven by export-crop production: the locus and agent in a pattern of selective redistribution, disconnected from the sphere of production. Obviously this type of process has numerous characteristics but central among these is a pattern of income distribution mostly unrelated to production and productivity. This characteristic is made possible in large part by the existence of multiple sources of parallel accumulation (or "coulage") in the shadow of the state. These aspects are not taken into consideration, as will be seen below, by studies such as the OECD's on equity and adjustment in Côte d'Ivoire. The above definition is suggested in Louis Gouffern, "Les limites d'un modèle. À propos d'État et bourgeoisie en Côte d'Ivoire," *Politique Africaine*, Paris, no. 6, May 1982: 19–34.

2 World Bank, *Adjustment in Africa: Reforms, Results and the Road Ahead*, Oxford, New York: published for the World Bank by Oxford University Press, 1994: 166.

3   François Régis Mahieu, "Variable Dimension Adjustment in the Côte
    d'Ivoire: Reasons for Failure," in *Review of African Political Economy,*
    no. 63, 1995: 9–26. As a "model" country, Côte d' Ivoire has certainly
    served as a terrain of experimentation for various strategies. According to
    F.R. Mahieu, Côte d'Ivoire has known a succession of anti-crisis products
    that serve to underline its position as a forerunner on the development
    market. As a result of this position, the country has been the object of an
    extensive literature riddled with numerous debates. On the recent evolu-
    tion of analyses of the Ivorian experience within the multilateral funding
    institutions, the following may usefully be consulted: Lionel Demery,
    "Côte d'Ivoire: Fettered Adjustment," in *Adjustment in Africa: Lessons
    from Country Case Studies,* edited by Ishrat Husain and Rashid Faruqee,
    World Bank, Washington, 1994: 72–152; and Christopher Chamley
    "Côte d'Ivoire: The Failure of Structural Adjustment," in *Restructuring
    Economies in Distress. Policy Reform and the World Bank*, edited by
    Vinad Thomas, Ajay Chhibber, Mansoor Dailami, and Jaime de Melo,
    published for the World Bank by Oxford University Press, 1991:
    287–308. A different perspective may be found amongst other sources:
    M.F. Jarret and F.R. Mahieu, "Ajustement structurel, croissance et répar-
    tition : l'exemple de la Côte d'Ivoire," in *Revue Tiers-Monde*, no. 32,
    1991: 39–62; Gilles Duruflé, *L'Ajustement structurel en Afrique*, chapter
    2, "La Côte d'Ivoire," Paris: Karthala, 1988: 87–148; Bonnie Campbell,
    "Indebtedness and Adjustment Lending in the Ivory Coast: Elements for
    a Structural Critique," in *Political Dimensions of the International Debt
    Crisis*, edited by B. Campbell, London: Macmillan Inc., 1989: 129–62.
    Finally, for an overview of research concerning the Ivorian adjustment
    experience one may consult *Le Modèle ivoirien en questions. Crises,
    ajustements et recompositions*, edited by Bernard Contamin and Harris
    Memel-Fôté, Paris: Karthala and ORSTOM, 1997.
4   I have kept the three periods proposed by Mahieu in his economic analy-
    sis of the Ivorian adjustment experience.
5   François Régis Mahieu, "Ajustement à dimensions variables en Côte
    d'Ivoire. Les raisons d'un échec," my translation from sections of the
    original, longer French version not included in "Variable Dimension
    Adjustment," 11–12.
6   Ibid., 12. Figures are in CFA francs. For this period, 100 CFA = 2 French
    francs and approximately 250 CFA francs = 1 US dollar.
7   Gilles Duruflé, *L'Ajustement structurel en Afrique. (Sénégal, Côte
    d'Ivoire, Madagascar)*, Paris: Karthala, 1988: 120–1 (my translation).
8   F.R. Mahieu, "Variable Dimension Adjustment," 12. The reference is to
    Bénié Kouadio "Restructuration et évolution de l'emploi dans le secteur
    public et para-public en Côte d'Ivoire," (unpublished paper, Abidjan,
    1989).

9   F.R. Mahieu, "Variable Dimension Adjustment," 13.

10 Ibid., 14–16.

11 M.F. Jarret et F.R. Mahieu, "Ajustement structurel, croissance et répartition : l'exemple de la Côte d'Ivoire," *Revue Tiers-Monde*, Paris, no. 32, 1991: 39–62.

12 Lionel Demery and Lyn Squire, "Macroeconomic Adjustment and Poverty in Africa: An Emerging Picture," *The World Bank Research Observer*, vol. 11, no.1, February 1996: 42.

13 Bastiaan A. den Tuinder, *Ivory Coast. The Challenge of Success*, A World Bank Country Economic Report Published for the World Bank by Johns Hopkins University Press, 1978.

14 World Bank, *Adjustment Lending : An Evaluation of Ten Years of Experience*. Washington, 1988: 77.

15 World Bank, Evaluation Department, *Trade Policy Reforms under Adjustment Programs,* 1992: 53.

16 J.P. Azam and C. Morrisson, *La Faisabilité politique de l'ajustement en Côte d'Ivoire et au Maroc,* OCDE, 1994: 11–12.

17 Harris Memel-Fôté, "De la stabilité au changement. La représentation de la crise politique et la réalité des changements," presented at the International Conference, "Crises, Ajustments et Recomposition en Côte d'Ivoire, La remise en cause d'un modèle," Abidjan, 28 November– 2 December 1994: 63; and published, slightly modified, in *Le Modèle ivoirien en questions*, 611–31 (my translation).

18 J.P. Azam and C. Morrisson, *La Faisabilité politique,* 52 (my translation).

19 F. Bourguignon and C. Morrisson, *Ajustement et équité dans les pays en développement, une approche nouvelle*, Paris: OECD, 1992.

20 This analysis is developed in more detail in B. Campbell, "Note on Adjustment and Equity," in *Labour, Capital and Society*, McGill University, no. 26, April 1993: 102–13.

21 "Public enterprise reform changed gear in the 1987–91 period, with greater emphasis placed on divestiture, and not simply on restructuring. Between 1987 and 1989 almost 30 public enterprises were privatized. Several divestiture techniques were used, usually involving direct negotiations with potential buyers. These privatizations were conducted with little transparency, and little strategic study was pursued prior to privatization. In short, the privatizations were not well managed," Lionel Demery, "Côte d'Ivoire: Fettered adjustment" in *Adjustment in Africa*, vol. 2, *Lessons from Country Case Studies*, edited by U. Husain et R. Faruqee, World Bank, 1994: 101–2. When the privatization of Énergie Électrique de la Côte d'Ivoire took place in November 1990 and the Compagnie Ivoirienne d' Électricité was created – with 51 per cent of shares going to SAUR, a subsidiary of Bouygues – it appeared that certain members of the government sub-committee responsible for privatizations were directly

involved in the purchase of shares via certain investment committees. This incident suggested to certain British observers the existence of an "old boy network" actively in place in the distribution of shares and goods which had previously belonged to the public sector. *The Economist Intelligence Unit: Côte d'Ivoire: Country Report*, no. 4, 1991: 14–15.

22 Richard Crook, "Côte d'Ivoire: Multi-party Democracy and Political Change. Surviving the Crisis," in *Democracy and Political Change in Sub-Saharan Africa*, edited by John A. Wiseman, London: Routledge, 1995: 14–15. Quotations from B. Contamin and Y Fauré, *La Bataille des entreprises publiques en Côte d'Ivoire*, Paris: Karthala.1990: 37.

23 F.R. Mahieu, "Variable Dimension Adjustment," 17.

24 Elliot Berg, *Rethinking Technical Cooperation*, 270.

25 Bruno Losch "À la recherche du chaînon manquant. Pour une lecture renouvelée de l'économie de plantation ivoirienne," in *Le Modèle ivoirien en questions: Crise, ajustements et recompositions*, 224 (my translation).

26 Ibid., 225 (my translation).

27 In its attempts to press the government to disengage from the Caisse, the World Bank had produced a review of Ivorian agriculture in February 1995. It reported that, calculated in French francs, planters' earnings had fallen in real terms, even though in absolute terms they might have increased by a total of more than 50 billion CFA. Between 1970 and 1988, it added that the Caistab had accumulated CFA Fr. 2.3 trillion, mainly through export taxation. However, the Caisse's board had proved incapable of guaranteeing producers prices or of doing anything to prevent rural impoverishment when world agricultural prices were low, as they were between 1987 and 1993. *The Economist Intelligence Unit: Côte d'Ivoire, Mali: Country Report*. 2nd quarter 1995: 15.

28 Bruno Losch, "Le Complexe café-cacao de la Côte d'Ivoire. Une relecture de la trajectoire ivoirienne," (2 volumes), doctoral dissertation, Faculté des Sciences économiques, Université de Montpellier 1, France.

29 The agreement, reached in July 1995, was only reported in late August. It was expected to lead to supplementary loans from France (60 million dollars) and Germany (20 million dollars) in support of the reform. *The Economist Intelligence Unit: Country Report: Côte d'Ivoire, Mali*, 4th quarter, 1995: 15.

30 The audit undertaken by Arthur Andersen at the request of the Bretton Woods institutions revealed the extent to which the funds of the Caisse had been dilapidated during its final years. In 1997, the Caisse declared a profit of 10.3 billion CFA francs but the auditors suggest that the figure was 71.2 billion. For the first four months of 1999, the Caisse declared a deficit of 3 billion CFA francs while the auditors put forward a profit of 23.5 billion (*Jeune Afrique*, no. 2031, 14–20 December 1999: 80–1).

31 From a quite different perspective, cocoa and coffee producers' co-operatives linked in the Syndicat national des producteurs (SYNAGCI),
opposed the reforms, which, since they enabled exporters to deal directly with individual planters, appeared to weaken co-operatives. Synagci
asked the authorities to provide financial support to co-operatives –
now at risk of being swallowed up by large private concerns – in order
to enable them to compete fairly and thus help preserve the livelihood
of small farmers. The pressure of the co-operative movement should not
be overestimated, however, as it has been kept weak in the past – controlling only approximately 20 per cent of sales. Again, from another
perspective, French importers of Ivorian cocoa, represented in the Association française de commerce de cacao warned that breaking up the
Caisse system could well create more problems, such as the dilution of
quality, than it is intended to solve (*The Economist Intelligence Unit:
Country Report: Côte d'Ivoire, Mali*, 3rd quarter 1995: 15; and 2nd
quarter 1995: 16).

32 Bruno Losch, Introduction, "Le Complexe café-cacao de la Côte d'Ivoire"
(quotation translated by Claude Lalumière).

33 According the Economist Intelligence Unit, as of 1995, at least twenty opposition journalists had gone to prison for offending the president of Côte
d'Ivoire; several rivals had been removed from political life on the dubious
grounds that their parentage was not "pure" Ivorian; and, at all levels of
Ivorian life, opponents were under threat. These trends were to increase
considerably over the following years. The London-based human rights
group Amnesty International had challenged the former government over its
intolerant stance, which, the organization alleged, had put more than 200
opposition supporters behind bars from September 1994 to September
1995. The same source continues, "Whatever the cause of Mr. Konan
Bédié's behavior may be, he seems determined to build himself a cast-iron
edifice of political security, even if it costs Côte d'Ivoire its relatively good
reputation for democratic and human rights," *The Economist Intelligence
Unit: Country Report: Côte d'Ivoire, Mali*, 3rd quarter, 1996: 4.

34 World Bank, *Adjustment in Africa*, 219.

35 Ibid., 183–4.

36 Mick Moore, "Declining to Learn from the East? The World Bank on
'Governance and Development,'" in *I.D.S. Bulletin*, vol. 24, no. 1, 1993:
39–43.

37 Thomas J. Biersteker, "Reducing the Role of the State in the Economy: A
Conceptual Exploration of I.M.F. and World Bank Prescriptions," in
International Studies Quarterly, no. 34, 1990: 477–92.

38 Ibid., 490.

39 See, for example: World Bank, *The State in a Changing World*. World
Development Report 1997, Oxford University Press for the World Bank,

1997. This particular conceptualization of the state is analysed in detail in B. Campbell, "New Rules of the Game: The World Bank's Role in the Construction of New Normative Frameworks for States, Markets and Social Exclusion," in *Canadian Journal of Development Studies*, Ottawa, vol. 21, no,1, March 2000.

40 World Bank, *Adjustment in Africa*, 30.

41 Ibid., 166.

42 These proposals were put forward by the minister of the budget of the transitional governement in a 15 February 2000 interview: "Entretien avec M. Mamadou Koulibaly, ministre du budget du gouvernement de transition de la République de Côte d'Ivoire," by Bernard Contamin and Bruno Losch, in *Politique Africaine*, Paris, no. 77, March 2000.

Introducing Race As a Variable Into the Political Economy of Kenya Debate: An Incendiary Idea

MICHAEL CHEGE

The debate on whether indigenous capitalism in Kenya could underwrite the economic transformation of the country, with or without the support of international capital, was all the rage in the late 1970s and early 1980s.[1] Writing in what appeared to be the terminal phase of it, Gavin Kitching predicted that the debate would end – like the famous "Brenner" controversy on the origins of agrarian capitalism in Europe – in mutual exhaustion and with no identifiable victor.[2] In Kitching's view, two major factors had inexorably steered the debate to a dead end: first, inability to acquire hard data on the inner strategies and thinking of the Kenyan African bourgeoisie; and, more importantly, the absence of a clear program of action for working class mobilization towards a socialist society, which some participants appeared to advocate. As events have since proved, Kitching was wrong. Old academic debates never die. They are just resurrected in a new intellectual attire and fitted with a trendy jargon. In the wake of the resurgent global euphoria on free enterprise as the engine of economic growth, academic discussion on African capitalists has rebounded with a vengeance.[3] It may well be that the salvation of African capitalism will benefit from such a resurrection, but the resurrected Lazarus in the debate also brings the added risk that Marx detected in *The Eighteenth Brumaire of Louis Bonaparte*: "All important events and personalities in history appear as it were twice, the first as a tragedy, the second as a farce."

This paper examines the increasingly popular rediscovery of race and culture as determinants of entrepreneurship in Kenya. To distinguish genuine economic knowledge from the tendentious race- and culture-based arguments that have now resumed a prominent role in comparative development studies, it is necessary to return to the fundamental rules that govern the formulation of tenable hypotheses and to the empirical proof of cause-effect propositions. Otherwise, slipshod arguments on culture, race, and the political economy of capitalism in Kenya or elsewhere run the risk of generating more ethnic heat than light. In the charged racial atmosphere of the late twentieth century, this may lead to grave social consequences. It could also postpone the answer to the problem of uneven distribution of entrepreneurial talent and rewards – not least between African communities themselves – which is among the thorniest issues in African development today.

Though dormant for a while, the race-and-economy debate in Kenya has a rich colonial ancestry in which the contribution of immigrant races – European and Asian – purportedly eclipsed that of Africans.[4] Joining it from the conceptual terrain of culture-and-economics in the new American right, Robert Kaplan asserted in 1992 that "Kenya (was) buttressed for decades by a white business community and Asian shopkeepers from the Indian subcontinent ... For decades it was the Asians who constituted the Kenyan urban middle class lying between the thin stratum of wealthy Africans and the mass of African peasantry below." He proceeded to contrast "the jealousy of an African underachieving culture" with the Asian "iron-tight family structure, allowing for enviable work habits and economic success."[5] And in a widely quoted series of articles, Keith Richburg, the *Washington Post* correspondent in Nairobi from 1992 to 1995, contrasted the high managerial capability of East Asian bureaucrats with the incompetence of African development managers, even in stable countries like Tanzania that had received record levels of external development assistance.[6]

In the academic world, David Himbara, with a book published in 1994,[7] made a resounding entry into the seemingly defunct debate on Kenyan capitalism. Railing against the neglect of the contribution made to Kenya's overall development by Kenyans of Indo-Pakistani origin, he claimed – on the basis of a sample of one hundred companies drawn from the register of the Kenya Association of Manufacturers (KAM) – to have "confirmed" his hypothesis that "relative development success in Kenya was mainly due to Kenyan Indian capitalists" and, secondarily, to the contribution of remnants of British administrators and the international development brigades that had saved the state from the "total collapse" that African administrators had allegedly set in motion right from the dawn of independence in 1963. Whether in commerce, the parastatal firms, or in government, African-run enterprises seemed perennially prone to "mediocrity," "total collapse," or "disaster" – the singular exception being their "success" in handicrafts and the so-called *jua kali* "informal sector." As with Kaplan, the singular cause for Asian business success in Kenya is reported to be "commercial skills ... sheer determination and hard work ... general efficiency and a competitive edge ... and the role of family units."[8] This is contrasted with the "lack of a business culture among Africans" and the "traditional ... cultural values" that consistently sabotaged all African entrepreneurial initiatives except the very few in which "black skinned" Africans had the wisdom (or luck) to go into partnership with the more talented white or Asian business managers.[9] Having ostensibly began as a refutation of the 1970s authors – notably Michael Cowen, Colin Leys, and Nicola Swainson – the last two of whom had argued against the "classical" dependency position that accumulation in the global periphery was impossible against the backdrop of a domineering multinational capital – the book ends up awarding credit for Kenya's economic "exceptionalism" (such as it is) to Asian capital (a neglected racial minority), not the "virtually extinct" and mainly Kikuyu African bourgeoisie which had featured in the 1980s publications. Himbara depicts the African bourgeoisie of the Kenyatta years (1964–78) as an ephemeral Kikuyu artificiality that withered immediately when its life support to "political handouts" was disconnected under Moi's rule. What the Kenyan-Asian capitalist class now required to blossom and transform Kenya economically, he argues, is a network of supportive state structures that has unfortunately been hostage to African incompetence and bureaucratic corruption since independence, unlike in Asia.

In a recent rejoinder to this line of analysis, Michael Cowen and Scott MacWilliam, have returned to the fray with a monograph contending that demeaning remarks about "indigenous classes of capital" have been standard baggage of ill-informed Marxist development discourse since the days of the Comintern, as demonstrated by the aspersions cast over native Indian capitalists (in India) in the 1930s and over the aspiring Afrikaner bourgeoisie in South Africa of the 1940s.[10] Cowen and MacWilliam stay clear of name-calling or assigning ethnic blame, the dominant tendency of their argument being to set the record straight, using classical Marxist analytical categories on class and what they call the "layering of capital" by successive generations of accumulators. On the whole, they remain sanguine about the prospects of capitalist development in the global periphery, Moi's Kenya included, provided that appropriate political conjunctures, fusing capital and state, are found. Both therefore cite the pivotal role of access to state power in defining the existence of a bourgeoisie and reiterate the agrarian origins of the Kenyan African capitalists – as opposed to manufacturing, on which Himbara's conclusions are erected.

Kenyan Capitalists received fulsome praise in leading North American journals; one reviewer called its writer "acute and bright," the other chimed in with the verdict of "a provocative and well researched analysis of Kenya's rise and fall."[11] In Kenya itself, partisan arguments by African and Asian racial extremists resumed centre stage from March to June 1996, both sides ironically drawing sustenance from Himbara's conclusion that Kenyan Asians provided the bedrock of the country's economic prosperity. The vituperative name-calling – Asian extremists berating "indolent blackies" and boasting control of "85 percent of the economy," their African counterparts demanding expulsion of "Asian exploiters" – dominated press statements and rebuttals.[12] In both its rabble-rousing and intellectual modes, the resurrected debate on Kenyan capitalism had acquired a new lease on life.

POLITICS, EVIDENCE, AND METHOD ONCE AGAIN

In his enduring work, *Witchcraft, Oracles, and Magic Among the Azande*, E. Evans Pritchard argued that the fundamental distinction between science and magic was not to be found over conceptual differences in interpreting basic cause-effect relationships. Both approaches were often in accord, for instance, that if untreated, a poisonous snake bite leads to the death of the human victim, but they differed irremediably on the *substantive understanding* of why one individual sustained the snake bite – as opposed to many others who had walked on the same path as the unfortunate person. While "rational" analysis is open-ended in its response to that question (offering as explanations, chance, high probability of getting bitten in certain places and times, etc.), magic is a "closed" system that consistently assigns causes to nefarious and fiendish outsiders, human or spiritual.[13] While rational analysis seeks to decipher systematic patterns in explaining observed phenomena, magical interpretations are entirely pragmatic – and therefore subject to varying, not to say contradictory and ad hoc, reasoning – constantly dodging contradictory facts. This approach is close to Popper's attack on "closed belief systems," including conspiracy theories in the wider social setting, which advance conjectures and propositions that are invulnerable to refutation by contradictory evidence or fresh theory – the generic mark of true science.[14] And in a widely read extension of this argument, Imre

Lakatos warns against "naive falsification" based on muddled theoretical premises, faulty apparatuses, and biased gathering of data.
Lakatos upbraided the introduction of utopian and ad hoc conditionalities (the same thing Pritchard had said of oracles and magic) to
avoid contradictory evidence and refutation.[15]

Like their 1960s predecessors, some of the contemporary studies
on the ethnic and cultural origins of entrepreneurship are of the
closed system variety and are auto-sealed against refutation. David
McClelland's 1960s postulate, for example, was based on early parent-
child relationships that nurtured an individualistic and acquisitive
trait.[16] By this reasoning, however, every successful capitalistic endeav-
our could be traced back on a post hoc basis to the "right" parental
nurture whether this involved stern rules, hardship, or affection – each
of which, after its own fashion, can inculcate a self-assured personal
drive in the growing child. The same could be done with business failure. Compared to the newly resurrected race-and-economy genre,
however, some of the older thinking seems highly circumspect in its
use of patchy data and in how carefully it qualified its conclusions.
Thus Bauer and Yamey, who could justly claim paternity to the contemporary creed in all-purpose markets as an engine for growth in
Africa, considered extended families in much of the developing world
to be a handicap to entrepreneurship. However, while acknowledging
that family-based immigrant trading groups, like the "Indians" in East
Africa and the "Lebanese" in West Africa, had pioneered the establishment of rural markets, they also denounced ethnocentric prejudice
against Africans whose agricultural productivity was already rising as
a result of the new international division of labour, the acquisition of
modern skills, and the farmers' natural instinct for profit. Still, Bauer
and Yamey believed that "force of custom, rigidity of status ... collec-
tivism of the extended family, the clan, village or tribe" were definite
barriers to indigenous commercial progress.[17] Thus while closely knit
families were an asset to immigrant entrepreneurs, they were the bane
of the Africans.

If the assumed causal linkage between being of Kenyan Asian
descent (and its heritage of family cohesion and industriousness) and
"success" in business is to be unmistakably established, the two variables need to be more precisely defined and measured. For the argument to be irrevocably proven, "Asianness" must be perfectly co-
extensive with success observed in all business categories that "Asians"
and other groups engage in on an equal footing. If significant variance
in achievement within the group itself is detected, however, then variables other than race and culture must be sought. In fact, being Asian
– the supposed precondition of "success" in "accumulation" – is not

as unproblematic and straightforward as Himbara and Kaplan assume. As a term of identity, "Asians" in East Africa acquired currency only after Pakistan's partition from India in 1947; it is a convenient short-hand incorporating all residents from the Indian subcontinent and countries beyond it. Like "African" (or indeed "European") in Kenya, it is a category of convenience conflating a plurality of multiple and often rival identities.[18] On the strength of past ethnographic and sociological data in East Africa, there is evidence to support great variations in "Asian" business specialization and incomes, corresponding to religious sects, caste, and regions of ancestral origin in the Indian subcontinent. The British sociologist, H.S. Morris, the leading authority on this subject through the early 1970s, observed this caste-grounded division of labour: Goans, Sikhs, and Brahmins in different branches of public service; Lohanas, Patidars, and Ismailis in industry; Sunni Muslims and Sikhs in engineering and the automobile industry.[19] There were and remain vast difference in inter-sectoral (and hence inter-communal) incomes that are better explained by path-dependent business skills, rather than the elusive "Asian" race and culture. Not all Kenyan Asians in any case are prospering industrialists; many – perhaps most – are of moderate means and are still in retail trade, the professions, and even wage employment. For academic work appearing in the 1990s, surprisingly, not a word is said about the glaring absence of Asian women in medium or large-scale businesses compared to their African and white counterparts.[20] The arbitrariness in defining who is an Asian is also evidenced by the exclusion of Kenyans of Arabic and Iranian descent – about half as many as the 76,000 residents of Indo-Pakistani origin in 1989. Given especially the religious and cultural overlap between them and those of Indo-Pakistan origin, their absence in the large-scale industrial sector may suggest that explaining business success or failure as a function of ethnicity and culture has an unusually weak predictive power.

The lack of precision is even greater in the definition of what constitutes "success." Despite its fleeting usage of paleo-marxist jargon – "bourgeoisie," "class," "accumulation," etc. – business achievement by Himbara is not measured by what ought to be the standard Marxist yardstick of increased surplus value, and hence higher capital accumulation: the replacement of absolute surplus value by relative surplus value, primarily through on-firm technical change.[21] In a sense then, Cowen and MacWilliam are wrong in faulting Himbara for reproducing the official line of the Comintern on the impotence of indigenous capitalism – a line that had been severely contested by the heterodox Marxism of India's M.N. Roy.[22] Himbara professes no interest in any economic theory, Marxist or neo-classical, as a tool of analysis and is markedly impatient with both. Other than "test" the two positions on the trajectory of Kenyan capitalism, he considers received theories as obscurantist and diversionary from the most urgent task – that of data gathering to right an academic injustice.[23] The race and culture genre, academic or journalistic, is also not seriously interested in validating business "success" by standard accounting methods, in the performance yardsticks of neo-classical economics such as rates of return on capital, or in total factor productivity. At its simplest, standard financial management assesses corporate performance on either (i) the appreciation of total net assets, especially in openly traded stock, or (ii) dividends earned per unit of investment at market value – the price-earnings ratio. None of that is attempted by way of proof. Conversely, other than the press, select interviews, and one-sided government statements, no objective criteria of any sort is used to prove that African performance in the private and parastatal sector ranges "from mediocre to total failure."[24] Instead, the sample of one hundred companies on which Himbara's case of Asian hegemony in the Kenya economy is based contains a double bias: membership in the KAM (which is not the universe of manufacturing in Kenya) and the inbuilt surviving-big-firms' capacity to confirm "success," since bigness is the obverse of the survival that produced it. In these circumstances, no effort is made to examine Coughlin's plausible thesis that, despite its evident economic and structural handicaps, Kenya's industrial structure could be reconfigured and guided to achieve economies of scale and international competitiveness by government policy.[25] In the end the only substantive logic that underlines the selection of the one hundred companies, and the accolade of success they are given, is not economic analysis, not profitability, and not efficiency in productivity but precisely the one used by Sir Edmund Hillary on scaling the Everest: because they are there.

As is well-established by now, faith in manufacturing as the foundation of other economic activity is subject to dispute, in rich and poor countries.[26] For all the hubris about the pivotal role of the Asian manufacturers as the true anchor of Kenyan "exceptionalism," it should be noted that the contribution of manufacturing to GDP has consistently ranged from 8 to 12 per cent since independence. More importantly, some 60 per cent of value added in Kenyan manufacturing in the 1980s was in fact attributed not to the import-substituting firms of the kind that dominate the KAM but to the food and beverages processing sub-sector that is dominated by a combination of multinationals and parastatal enterprises (e.g., Kenya Breweries, British American Tobacco, Kenya Cooperative Creameries).[27] Given the critical role of agriculture and agricultural processing in the country, it makes no sense to omit the factories whose output is normally enumerated under agriculture – like the forty-five factories of the Kenya Tea Development Authority, an African-run organization that, David Leonard informs us, is "the largest tea corporation in the world"[28] – or those of Kenya Cooperative Creameries and the coffee industry – just because they are not in the KAM register, which is essentially a lobby of the import-substitution interests.

The statistical hat trick under which probably one half of the 12 per cent of GDP located in manufacturing (and owned by Kenyan Asians) becomes representative of "accumulation" and "exceptionalism" of the Kenyan economy, leaving out some 35–40 per cent the GDP earned from agriculture, is justified in the most cavalier manner. To Kaplan the Kenya economy is evidently all urban. For Himbara, agriculture "was in a state that rendered it inappropriate as a subject for survey," citing newspaper reports of a riot among tea farmers in Murang'a, government banishment of farmers organizations for "corruption," and the transparently inaccurate statement that "sectoral regulatory agencies like the Kenya Tea Development Authority and the Kenya Coffee Growers Association were either under official investigation or ... not functioning at all."[29] The second reason given in defence of the biased sample – African managerial incompetence in assembling rural data and the poor statistical sources at Kenya's Central Bureau of Statistics (CBS) – is best refuted by Judith Heyer of Somerville College, Oxford, whose research in rural Kenya goes back to 1964:

CBS is a large organisation whose capacity has been built up over a considerable period of time, the product of experience as well as training, and institutional as well as individual development. CBS has a most impressive capacity to do a great deal of high quality, detailed, continuing work on matters of central concern to the Kenya government ... It also has the most impressive capacity to conduct rural and urban surveys, and to provide technical advice on statistical matters ... It has an unusually enthusiastic, committed and highly motivated staff.[30]

None of this excuses the administrative depravity of the Moi years within CBS, but it does introduce a sense of proportion. Written after an extensive survey and seminars with CBS staff in 1989, at exactly the same time that Himbara saw that agency disintegrating under the weight of African inefficiency, surviving only courtesy of a handful of Western expatriate managers, it says much about the self-confirming character generically assumed by oracles and closed systems analytical models.

RACE AND CULTURE AS DETERMINANTS
OF ECONOMIC SUCCESS

The rambling literature on the socio-cultural origins of economic decay in Kenya, especially over the Moi years, can be divided into four areas of concentration: (i) the basis of the robust macroeconomic indicators in the "miracle years" from 1964 to 1988, (ii) repeated failure of African entrepreneurship, (iii) problems in the parastatal sector, and (iv) corruption and inefficiency in the public sector under African management.

1 Origins of Kenyan "Exceptionalism"
in the "Miracle" Years

Because in history disaster tends to provoke post hoc aspersions against any preceding it, doubts have been expressed yet again as to whether Kenya's outstanding economic performance in the decade after independence owed anything to African entrepreneurship and state management. This is the import of Himbara's data, culled from a sample of one hundred (out of six hundred) companies with a capital value of at least 100 million Kenya shillings in the KAM register, 85 per cent of which turned out to be owned by Kenyans of Indo-Pakistani descent. On the whole, Asian firms in the sample were less susceptible to bankruptcy than African and European-owned ones. In quick succession, Kenyan Asians were then designated as the only authentic class of local "accumulators" – "pioneers of accumulation" with business roots going back to the last century "who spearheaded accumulation in almost all historical phases" before and after independence. In contrast to the pathetic Kikuyu political capitalists, Kenyan Asian entrepreneurs are uniformly paraded as "enterprising" and "experienced."

Ethnic adulation, however, is not a recognized method of explaining sources of high economic growth. The most objective approach in pinpointing the sectoral origins of Kenya's most robust phase of economic expansion would have been to calculate total factor productivity (TFP) by sector.[31] Rising TFP – reflecting the ability to squeeze more output out of the same (or lower) factor inputs – has an added advantage: it serves as a proxy for the technical innovation and "ingenuity" Africans are said to lack. Although we have not encountered a full scale evaluation of this kind in Kenya, available evidence provides little comfort to the opinions of Himbara and Kaplan. In assessing the country's outstanding performance from 1964 through the mid-80s, the engine of growth by all professional accounts lay not in immigrant groups but in African-run smallholder agriculture – the supposed source of African cultural and economic pathology. Despite the many tribulations visited this sector by the Moi regime, this was still the case in the mid-1990s, when the combined efforts of domestic agrarian opposition and stop-go economic liberalization imposed by Western donors were beginning to show some gradual positive results.

Despite officially sanctioned price distortions against farming, and the incentives extended to manufacturing by the state, small-scale farmers maintained efficiency superiority in production over domestic industry – not to mention foreign competitors – by a wide margin. After assessing inter-sectoral usage of labour, imports, and capital per unit of output in 1975, a major World Bank survey remarked that "investment in agriculture contributed more to development at less cost, than any other kind of investment."[32] It was known by the mid-1970s that sections of the tariff-protected import-substitution industries in Kenya were characterized by negative value-added and used more foreign exchange than they generated.[33] Despite the bombast on inefficiency of African producers compared to their counterparts in Asia and elsewhere, arabica coffee production in metric tons per hectare in Kenya's Central Province – the hub of the country's smallholder commercial agriculture – averaged 897 from 1979 to 1989, compared to 691 for Colombia, 669 in India, and 623 in Indonesia.[34] As an efficiency index, output per hectare is of course inadequate because it ignores other factors and intermediate inputs. But from the work of Barbara Grosh we have evidence of remarkable decline (87 per cent) of real unit costs of production of capital employed in the tea industry from 1964 to 1987 and of even greater efficiency in annual operating costs.[35] In the coffee sector, research demonstrates that for all their problems, co-operatives in Kenya's Central Province had, by most criteria, an overall efficiency edge in the continent.[36] By the 1990s, horticultural exports by large and small scale farms was cited as a successful example of diversification of agricultural exports, having grown from nothing at independence in 1963 to 4 per cent of total exports in 1987 – about the same ratio as Kenya's manufactured exports net of re-exports.[37]

In an increasingly globalized market, the acid test of sectoral efficiency remains the ability to expand market share in the face of external competition. Kenya farmers doubled their global market share of tea and coffee (very small proportions of which are domestically consumed) from 1967 to 1987, while the ratio of exported to total manufacturing fell from 20 per cent in 1964 to 10 per cent in 1984.[38] Despite the buffeting it had received from the Moi government, Kenya's (predominantly smallholder) sector produced a record

244,500 tonnes of tea in 1995, threatening to overtake Sri Lanka as the world's second largest source of black tea.[39]

While reproaching the independent Kenyan government for its incompetence and inability to secure protected national and African regional markets for local manufactures, Himbara asserts that the decline of Kenyan Asian external markets was occasioned by the collapse of the East African common market in 1977 – a reflection of economic ineptitude attributed to Kenya's political leadership.[40] In fact, as Sharpley and Lewis demonstrate, the loss of regional market share of Kenyan manufactures was already in progress as early as the mid-1960s, the heyday of East African co-operation. The principal reason, a World Bank industrial sector review in 1983 remarked, was "high cost and low quality of Kenyan consumer goods" that had led to the poor competitiveness of the country's manufactures.[41] The linkage between lack of competitiveness in the manufacturing sector and industrial protection was underscored by Arvind Barve, previous head of the Kenya External Trade Authority, a Kenyan Asian, and one of the most accomplished public servants ever to work in the trade sector.[42] The two subsectors of Kenyan industry that demonstrated capability to expand external market shares – refined petroleum products and cement – were dominated by multinational corporations with substantial African and foreign management.

Moreover, it is analytically fatal to trumpet the supremacy of manufacturing in moving the economy, independently of inter-sectoral resource flows. For Kenya, it is worth noting that most expansion in the industrial and consumer goods sector – 69 per cent of manufacturing output from 1964 to 1984 – was derived from domestic demand in the captive African consumer sector in agriculture.[43] As Cowen and MacWilliam observe – citing John Zarwan's work on Oshwal (Asian) commerce and industry in Kikuyu country – this trend is the exact opposite of what Himbara and Kaplan propose.[44] Yet in the interest of import substitution, the Kenyan government, like that of most developing countries in the 1960s on, instituted a range of policies – a moderately overvalued exchange rate, quantitative import controls, high import tariffs on consumer goods, low capital goods taxation, submarket interest rates, and fiscal subsidies – all with the goal of stimulating local manufacturing. In an economy with only two categories of tradables – farm goods and manufactures – these policy instruments penalized agriculture to the same extent that they subsidized industry. For that reason, household expenditure analysis from Central Kenya on the proceeds of the 1975-83 coffee boom, as conducted by Bevan, Collier, and Gunning, reflected short-run income redistribution from farmers to construction and the protected import-substitution firms that Himbara credits with "spearheading accumulation."[45] With a smallholder coffee sector savings ratio estimated by the Bevan-Collier-Gunning study at 60 per cent in those years – higher than that of South East Asia or Nairobi's KAM factories at their best – it is evident that "accumulation" – understood more precisely as generation of investible surplus above consumption – was first taking place in small-holder commercial agriculture. By putting pressure on the supply of investment goods (in a protected market), the coffee farmers ended up tilting the domestic terms of trade against themselves even more.

Sharpley has estimated net capital outflows out of agriculture via adverse internal terms of trade incurred through such regulatory poli-cies at an average of 58 per cent of Kenya's gross capital formation from 1964 to 1977, and just as substantial in the 1980s.[46] World Bank efforts to dismantle this structure and replace it with a more interna-tionally competitive one in the 1980s and 1990s met little success. This is because, as a Bank study in 1994 remarked, "the uneasy yet mutu-ally accommodating relationship between Asian-Kenyan entrepreneurs and African Kenyans in political power created a highly protected, uncompetitive and oligopolistic industrial structure."[47] These "sweet-heart deals" are the opposite of the statistical and political trends in the relationship between the Moi state and export-crop agriculture. The fierce manner in which kinship-based Asian cartels sought to protect their privilege in the face of economic liberalization in the 1990s should not be underestimated.[48]

2 African Entrepreneurship

Oracular, self-confirming observations are amplified in explaining the failure of African entrepreneurs in two periods: following the Second World War, and then after independence in 1963. It bears recalling that, in modern business analysis, wider opportunities and a free, "enabling environment" play a greater role than individual enterprise in explaining commercial success.[49] The racially discriminative nature of colonial business and agrarian law and its impact on Kenyan Africans have been detailed by Yash Ghai and J.P.W.B. McAuslan, while David Throup has described efforts to ameliorate the situation in the closing years of the Mitchell governorship (1948–52) as "too little, too late."[50] In the eyes of the new revisionist history, however, obstruc-tion of African business under colonial rule was a carefully cultivated "myth" – citing as evidence the limited credit and training opportuni-ties open to Africans since the Mitchell years – wholly oblivious to the impact of the systemic injustices of the era and the rebellion they pro-voked in Mau Mau.[51] This anti-African bias is most evident in the analysis of the famous late–1940s struggle between British colonial authorities and the Kikuyu over control of the two dried vegetable factories at Karatina and Kerugoya, cited in history as one contributing factor to the discontent that fuelled the Mau Mau revolt. Fed by Kikuyu outgrowers, and established by the colonial government to supply dried vegetable to the British forces in the Middle East, the firms were a commercial and agricultural success when, in a move that anticipated the problem of state divestiture in the Moi years, the government resisted local demands to transfer total factory ownership to the United Companies of Mumbi, a Kikuyu public company that had collected 600,000 Kenya shillings (51 million at 1994 prices) from ex-soldiers gratuities and farm savings.[52] Pleading lack of business experience among the Kikuyu, and facing an imminent growers' boycott, the government closed the factories in 1946, after a futile "propaganda" campaign (as Rosberg and Nottingham describe it) against the buyers and Kikuyu business capability – as if banishment from business would have given Africans the commercial experience they were said to lack. Against the wider restrictions facing Kenyan Africans in the 1940s, one would judge this degree of determination and funds mobilization as symbolic of entrepreneurial ferment. Indeed it would be worth comparing these funds, as a proportion of Kikuyu incomes, to the savings ratio of demobilized Kenyan Asians and Europeans – not to mention other Africans – that went to the formation of joint-stock public corporations. In the new upside-down world of Kenyan business history, the Kikuyu factory-buying effort is portrayed as evidence of African economic naiveté, and, like among Evans-Pritchard's Azande, the biased but confirmatory *opinion* of colonial propaganda that Kikuyu lacked business experience is itself cited as *evidence* of the new bias that they could not then match the commercial acumen of Asians and Europeans and cannot therefore possibly do so now.

The same strategy is pursued in announcing the demise of the African post-independence business class, solely by dint of its absence in manufacturing and high public office – a result of its enforced economic exile and expropriation under the Moi government, as evidenced by the case of Madhupaper International in 1989.[53] In his 1990 sample of thirty-six successful entrepreneurs in Sub-Saharan Africa, however, Keith Marsden located three Kikuyu-owned firms specializing, respectively, in leather manufacturing, horticultural export, and the hotel industry.[54] As the grip of the Moi government on the agricultural processing sector began to weaken in the 1990s, the result of domestic political pressure and donor conditionally, three African-owned companies opened coffee mills at Thika, near Nairobi.[55] One of the largest financial and trading conglomerates in Eastern Africa, comprising the Insurance Company of East Africa, AM Bank, and First Chartered Securities, was African-owned, and its owner was a candidate for *Forbes* magazine's list of the richest people in the world.[56] To sustain the fiction of consistent African business failure, African commercial success is parried whenever encountered or, in Himbara's case – downplaying the profitable African-run (or owned) Unga Ltd, Alliance Hotels, and Kenya Breweries – attributed to non-African managers. The latter is a typical Lakatos case of ad hoc dodging of refutation since no corresponding credit is given to African managers (or labourers) employed by "successful" Asian firms. Conversely, Himbara and Kaplan see no failed Asian enterprises, though they are well documented by Coughlin, for instance, in the textile sector.[57] Then there is the ultimate irony. Contrary to the supposed African ineptitude, the spectacular binge of early 1990s multinational takeovers – involving Union Carbide, Marshalls Motor Company, Twentieth Century Fox, Firestone International, etc. – by a group of Kenyan Asians in alliance with top Kalenjin politicians, using commandeered state resources, are proudly paraded as "the latest trend in (Kenyan Indian) patterns of accumulation" to illustrate Asian business acumen.[58]

3 Collapsed Parastatals

While not entirely wrong, the popularization, by the Bretton Woods institutions, of the notion that state-owned enterprises were partly responsible for the mounting African fiscal deficit and internal price distortions comes in handy to those with preconceived biases. In a painstaking financial analysis of thirty-two Kenyan public enterprises – covering agriculture, finance, energy, and infrastructure and accounting for 90 per cent of all government-funded corporations in Kenya – Barbara Grosh revealed a wide variation in their performance from 1963 to 1988.[59] Subjected to the criteria of rate of return on investment (i.e., pre-tax profits plus interest payments as a percentage of long-term investment) and using external-audit and other reports, Grosh found that half the companies passed the test of "efficiency and profitability," in some cases (notably in finance, manufacturing, and agricultural processing) outperforming the private sector. In the remaining half of the firms, problems of under-capitalization accounted for more losses than did the much-touted African corruption and mismanagement. Over these years, economically disastrous performance was an isolated phenomenon that had crept in especially during the Moi years. Since the publication of the Grosh book, the ruin of the parastatals has of course accelerated: the Kenya National Assurance,

Kenya Housing Corporation, and Nzoia Sugar Corporation have gone into receivership, as should have the National Bank of Kenya and Kenya Railways. Any objective analysis of the parastatal sector must therefore account for inter-firm variation as well as the managerial differences between the Kenyatta and Moi years. For the picture is infinitely more nuanced than is suggested by the cavalier pronouncement that "hardly any observer had been able to candidly ask the progress, if any, being made by public corporations ... (since) most parastatals existed in name only."[60]

Against the backdrop of the presumed African ingenuity deficit in the public enterprise sector, special mention must be made of the entrepreneurial and innovative capability displayed by Charles Karanja, who, with "a ruthless commitment to efficiency that characterized his career," steered the Kenya Tea Development Authority (KTDA) – the organ of small scale tea farmers – from a fledgling institution in 1964 to become "the world's top producer of quality tea."[61] Under his tenure, foreign managerial assistance fell to nought. At the same time, KTDA unit costs fell by 90 per cent from 1965 to 1988, with farmers earning upwards of 85 per cent of border export tea prices. Not only had smallholder tea production efforts previously failed in South Asia but the Kenyatta government faced stiff opposition from the donors – including the World Bank and the Commonwealth Development Corporation – who had doubts about its financial viability and the competence of African smallholders. Despite much buffeting by the Moi government, household incomes from Kenya tea rose to thrice the national average in 1995. Grosh reports a 4 per cent annual rate of return on capital at KTDA, while a World Bank evaluation estimated KTDA's social cost/benefit ratio at 28 per cent annually; performance in most, though not all, state-run bodies in the banking and industrial sectors outstripped the private sector.[62] However, in Himbara's assessment, backed essentially by press headlines, the record of KTDA and other "state parastatals had ranged from mediocre to total failure."[63]

4 Financial Corruption in Government Ministries

In his umbrage against the 1970s writings promulgating the extreme dependency of Kenya – notably those of Kaplinsky – Leys had noted their tendency to disparage any economic progress involving colonialism and multinational corporations, and their African "auxiliary bourgeoisie," as transitory, unbalanced, and doomed, especially when data indicated otherwise.[64] In the age of right-wing triumphalism, the shoe is now on the other side as, in Azande oracular style, colonialism, international corporations and donor agencies – the World Bank, IMF, Canadian International Development Agency (CIDA) – are portrayed as saviours in comparison to the malignant African development managers and their traditional following. The resulting lack of any sector-based or inter-temporal sense of proportion leads to the most unconscionable conclusions.

Thus even though Kenya's receipts of official development assistance per capita from 1981 to 1985 ($24.30) and aid ratio of GDP (7 per cent) were typically about or below average for Sub-Saharan Africa, the revisionists now contend that Kenya's relative prosperity owed much to special favours from Western donors. Whereas Tignor, looking at the ill-advised European official discrimination against Asian manufacturers after the Second World War, was convinced that "economic and financial experts in (colonial) Kenya were individuals with modest expertise in economics" and management, we are now informed that independent Kenya inherited a "remarkable state apparatus that had successfully marshalled ... development since the 1940s."[65] There is no room here for the well documented corruption of colonial European and Asian civil servants, or for Governor Baring's secret payment of 20,000 UK pounds to Justice Thacker (who returned a guilty verdict against Jomo Kenyatta and his associates at the infamous Kapenguria trial of 1953).[66] Richburg and Himbara lecture Africans on public infrastructure efficiency in South East Asia, oblivious of the congestion and power failure in Bangkok, coastal China, Djakarta, and Manila resulting from what Jim Rohwer, an expert in the region, calls "bad government ... and the colossal sums of expenditure ... inviting proportionally colossal bribes."[67] At this rate, it was only a matter of time before Kenya's monumental Goldenberg scandal, in which the state lost GDP $455 million (12 per cent of GDP) from 1991 to 1993, was foisted by Himbara on African bureaucratic inefficiency in the Kenya Treasury, even though the perpetrators were known to be Kenyan Asian "bankers" in league with the political barons of the ruling Kanu party.[68] Despite corruption at the Nairobi Treasury, such disparagement of Kenya's finance managers does injustice to the well-documented integrity of such officials as Harris Mule and the controller and auditor general, D.G. Njoroge.[69] To put the matter in perspective, not only had the World Bank judged Kenyan public financial management in the 1970s "excellent and particularly praiseworthy" but the IMF was then using Kenyatta's Kenya as a model in its fiscal policy workshops.[70] So much for uniform African financial mismanagement in Kenya since independence.

CONCLUSION: "ARISE LAZARUS!"

From the foregoing, it ought to be evident that credit for economic growth in Kenya could be claimed (if unevenly, depending on the era and the sector) by citizens of African, Asian, and European origin; the destruction that followed "the miracle years" was also wrought by a multiracial but African-led group with prominent Asians and whites. This reduces the significance of culture and race as predictors of overall economic performance and management. Warning about the potential for abuse inherent in the resurrected development literature on "culture" as a determinant of business behaviour, Mick Moore remarks that "the social barriers paradigm is in most respects misconceived, and based on virtual ignorance of the world of business. In so far as the major propositions can be tested, they are empirically false. It appears in retrospect as a classic case of the world being constructed on doctrinal lines to the neglect of evidence."[71] For Africa, especially, it should never be forgotten that this is not the first time that the cultural stereotype has been called upon to explain the continent's relative backwardness (according to Western criteria). As Leys remarked in 1974, speaking of "tribalism" as a peculiarly African affliction: "People (in the past) frankly declared that Negroes had smaller brains."[72] In 1996 an economics professor at the University of New Orleans resumed the defence of the smaller brains thesis, not long after Herrnstein and Murray had propounded the argument that Asian-Americans by a large margin outperformed African-Americans in IQ scores (and economic aptitude), concluding that the cause was essentially genetic.[73] In a sense we are back to square one, and not least due to the incredible chicanery of the predators who claim to rule such states as Kenya, Nigeria, Zaire, and Cameroon and their local and external mentors – all of whom provide ample daily evidence of African caprice and nihilism in the midst of poverty.

Times are hard for Africa, Africans, Africanists, and African studies. This may explain why, apart from isolated cases like Kenya, the growing culture-and-capital debates are not an intellectual priority as yet. Still, Kenya has been a trendsetter more than once. For that reason and for the sheer degree of desperation in African development generally, we must nevertheless continue the search for objective explanations of not only why African countries have fallen so much behind South East Asia in the struggle for economic development but also why there are such glaring differences in material achievement between immigrant groups (like "Asians" and "Lebanese") on the one hand and Africans on the other – and between the African communities themselves.

Economic inequalities at these two levels, and the shrewd manner in which the Moi regime has exploited them for its own ends, lay behind the tragedy of Kenya in the 1990s. Two explanatory factors stand out. At one level, the latitude of a supportive law-driven governance framework, deregulation, and a stable macroeconomic environment, as argued by the World Bank, should not be underestimated whatever one thinks of the IFIs. Secondly, and perhaps more importantly, at the community level "social capital" may be a more appropriate development determinant (especially when added to the right legal and macroeconomic policies) than the amorphous culture. Social capital is premised on the intensity of voluntary civic engagement by private citizens; it is therefore a malleable human artefact; it makes for a rapid "supply response" to new opportunities; and, like physical capital, it is subject to depreciation if not kept in good repair.[74] The interface between these factors may explain better the commercial differences between various "Asian" communities in Kenya as well as the variations in entrepreneurship within African communities. That task is yet to be broached, but it now should be. In its current decrepit status, the last thing the Kenyan economy needs is the inflammatory racial language produced by some of the protagonists, and by their acolytes in Nairobi and North America.

NOTES

1 See the chapters by Michael Cowen, Colin Leys, Raphie Kaplinsky, and John Henley in Martin Fransman (ed.), *Industry and Accumulation in Africa*, London: Heinemann, 1982: 142–231; and the contributions on agrarian capitalism in Kenya by Peter Anyang' Nyong'o, Michael Cowen, Apollo Njonjo, and Mukaru Nganga in *Review of African Political Economy*, no. 20, January 1981.

2 Gavin Kitching "Politics, Method and Evidence in the Kenya Debate," in Henry Bernstein and Bonnie Campbell (eds), *Contradictions of Accumulation in Africa*, London: Sage Publications, 1985. Revisiting the debate in 1994, Colin Leys makes efforts to bring in the dimension of the political strategies of the African capitalists; in Colin Leys "Learning from the Kenya Debate," in David E. Apter and Carl Rosberg (eds), *Political Development and the New Realism in Sub-Saharan Africa*, University Press of Virginia, Charlottesville, 1994: 220–43.

3 See from very different perspectives: Colin Leys, "Learning From the Kenya Debate," Colin Leys and Bruce J. Berman (eds), *African Capitalists in African Development*, Boulder, CO: Lynne Rienner, 1994; Keith Marsden, *African Entrepreneurs: Pioneers in Development*, IFC Discus-

sion Paper no. 9, Washington, DC: World Bank, 1990; and Mamadou
Dia, *Africa's Management in the 1990s and Beyond,* Washington, DC:
World Bank, 1996: 155–219.

4 Writing in 1956, for instance, Ernest A. Vasey, the influential colonial
finance minister, remarked that "the Europeans who brought the technical knowledge and the Asians who came as artisans found an African
people primitive in every sense of the word ... Our European population
was the main spearhead of our development ... Our Asian population
provided largely the distributive and commercial sector of our economy."
See Vasey, "Development: Economic and Political Planning in Kenya,"
East African Economic Review, vol. 2, no. 2 January 1956: 83–4.

5 Robert D. Kaplan, "Continental Drift: Africa's Dysfunctional Politics,"
New Republic, 28 December 1992: 16–18.

6 *International Herald Tribune,* 14 July 1992. This article was extensively
cited by Lee Kwan Yew, the founding leader of modern Singapore, in his
advice to a select group of development-minded African leaders in Singapore in November 1993, according to the *Newsletter of the African
Association of Political Science,* December 1993.

7 David Himbara, *Kenyan Capitalists, the State, and Development,* Boulder, CO, and London: Lynne Reinner, 1994.

8 Ibid., 35.

9 Ibid, 90.

10 Michael Cowen and Scott MacWilliam, *Indigenous Capital in Kenya:
The Indian Dimension of the Debate,* Helsinki: Institute of Development
Studies, 1996.

11 *International Journal of African Historical Studies,* vol. 28, no. 3, 1995:
629; *Foreign Affairs,* vol. 73, no. 6, November 1994. For an informed
and sober dissent on the book, see Henry Rempel's review in *Canadian
Journal of African Studies,* vol. 30, no. 1, 1996, 130–1.

12 See *Economic Review,* (Nairobi) 10 June 1996; *Sunday Nation* (Nairobi),
2 June 1996; BBC African Service, "Focus on Africa," 14 June 1996;
Moyiga Nduru, "Kenya Politics: Asian Community Seeks to Set the
Record Straight," *Interpress Service,* 8 August 1996.

13 E. Evans Pritchard, *Witchcraft, Oracles, and Magic Among the Azande,*
Oxford: Oxford University Press, 1937: 540–1.

14 Karl Popper, *Conjectures and Refutations: The Growth of Scientific
Knowledge,* London: Routledge and Kegan Paul, 1969; and Brain Magee,
Modern British Philosophy, London: Secker and Warburg, 1971: 67–8.

15 Imre Lakatos, "Falsification and the Methodology of Scientific Research
Programs," in I. Lakatos and A. Musgrave (eds), *Criticism and Growth
in Knowledge,* Cambridge University Press, New York, 1970: 91-196.

16 David C. McClelland, *The Achieving Society,* New York: The Free Press,
1961. Anticipating Herrenstein and Murray, *The Bell Curve,* New York:

Free Press, 1994, McClelland (340) berated "primitive cultures," like those of the Yoruba and US "Negroes," for a low n-achievement compared to other ethnic groups.

17 Peter Tamas Bauer and Basil S. Yamey, *The Economics of Under-developed Countries*, Chicago: University of Chicago Press, 1957: 102–3.

18 Masakazu Yamazaki, "Asia, A Civilization in the Making," in *Foreign Affairs*, vol. 75, no. 4, 1996, makes an eloquent case against "Kiplingesque assumptions about an Asian civilization, whose existence it fails to demonstrate" given the extreme cultural and economic diversity that is found in the Asian continent, past and present.

19 H.S. Morris, *The Indians in Uganda*, Chicago: University of Chicago Press, 1968; "Indians in East Africa: A Study in a Plural Society," *British Journal of Sociology*, vol. 7, no. 3, 1956; "Communal Rivalry Among Asians in Uganda," *British Journal of Sociology*, vol. 8, no. 4, 1957. See also Shiva Naipaul, *North of South*, London: Penguin Books, 1978: 117–18, for communal and commercial cleavages among Kenyan Asians.

20 Dorothy McCormick brings this out in "Women in Small-scale Manufacturing: The Case of Nairobi" (Paper read at the Annual Third World Conference, Chicago, Illinois, 1988). This opens the mono-causal race-culture hypothesis to even more absurdities: by its logic Asian women who reproduce and nurture the habits of thrift and hard work in the young could then be accused of deficiency in a business culture.

21 Karl Marx, *Capital, Vol. 1*, Harmondsworth: Penguin Books, 1976: 429–38.

22 Cowen and MacWilliam, *Indigenous Capital in Kenya*, 23–80.

23 Himbara, *Kenyan Capitalists*, 18–19. We also know from the basic methodological texts that data gathering outside a paradigmatic framework is an impossible, even risky, task. See Thomas S. Kuhn, *The Structure of Scientific Revolutions*, Chicago: University of Chicago Press, 1970: 43–51.

24 Himbara, *Kenyan Capitalists*, 51.

25 Peter Coughlin, "Toward a New Industrialization Strategy for Kenya," in Peter Coughlin and G.K. Ikiara (eds), *Industrialization in Kenya*, Nairobi: Heinemann, 1988: 275–302.

26 See "Manufacturing Myths," *The Economist*, 9 November 1991.

27 World Bank, *Kenya: Re-investing in Stabilization and Growth*, Washington, DC: The World Bank, 1992: 184.

28 David Leonard, *African Successes: Four Public Managers in Kenya's Rural Development*, Berkeley: University of California Press, 1991: 1.

29 Himbara, *Kenyan Capitalists*, xi; firstly as we shall see, the bluster of the Moi government against corruption in organized agriculture need never

be taken at face value. Neither the Coffee Growers Association (an effective farmers' lobby deregistered by Moi in 1988) nor the KTDA ever were "regulatory agencies." At the same time that research in the agricultural sector was said to be impossible, Barabara Grosh was completing her outstanding Berkeley dissertation that included a detailed survey of agricultural parastatals, whose results contradict the theme of African mediocrity. This author was working on the structural transformation of the coffee sector from 1986 to 1990.

30 Judith Heyer, *Kenya: Monitoring Living Conditions and Consumption Patterns*, Geneva: UN Research Institute for Social Development, 1990: 85-6.

31 Robert M. Solow, "Technical Progress and the Aggregate Production Function," *Review of Economics and Statistics*, no. 39, 1957.

32 World Bank, *Into the Second Decade,* Baltimore: Johns Hopkins University Press, 1975: 29.

33 M.G. Phelps and Bernard Wasow, "Measuring Protection and Its Effects on Kenya," Nairobi: IDS working paper no. 37, 1972.

34 FAO, *Production Yearbook*, 1979–89. Central Province statistics from *Coffee Board of Kenya Annual Reports*, 1979–89.

35 Barbara Grosh, "Performance of Agricultural Public Enterprises: Lessons from the First Two Decades of Independence," *East African Economic Review*, vol. 3, no. 1, 1987: 43.

36 Bjorn Gyllstrom, *State Administered Rural Change: Agricultural Cooperatives in Rural Kenya,* London: Routledge, 1991: 7, 170–84.

37 M.O. Schapiro and S. Wainaina, "Kenya: A Case Study of Production and Export of Horticultural Commodities," in World Bank, *Successful Developments in Africa,* EDI Policy Series, no. 1, Washington, DC: World Bank, 1989.

38 Jennifer Sharpley and Stephen Lewis, "Kenya: Manufacturing Sector to the Mid–1980s," in Roger C. Riddell (ed.), *Manufacturing Africa,* London: James Currey, 1990: 213.

39 *Financial Times*, 20 June 1996.

40 Himbara, *Kenyan Capitalists,* 138–40.

41 World Bank, *Kenya Growth and Structural Change,* Washington, DC: World Bank, 1983: xix.

42 Arvind Barve, *The Foreign Trade of Kenya,* Nairobi: Transafrica Publishers, 1984: 65–77.

43 Sharpley and Lewis, "Kenya; Manufacturing Sector to the Mid–1980s," 214.

44 Cowen and MacWilliam, *Indigenous Capital in Kenya,* 122–4.

45 D.L. Bevan, P. Collier, and J.W. Gunning, "Consequences of a Commodity Boom in a Controlled Economy: Accumulation and Redistribution in Kenya," *World Bank Economic Review*, vol. 1, no. 3, 1987.

46 Jennifer Sharpley, "Resource Transfer Between the Agricultural and Non-Agricultural Sectors," in Tony Killick (ed.), *Papers on the Kenyan Economy*, Nairobi: Heinemann, 1981.

47 Gurushri Swamy, "Kenya: Patchy, Intermittent Reform," in Ishrat Hussein and Rashid Faruqee (eds), *Adjustment in Africa: Lessons and Country Case Studies*, Washington, DC: World Bank, 1994: 198.

48 See Peter Coughlin, "Toward a New Industrialization Strategy for Kenya," 281–2; and "US Businessman Gambles on Kenya," *USA Today*, 30 October 1995, for the extent to which some of the Asian companies will go to ward off competition.

49 See from very different yet relevant historical circumstances, David Landes, *The Unbound Prometheus*, Cambridge: Cambridge University Press, 1970: 15–25. The World Bank's *World Development Report, 1991*: 70–87, estimated that returns of capital investment could be raised by as much as 50–200 per cent by the elimination of policy and institutional distortions.

50 Yash P. Ghai and J.P.W.B. McAuslan, *Public Law and Political Change in Kenya*, Nairobi: Oxford University Press, 1970: 97–124; and David W.Throup, *Economic and Social Origins of Mau Mau*, London: James Currey, 1987: 209-19.

51 Himbara, *Kenyan Capitalists*, 75-6; compared to Greet Kershaw, *Mau Mau From Below*, London: James Currey, 1997: 122–3, 133–4.

52 Carl G. Rosberg and John Nottingham, *The Myth of Mau Mau: Nationalism in Kenya*, Nairobi: East African Publishing House, 1966: 235–7; David F. Gordon, *Decolonization and the State in Kenya*, Boulder, CO, and London: Westview Press, 1986: 223–4; John Spencer, *James Beauttah: Freedom Fighter*, Nairobi: Stellascope Publishers, 1983: 57–8. Beauttah was treasurer of the United Companies of Mumbi and a prominent official of Kikuyu Central Association and the Kenya African Union.

53 *Weekly Review*, 31 March 1989, 10-16.

54 Keith Marsden, *African Entrepreneurs*, 34, 53, 65.

55 *Economic Review*, 29 January 1996.

56 *Economic Review*, 15 January 1996, 12.

57 Peter Coughlin, "Gradual Maturation of an Import-Substitution Industry," in P. Coughlin and G.K. Ikiara (eds), *Kenya's Industrialization Dilemma*, Nairobi: Heinemann, 1991: 127–52.

58 Compare Himbara, *Kenya Capitalists*, 65-6, with "The New Capitalism and its Cronies," *Africa Confidential*, 2 December 1994, and "Sacrificial Lambs if Moi Fails," *Africa Analysis*, 11 December 1992.

59 Barbara Grosh, *Public Enterprises in Kenya; What Works, What Doesn't and Why?*, Boulder, CO, and London: Lynne Rienner, 1991.

60 David Himbara, "Myths and Realities in Kenyan Capitalism," *Journal of Modern African Studies*, vol. 31, no. 1, 1993: 97–8.

61 Leonard, *African Successes*, 131.

62 Grosh, *Public Enterprise in Kenya*, 34–6, 56–90, 105–17.

63 Himbara, *Kenyan Capitalists*, xi and 51.

64 Colin Leys, "Kenya: What Does Dependency Explain?" in Fransman, *Industry and Accumulation*, 230.

65 Robert Tignor, "Race, Nationality and Industrialization in Decolonizing Kenya," *International Journal of African Historical Studies*, vol. 21, no. 1, 1993: 33; and Himbara, *Kenyan Capitalists*, 154.

66 Richard Frost, *Race Against Time*, London: Rex Collings, 1978: 39, 44; Charles Douglas-Home, *Evelyn Baring: The Last Proconsul*, London: William Collins, 1978: 247. This of course does not excuse corruption in the African District Councils, also well recorded.

67 Jim Rohwer, *Asia Rising*, New York: Simon and Schuster, 1995: 267.

68 See Sarah Elderkin's detailed investigative reports in *Daily Nation*, 1–9 August 1993; also *The Independent* (London), 8 June 1993.

69 Leonard, *African Successes*, 183–201.

70 World Bank, *Kenya: Into the Second Decade*, 42; and IMF, *Financial Policy Workshop: The Case of Kenya*, Washington, DC: IMF, 1981.

71 Mick Moore, "Societies, Polities and Capitalists in Developing Societies," *Journal of Development Studies*, vol. 33, no. 3, 1997.

72 Colin Leys, *Underdevelopment in Kenya*, London: Heinemann, 1974: 198.

73 See *Chronicle of Higher Education*, 1 November 1996. Richard Herrnstein and Charles Murray's *The Bell Curve*, 288–9, states that African IQs are probably inferior to those of Asian Americans.

74 Robert Putnam, *Making Democracy Work: Civic Traditions in Modern Italy*, Princeton: Princeton University Press, 1993.

World Economy: Ideologies, Perspectives, and Strategies for Change

Introduction

In part three, we turn our attention to strategic questions in the politics of transformation. These articles address global hegemonic forces and institutions, the politics of justice, and the theory and practice of social movements.

Manfred Bienefeld's "Development Theory: A New Hegemonic Ideology?" asks a provocative question. Why is it that, over recent decades, a concept "so weak and implausible" as the neoliberal "manufactured consensus that both reflects and rationalizes the accelerating advance of market forces around the world" could claim pride of hegemonic place in development policy and theory? Bienefeld considers what is necessary for an ideology to obtain hegemony. He then proceeds to examine the content of the pro-market bent of development theory in detail and, in the process, unravels its contradictions. While convinced of the need for radical transformation, Bienefeld also explores the difficulties and constraints involved in creating an effective alternative to the destructive forces of the global market.

In the next article in this section, Abigail B. Bakan considers the world system from the perspective of global trade and investment arrangements. In "Capital, Marxism, and World Economy: APEC and the MAI," she makes the case for a Marxist analysis of the global market, focusing on two particular multinational trade organizations. The MAI and APEC were inspired by an ideological celebration of the market, and a revamped commitment to modernization theory. The success of popular opposition in promoting the demise of the Multilateral Agreement on Investment (MAI) was a contributing factor in the emergence of a movement for global justice that found its voice in Seattle against the World Trade Organization meetings at the end of 1999. The Asia Pacific Economic Co-operation group (APEC) was initiated in 1989 to ensure increasing free trade in an era of the "miraculous" growth of the Asian economies. As we enter a new millennium, the Asian miracle has been replaced by crisis, and one of APEC's principle host states, Indonesia, has seen its once powerful dictator, Suharto, toppled through popular revolt. Bakan makes "a general case for a Marxist analysis of international trade and investment agreements in the contemporary system" and at the same time provides "a particular consideration of the applicability of such an approach to APEC and the MAI."

Phil Goldman, in "Amnesty: An Essay in Law and Politics," shifts our attention from the economic to the juridical realm. He presents a series of observations and reflections "on the problems of doing justice to victims of political violence." Goldman focuses on amnesty not only in its formal definition; he also pursues its implications for legal inquiry and in terms of the centrality of violence in the political realm. This is an article that combines tragic personal experience with insightful inquiry regarding the pursuit of human justice. Goldman considers the juridical and political context of memories of political violence and concludes with a particular focus on conditions in post-apartheid South Africa.

The remaining two articles in this section look at the prospects and problems of social movements, in theory and in practice. In "The Rise and Fall of New Social Movement Theory?" Laurie E. Adkin considers both the "prophesy" of new social movement theory (NSMT) as it was presented in the 1970s and the 1990s argument that challenges NSMT for being "nothing but nostalgia." Adkin takes issue with both interpretations. She takes us through an impressive review of several decades of debates in the literature, paying particular attention to the theoretical contributions inspired by Alain Touraine and to social movement experiences in France and Ontario, Canada.

In the final article in this section, "The Social Economy of Québec: Discourse and Strategies," Marguerite Mendell considers the implications of a particular example in radical social movement practice. She explores the labour movement's community economic initiatives in Québec. Mendell edited a collection with Colin Leys in 1992 (*Culture and Social Change*) that resulted from an exchange among social movement activists and academics from Ontario and Québec. Here, she picks up the thread of the Québec context. Mendell identifies the June 1995 Women's March Against Poverty as an important turning point. Moreover, she sees important social and theoretical implications to this new dialogue. According to Mendell, the notion that a free market economy "would replace indolence with innovation, dependency with entrepreneurship" has been fundamentally shaken through the Québec experience.

From the macro level of the world economy to the micro level of the lived experiences of victims of political violence and the strategic orientations of social actors, this section addresses some of the most central practical issues in the project of critical political studies. While diverse in substance, these articles share an engagement in the challenge of achieving a world where social justice is not only a passing thought but at the centre of society's priorities.

Development Theory:
A New Hegemonic Ideology?

MANFRED BIENEFELD

In the last twenty years, development theory, like development policy, has been overwhelmed by a manufactured consensus that both reflects and rationalizes the accelerating advance of market forces around the world. But, no matter how often the universality of this new hegemonic ideology is proclaimed, skepticism remains widespread outside of the corridors of power. This is likely to remain so as long as the resulting policies continue to wreak havoc with so many people's lives, and as long as the theoretical, empirical, and historical foundations of this ideology remain so weak and implausible. Indeed, what needs to be explained is how such a tendentious, selective and, implausible account of global change could provide the intellectual foundations for the reassertion of a discredited, fundamentalist version of bourgeois ideology?

To be hegemonic, an ideology must provide people with a way of understanding the world that leads them to accept the legitimacy of the existing order, either because it is deemed relatively desirable and just or because it is regarded as natural or beyond challenge. In either case, the existence of such an ideology – by ensuring that fundamental critiques of the status quo will appear perverse, misguided, or unrealistic – allows social and political stability to be maintained with a minimum of coercion. That is why the celebration of the development of a global market economy is backed by two complementary claims: globalization is good for us because it promotes growth and enhances human welfare; and it is inevitable, hence it is foolish to stand in the way of these historic forces for progress. There is little doubt that this view appears to be assuming hegemonic status in the mid 1990s, as more and more people seem to be persuaded of its wisdom or resigned to its coercive inevitability. Increasingly unable to imagine a successful alternative, the opposition's ranks are thinning, while those of the cynics, the defeatists, and the hucksters are swelling. As globalization comes to be more and more universally espoused by democratically elected governments around the world, it may seem as if the "end of history" is at hand. But those preparing to celebrate this ultimate victory of bourgeois ideology have forgotten that history is a dialectical process; every action begets a reaction.

Although these naive neoliberal dreams are bound to be disappointed, that is no longer simply a cause for celebration since the relentless pursuit of those dreams over so many years has, by now, created imbalances and contradictions that will prove difficult, costly, and dangerous to resolve. If we are lucky, Polanyi's "double movement" may see societies rebuild their capacity to manage competitive markets in the public interest, after only a brief period of limited political instability and conflict. If we are not, we stand on the threshold of a darker age, in which insecurity will feed intolerance, fear will breed hate, and the consequent repression will fuel fanaticism and cynicism; although it is also bound to call into existence new reservoirs of heroism and idealism. History, in other words, is very much alive, and in grave danger of repeating itself.

As the spectre of ungovernability looms, the claims made in the name of the neoliberal[1] ideology are being constantly adjusted. The positive claim that it is irrational to oppose the neoliberal agenda because it is known to serve the public interest is becoming less prominent in the face of persistent and growing economic instability, rising inequality, and the progressive dilution of substantive democratic rights. Meanwhile the negative assertions that there is no alternative and that opposition to this agenda is futile in today's world are in the ascendant. Unfortunately this shift is also reflected in the actions that are taken to buttress this rhetoric. Thus, aid flows have declined so far that they are now lower (as a proportion of GDP) than at any time since the 1950s, in spite of evidence showing that poverty and inequality remain chronic, and growing, problems. At the same time, increasing efforts are going into the construction of institutional and regulatory mechanisms that are, in part, explicitly designed to lock in those neoliberal reforms by exposing countries that are not prepared to provide a level playing field for private corporations to the threat of escalating international sanctions. In the background, there is growing evidence that, if political tensions continue to rise, large parts of the bourgeoisie will be prepared to shed its liberal veneer and welcome an iron fist that promises to restore order, profitability, and their right to enjoy their accumulated wealth, undisturbed by those nasty and disheveled homeless people or by the beggars overrunning the city streets. Their preferred solutions to such problems are increasingly clear: gated, secure communities; a proliferation of private schools, clubs, resorts, and shopping centres; tough law enforcement to "clear the streets" of riff-raff; permanent curfews for juveniles; draconian "three strikes and you're out" laws; and overflowing prisons that become profit centres for major corporations.[2]

If there is a victory that lies at the end of that road, it is surely a pyrrhic one – a hollow victory of form over substance. While such societies may appear peaceful on the surface, and although their crime rates may be suppressed for a time, this will not be a society at peace. It will not be a society in which the dominant ideology could claim to be hegemonic, because that would be true only if it were able to secure the willing consent of the governed to a degree that allowed existing social and economic structures to function and to reproduce themselves with a minimum of coercion. Instead, in such societies, coercion is bound to become an ever more prominent control mechanism. Indeed, in such societies, coercion is presently becoming increasingly important. I refer to, especially, the silent coercion embedded in overflowing prison systems; the coercion implicit in the proliferation of homelessness, poverty and hunger; and the coercion and intimidation associated with more aggressive policing, and with the explosive growth of private security systems and guards, as well as the relentless expansion of "private spaces," in which citizens' rights are often sharply curtailed. There is little indication that these trends are about to be reversed. In fact they appear to be intensifying in the late 1990s.

That is the situation in the industrial world; the developing world is far more polarized and unstable. In most places, the neoliberal ideology may be dominant, but it is not even close to being hegemonic. In fact, the gulf between the official discourse and popular opinion is widening almost everywhere, especially now that the "Asian miracle" has been so badly tarnished by a maelstrom of financial instability. Certainly, both in the developing world and in the transition economies of Eastern Europe, the early euphoria that followed democratization in the 1980s and early 1990s has given way to more sober assessments of the narrow limits within which these democratic rights are exercised when economies are so deeply integrated into an increasingly unstable world economy.

In a growing number of developing countries, the threat of serious social or political instability is not merely a hypothetical possibility. In many it has already arrived; and in many others it looms ominously on the horizon, as the contradictions continue to grow. In this context the neoliberal ideology's erstwhile dreams of hegemony are rapidly receding. The truth will come out. The emperor is naked; the promises are empty; the new mountains of (bond) debt are reaching to the heavens; and large numbers of banks are teetering on the edge, as wildly inflated stock and property markets discover the laws of financial gravity. And to all of this, the high priests of neoliberalism have only one response: "More of the same!" At first glance, they may be reminiscent of the gambler mortgaging his house to raise the stakes in a desperate effort to recover previous losses, but, on closer inspection, it becomes clear that it is casino operators who are promoting this "solution." This should not come as a great surprise, since they are "doing very well" out of the present situation, and since their proposed solution would give them even greater freedom to exercise their judgments, free from "political meddling" or "interference" from those who do not share their priorities and values. What should be surprising is that their advice is still taken so seriously. But, here too, that is now almost entirely due to their power to punish those who fail to do so, and not to the strength or persuasiveness of the claim that their activities will serve the public interest, as neoliberal ideology would suggest.

Even Asia, yesterday's shining beacon of hope, the (largely mythical) market-driven model to which all were supposed to aspire, has been transformed almost overnight into a place where statist intervention and corruption prevail. The Mexican minister of finance is suddenly giving advice to the Thais, and no-one is laughing – yet. But the balloon is bleeding air and the hot air of promises is barely keeping things aloft. Hegemony is not on the cards any longer, no matter how often the mantra of liberalization is repeated. It is time to ask: What story will come next? And can the rising opposition be united by a counter-hegemonic ideology? Those questions will accompany us into the new millennium. They are the same questions that ushered in the one that is now dying. No wonder the belief in progress lies in tatters.

At this juncture, a counter-hegemonic ideology has one central task, namely, to rebuild the foundations for social solidarity in order to increase the scope for collective action in the public interest. Unfortunately, to do that, we must change the world; and to change the world we need social solidarity and collective action. In short, we need both Hegel and Marx; but, most importantly, we need hope, idealism, and courage. In one sense, we might say that "society now needs a long-run communalism to supplement its short-run individualism."[3] In another, we might say that we need to restore the balance of power to rebuild the material foundations for a new ideology. We need a revolution to reverse the right-wing revolution that has shifted power so radically and so unwisely into the hands of private property and finance and that has undermined public authorities, collective rights, and the very ideals of an encompassing citizenship that implies a shared, mutual responsibility for one's fellow citizens. Instead we are reduced to consumers and clients, whose rights are largely measured by their ability to pay, in a world where income disparities have exploded in an orgy of greed and excess. No wonder even those who are leading us into this wilderness are occasionally heard to wonder whether it can last. Well, the answer is: No! It cannot last. But what will come after is far from clear; although we do know that, whatever it is, it will be largely determined by us, as citizens.

FAST FORWARD TO THE PAST: THE RISE OF THE NEW "OLD" HEGEMONIC IDEOLOGY

The extent of the transformation that has occurred in the global economic policy debate since the Second World War, and in the hegemonic ideology within which that debate is embedded, is difficult to exaggerate. It all began with the initial Bretton Woods Agreement, which sought to lay the foundations for a stable and liberal global economy. However, it did so on the basis of a cautious Keynesian/New Deal consensus: it was essential to design a system that would protect the world from the destabilizing international capital flows and the unrestrained speculative bubbles that had, in the past, made economies so unmanageable that euphoric prosperity had become the midwife of depression and war. That is why that initial agreement had made provision for permanent capital controls, and why its architects had opted for the relatively inflexible par-value system[4] to govern exchange rate movements.

In stark contrast to this postwar understanding of the international political economy and the desire of the new order's architects for monetary and exchange rate stability, a recent history of the international monetary system, commissioned by the IMF to commemorate its fiftieth anniversary, clearly welcomes the return to the conditions of the nineteenth century that has occurred over the past decades. Its author even describes the nineteenth century as "the golden age" and argues that "[t]he very rapid development of international financial markets has been more effective than the intentions of politicians or the discussions of technocrats in obliging governments to rethink their approach to policy. The world is moving once again, after an interruption of three quarters of a century, closer to the free international flow of capital that characterized the era of prosperity and stability at the end of the nineteenth century."[5] In one important sense, the author is quite right. These changes did not happen on the basis of some rational decision making process, democratic or otherwise. They did not happen because the world had reached a better understanding of the economic process, or because there had been a decision to alter our social or political priorities. They happened because some people, institutions, and interests were able to take advantage of ambiguous rules, of contradictions, and of complacency to advance their interests. Their actions changed things gradually, often by default; but, over time, the steady dismantling of certain safeguards and rules accelerated the policy drift that served to further enhance the power of those interests.[6] In time, the process comes to feed on itself, as old policy instruments are overwhelmed by increasingly unstable markets, even as armies of myopic economists grossly misuse their static models of perfect competition to derive real-world policy prescriptions that extol the long-term virtues of the competitive market to a degree that goes far beyond anything that their theories could legitimately support.[7] Ironically, the indefensible policy prescriptions that result from this process often appear to be validated by subsequent events because they turn into self-fulfilling prophecies, as when the pervasive deregulation of international financial markets actually destroys the utility of previously important and effective economic policy instruments, making the task of prudent national macroeconomic management far more difficult.

All of this puts a greater premium on the effective supervision of global markets, but the institutions charged with that task are both misconceived and inadequate. That is true for a number of reasons: first, they are not embedded in, or guided by, any meaningful political process that could legitimate the value judgments, the priorities, or the risks embedded in their regulatory actions or their policy prescriptions; second, the markets that they have been asked to regulate are too complex and too anarchic to be regulated effectively, and a law can only be effectively, or efficiently, enforced when most people choose to obey it because they understand it to be in the social interest, and therefore in their interest; and, third, institutions must ultimately exercise control through the very same national authorities whose capacities have been so sharply eroded. Thus, " the influence of the institution [the IMF] at the heart of the international financial system [now] depends largely on its ability to provide speedy, accurate, and persuasive economic analysis. This is the consequence of the emergence of capital markets, which make it impossible for the international system, to police and control national policies, as it had done until the 1960s."[8]

In such a world, it becomes increasingly difficult to address impending crises, because the mere discussion of such a possibility could trigger the crisis that is to be averted. Indeed, "the difficulty posed to policy discussions by the sensitivity of markets and the volatility of international capital." is thought to be a "particularly acute problem" now facing the IMF.[9] And such problems loom even larger for a national government that might wish to consider the reintroduction of capital controls to curb the destructive effects of destabilizing, speculative flows of "hot money." These could be severely punished by those same capital markets for even considering such a possibility. In this way, policy instruments that might have been economically beneficial, or that might be preferred on social or distributional grounds, have been ruled out because inferior policies have allowed the world to change in ways that make them increasingly ineffective. At some point, those inferior policies thus come to appear justified because, by then, "there is no alternative." Such self-fulfilling prophecies abound, especially in the developing world.

The extent of the change that has occurred in the hegemonic ideology's definition of what constitutes sound economic policy is truly stunning. Arthur Lewis, writing about economic policy choices soon after the Second World War, began a monograph entitled *The Principles of Economic Planning* by listing the main reasons why excessively deregulated markets will be dynamically inefficient and socially undesirable in the real world. He concludes this very brief summary as follows: "It has been possible to state the counts in this indictment of laissez-faire so briefly because they are now accepted by most serious political thinkers. There are no longer any believers in laissez-faire, except on the lunatic fringe. There are many who denounce planning in fierce language, and who appear by implication to be arguing for laissez-faire, but, on closer inspection there are always a few pages ... which give the game away. The truth is that we are all planners now."[10] And these views helped to usher in a world in which relatively sovereign national governments were allowed to make pragmatic use of a wide range of economic policy instruments that would allow them to stay close to their full employment growth paths. In the politically charged atmosphere of the day, there simply seemed to be no alternative. Indeed, in the context of Western Europe's reconstruction, it has been said that "high and increasing output, increasing foreign trade, full employment, industrialization and modernization had become ... inescapable policy choices, because governments could find no other basis for political consensus."[11] And much the same could have been said about the developing world, especially in those places where national independence struggles had only recently given people the opportunity to manage their own national economies. Of course, in these latter cases, the obstacles tended to be greater, and the possibility of failure, more real.

Under these conditions, pragmatism ruled supreme. Indeed, the Bretton Woods institutions played only a marginal role in Western Europe's reconstruction, largely because their assistance would have required recipient governments to abandon many of the policy instruments they were using so successfully to rebuild their economies and to manage their precarious political balances. While "Bretton Woods depended on the concepts of universality, equality, and progressive liberalisation,"[12] it soon turned out that the resulting rules and "institutions ... were fundamentally unsuited to the combination of the political climate of the early Cold War and the prevalence and persistence of the managed exchange and trade regimes inherited from the 1930s and the experience of the war. The Marshall Plan, and the initiatives associated with it ... produced a much more effective immediate mechanism for promoting recovery."[13]

Moreover, the important point about Marshall Aid was not only that it provided the reconstructing economies with grant aid to relieve the balance of payments problems created by their rapid growth but that "it allowed ... governments to continue to pursue by means of an extensive array of trade and payments controls the extremely ambitious, expansionist domestic policies which had provoked the 1947 payments crisis."[14] Moreover, the rapid and sustained growth that resulted from this enforced pragmatism was a critically important aspect of the period of unprecedented growth and prosperity that characterized the global economy for the largest part of the quarter century from 1948 to 1973. The contrast with the gloomy and ultimately disastrous aftermath of World War I could not have been greater. It is a sobering thought that this "golden age" came as an almost complete surprise to almost everyone – and that we do not appear to have learned much from the experience. A generation later pragmatism has once more given way to the ideological fervor of those whose faith in markets appears to know no bounds. They also seem destined to be thoroughly surprised by what the future will bring, only this time it is unlikely to be a pleasant surprise.

Gradually growth, prosperity, and domestic stability allowed more and more countries to enter into the internationalist spirit of Bretton Woods, but, once again, they did so gradually and pragmatically. Trade barriers were gradually lowered, leaving plenty of room for exceptions and for flexibility; currencies became gradually convertible, but capital controls remained in place for a long time; foreign direct investment was encouraged, but in ways that allowed recipient countries considerable freedom in managing the nature of its links to their domestic industrial structure; and exchange rates continued to be managed within a par-value system, which sought to reduce instability by giving governments an incentive to manage their domestic economies within that given framework.

Once the decision had been taken to go for fixed exchange rates, both the need for, and the nature of international economic management followed logically from the conventional wisdom of the day about domestic economic management. The major countries had a collective responsibility to maintain the right level of demand in the world economy as a whole ... if the risks were on the inflationary side, it was the countries with balance-of-payments deficits that should take restrictive action. And if the risks were on the deflationary side, it was the countries in balance-of-payments surplus that should take expansionary action. This was the logical thread running through the Bretton Woods agreements, echoes of which could still be heard in the 1970s.[15]

Unfortunately, although "this approach seemed to be working rather well ... in the 1950s and 1960s," national economies did not manage their domestic economies to avoid the emergence of underlying imbalances and tensions.[16] In time, this led to a dramatic policy reversal.

It would be hard to exaggerate how completely this conventional wisdom about international economic management had been overturned by the early 1980s – although this is still often obscured by ritual references to the virtues of economic cooperation ... The slogan ... became: "If each country gets its fundamentals right, the world will look after itself".

This change in the conceptual approach to international cooperation was part of a wider change in attitude toward the management of free-market economies, which is well captured in the aphorism: "Governments do not solve problems, they are the problem." At the international level, moreover, the case for the ... [earlier] ... approach was to some extent undermined by its own apparently brilliant success. As a quarter of a century rolled by with almost uninterrupted growth, expanding trade, and no major breakdowns, memories of the horrors of the 1930s faded.[17]

The apparent ease with which this consensus was so dramatically transformed, despite the palpable, long-term success of the previous policy regime, is extraordinary and should serve as a cautionary tale for those who want to believe that economics is a science that progresses over time to a higher understanding of the economic process. In this case, it was not just the speed of the transformation that raises questions on this score, it was also the fact that the new consensus was virtually identical to the one that had been so reluctantly abandoned in the aftermath of the disastrous events of the 1920s and the depression that followed.

The noneconomist historian, reviewing this period, might well be tempted to draw rather unflattering conclusions about our profession. Using our own terminology, he might unkindly suggest that the elasticity of conventional economic wisdom with respect to events appears, after a lag, to have been very close to one. He might raise doubts as to whether, on the record, economics has yet become a science that can assimilate new observations constructively into an agreed body of thought. Or, trying to be fair, he might suggest that if there is such a body of progressively evolving established doctrine, then economists appear to have been singularly unsuccessful in getting it across to public opinion and political leaders.[18]

In fact, this historian should ask a different question: one that would lead the author to enter the realm of political economy, and thus reach a better understanding of such transformations. The truth is that hegemonic ideologies must constantly evolve, partly in order to ensure that the systemic picture which they present to the world remains sufficiently widely accepted for them to remain hegemonic, and partly because the picture that they present must ultimately be compatible with a reality that is, itself, constantly changing in response to shifts in the balance of power between various economic, social, and political actors. To ensure that things are not too simple, the two dimensions of this process are interdependent, so that the weakening, or the consolidation, of a hegemonic ideology will, in turn, affect the balance of forces that will ultimately help to shape the real world.

In this case, the central driving forces behind this reconstruction of the hegemonic ideology are to be found in the interest of the United States, whose economic position was eroding dangerously by the early 1970s,[19] and in the interests of capital, which saw its power eroding, along with its rates of return, because it was forced to reach explicit, politically derived compromises with other interest groups in its relatively sovereign "home states." In addition, capital was also faced with less serious, but increasingly worrisome, nationalist challenges from more and more developing countries, as governments learned to defend their national interests more effectively in bargaining over natural resource rents, market access, and technology transfer.

The counter-attack took many forms and proceeded on a variety of fronts. By the end of the 1960s capital was beleaguered and on the defensive, hemmed in by national governments, trade unions, and an increasingly vocal civil society demanding change on many fronts, including, among others, the environment, nuclear disarmament, poverty and international development. By the end of the 1970s, the world had been transformed: by the oil crisis, the explosive growth of the Eurocurrency markets, and the effective demise of the Bretton Woods system of international policy coordination. Violent fluctuations in the main economic variables had created such instability that political compromises and the mechanisms for national economic management were simply swept away. Not only did the economic policy instruments that had served the world so well for more than twenty years cease to function in this newly turbulent world but that turbulence immediately proceeded to generate mountains of debt – private debt, corporate debt, consumer debt, public sector debt – with consequences that would prove even more disastrous in the years to come.

By the end of the 1980s, this process had produced "the lost development decade" in Africa and Latin America and the "Reagan boom" in the US, the latter being the mirror image of the former. In the words of the IMF's historian of the world monetary system, the "bizarre combination of fiscal stimulus and monetary restraint" that had driven real interest rates to extortionate levels by 1981, had "created one of the most serious recessions in modern times."[20] Moreover, these policies had pushed the US "onto a course that distorted the international distribution of growth and the whole international order."[21] Debtors were crucified in this process, and none more so than the indebted developing world; but the turn of the industrial country governments would come soon enough. For now, as massive quantities of finance started flowing out of the developing world into the US, the US government denied any responsibility. Paul Volcker, then head of the Federal Reserve and in many respects the initial architect of those high real interest rates, had become seriously concerned about the adverse consequences of US economic policy by 1983. His warnings that the continued rise of the value of the dollar would create major problems fell on deaf ears. Later he would write in his diary: "Yet there was an administration that simply didn't seem to care ... the strength of the dollar came to be cited by some officials as a kind of Good Housekeeping Seal of Approval provided by the market, honoring sound Reagan economic policies."[22]

This party would not end for some time. No wonder it was fashionable to celebrate the magic of the market in Washington in those days, although what was happening was not magic at all. It was simply extortion on a grand scale. The simple extraction of money, massive as it was, turned out to be the least important aspect of these events. The far more important aspect was the use to which the creditors would put the leverage they now had over these hapless debtors. In fact, this leverage became the central instrument for promoting, and ultimately installing, the new hegemonic ideology in much of the developing world. Indeed, given the circumstances under which this miracle was achieved in the developing world, and the extent of the apparent success of the transplant, it now frequently appears as if the truths of the development debate have come to constitute the core of the new hegemonic ideology that now rules the world. There is a small element of truth in this assertion. The developing world has indeed been used shamelessly as a laboratory by radical neoliberal policy wonks, and many developing country governments now espouse these policies with considerable ferocity. Ultimately there can be no doubt, however, that this ideology has been promoted most aggressively from the centre of global economy. Those who have benefitted the most turn out to have been its most persistent supporters. No mystery there, either.

In fact, the most revealing and most important common denominators that underlie all of the processes through which capital has restored its dominance in the global economy involve the systematic promotion of private property rights over public rights and the privileging of individual over collective and social rights. James's history of the IMF agrees. "The redefinition of the Fund's role reflects a general shift in the global allocation of responsibilities between the public and the private spheres, with an increasing preponderance of the latter – the general transfer of ... choice to the collective outcomes of millions of independent decisions."[23]

Of course those independent decisions that now account for more and more "choices," are made strictly in accordance with the effective purchasing power wielded by those countless individuals. This is an important caveat in a world in which income disparities have grown so dramatically, both between rich and poor countries and between individuals within countries. In the US, an index of social well being that has been published by Fordham University for many years, has fallen to 38 in the mid 1990s. It stood at 73 under Nixon/Ford; then fell to 43 under Reagan; and suffered further small declines under both Bush and Clinton.[24] The reality is that most working people around the world are experiencing increasing social and economic insecurity, very large numbers are seeing declines in wages and incomes, and virtually all are witnessing a steady decline in the social and economic infrastructure. It is here that we must seek the reason why the world's hegemonic ideology has returned to the crude homilies of nineteenth-century individualism. A hegemonic ideology that has to make such a deplorable and contradictory reality acceptable can only do so by presenting it as the inevitable result of impersonal forces that people are both powerless and foolish to oppose and that will, in any case, serve their best interests in the long run, if they are wise enough to let them run their course. Such a reality could not be made acceptable to most people if it were seen as the direct result of conscious policy choice. That is the reason why the ideology of the nineteenth century turns out to be so surprisingly suitable for an age that is, in every other respect, so utterly different. The similarity lies in the underlying realities that are to be rationalized.

Moreover, if the expansion of private property rights, to the detriment of public or collective rights, does lie at the heart of the current global transformation, then the nation-state, in some form or another, moves to center stage, since public rights have long been largely constituted primarily within the framework of such states. It should thus come as no surprise that the nation-state has become a central focus for the hostility of those anxious to promote the expansion of private power. A 1994 *Business Week* editorial provides some insight into the reasons why this is so. The editorial urges President Clinton to accept that "the main element in any U.S. foreign policy must now be 'enlargement' – [the] unyielding promotion of an open global-market economy," but warns him that, in order "to guarantee the spread of market economies overseas, the U.S. must also contain the forces of reaction" which "won't be easy ... [because] those dispossessed on the road to capitalism" will inevitably object, and they will generally do so as "nationalists." That is why the US must be prepared to take a hard line "to preserve ... nascent market economies and to contain the nationalists who threaten them."[25]

DEVELOPMENT AND
THE NEW HEGEMONIC IDEOLOGY

For the developing world, the shift in the global balance of forces described above has had a dramatic effect. In most cases the impact on its economies and societies has been negative; in many it has been devastating. On the other hand, it is also true that a few Asian states were able to take advantage of these changes to implement dynamic and highly successful national development strategies that have transformed them into industrial powers in the space of one generation. Generalizations about "the developing world" are therefore perilous, and always in need of qualification. It is nevertheless possible to suggest that the apparently widespread acceptance of the new hegemonic ideology's celebration of market forces is neither stable nor deeply rooted. Indeed, despite the fact that governments espousing these policies are now frequently elected, there are very few places in which one could say that these policies enjoy popular support. In most such cases, apathetic electorates are weakly endorsing these policies, largely out of the legitimate fear that things would get even worse if they did not – and because the opposition is generally deeply divided and bereft of any vision that could capture people's imaginations or restore their confidence that "an alternative" exists.

This is not generally a stable equilibrium position. In more and more places apathy is turning into anger, and that is fraying the bonds of citizenship. Social disintegration and political tension have become increasingly serious concerns from Russia to Mexico and from Nigeria to many parts of the industrial world. These issues, especially when they become overt, serve as a reminders that laws and contracts become unenforceable (at reasonable cost) unless the bulk of the population recognizes them as legitimate – and ultimately just. Indeed, it is the central task of a hegemonic ideology to explain the world to people in such a way that they will reach exactly this conclusion. When they do not, this constitutes prima facie evidence that a society's leading ideology has ceased to be hegemonic. In such societies, "the centre will not hold." And that is the world that awaits all too many people both in the developed and the developing worlds.

Returning to the earlier point that a hegemonic ideology must be adapted to suit the changing reality that has to be rationalized and made acceptable to people, it now appears that the contradictions and problems of this reality are frequently outstripping the capacity of today's dominant neoliberal ideology to remain (or to become) hegemonic. This creates an unstable situation that can only be resolved in one of four ways if it is not merely to slide into anarchy. Reality may change to moderate the problems that presently undermine the credibility of the dominant ideology; more intense efforts at persuasion may succeed in "teaching" the people to accept the present situation, either as desirable or, at least, as a necessary, unavoidable, and/or temporary evil; those in power may simply "hold the line," waiting for people to resign themselves to their problems, while increasing their reliance on coercion as a means of obtaining compliance, although this is costly and may simply accelerate the slide into anarchy; or, finally, the people may rally around a counter-hegemonic ideology which creates some space for the implementation of alternative policies.

The first three responses are being actively pursued almost everywhere in the developing world, and these concerns focus on the question of good governance, which is generally taken to mean governance that allows "sound market oriented policies" to be legitimated through some sort of democratic process. The fact that, in order to be successful, this legitimation must be achieved without triggering violent opposition movements or processes of social disintegration is generally neglected in these discussions. The responses that are mobilized under this heading often involve a mixture of policies to mitigate the welfare impact of market deregulation and the roll-back of the public sector; to buy off the losers and take steps to mobilize the "winners," ensuring their vocal support of the policies; to persuade more people that "there is no alternative" and that those who fail in this system are ultimately personally to blame, since those who work hard and get the "right" skills can prosper in this brave new world; and to gain public support for the increasing use of force against the "terrorists" and "social deviants" who insist on standing in the way of progress. These are powerful instruments, and, in different countries, they are succeeding to varying degrees in maintaining a balance, though often a precarious one. Optimists, and those who have faith in the market, will believe that these responses are adequate and that they are likely to lead to stable equilibria in most places in due course. The trouble is that time is probably not on their side. Very few countries have actually achieved such a balance. Even in many industrial countries, where such a balance had long been achieved, there are increasing signs of stress and disintegration. But the biggest problem is that such optimism is simply not credible; neither history, nor theory, nor an understanding of global economic processes would lend much support to such ideological dreams.

The truth is that largely unregulated global markets will not generally allow weak, divided, and poor societies to mobilize resources in a socially efficient manner, especially if the deregulation of financial and capital markets allows wealthy citizens to escape the risks and difficulties of such a desperately difficult enterprise by evading taxes and by limiting their exposure to the domestic economy through asset diversification. If, in addition, all resources are privately owned in such a setting, resource rents will accrue to a few individuals, or to foreign owners, leaving even less of an economic base from which a society could begin to finance the cheap, efficient and widely accessible social and economic infrastructure that is a vital prerequisite for development. Moreover, the financing of such an infrastructure requires a political base that is made up of citizens and firms that have enough of an interest in, and enough of a commitment to, the long-term development of their society to support such an initiative politically, financially, and through taxes that are willingly paid because they are understood to serve society's long-term interests. Unfortunately, the policies now being promoted systematically undermine such possibilities. They promote the liberalization of finance and trade with little regard for the special problems of mobilizing finance for long-term development or the importance of learning effects and externalities in the industrial sector; they foster and encourage individualistic attitudes that tend to undermine the moral authority of government and the public sector; and they promote privatization without due regard for the longer term or the social and distributional reasons why public services may be more desirable and even more efficient. However, the greatest problem with these policies is their relative disregard for the ability of governments to manage economic processes in accordance with changing domestic social and political circumstances and priorities. That is why such policy regimes will only rarely turn out to be compatible with social or political stability, and why, in turn, even the allocative efficiency that is the primary concern of those policies will tend to be ill-served by them. Instability is a mortal enemy of efficiency.

The fact that the most successful developing economies of East Asia have been extremely statist in their approach to economic policy, and have only very gradually acceded to the strident demands for liberalization to which they have now been subjected from outside agencies for almost two decades, should serve as a powerful reminder of the importance of taking a coherent, strategic approach to national development. The World Bank's recent attempt to argue that these models do not hold any lessons that would justify a re-examination of their standard policy advice[26] is so disingenuous and unpersuasive that it is actually very instructive in revealing more clearly the deeply ideological nature of this institution's policy pronouncements.[27] Any objective appraisal of the East Asian NICs would conclude that their experience strengthens the hypothesis that successful development must focus on the development of a national technological base that can eventually both generate and appropriate significant technological rents. Only then can an economy hope to be able to remain internationally competitive while paying its labour a wage above the desperately low minimum that necessarily prevails in a global economy where labour will long be in surplus.[28]

For all of these reasons, the optimists are not on strong ground in believing that the policies advocated and defended by today's dominant ideology are likely to produce outcomes that will allow that ideology to become truly hegemonic in most cases. It is far more likely that the disappointments that have been such a feature of the adjustment process will continue long into the future. However, if that is so, how are we to understand the continued pursuit of these policies?

The answer lies in the earlier identification of the promotion of private property rights as the central mechanism through which capital is seeking to gain relatively free and unrestricted access to all of the world's resources and markets. Viewed from this perspective, the adjustment policies that are reflected in today's dominant, possibly hegemonic, ideology have been an astonishing success. Indeed, the most pessimistic exponent of dependency theory could not have imagined a more extreme result than the one that has actually materialized. Today one can truly say that international (or comprador) elites are managing the assets and resources of "their" countries in ways that serve to an unprecedented degree their narrow interests, and with very little regard for the general welfare of the rest of their populations. Moreover, they are actively collaborating in the implementation of policy regimes and an international institutional structure, making it increasingly difficult for those populations to alter this situation. Moreover, the fact that their counterparts in the developed world are also increasingly prepared to neglect the welfare of their fellow citizens augurs ill for those who think this is a temporary phase.

TOWARDS A COUNTER-HEGEMONIC IDEOLOGY

The fourth response to the fact that there is little prospect of achieving a stable equilibrium in the political economies of most developing countries pursuing today's dominant, neoliberal policy regime was said to involve the development of a counter-hegemonic ideology that could allow one to increase the scope for considering alternative policy approaches; to say that this is no easy task is a considerable understatement. The obstacles that stand in its way are formidable, but this cannot be a reason for shying away from the task. There is, in fact, no alternative, unless one is prepared to accept a situation that is deeply unjust, extremely unstable, and full of danger.

A counter-hegemonic ideology must provide people with a different way of understanding the world in which they live; a way of defining their interests, and of evaluating their circumstances; a way that is internally consistent and that provides people with a foundation for social solidarity and ultimately with a basis for political engagement. Moreover, it has to take the current contradictions as its point of departure and provide a more plausible explanation of the consistently disappointing outcomes being experienced by so many people. It must then use that analysis to define an alternative vision that is both realistic and attractive. Ultimately the central issue that has to be addressed is that of defining a basis for social solidarity in a polarized, unstable society; in an environment in which "politics" has often become a dirty word, often for good reason; and under circumstances where political opposition is often treated with extreme hostility, even in places where democracy ostensibly allows for political opposition.

This is not the place to attempt to articulate such an ideology. It would necessarily differ across time and space and would, in any case, have to build on the cultural and social realities of any given society. Here I would merely like to reflect on some of the factors that could improve the prospects of such a project in a given society and on some of the ways in which international solidarity links could be of help in supporting such processes.

First, it is extremely important to sustain a critical body of carefully researched and clearly presented literature that provides people with facts and materials that allow them to deepen their understanding of the processes that they are ultimately trying to judge and change. Given the enormous preponderance of the orthodox arguments in the official literature, it is very important to ensure that people can exchange views and interact with work that is not subject to the same biases and distortions. While the World Wide Web is clearly an important vehicle for such efforts, it is important to try to develop the personal networks that allow the information on the Web to be evaluated and used more effectively. Second, it is essential to engage in the debate regarding the ways in which the international institutional framework is being restructured; this broadly defines the constraints within which individual societies must ultimately seek to identify and implement more suitable policy alternatives. Third, we need to engage politically in activities that expand the constraints within which people must struggle for their right to develop alternative visions.

Ultimately, thoughts about such alternatives must build on those things that have been learned about development. We have learned that development is a slow and painful process that requires social cohesion, political stability, and economic flexibility; that development is largely financed from within; that external resources can play a useful role but also carry significant risk; that culture provides the medium within which development necessarily has to occur, and that this both limits and shapes the resulting process of social and economic change; that culture changes only slowly, and that it has an intrinsic value that must be accounted for by those who seek to use cultural change to accelerate economic growth; that markets are social institutions whose effectiveness depends on the institutional, the ethical, and the regulatory frameworks within which they function; and, above all, that an economy's (or a society's) integration into the international economy is a dangerous and ambiguous process that juxtaposes potential gains against potential losses, and that these losses can become catastrophic if they destroy a society's internal coherence, or make it impossible for that society to reconcile economic demands or policies with its domestic political and social realities.

We now understand that development is a social undertaking that entails enormous risks and requires huge investments aimed at the generation of joint, long-term gains for society as a whole, and that only a belief in such gains, and in such a common social project, could provide the ideological and the material base for such an undertaking. We have come to understand that the financing, the management, and the coordination of this collective investment in development represents a gargantuan task that requires strong and effective public institutions, a strong sense of identity, commitment on the part of both bureaucrats and citizens, financial mechanisms that can raise the necessary funds and manage and allocate the resulting risks both equitably and efficiently, and an ability to manage the risks implicit in the economy's insertion into a hostile, competitive, and volatile international economy. These are the lessons to be drawn from the experience of the currently industrialized countries, and they are also the lessons that are to be derived from the experience of the East Asian NICs. Of course, the way in which those lessons should be applied to any particular situation today cannot be read off from these conclusions. That must depend on a number of factors, including the society's priorities, resources, risk preferences, and political configuration.

Much of this discussion has focused on the nation-state, and this is as it should be. The nation-state remains one of the most important vehicles for the development of social solidarity, especially if that solidarity is to be based on an inclusive concept of citizenship that, at least, creates the possibility of striving for a relatively egalitarian, non-racist, and non-sexist society. Moreover, because the nation-state remains an important vehicle for the collective mobilization of resources for development, its capacity to do so must be protected and rebuilt whenever possible. Efficiency must clearly be considered in making such choices, but so must the role that the collective provision of services can play in integrating a society and in giving material content to one's sense of citizenship.

It is important to remember that the central thrust of the new development theory has been its systematic destruction of the nation-state as an effective mechanism for social and political mobilization in the pursuit of collective welfare gains. The state has been undercut ideologically, materially, and institutionally, while attention has been focused on the private sector, NGOs, and civil society; but the problems encountered by these actors have merely reminded us of the important mobilizing and coordinating role that successful states have always played in the development process. Certainly the generalized claim that state activities are always wasteful or unnecessary is without merit or foundation.

Politics and the state are ultimately the manifestation of concerted social action. While the outcomes of such activities in terms of efficiency, fairness, justice, or representativeness will always be somewhat unpredictable and imperfect, the vital importance of politics and the state cannot be denied. Only those who believe in the fiction of a self-regulating market have any basis for the belief that government is the primary problem of underdevelopment. Indeed, insofar as the state is a problem – and many states have been highly imperfect – the task must be to improve their performance, not to denounce it and to replace it with markets or NGOs, whose strengths and weaknesses have commonly been too imperfectly assessed or understood. There is no plausible empirical or theoretical foundations for such ideological policy prescriptions; all privatization proposals should be resolutely exposed as ideological unless a careful assessment has made a case for such a policy change in a particular area of the economy, or the society. Meanwhile, the material and institutional base of most states is being eroded by privatization, by downsizing, and by contracting out mechanisms. This generally undermines public sector capacities and morale, which reduces the likelihood that civil servants will act in the interests of society. As the effectiveness of states is diluted, the public choice mentality that underpins these policy prescriptions appears to be vindicated. Another self-fulfilling prophecy rears its ugly head: the state gradually becomes an ineffective policy instrument that is staffed by people with little commitment to public service, working in institutions that are understaffed and constantly being reorganized. In this way, public choice theory is set to become yet another self-fulfilling prophecy.

Finally, internal economic linkages within a state need to be assessed in ways that take their potential political significance into account. A politically and socially stable, representative state is more difficult to sustain when a society's material base is highly fragmented and agriculture, industry, and services are not essentially interdependent. Under such conditions it would be more difficult to mobilize the finance necessary for long-term investment in infrastructure, human development, or the development of industrial technological capabilities. Such a society would have more difficulty responding flexibly and effectively to sudden disturbances since that invariably requires agreement about how the resulting short-term pain should be distributed.

Such developments as privatization, state downsizing, diminished representativity, and so forth are altering the material foundations for the social solidarity that has to be the object of any counter-hegemonic ideology. Unfortunately, this makes the task of rebuilding the social, political, and ideological foundations needed for a more coherent, more humane, and more predictable development process increasingly difficult. The problem is not that this is not known. It is that certain powerful interests have chosen to distort the lessons of history, so that they can continue to shift power towards private property rights, while claiming that their actions are designed to promote "development." For the moment it is not easy to see how these trends can be reversed in the short run, especially since this is a self-reinforcing process that continually increases the power of private property.

History tells us that capital will become more circumspect and more willing to compromise when it is forced to do so and that, in this scenario, prosperity and human happiness need not be destroyed. Indeed, the last time it was forced to work extensively with labour and other social forces within relatively sovereign nation-states, the world enjoyed its most successful period of economic growth, welfare diffusion, and political stability. Let us hope that it does not take another war and a long depression before those lessons can be learned once more.

NOTES

1 The term neoliberal occasionally gives rise to confusion. It is essentially derived from the economic debate and refers to a relatively fundamentalist espousal of the laissez-faire doctrines associated with economic liberalism in the eighteenth and nineteenth centuries. In the United States, the same concept is probably best rendered by the term "neo-conservative." This is so for two reasons. First, in the United States the word conservative has increasingly been appropriated to describe "economic liberals" who espouse "free markets" above all else. This has created much confusion, since it seems to leave the language without a word for those who are conservative, in the sense that they fear, or oppose, the erosion of existing social institutions, ethical standards, behavioral norms or value systems. The fact that this erosion is often primarily due to the operation of unrestrained market forces merely intensifies the problem and explains, in part, the deeply paradoxical (oxymoronic?) nature of much

of America's conservatism. Second, in the United States, the meaning of the word liberal is primarily derived from the political sphere, and is used to refer to people who oppose conservatives in their unrestrained espousal of market forces. To complete the confusion, it is generally assumed that because this form of liberalism is opposed to conservatism in such an economistic sense, it must also be opposed to its apparent efforts to defend existing social institutions, ethical standards, behavioral norms and value systems. For the free marketeers there is method in this madness, since it allows them to present themselves as the friend of the increasingly beleaguered "common man," as he tries to make sense of an increasingly unstable world in which the icy waters of commercial calculation threaten to destroy "the world as he knows it." Even better, from their point of view, is the fact that this allows the liberals to be portrayed as the agents of the destruction of that world, leaving the role of market forces largely unexamined and marginalized. In this paper I will use the term neoliberal as defined in this footnote. I hope that this brief discussion will allow it to be reconciled with American usage.

2 This most disturbing development is, as so often, most advanced in the United States. The conflicts of interest that are raised by these developments are, of course, monumental.

3 R.N. Cooper, writing in *Foreign Affairs*, September/October 1996: 138, uses this phrase in a review of Lester Thurow's *The Future of Capitalism: How Today's Economic Forces Will Shape Tomorrow's World*, New York: William Morrow, 1996.

4 This "fixed" exchange rates in terms of the US dollar, which was, in turn, linked to gold by the US government's commitment to buy gold at a fixed price, $32 an ounce, at any time. Exchange could be altered, but only if an economy was experiencing a "fundamental disequilibrium," and only with the agreement of the IMF and, through it, of most of its trading partners.

5 H. James, *International Monetary Cooperation since Bretton Woods*, Oxford, UK: Oxford University Press, 1996: 459.

6 This support is not necessarily confined to the most obvious interests, such as the more aggressive internationally oriented financial institutions. Although these interests did benefit massively from such changes, and although their support was undoubtedly of central importance, it is necessary to remember that other interests, including other business sectors, governments, and even trade unions, often stood to benefit from the liberalization of international financial flows in the short run.

7 See F. Hahn, "Reflections on the Invisible Hand," *Lloyd's Bank Review*, April 1982, for an excellent discussion of this issue with specific reference to the policies of Thatcher's British government.

8 James, *International Monetary Cooperation since Bretton Woods*, 612.

9 Ibid., 599.

10 William Arthur Lewis, *Principles of Economic Planning; a Study Prepared for the Fabian Society*, London: Dobson, 1950: 14. Such sentiments were indeed commonplace at the time. Thus Jacob Viner, writing in 1951, said: "The world has changed greatly, and is now a world of planned economies, of state trading, of substantially arbitrary and inflexible national price structures, and of managed instability in exchange rates. The classical theory is not relevant for such a world, and it may be that for such a world there can be no relevant general theory." Jacob Viner, *International Economics*, Glencoe, Ill.: Free Press, 1951: 16.

11 A. Milward, *The Reconstruction of Western Europe*, London: Merlin Press, 1984: 466.

12 James, *International Monetary Cooperation since Bretton Woods*, 58.

13 Ibid., 83.

14 Milward, *The Reconstruction of Western Europe*, 466.

15 S. Marris, "Managing the World Economy: Will We Ever Learn?" *Princeton Essays in International Finance*, no. 155, October, 1984: 5-6.

16 I discussed the nature of those tensions and the problematic ways in which they were ultimately resolved in M.A. Bienefeld, "The International Context for National Development Strategies: Constraints and Opportunities in a Changing World," in M.A. Bienefeld and M. Godfrey (eds), *The Struggle for Development: National Strategies in an International Context*, Chichester, UK: Wiley, 1982.

17 Marris, "Managing the World Economy," 7.

18 Ibid., 10–11.

19 The above paper includes an extensive discussion of the way in which the increasing tension between the US, on the one hand, and Europe and Japan, on the other, played a central and determining role in bringing about the oil crisis, and of the subsequent upheavals that tore apart the par-value system, the "managed global economy" and, ultimately, the social-democratic compromises that had been at the heart of the earlier "consensus."

20 James, *International Monetary Cooperation since Bretton Woods*, 419.

21 Ibid., 415.

22 P. Volcker and T. Gyohten, *Changing Fortunes: The World's Money and the Threat to American Leadership*, New York: Times Books, 1992: 237.

23 James, *International Monetary Cooperation since Bretton Woods*, 613.

24 Fordham University Institute for Innovation and Social Policy, "Annual Index of Social Health," quoted in *The Nation*, 11 November 1996: 7.

25 *Business Week*, "Editorial," 17 January 1994: 102.

26 World Bank, *The East Asian Miracle: Economic Growth and Public Policy*, Washington, DC: World Bank, 1993.

27 For trenchant critiques of the above World Bank Report, see Robert
    Wade, "Japan, the World Bank, and the Art of Paradigm Maintenance:
    The East Asian Miracle in Political Perspective," in *New Left Review*, no.
    217, 1996; World Bank Operation Evaluations Department, *World Bank
    Support for Industrialization in Korea, India and Indonesia,* Washington,
    DC: World Bank, 1992, executive summary and chapter 4: 1–7, 53–7;
    Sanjaya Lall, "'The East Asian Miracle': Does the Bell Toll for Industrial
    Strategy?" *World Development*, vol. 22, no. 4, April 1994; Dani Rodrik,
    "King Kong Meets Godzilla: The World Bank and the East Asian Mira-
    cle," Center for Economic Policy Research Discussion Paper no. 944,
    London: CEPR, 1994; and Ajit Singh, "How Did East Asia Grow so Fast?
    Slow Progress Towards an Analytical Consensus," UNCTAD Discussion
    Paper no. 97, Geneva: UNCTAD, February 1995.
28 This conclusion receives strong support from Paul M. Romer, "Two
    Strategies for Economic Development: Using Ideas and Producing Ideas,"
    Proceedings of the World Bank Annual Conference on Development
    Economics, Washington, DC: World Bank, 1992.

Capital, Marxism, and the World Economy:
APEC and the MAI[1]

ABIGAIL B. BAKAN

In the twenty-first century, it it is widely accepted that we live in a new era in the world economy. One of the most notable features of the times is the apparent proliferation of international trade and investment agreements, organizations, and accords, notably the World Trade Organization (WTO), which became a target of anti-corporate protest when its representatives met in Seattle, Washington in November-December 1999. Other trade arrangements include the move towards a single European common market and the establishment of the Euro currency, the North American Free Trade Agreement (NAFTA), the proposed Free Trade Area of the Americas (FTAA), the Asia Pacific Economic Cooperation (APEC) trade forum that spans North America and Asia, and the now defunct Multilateral Agreement on Investment (MAI) under the auspices of the Organization for Economic Cooperation and Development (OECD).[2] It is clear that the world's ruling groups are moving with considerable vigour to shape and reshape the terms of international trade and investment.

For some analysts, such agreements are easily explained as characteristic of a fundamentally new era of globalization. The decreasing relevance of the individual nation-state is taken to be the hallmark of the times, and international economic alliances among states are read as one symptom of the necessary adjustments to new conditions.[3] The claim has commonly been made that Marxist theory no longer fits the bill. Instead we need a new methodological approach that can cut "across the ancient battle lines of right and left."[4]

The following argument presents a rather different claim. Marxism, understood as a method for explaining capitalism and its accompanying contradictory dynamics, is in fact uniquely suited to guide us in understanding the current global crisis. More specifically, taking two of the largest and most important recent international trade and investment agreements as examples, the applicability of the Marxist method can be demonstrated in concrete terms.

There is little doubt that we are living in an era of dramatic and profound change in international economic and political relations. To repeat old dogmas would be the furthest thing from serious or fruitful analysis. Moreover, the collapse, after the end of the Cold War, of Stalinist hegemony in left intellectual life is a development any progressive thinker or social activist should welcome.[5] The development of new international economic relationships among states, like any new feature of the capitalist world system, does not necessarily negate the contribution of classical Marxism. On the contrary, explaining the nature of and changes in relations of production and exchange provided the substance of Marx's lifelong inquiry. Contemporary trade and investment agreements themselves are less a feature of a new and qualitatively distinct era than of an advanced – and therefore massive and also particularly volatile – form of the relationship between nation-states and global competition that has characterized capitalism from its inception.

Objectively, this is what the agreements are all about. There are numerous elements within the new trade and investment agreements, however, that indicate something distinctive on the subjective plane: a conscious incorporation of the key features of advanced capitalism on the part of the advocates. What was once called "modernization theory" in the study of the political economy of development, has returned like a ghost to haunt the world's poorest and most exploited. This applies not only in the Third World but also within the First World, as reflected in the strategic aims of the new agreements.

Walter Rostow was the theorist most closely identified with modernization theory in its heyday in the post-war era.[6] By the mid-1970s, there was probably no single body of ideas in international political economic theory more profoundly challenged, both on a theoretical level and in terms of its practical failures.[7] Yet Rostow seems to have returned to take back the pride of place he and his followers once held in the 1950s. Increasingly, restructuring policies dictated by the International Monetary Fund and the World Bank compel debt-burdened Third World states to dismantle the usually minimal local state mechanisms in place, ostensibly to make greater room for the unhindered intervention of market forces. The caretaker of the office, John Maynard Keynes, seems to have been usurped by the return of Mr Rostow.

The "Euro-debates" and the implications of NAFTA have been the subject of considerable analysis from a critical left perspective for several years.[8] Recently, the WTO has been the subject of extensive analysis.[9] Two other agreements, APEC and the MAI (within both of which Canada has been a prominent player), have received less analytical attention. These will provide a focus for the following discussion. Both of these trade groups experienced a dramatic rise in global prominence in the mid-1990s, only to be curtailed or halted by international crisis and disunity by the end of the decade. By addressing APEC and the MAI in particular, attention can be turned to specific features of the capitalist system today. The assumption is that the essential dynamics of this system continue to be more the same than different than those originally explained by Karl Marx. Further, these agreements indicate a moment in that system which is in many respects more transparent than the capitalism of Marx's day.

One of the most striking features of these agreements is the elevation of the discourse of "rights" to apply to capital personified on a global scale. The concomitant denigration, or rendering non-existent, of similar rights for workers and the poor the world over is no less subtle. The emphasis on the mobility rights of capital in these agreements, as contrasted with the restricted mobility of labour, particularly unskilled labour, on a global scale is one of the most notable examples of this phenomenon.

The argument that follows is divided into two parts: one, the general case for a Marxist analysis of international trade and investment agreements in the contemporary system; and, two, a particular consideration of the applicability of such an approach to APEC and the MAI.

MARXISM AND GLOBALIZATION

In the days of Karl Marx and Frederick Engels, capitalism was in its infancy. The system is now showing all the signs of old age, including the emergence of various long-term chronic illnesses. Some of its faculties, however, like many an aging organism, remain intact. Certainly, capitalism as a system has now expanded to every corner of the globe. This is true whether it is in its old capital form, as in much of Western Europe; its new capital form, in what were once called the miracle states of the "Newly Industrializing Economies" (NIES); the many variants of old and new capital which mark much of the Third

World, the former East Bloc states, and North America; or the remaining state capitalisms of nations such as China, Cambodia or Vietnam, which adhere to the name of socialism but not to its liberating elements.

There is a hunger that is driving the system to seek more and more of its ultimate curative potion – profits based on the exploitation of labour. Respect for the boundaries of nation-states is clearly no barrier to the drive for profit. The quest for international markets, raw materials, and investment sites is not, however, a new characteristic. In Marx's day, capitalism was no less desperate to seek profits outside the borders of any single nation-state than it is today. Marx and Engels argued that capitalism is driven not only on the basis of the exploitation of labour but also through the division among capitals that compels competition. This is true of competition within the borders of a single nation-state and across the borders of nation-states. On this, Marx was explicit. Indeed, he predicted features of the world market we continue to see today, including, for example, the universalization of consumption patterns.

The need of a constantly expanding market for its products chases the bourgeoisie over the whole surface of the globe. It must nestle everywhere, settle everywhere, establish connections everywhere. The bourgeoisie has through its exploitation of the world market given a cosmopolitan character to production and consumption in every country. To the great chagrin of the Reactionists, it has drawn from under the feet of industry the national ground on which it stood. All old-established national industries have been destroyed or are daily being destroyed. They are dislodged by new industries, whose introduction becomes a life and death question for all civilized nations, by industries that no longer work up indigenous raw material; industries whose products are consumed, not only at home, but in every quarter of the globe. In place of the old wants, satisfied by the productions of the country, we find new wants, requiring for their satisfaction the products of distant lands and climes. In place of the old local and national seclusion and self-sufficiency, we have intercourse in every direction, universal interdependence of nations.[10]

From the earliest developments of merchant capital, the mobility of capital across national boundaries has been a characteristic feature of the system. It is simply not historically accurate to presume that early capitalism was marked by nation-states *par excellence* without globalization, and late capitalism by globalization without nation-states. Therefore, the new trade and investment agreements are not notable because they facilitate internationalization of capital and commodities across borders of states previously impermeable to capital; nor, however, are these new agreements only window dressing, purely redundant to prior practices.

As Marx elaborated in detail, capitalism does not emerge without contradictory pressures. Internationalization presents one set of pressures; the move towards the consolidation of nation-states, another. These latter include isolating sections of land and territory, regulating the emergent borders with the legislative and military arms of the state, the development of the home market, creating barriers to foreign competition, and control of the wage rates, mobility, and citizenship rights or of subject obligations of the workers within those borders. National peculiarities are not fictive institutional affects, as there are real differences in how nations are organized. These differences can be expressed in the use of various forms and ideologies of oppression, the assignment or limitations of rights, and the invention of national traditions.[11] The growth of nations and the internationalization of capital develop in relation to one another; the specific nature of this relationship varies historically. It is, in other words, a dynamic relationship rather than a static one.

Seen in this light, what the new trade and investment agreements facilitate is the increased ability of capital to cross national borders with fewer restrictions, often under the welcome watch of the ruling classes of the receiving nation-state. They codify a level of agreement that attempts to secure more momentum to one element, international accumulation and trade, and to diminish some aspects of the other, specifically economic protectionism. The scale and reach of the units of capital and the market in the world system today have compelled the adjustment of the system well beyond the boundaries of national markets. There have been variations in the pattern, and, sometimes, regarding the economic cycle of expansion and crisis, these have been dramatic. However, this general trend in its current manifestation has been in place since at least 1957, with the original formation of the European Common Market.

Despite contemporary changes, profit has never been respectful of sovereignty as an abstract principle. Expansionist practices and policies beyond national borders developed with the emergence of nation-states. Manufacturing and industrial capital and international trade arose, if unevenly, over the period roughly spanning the sixteenth and seventeenth centuries. In Marx's words:

The sudden expansion of the world-market, the multiplication of circulating commodities, the competitive zeal of the European nations to possess themselves of the products of Asia and the treasures of America, and the colonial system – all contributed materially towards destroying the feudal fetters on production. However, in its first period – the manufacturing period – the modern mode of production developed only where the conditions for it had taken shape within the Middle Ages ... And when in the 16th, and partially still in the 17th, century the sudden expansion of commerce and emergence of a new world-market overwhelmingly contributed to the fall of the old mode of production and the rise of capitalist production, this was accomplished conversely on the basis of the already existing capitalist mode of production. The world-market itself forms the basis for this mode of production.[12]

It should not be assumed that the early period of competitive capitalism was one in which the free market ruled supreme, without the aid of state intervention. Indeed, the "Joint Stock Company was the answer of the merchants in the sixteenth and seventeenth centuries to the problem of how to raise the huge sums of money needed for such vast undertakings as trading with America, Africa and Asia represented."[13] This is not to suggest that the system of capitalism has not changed since the sixteenth century, nor to maintain that Marx predicted modern trade agreements when he first drafted Capital. The point is that contrary to the claims of many contemporary globalization theorists,[14] varying tensions between the nation-state and the world economy are characteristic of capitalism in general. The task at hand is to specify the nature and contradictions of this dynamic relationship.

One of the specific features of the current period of globalization is the growing class contradiction regarding mobility rights. While the international mobility rights of corporations are increasing, the rights of workers to travel across borders is tending to decline. Determination of mobility rights of labour, as opposed to the mobility of capital, continues to be virtually the exclusive jurisdiction of sovereign states.[15] The rhetorical "global ethic of humanitarianism" notwithstanding, refugee policy, for example, "is one of the areas in which the state is exercising ever-increasing control."[16] According to the United Nations report of the Special Rapporteur on Human Rights for Migrant Workers, in 2000, there was an estimated 120-130 million "people outside their country of origin." Of these, approximately 21.5 million were refugees, and an additional 30 million displaced persons.[17]

Two processes that characterize mobility rights, or their absence, in contemporary global capitalism are related: increasing relaxation of restrictions on the mobility of capital and rising pressure for labour to emigrate under tightening conditions of state control. The dislocating impact of restructuring policies on Third World populations creates vast pools of labour migrating from rural to urban areas domestically, and then, for example, from Third World to First World regions.

Migration in search of work is a condition provoked by the commoditization of land, removing rural populations of their means of livelihood and at the same time creating a reserve army of labour.[18] The scale of global migration has changed considerably over various phases of the development of capitalism. From its inception, however, capitalism has been characterized by the creation of a mass migrant labour force in search of employment. This is what Marx referred to as the "relative surplus population," a dislocated agricultural workforce, "constantly on the point of passing over into an urban or manufacturing proletariat, and on the look-out for circumstances favourable to this transformation."[19]

The term "globalization" then, in contemporary conditions, refers primarily to the ease of access of capital to world markets. For increasing numbers of persons finding themselves stateless, or without the designated rights to state residence, being human citizens of the planet in a globalized world offers little comfort. The basic division of capitalism into classes, between large corporate monopolies on one side and a labouring class lacking access to or control over the basic means to acquire subsistence on the other, is increasingly manifest both within nation-states and as an integrated feature of the world economy.

MARXISM, APEC, AND THE MAI

APEC and the MAI represent two of the largest of the recent international trade and investment agreements. They are examples not only of globalization, the point that is commonly emphasized in the literature,[20] but also, arguably, of the continuing role of nation-states and national capitalist classes within the world economy today. A brief consideration of each of these agreements from such a perspective follows.

I APEC

In November of 1989, the Asia Pacific Economic Cooperation trade group held its first official meeting in Canberra, Australia. In November 1997, Canada was host to the Ninth Ministerial Meeting of APEC Economic Leaders in Vancouver, British Columbia. In 1998, APEC leaders met in Kuala Lumpur, and in 1999 in Auckland, New Zealand. Since then, meetings have taken place in Kuala Lumpur, New Zealand, and Darussalam.

The twenty-one member economies, including the US, Canada, Mexico, Australia, Japan, China, and the once mighty "Asian Tigers" had a combined Gross Domestic Product (GDP) of over US$16 trillion in 1998, representing 42 per cent of global trade.[21] The general slogan put forward by APEC to summarize its mandate is precise and to the point: "APEC means business."[22] As one APEC statement summarized:

Although APEC is an official dialogue between Asia Pacific economies, it has been driven by the needs and interests of the private sector from the start ... [S]pecialist regional bodies and individual business representatives provide expert advice to governments and to meetings and conferences throughout the APEC network. Continual dialogue and feedback, from working-level officials up to APEC Leaders, ensures that governments in the region know how to make Asia Pacific an easier place in which to conduct business.[23]

The essential basis of APEC is to facilitate greater mobility and access of international trade flows among the member states, "liberalizing trade and investment unilaterally and under the multilateral framework." To that end, the elimination of "various constraints and bottlenecks associated with infrastructure, [and] technological capability to undertake transition and structural change," particularly among less developed APEC states, is the hallmark of the accord.[24] The stated goal is to see free and open trade and investment within APEC by 2010 for the developed member states, and by 2020 for the developing member states. These target dates were set at the 1995 Osaka meeting.

The entire agreement is based on a profound commitment to the goals of 1990s-style modernization theory, or neoliberalism: restructuring, privatization, deregulation, downsizing, slashing of the social wage of the state, flexible labour markets, and competitive advantage. As APEC puts it, "Issues directly related to poverty alleviation and social issues have by and large not been directly addressed by APEC. The basic premise underlying APEC's economic and technical cooperation has been that economic growth and development is the best approach to eradicate poverty on an economy-wide basis and accordingly has been the priority in terms of addressing the issue of equitable development."[25] The return of the influence of classical modernization theory is striking. However, there are two related and distinctive adjustments of traditional Rostowian development theory to current times: one, initial take-off is seen as essentially motivated by any section of capital, indigenous or exogenous, that can generate sufficient investment; and, two, the market is described in both national and international terms.[26] Periodic references to the inevitable trickle-down effect of improving the business environment pay homage to the barrage of public criticism that the APEC leaders have attracted in the Philippines, Canada, South Korea, and elsewhere.[27]

APEC was established on the basis that the Asian boom economies were the driving force of the world system;[28] however recent summit meetings have taken place in the midst of the spread of the most serious financial crisis faced by the region. The spread of "Asian flu" clearly took the APEC leaders by surprise during the 1997 summit. They were forced continually to assure themselves and the media that the collapse of one currency after another was well under control and would soon be reversed.[29] Indeed, given that Asia has accounted for two-thirds of global economic growth since 1990, crisis management was the order of the day.[30] Despite the efforts of APEC leaders to put on a bold face, one month after the November 1997 summit, the International Monetary Fund revised its World Economic Outlook report, originally released in October 1997, with new, and lower, economic projections. The shift was a direct result of the financial fallout from the Asian economies. The central role of the Japanese economy in the international system was seen as the key risk factor, a projection that has proven to be painfully accurate.[31]

Subsequent summit meetings of APEC leaders in Kuala Lampur and Auckland took place in a changed international context. Now, global trade liberalization was failing in the face of economic crisis and national protectionist strategies. Despite the best efforts of the neoliberal free trade advocates, state-led economic stimulation strategies were being adopted in the crisis-ridden Asian states, including Japan.[32] The priority of the market and increased profits remained, but nation-states were not prepared to take the political risks involved in serious economic crisis. Moreover, there was now the example of Indonesia, a prominent APEC member that witnessed a revolutionary challenge to President Suharto in 1998, largely in direct response to the impact of restructuring policies on the poorest sections of the population.

The inability of the global trade agreement to offset the decline of the currencies of the individual nation-states is one critical indicator of the continued impact of states within the international system. Writing in late May of 1998, Dato Noor Adlan, then Executive Director of the APEC Secretariat, was compelled at least partially to acknowledge the claims of the critics.

Some recent commentaries contend that APEC has been conspicuously missing from the international response to Asia's financial crisis, and that this alleged absence somehow confirms APEC's broader irrelevance ... While individual APEC members are, of course, engaged in responding to the crisis, whether as affected economies pursuing adjustment programs or as supporting-partner economies, APEC as a multilateral organization has not been in the forefront of the international response to the immediate crisis. That much is true.[33]

Even in headier days, however, the APEC forum had incorporated the centrality of nation-states into the fabric of its terms of collusion. The vast variation among the member states, particularly between developed and developing economies, is a central feature of APEC concerns.

The largest single member state among the APEC twenty-one is the People's Republic of China. China has welcomed US capital with bold determination since the 1970s, marked in particular by the dramatic visit in 1971 of US President Richard Nixon to Mao Zedong's welcoming entourage.[34] In 1977, the last year prior to China's major economic reform period, the sum of the country's imports and exports, which together constitute its total trade turnover, was less than US$15 billion. China at that time was the thirtieth largest exporter in the world. By 1993, the comparable trade turnover figure was US$196 billion, and China now ranked as the tenth largest exporter. In the mid-1980s, China became the largest borrower from the World Bank; and by 1989 Beijing had surpassed New Delhi, India, in becoming the largest recipient of official bilateral and multilateral aid, receiving US$2.2 billion a year.[35]

Two things stopped China from becoming the largest single force in Asia for the attraction of foreign direct investment: its own population's restiveness with the lack of internal democratic practices and the remnants of a stagnating state capitalist economy. The high point of conflict regarding the former was the massive student protest at Tienanmen Square in May and June of 1989. It was met with military repression and a bloodbath taped live on CNN that could not be ignored even by business pundits without risking the ire of their own populations.

China's move into the world market was temporarily halted. Washington banned military sales and all high-level military exchanges and recommended that US banks suspend lending agreements; it was not long until the EC banks followed suit. In July, at the G7 meeting in Paris, Japan also suspended new loans. The Asian Development Bank and the World Bank stopped new lending, negotiations over China's application to the General Agreement on Tariffs and Trade (GATT, which has now been replaced by the WTO) was suspended, and the IMF halted technical assistance projects.

The punishment meted to China from global investors was not severe compared to sanctions taken, for example, against Iraq during and after the Gulf War, but neither was it without consequence.[36]

China won back considerable favour on the global marketplace, however, by refusing to exercise its veto in the UN Security Council on the occasion of the US request for United Nations support for the war in the Gulf against Iraq and Iraqi-occupied Kuwait in 1991. As Rosemary Foot has summarized, "[T]he Gulf war was used to demonstrate how valuable and cooperative China could be: it voted for all ten UN resolutions that ordered military and economic sanctions against Iraq and abstained on resolution 678 that permitted the use of force to compel an Iraqi withdrawal from Kuwait. Such cooperative or, rather non-obstructive behaviour reaped a number of diplomatic and economic rewards."[37]

Thus, with the first difficulty apparently attended to, the next issue was on the agenda: opening up the internal market to attract foreign investment. Enter APEC. In November 1991 China joined APEC, agreeing to accept concessions to Taiwan and Hong Kong in the process, but at the same time gaining access to the world's largest international trade accord. For China to be an enthusiastic participant in a major trade arrangement with the US, Canada, Japan, Indonesia (still at the time under the leadership of China's erstwhile enemy Suharto), and South Korea should give pause to those who still wish to maintain there is any socialist character to the People's Republic.[38]

APEC is boldly committed to "the important contribution of the private sector to the dynamism of APEC economies." Despite massive expansion of the private market, the largest sections of China's industry and its banking system remain state-regulated.[39] China's president, Jiang Zemin, is committed to eliminating this tension by clearly favouring privatization, but he also faces the challenge of provoking the type of unrest encountered by his predecessor, Deng Xiaoping. China's November 1999 bilateral trade agreement with the United States, a precondition to its entry into the World Trade Organization, is a further indication of the course Zemin is intending to follow.[40]

The case of China indicates that individual APEC states maintain their own specific national interests within the globalized economy, and within APEC itself. Canada, the US, Japan, and Australia are all competing for Asian markets; Singapore, Indonesia, Hong Kong, the Philippines, South Korea, and Taiwan and other smaller economies are highly dependent on foreign markets and foreign investment. Despite the bold claims of APEC, the barriers to trade integration continue. In the meantime, APEC has developed an international bureaucracy simply to be able to devise common statistics to measure exchange rates, while plans to enter into major investment deals have been stalled by the impact of the crisis.

The emphasis on the mobility of commodity trade and investment opportunities in APEC stands in sharp contrast to its minimal emphasis on labour mobility. Labour is seen simply as one of many market inputs. To the extent that labour is a concern, class divisions are accepted as permanent market factors. A clear distinction is made between highly skilled technical and managerial personnel, and unskilled, general labour. Education and training for the vast majority of citizens in APEC member states are perceived in APEC reports as an inevitable spin-off of increasing capitalization and rising productivity. The body of evidence demonstrating the devastating impact of such policies on living standards in countries which have been experimental models of IMF restructuring policies is, of course, entirely ignored.[41] To the extent that border controls for labour are challenged, it is only in relation to the movement of managerial personnel associated with the tasks of corporate administration. The class orientation in this dimension is explicit: efforts to "promote international labour mobility, particularly of professionals" is stated as one significant goal of APEC countries.[42]

Finally, and notably, gender issues do figure into APEC deliberations. Here however, the class divide is no less obvious. Related to the issue of professional cross-border mobility, particular concern is raised regarding "the case of professionals in dual-income families, whose spouses are often professionals" and the need to achieve easy access to visas for "temporary overseas assignments."[43] When attention shifts to the low-paid or unemployed women workers in unregulated industries, APEC commentators make scant reference, stressing only the improvement of output and productivity and the elimination of government waste on social programs.

The living and working conditions of Asian women workers, at home and as migrant workers, is strikingly absent in APEC deliberations. Today, Asian women are the fastest growing section of migrant workers in the world. According to the International Labour Organization, there are currently at least 1.5 million Asian women working abroad. Further, the activities of "illegal recruitment agencies, overseas employment promoters, manpower suppliers and a host of other legal and illegal subsidiaries" are central to this process.[44]

As an international alliance of ruling classes, APEC represents an extension of what Marx identified as the personification of capital, but here it appears on an international scale.[45] Issues of workers' rights, human rights, or women's rights are given at best token recognition. Referred to rhetorically, such rights are presented as an inevitable effect of capital productivity. Any deeper consideration is entirely ignored.[46] A similar pattern is seen in the aborted negotiations regarding the Multilateral Agreement on Investment (MAI).

2 The MAI

The MAI was distinct from other international economic arrangements in that its focus was specifically on investment rather than commodity exchange. Negotiations for the MAI came to a halt when France withdrew its participation in the fall of 1998. On 3 December 1998, the OECD issued a press release indicating that negotiations were stopped indefinitely.[47] The failure of the MAI indicated the impact of public pressure on national participating states. The MAI's demise signalled the growing popular resistance to international free trade agreements that would ultimately find mass expression in Seattle, Washington, in November–December 1999, when over 50,000 participants from the US and other countries successfully stopped the summit meetings of the WTO.[48] The MAI's demise also indicated the continuing importance of nation-states to international economic policy formation and the lack of uniformity of purpose among states, even in an era of globalization.

The MAI was intended to be a closed-door operation. It was launched in May 1995 under the auspices of the OECD, whose twenty-nine member states and the European Commission met regularly through the MAI Negotiating Group. The original aim was to develop a massive new international investment accord to become operative by May 1998.[49]

For the purposes of this discussion, the stated aims of the accord – in terms normally associated with issues of civil rights – are particularly interesting: "non-discrimination" against foreign corporations and investment "protection" against expropriation without compensation were the principal objectives of the MAI.[50] The use of such categories to apply to corporations in legal discourse of advanced capitalist democracies is not new, but the MAI took the Marxist notion of the personification of capital to new heights. This is both because of the size and scope of the agreement, and because of the clarity of purpose with which the MAI was developed. Though the MAI died on the international order paper, as it were, it re-emerged in a new form as part of the WTO General Agreement in Trade in Services (GATS). Unlike more classic trade deals that involve commodities, the MAI and the subsequent GATS element of the WTO enabled member states within the accords to challenge services and virtually every other human activity if these are seen to act as a "barrier" to the investment opportunities of multinational corporations.[51]

Unlike APEC, which prides itself in combining under a single rubric the advanced and less advanced capitalist states in a united regional bloc spanning the Pacific region, the MAI was an alliance of the most advanced nations of the world. The MAI was designed to be resistant to international competition, particularly from the South. Modernization theory was again implicitly applied, but without the pretense of a prescriptive model for "traditional" economies. Other aspects of the MAI are all too familiar. Like APEC, the MAI was constructed from a perspective that celebrates the free market, looks to the benefits of unfettered capital investment, and seeks to facilitate the free movement of corporate capital across international borders.

The enthusiasm of the Canadian government for the MAI was ultimately tempered by political opposition, but Canada originally was a particularly active, and aggressive, advocate of the deal. The lines of considerable domestic debate follow closely on earlier political polarizations that surrounded the Free Trade Agreement (FTA) between Canada and the US, signed in January of 1989, and the extension of that accord into the North America Free Trade Agreement (NAFTA) which came into force in January of 1994. Business interests and the parties that favour them, principally now the ruling federal Liberal Party in Canada, were enthusiastic supporters of the MAI; the major trade union federations and the labour party to which they are affiliated, the New Democratic Party, its staunch opponents. An editorial in the pro-business daily newspaper *The Globe and Mail* stated the former case clearly:

Internationally, flows of foreign direct investment (FDI) have grown nearly three times faster than trade in goods and services since 1980 ... Canada benefits strongly from FDI ... Creating a consistent and transparent international climate for foreign investment – the objective of the MAI – is thus in the interests of all. By removing the risk of discriminatory treatment against foreign investors or the danger of uncompensated nationalization of assets and by creating a strong dispute-settlement mechanism, the international community lowers the risk of investing abroad and allows more money to flow to where it will do the most good.[52]

While APEC was established on the hopes of a generalized and unrelenting expansion of the Asian miracle, the driving vision of the MAI was the US economic boom. The US, though growing only at a rate of 2.3 per cent a year in the late 1990s, experienced a prolonged period of economic expansion. Only in 2001 did predictions turn to signs of recession. US multinationals and the US government have been seeking the elimination of investment barriers in order to increase

American corporate access to international markets in the most advanced economies in the world. Canada, a smaller economy but similarly competitive on a world scale, has been desperate to follow suit. The initial enthusiasm of the governments of both the US and Canada for the MAI, and more recently for the WTO and the Free Trade Area of the Americas (FTAA),[53] expresses this underlying economic drive.

The MAI was originally developed to ensure the mobility of capital into the domestic markets of other capitalist economies. The fear of "discrimination" against foreign-owned corporations from states, in the name of protecting less competitive national corporations, motivated the terms of the MAI. The MAI would have extended what had already been codified on a more limited scale in NAFTA. The wider reach of the accord, however, elevated the "rights" of corporations to an international level. Any government which signed onto the MAI agreed to treat foreign corporations on a par with national ones. The MAI began by including the OECD states: 477 of the Global Fortune 500 are based in these states, comprising 95.4 per cent of the largest transnational corporations.[54] However, an accession clause was added to allow non-OECD countries to join the MAI on certain specified conditions.[55]

The implications of the agreement are of interest from the standpoint of current debates on globalization, particularly in light of international public opposition sparked by the WTO "millennium round" meetings in Seattle in 1999. The MAI was drafted with full recognition that transnational corporations control the direction of their profit flows, and that corporations bear "nationalities" associated with their "foreign" status when investing in another country. Contrary to globalization theorists who maintain that the size and scale of capital today works in contradistinction to nation-states, the MAI was motivated by a concern to prevent other nation-states from laying claim to control over the "rights" of the home state's corporate profits. The WTO has encountered opposition not only among populations of member states who object to the domestic implications of corporate control but also among leaders of Third World nations within the WTO. The dominance of advanced states acting as the defenders of multinationals with home offices based within their borders is now widely recognized. Globalization in other words, has to do with the global, or imperialistic, reach of multinational corporations based in certain nation-states, not the delinking of multinationals from states per se.

The protection of the "rights" of the parent corporation to invest and return profits, free of the fetters of nationally enforced policies such as taxation, were central to the concerns of the MAI. The agreement sought to prevent "discrimination" on the grounds of being foreign; the threat of expropriation was particularly clear, even gradual or "creeping" expropriation.[56] Like a corporate code of civil rights, the draft MAI document read as if corporations are living beings, with home citizen states and the risk of facing prejudice and bias when travelling in foreign lands.

The most articulate challenge to Canada's participation in the MAI was put forward by Tony Clarke and Maude Barlow.[57] Referring to the MAI as "NAFTA on steroids,"[58] the debate was framed primarily in terms of the threat the accord would pose to the sovereign status of the Canadian state. There is an historic popularity of left nationalism among the English Canadian progressive community. However, it is not the Canadian state whose interests were threatened by the implementation of the MAI. What was codified in the MAI with reference to foreign investment was not new, especially in the post-NAFTA period. Moreover, as in NAFTA, national exemptions could be written into the agreement. The Liberal government, in its defence of the MAI, could point to the fact that Canada is one of the most developed economies in the world. This economic status has certainly not been hampered by large amounts of foreign capital investment.[59]

Foreign investment in Canada, like foreign investment in the US and Western Europe, is linked to an industrially advanced economy. Rather than producing a chain-like dependency drawing capital and commodities outside the domestic market, foreign investment is attracted to the large, stable, and economically advanced market within the investment zone.[60] There are examples, notably the erstwhile "miracle" economies of Asia and Latin America, where large amounts of foreign investment have not generated an inevitable weakening of the domestic economy despite increasing dependence on international markets. Certainly, earlier critics of dependency theory came to grips with the limits of such a claim some years ago.[61]

The argument originally put forward against the MAI by left nationalist critics was flawed analytically; moreover, it does not stand up empirically. In the case of Canada, between 1980 and 1997, foreign direct investment increased by almost 50 per cent. Over the same period, however, Canadian corporate investment abroad increased by 300 per cent.[62] The Canadian state's interest in the MAI cannot be explained on the basis of a primary motivation to secure the profits of foreign corporations investing within Canada. In fact, major foreign interests were already operating at low-risk terms under prior agreements including NAFTA.

To challenge the MAI on these terms placed its opponents in a contradictory theoretical space. Opposing corporate rule within Canada and internationally pulled them towards a class analysis; yet calling for increased Canadian sovereignty tended to blur class divisions and paint Canada as a unified whole, facing exceptional international discrimination. To their credit, in a subsequent publication, Maude Barlow and Tony Clarke take considerable steps towards the resolution of this contradiction. Their recent book, *Global Showdown: How the New Activists Are Fighting Global Corporate Rule*,[63] all but sheds any memory of left nationalism and soundly lambastes the corporate domination of the Canadian state. There is also a clear recognition of Canada's role as far more than a junior player in the new, post-MAI, free trade negotiations. The authors expose Canada's lead in the international efforts to restore an MAI, playing a major role in advocating the General Agreement on Trade in Services (GATS) within the WTO and in the terms of the negotiations leading to the Free Trade Area of the Americas agreement.[64]

A focus on issues of class and capital accumulation serves to strengthen this critical perspective. This is the focus that has started to capture the imagination of critics of the WTO.[65] As an advanced OECD capitalist state, the interests of the Canadian business class and the Canadian state in the MAI followed from perceived opportunities to reap greater profits for Canadian corporations investing abroad, unfettered by the restrictions imposed by host states.

Moreover, a tactical alliance with local Canadian capital against foreign capital in order to oppose the MAI was strategically problematic. Rather than suffering a lack of sovereignty, this already sovereign state has demonstrated its competitive capitalist, and imperialist, nature all too clearly. Canada's corporate elite have displayed a record, historically and recently, that places it well on a par with its global competitors.

That Canada is a major capitalist power seems to be a point well understood within the international community. The United Nations Human Development Index has, in a sense, selected Canada as the best example of capitalism anywhere in the world: Canada has been repeatedly granted the status of the best country in the world to live over recent years.[66] The point to emphasize here is that the MAI, which advocated the full freedom of international corporate investment regardless of the interests or rights of working people as labourers or citizens, was consistent with the interests of the Canadian capitalist state. To challenge the MAI on the grounds of Canadian nationalism, and thus blur the class distinctions within Canada, places those who stand to lose from its implementation at a disadvantage; if, however, focus is shifted to those at the bottom of society – workers, Native people, Somalis and other peoples of the Third World, and most women and immigrants, etc.[67] – there is a common thread of interests potentially uniting those who suffer at the hands of the Canadian corporate elite and the state that supports it, both within Canada and internationally.

It should not be concluded from this argument that sovereignty of nation-states was immaterial to the MAI negotiations. The MAI was a treaty of advanced states, each of which has interests, though to varying degrees, in expanding the reach of their most prosperous multinationals unhindered by the regulations of other host states. Canada is on the side of the predators; but weaker states, first excluded from the MAI negotiations, and later marginalized in WTO deliberations, are indeed faced with the threat of imperialist expansion.

The United States is another, and certainly a larger, predator; it was in fact originally the primary advocate in the MAI negotiations. It also remains, despite its relative decline in global hegemonic influence since the end of the Vietnam War, the single most aggressive world power. Originally, the European Commission had proposed a global investment treaty like the MAI as part of the operations of the new World Trade Organization (WTO). However, the US representatives balked, fearing "that opposition from developing countries ... would 'water down' any consensus that might be reached on an investment treaty."[68] Later, the US changed its tune, and attempted to bring in MAI-style protections of multinational corporate investments within the WTO.

Once again, it is instructive to return to a consideration of Marx's analysis of capitalism. The centrality of class divisions is obviously a premise which informs Marx's work. Such an analysis requires in contemporary conditions the same sensitivity to historical specificity, exception, change, and contradiction that Marx was able to apply to conditions of emergent nineteenth century capitalism.[69] This is not an easy or simple task, but difficulty in accomplishment does not make it any less strategically important.

IN CONCLUSION:
CAPITAL AND CLASS IN GLOBAL PERSPECTIVE

APEC and the MAI represent, in sum, the equivalent of international bosses' agreements. Those who support the rights of workers, the poor, and the oppressed should oppose the continuance and implementation of APEC and celebrate the demise of the MAI. But to challenge capital effectively, we have to understand it. The case that has been presented above is that Marxism is the most effective means by which to do so. As capital finds its profit base in crisis, national competition increases. At the same time, borders are broken or opened to capital to allow for greater mobility for investment and trade. Millions of workers and the poor lose their homes and their livelihoods in the process, yet the system becomes only more oppressive to those it victimizes. For those who suffer the consequences of global capital, the repressive regulation of borders at the hands of specific nation-states only tightens.

Marxism can reclaim its ideological position as the method most uniquely suited to explain capitalism, in all its complexity, including its massive wealth and its tragic inhumanity. Of course, it would be a nonsense to presume that there is only one Marxist interpretation. A common reading of Marx regarding global conditions, even among his adherents, is that it was not Marx himself who developed the methodological tools for explaining international political economy. Instead, it is presumed that Marx's emphasis on "a closed system, which, rightly or wrongly, came to be taken among many of his followers to coincide with the national economy"[70] is ill-suited to current times. In the foregoing discussion, I have attempted to demonstrate that, in fact, within Marx's original method the tools to understand contemporary global relations not only exist but can serve us well. The specific examples of APEC and the MAI have been selected as case studies, looked at through the lens of classical Marxism.

Marxism is not only a method of calculated critique, but ultimately a philosophy of liberation. Marx watched capitalism at its dawn, and he sought to understand its every moment, no less its capacity for productive expansion than its vicious brutality. As we begin a new millennium, we might do well also to remember Marx's optimism: there is really nothing to lose but the chains, and there is a world, a very big world, yet to win.

NOTES

1 I would like to thank Marcus Pistor for his expert research assistance in the preparation of this article.

2 The term "agreement" is used generically to apply to these various accords, as it aptly addresses the efforts on the part of formally appointed government representatives to arrive at common economic codes of operation, as opposed to the traditional anarchy of the free market. However, the two main accords which are the focus of this discussion indicate the problematic nature of the term. While the MAI included the name "agreement" in its title, it remained unsigned and collapsed under strained negotiation; APEC, while much further advanced, is non-binding and therefore begs the definition of an agreement. Despite these provisos,

for the purposes of this discussion the term "agreement" seems more suitable than any other.

3　Nigel Harris, *The New Untouchables: Immigration and the New World Worker*, Harmondsworth: Penguin Books, 1996: viii; for further elaboration specifically in regards to global migration, see page 20.

4　Ibid., viii.

5　See Abigail B. Bakan, "On the Relevance of Marxism," in Bruce Berman and Piotr Dutkiewicz (eds), *Africa and Eastern Europe: Crisis and Transformations*, Kingston: Centre for International Relations and Program of Studies in National and International Development, 1993.

6　See W. W. Rostow, *The Stages of Economic Growth: A Non-Communist Manifesto*, Cambridge: Cambridge University Press, 1960, and the debates pursuant. A comprehensive and reflective summary is to be found in Colin Leys, "The Rise and Fall of Development Theory" and "Samuel Huntington and the End of Classical Modernization Theory," in *The Rise and Fall of Development Theory*, London: James Currey, 1996: 3–44, 80–103.

7　See for example, Kenneth E. Bauzon, "Development Studies: Contending Approaches and Research Trends," in Kenneth E. Bauzon (ed.), *Development and Democratization in the Third World: Myths, Hopes and Realities*, Washington: Crane Russak, 1992: 35–52; and James Manor (ed.), *Rethinking Third World Politics*, New York and London: Longman, 1991.

8　See, for example, Peter B. Kenen (ed.), *Managing the World Economy: Fifty Years After Bretton Woods*, Washington, DC: Institute for International Economics, 1994; A. S. Milward, *The European Rescue of the Nation-State*, London: Routledge, 1992; B. Connolly, *The Rotten Heart of Europe*, London: Faber, 1996; Alex Callinicos, "Europe: The Mounting Crisis," *International Socialism Journal*, series 2, no. 75; 23–60. On the FTA and NAFTA, particularly from the point of view of debates in Canada, see Duncan Cameron and Mel Watkins (eds), *Canada Under Free Trade*, Toronto: James Lorimer and Co., 1993; and Michael D. Henderson, *The Future on the Table: Canada and the Free Trade Issue*, Toronto: Masterpress, 1987.

9　See for example Steven Shrybman, *The World Trade Organization: A Citizen's Guide*, Toronto: Canadian Centre for Policy Alternatives and James Lorimer and Co. Ltd., 1999; Susan George, "Globalising Designs for the WTO: State Sovereignty Under Threat," *Le Monde diplomatique*, July 1999. <http://www.tni.org/george/wto/lemonde.htm>; and Abbie Bakan, "After Seattle: The Politics of World Trade," *International Socialism Journal*, series 2, vol. 86, Spring 2000: 19–36.

10　Karl Marx and Frederick Engels, "Manifesto of the Communist Party," English translation according to F. Engels, London 1888, in Karl Marx and Frederick Engels, *On Colonialism*, New York: International Publishers, 1972: 12.

11 See for example, Thomas C. Holt, *The Problem of Freedom: Race, Labor, and Politics in Jamaica and Britain, 1832–1938*, Baltimore and London: Johns Hopkins Press, 1992; Benjamin B. Ringer, *We the People and Others: Duality and America's Treatment of its Racial Minorities*, New York and London: Routledge, 1983; and Kees van der Pijl, *The Making of an Atlantic Ruling Class*, Thetford: Verso, 1984.

12 Karl Marx, *Capital: A Critique of Political Economy, Volume III: The Process of Capitalist Production as a Whole*, Frederick Engels (ed.), Moscow: Progress Publishers, 1959: 334–5.

13 Leo Huberman, *Man's Worldly Goods: The Story of the Wealth of Nations*. New York and London: Monthly Review Press, 1936; rpt. 1968: 93.

14 See, for example, Scott Lash and John Urry, *The End of Organized Capitalism*, Madison: University of Wisconsin Press, 1987; and Alain Touraine, *Return of the Actor: Social Theory in Postindustrial Society*, Minneapolis: University of Minneapolis Press, 1988.

15 The obvious exception here is in the European Union. However, even in this case, the mobility rights associated with capital remain far greater and more flexible than the right of labour to travel across borders. Moreover, the conditions pointing towards a lower standard of living and declining social wage for workers under the Maastricht Treaty is in sharp contrast with increased corporate profitability. This contrast indicates that the balance of "rights" in the European context is not fundamentally contrary to this general pattern.

16 Tanya Basok, "Refugee Policy: Globalization, Radical Challenge, or State Control?" *Studies in Political Economy*, no. 50, Summer 199: 133.

17 Report of the Special Rapporteur, Ms Gabriela Rodriquez Pizarro, United Nations Economic and Social Council, Commission on Human Rights, 56th Session, 6 January 2000. E/CN.4/ 2000/82. (G0010036.pdf).

18 For a concise summary of this process, see Susan George, *The Debt Boomerang: How Third World Debt Harms Us All*, Boulder and San Francisco: Westview Press, 1992: 110–35.

19 Karl Marx, *Capital: A Critique of Political Economy, Volume I: A Critical Analysis of Capitalist Production*, Moscow: Progress Publishers, 1959: 601.

20 See for example Peter J. Katzenstein, *Regionalism in Comparative Perspective*, Oslo: Advanced Research on the Europeanization of the Nation State, January 1996, Working Paper no. 1; Gary Hufbauer, "Whither APEC?" *Journal of Asian Economics*, vol. 6, no. 1, Spring 1995: 89–94; Richard Higgott, Richard Leaver, and John Ravenhill (eds), *Pacific Economic Relations in the 1990s: Cooperation or Conflict*, New South

Wales: Allen and Unwin, 1993; and Tony Clarke and Maude Barlow, MAI: *The Multilateral Agreement on Investment and the Threat to Canadian Sovereignty*, Toronto: Stoddart, 1997.

21 The APEC member countries are Australia, Brunei Darussalam, Canada, Chile, People's Republic of China, Hong Kong, Indonesia, Japan, Republic of Korea, Malaysia, Mexico, New Zealand, Papua New Guinea, Peru, Republic of the Philippines, Russia, Chinese Taipei, Thailand, United States, and Vietnam. For sources see Asia Pacific Economic Cooperation, "An Introduction to APEC," n.p.; APEC Economic Committee, *State of Economic and Technical Cooperation in APEC*, Singapore: APEC Secretariat, November, 1996; and APEC home page: <http://www.apecsec.org.sg/member/membec_report.html>.

22 APEC home page, February 2000, "Executive Summary"; <http://apecsec.org.sg/ExecSummary.html>.

23 APEC, Division of the Department of Foreign Affairs and International Trade, Government of Canada, "APEC and Business," 1997.

24 Pacific Economic Cooperation Council, Philippine Institute for Development Studies and The Asia Foundation, *Perspectives on the Manila Action Plan for Asia*, Manila: Pacific Economic Cooperation Council, 1996: 5.

25 APEC Economic Committee, *State of Economic and Technical Cooperation in APEC*, 61; see also 24–53.

26 Ibid., 20-2.

27 During the 1997 APEC summit meeting in Vancouver, demonstrations outside the gated walls of the APEC conference took place throughout the week. On November 25, police responded by an unprecedented attack against protesters, without warning, breaking up the demonstration using tanks of pepper spray. The crowd of several thousand was dispersed after dozens were arrested and one person was hospitalized. Further investigations have raised suspicion of orders to suppress the crowd arising directly from the office of the prime minister, following negotiations to ensure the security of then Indonesian president Suharto. See *The National Features: The APEC Documents (CBC)*: February, 2000, <http://www.tv.cbc.ca/national/pgminfo/apec/docindex.html>, and W. Wesley Pue (ed.), *Pepper in Our Eyes: The APEC Affair*, Vancouver: UBC Press, 2000.

28 The APEC region was seen as increasingly becoming the "centre of gravity of the global economy." See APEC Economic Committee, *1995 Report on the APEC Regional Economy: Performance, Structure, Outlook and Challenges*, Singapore: APEC Secretariat, 1995: 3.

29 Laura Eggerton, "APEC soothes market storm: damage control takes precedence over freer trade," *The Toronto Star*, 26 November 1997: A–7.

30 This according to economists at the Union Bank of Switzerland. See Peter Cook, "Asian Fears May Just Be Shadow-Boxing," *The Globe and Mail*, 29 December 1997: B–1.

31 "IMF warns money crisis will spread," *The Toronto Star*, 21 December 1997: A-16; and APEC country reports, February, 2000: Japan: <http://www.apecsec.org.sg/member/jpec_report.html>

32 APEC country reports, February, 2000: Japan: <http://www.apecsec.org.sg/member/jpec_report.html>.

33 Dato Noor Adlan, "APEC and Asia's Crisis," *Far Eastern Economic Review*, 28 May 1998, Editorial, APEC: <http://www.apecsec.org.sg/97brochure/97brochure.html>.

34 Such a historic deal was this, that in the trade deal between Microsoft, owned by Bill Gates, the richest man in the world, and then flailing competitor, Apple, the latter's president Steve Jobs stated: "It's not like Apple is going to become like Microsoft; they're obviously going to compete. But it's crazy for the only two players on the desktop market not to be working together. It's a little like Nixon going to China. It's the right thing to do." From an interview, "'It's like Nixon to China': Steve Jobs on the Microsoft Deal – and Apple's Future," *Newsweek*, 18 August 1997: 26.

35 See Robert Benewick and Paul Wingrove (eds), *China in the 1990s*, Vancouver: UBC Press, 1995.

36 Rosemary Foot, "China's Foreign Policy in the Post–1989 Era," in Robert Benewick and Paul Wingrove (eds), *China in the 1990s*, Vancouver: UBC Press, 1995: 236–9.

37 Ibid., 240.

38 There is a fairly extensive literature challenging this assumption from a critical and progressive perspective. See for example, Grant Evans and Kevin Rowley, *Red Brotherhood at War*, London: Verso, 1984; Nigel Harris, *The Mandate of Heaven: Marx and Mao in Modern China*, London: Quartet Books, 1978; and Charlie Hore, *The Road to Tienanmen Square*, London: Bookmarks, 1991.

39 See *Economist*, 16 August 1997, 56.

40 Martin Crutsinger, "US, China Forge WTO Deal: Beijing to Cut Tariffs, Allow Greater Access to Markets," *The Toronto Star*, 16 November 1999: C–1,5.

41 See for example, Abigail B. Bakan and Daiva Stasiulis, "Structural Adjustment, Citizenship, and Foreign Domestic Labour: The Canadian Case," in Isabella Bakker (ed.), *Rethinking Restructuring: Gender and Change in Canada*, Toronto: University of Toronto Press, 1996; and Kathy McAfee, *Storm Signals: Structural Adjustment and Development Alternatives in the Caribbean*, Boston: South End Press and Oxfam America, 1991.

42 APEC Economic Committee, *State of Economic and Technical Cooperation in APEC*, 7; see also 32.

43 Ibid., 32. This orientation is further elaborated in the Framework for the
Integration of Women in APEC policy endorsed by APEC Ministers and
Leaders in September 1999, which explicitly advocates the involvement
of women in the business sector. See "APEC Leaders Encourage Continuing Growth in Women's Participation," APEC Media Release, 13 September 1999: <http://www.apecsec.org.sg/whatsnew/press/rel59_99.html>

44 L. Lim and N. Oishi, "International Labour Migration of Asian Women:
Distinctive Characteristics and Policy Concerns," Geneva: International
Labour Organisation, 1996:
<http://www.ilo.org/public/english/bureau/inf/pr/96-1.htm>. See also,
Daiva Stasiulis and Abigail B. Bakan, "Regulation and Resistance: Strate-
gies of Migrant Domestic Workers in Canada and Internationally," *Asian
and Pacific Migration Journal*, Fall 1997; and "Negotiating Citizenship
Globally: Migrant Domestic Workers as a Case Study," *Feminist Review*,
London, UK, no. 57, September 1997.

45 Karl Marx, *Capital: A Critique of Political Economy, Volume III*, 20–1.

46 Such a pattern is not, of course, unique to the formation of trade blocs.
See for example, Jacqueline Bhabha, "Embodied Rights: Gender Persecu-
tion, State Sovereignty and Refugees," *Public Culture*, no. 9, 1996: 3–32.

47 OECD News Release, 3 December 1998, Paris:
<http://www.oecd.org/news_and_events/release/nw98–114a.htm>.

48 See various articles, *The Economist*, 11–17 December 1999; *Newsweek*,
13 December 1999; *Time* (Canadian edition), 13 December 1999.

49 Department of Foreign Affairs and International Trade, Government of
Canada, "Multilateral Agreement on Investment (MAI): The Road to
Negotiations," n.p.: 9 September 1997: 1–2. The participating countries
in the MAI, in addition to the European Commission, were Australia,
Austria, Belgium, Canada, Czech Republic, Denmark, Finland, France,
Germany, Greece, Hungary, Iceland, Ireland, Italy, Japan, Korea, Luxem-
burg, Mexico, Netherlands, New Zealand, Norway, Poland, Portugal,
Spain, Sweden, Switzerland, Turkey, United Kingdom, and the United
States.

50 Department of Foreign Affairs and International Trade, Government of
Canada, "Multilateral Agreement on Investment (MAI)," n.p.: 29 May
1997: 2.

51 As Steven Shrybman summarizes it, "The WTO Services Agreement – The
MAI by Any Other Name," *The World Trade Organization*, 101.

52 Editorial, *The Globe and Mail*, "Y.E.S to M.A.I." 25 November 1997:
A-18.

53 See Abbie Bakan, "After Seattle: The Politics of World Trade," *International Socialism*, series 2, vol. 86, Spring 2000: 19–36.

54 Tony Clarke, "MAI-DAY: The Corporate Rule Treaty – The Multilateral Agreement on Investment (MAI) Seeks to Consolidate Global Corporate Rule," paper presented to the Common Front on World Trade Organization, Ottawa, Sierra Club of Canada, April 1997: 2.

55 OECD, *Multilateral Agreement on Investment: Consolidated Text and Commentary*, Paris: OECD, May 1997: 94.

56 Ibid., 33, 122.

57 Clarke and Barlow, MAI: *The Multilateral Agreement on Investment and the Threat to Canadian Sovereignty.*

58 Sergio Marchi and Maude Barlow, "Is the MAI Good for Canada?" *The Toronto Star*, 10 November 1997: A–18.

59 Department of Foreign Affairs and International Trade, "Canada's Investment Agreements and Negotiations," n.p.: 9 September 1997; and "Multilateral Agreement on Investment (MAI): The Facts," n.p.: 9 September 1997; see also Sergio Marchi and Maude Barlow, "Is the MAI Good for Canada?" *The Toronto Star*, 10 November 1997: A–18.

60 Regarding the Canadian example, see William Carroll, *Corporate Power and Canadian Capitalism*, Vancouver: University of British Columbia Press, 1986; Paul Kellogg, "Arms and the Nation: The Impact of 'Military Parasitism' on Canada's Place in the World Economy," Kingston: Ph.D. Dissertation, Department of Political Studies, 1990.

61 Not least, see Colin Leys, *The Rise and Fall of Development Theory.*

62 Department of Foreign Affairs and International Trade, Government of Canada, "Multilateral Agreement on Investment (MAI)," n.p.: 29 May 1997: 1.

63 Maude Barlow and Tony Clarke, *Global Showdown: How the New Activists are Fighting Global Corporate Rule*, Toronto: Stoddart, 2001.

64 Ibid., 90–6.

65 See, for example, Susan George, "Globalising Designs for the WTO," *Le Monde diplomatique,* July 1999, <http://wwwtni.org/george/wto/lemonde.htm>.

66 *United Nations Human Development Report 1997* (Cary, N.C. and Oxford: Oxford University Press, 1997). Also see website <http://www.undp.org/undp/hudro/97.htm>; for UNHD Reports, 1990–96, see <http://www.undp.org/undp/hydro/hdrsindx.htm>.

67 For more detail on some of these issues, see, for example Royal Commission on Aboriginal Peoples, Ottawa: Ministry of Supply and Services, 1996; and Peter Desberats, *Somalia Cover-Up: A Commissioner's Journal*, Toronto: McClelland and Stewart, 1997.

68 Tony Clarke, "MAI-DAY: The Corporate Rule Treaty," 1.

69 See for example, one of Marx's most brilliant studies of the anatomy of capitalist society, *The Eighteenth Brumaire of Louis Bonaparte*, Moscow and London: International Publishers, 1967.

70 Bjorn Hettne, "Introduction: The International Political Economy of Transformation," in Bjorn Hettne (ed.), *International Political Economy: Understanding Global Disorder*, Halifax and London: Fernwood Publishing and Zed Books, 1995: 9.

Amnesty: An Essay in Law and Politics

PHIL GOLDMAN

One of the difficult truths of contemporary political life is that there can be little if any justice measured out to the victims of great political crimes. The position can be argued in different ways. For example, truly horrific crimes necessarily escape redress because there is no proportionate penalty that can possibly make up for the evil committed. Even capital punishment is a diminished response to torture, rape, and murder committed on a large scale. Or, simply too many people are involved in carrying out the violence against the innocent to ever allow for rooting out enough of them to qualify as just retribution. Why so many necessarily remain beyond reach, aside from simply numbers, is that political systems, when they change, continue to rely on the same agents of power, especially the police. Finally, politics is largely about the future, about getting on with governing, and often this compels accommodation with the past and with the agents of political criminality who are too powerful to be judged and punished by any transparent judicial process.

The observations that follow are reflections on the problems of doing justice to victims of political violence. For the most part they are animated by a desire to explain to victims the limits of justice as most victims are likely to conceive of justice. My focus is on amnesty: the act of state that eliminates the possibility of pursuing violators by way of law. Readers should note, however, that, while I am treating amnesty as a formal doctrine, I am also concerned to view it as a process driven by specific considerations of both politics and law. For law, these include questions of evidence and testimony, the individuated character of legal inquiry, the assignment of legal responsibility, and the problem of judging with clean hands. For politics, there are issues of the centrality of violence in prosecuting its purposes, of the quest for transitional accommodations between winners and losers, and of the interests shared by competing political classes that seem to exclude continued considerations of the interests of victims of political violence.

As legal doctrine, amnesty stands as the most significant formal obstacle to accounting for past wrongs. It commands us, as a matter of law, to forgo redress, because the events complained of have no legal existence. No memory can be recounted that a court might hear. Amnesty is a challenge, above all, to the signification of memory. It is not the only challenge because testimony is difficult for both personal and political reasons, in addition to the legal burden that amnesty imposes. What follows from this is a recognition that the presentation of remembered events is problematic, and that bearing witness has a politics, entailing a mobilization of resistance to forgetting. It is a politics that is almost always discomforting because it is so often relentlessly accusatory – not only against the perpetrators but also against the silent. And so is it also a politics against any of us who would prefer to not be discomforted.

I MEMORY

It was a feature of almost all the former [gulag] camp inmates I have met immediately after their release – they had no memory for dates or the passage of time and it was difficult for them to distinguish between things they had actually experienced themselves and stories they had heard from others. Places, names, events and their sequence were all jumbled up in the minds of these broken people, and it was never possible to disentangle them ... I was horrified at the thought that there might be nobody who could ever properly bear witness to the past. But it later turned out that there were people who had made it their aim from the beginning not only to save themselves, but to survive as witnesses.[1]

[i]

Memory is a theme that emerges in most experiences with political oppression. The stark truths about state brutality surface with great difficulty. The state denies the existence of camps, or what they are about. It denies the claims of violence perpetrated against its own subjects. Too often, few remain to object. They have been "disappeared," leaving little of the trajectory of their final days. The survivors and those intimately connected with them and with the disappeared, the victims of an allegedly imagined process, are left most often to their own devices to register a different story.

It is not easy to recount what is most readily dealt with by repression. The memories are too painful. Often, there is need of psychological assistance in confronting past horrors. Witnesses subject to cross-examination also can be tripped up. Their grasp of detail is found faulty. Sequences do get jumbled, identities of perpetrators shown to be uncertain. Countries and judicial processes can be consequently brought into disrepute.

Catharsis is sometimes thought to be a product of exposing repressed events. Certainly, there are recorded moments of revelatory responses following the breaking of barriers of silence. "Suddenly a compulsion to speak of the unspeakable seemed to consume the Argentine imagination. The cathartic aspects of speaking the unspeakable that psychologists discovered almost a century earlier were rediscovered in Argentina, the centre of psychoanalytic thinking in Latin America."[2] These are significant moments, revealing to many in Argentina, in their political isolation, a fuller truth about terrors previously only imagined. However, we should take care not to underestimate the impediments to speech for many by romanticizing its effects for some. The concern is that a commitment to the value of speech is often too decontextualized. What are the real consequences of speaking? In some countries, the truth is sufficiently accusatory and pointed that the witness becomes targeted for retribution. So, who will protect the witness? What police force, what community will ensure safety? And, is there not also a stigmatization that comes from confessing to violation?

Women in the former Yugoslavia are encouraged by the international press to reveal details about rape. It is reported that not only are some paid for speaking with reporters but that they are paid more if they do not speak anonymously. The larger audience for these traumatic accounts rarely develop any insight into the consequences visited upon the women. We know that independent of broader public revelations, many women have been rejected by their husbands and families because of the shame and impurity attached to sexual violation. How much more difficult must it be for women to share their experiences in a public arena.[3] In South Africa, women wanting to testify before the Truth and Reconciliation Commission demanded special hearings and special panels to hear from women about human rights abuses. The Commission declined to move the hearings from the public arena given the importance attached to the political educative functions of the process. It also constitutes a difficult acknowledgement that testimony is a public act in which testifiers neither select the audience nor the terms of reference for hearing their words.

Despite impediments to testimony, there are some people, usually a small minority, whose dedication to truth-telling remains firm. They are not the easiest of people. We are frequently discomforted by their commitment to remembrance because we detect in that commitment a preoccupation with "vengeance" that has become normatively devalued. To take revenge is too primitive an inclination, too "Old Testament" ("an eye for an eye"), too feminine, too counterproductive, too dangerous.[4] Moreover, personalities afflicted by an unremitting accusatory anger are "prickly" and seem to demand a response by their very presence amongst us. Indeed, it is in the very nature of anger expressed that, unlike pain, it will brook no silence from its audience.[5] We prefer the witness who recounts his/her pain to the one who wants to know why we remained silent.

Understandably, most people not directly affected by the violence, would opt for the grace of an innocence conferred by ignorance. Many in Argentina, during the dark period of the dirty war, are said to have developed a "passion for ignorance," because they did not, and perhaps psychologically could not, know what was going on around them.[6] Moreover, in a state which strictly controlled the means of communication and was dedicated to a politics of disinformation, for those who preferred to not ask difficult or even obvious questions, it was easy to remain in the dark. But once this dark truth is spoken, the acknowledgement of their ignorance becomes an accusation of complicity. They are condemned to take refuge in ignorance and to find personal mechanisms to deal with lingering thoughts about "willful blindness." For outside observers, for example, it seems quite astonishing when well-placed white South Africans react with horror and surprise to revelations about police assassination squads. "Not even our wildest nightmares could have matched the horrifying reality of what was going on around us as we went about our normal business" writes John Battersby, the editor of the Sunday Independent.[7] Hannah Arendt's more critical view is that in politics silence is acquiescence.[8] If so, then naming the silence is accusatory. There is a large reservoir of complicity in unasked questions, questions which will take different forms in different societies. Where did the "disappeared" go? Why have they not returned? Where is their property? Who is living on their land, in their homes? What has become of their children? Who was raped? Who tortured? What did they do or was it just their turn? Why not me? And so, facing such resistance against knowing, the victim of the violence and the terror does not easily find an authentically receptive audience.

Standing out amongst the survivors are those who chose to resist the oppression and were harmed by their resistance – by exile, imprisonment, and/or physical attack – yet who do not seem caught up in coming to terms with their past. They are easier dinner guests. They do not want their lives to become defined solely by the role of witness. "Living well is the best revenge" is pre-eminently the perspective of those who remain animated by an alternative political vision.[9] This is likely a minority view, but perhaps it is more prevalent for those who have accepted some political responsibility for remaking the future. It may even be a necessary stance if the future must be built, somehow, in conjunction with agents of the past. This dilemma reasserts itself, in post-war Germany, in France, in Argentina, Chile, in Eastern Europe, in the former Soviet Union, and in South Africa. There is no shortage of reconciliation talk that focuses attention away from the past and onto the future. But for many victims, it is like bad medicine. How much memory will reconciliation cost? How many criminals will not thereby be removed from power and liberty? How much will the future thus be condemned to re-enact the past?

[ii]

For the most part, current debates over the disposition of the crimes and criminals of precursor regimes centre around the application of law. The demands are articulated in the language of justice and the particular processes of criminal trials. Means to formally register long-repressed truths are sought. Storytelling is not enough. The media representation of horrific experiences is never definitive. There is a shaky reality where images of certain atrocities blend with images of other atrocities. Law has distinct advantages over narratives produced by other means. It is focused. It deals only with the case at hand. It normally requires the attendance of both the accused and the accusers. It makes authoritative findings about credibility and chooses amongst competing narratives, again authoritatively. And it registers its findings of guilt on the bodies of the guilty. Law thus engenders a process full of measurable consequences and elicits expectations about deterring repetitions of political violence in the future. No wonder then that there is so much concern expressed about not arresting and prosecuting Hutu *genocidaires* in Rwanda or war criminals responsible for "ethnic cleansing" in the former Yugoslavia.

There is a further aspect of the application of law that is of special significance. The crimes alleged are said to have been committed, usually, against humanity, but are formally presented as having been committed against the state. It is the state that prosecutes, or in the case of international tribunals, some designated international sovereignty. The law speaks in the language of generality and incorporates particular harms visited on named persons or groups as instances of broader injury to the state. And so, as prosecutor, the state must make out a case. But what case? Is not the case provided by testimony of the victims? The answer is, only partly. For what is alleged is more than kidnapping, torture, rape, and murder. The allegations are broader: these crimes have been committed in the service of a larger political project. And it is normally not given to the victim to offer up enough by way of testimony about the larger animus behind the offences. Too little of the why of the assault is contained within the victims' experience of the assault. So the memories of the victims, however tested against evidence, are insufficient to make the case that the law requires the state to make.

The task of prosecution is an exercise in the political mobilization of a wide range of narratives and, where available, documentation. Each participant contributes something to the end result, but may find the discourse and findings discordant with or irrelevant to the recollections. Does it really matter to the Muslim woman in Bosnia that the boy next door who sexually assaulted her played a role in a political strategy of communal destruction? So what if they never get the leaders? What matters first is that they get the neighbour. The task of establishing the broader connections is not hers, or at least not hers alone.

There is also a remarkable sameness to victim narratives about violations of their bodies. The accounts do not register details of time and space. What matters is the pain and the destruction it produces. In a world replete with politics, what is recounted is so personal and isolated as to have almost no connection with the larger universe. But insofar as politics has a place in this hidden world, it is in the moments that re-enact the connections between pain and power. "Testimony given by torture victims from many different countries almost inevitably includes descriptions of being made to stare at the weapon with which they were about to be hurt: prisoners of the Greek Junta (1967–71), for example, were made to contemplate a wall arrangement of whips, canes, clubs, and rods, were made to examine the size of the torturer's fist ... [T]orture is a process which ... announces the conversion of every conceivable aspect of the event and the environment into an agent of pain."[10] There is little that is reported to be haphazard about this process. It is an organized and systematic demonstration of power. In the Philippines the torturers referred to the torture room as the "production room"; in South Vietnam, as the "cinema room"; and in Chile, as the "blue lit stage."[11] So the description of the process seems to ultimately focus on its setting, which becomes the metaphor for the pain.

However, the palpability of the experience of violence is, in itself, inexpressible. It is Elaine Scarry's view that physical pain ensures its unshareability through its resistance to language.[12] And because of the absence of the resources of speech, the articulation of pain necessarily invokes a limited reservoir of metaphors and analogies and most often requires someone not in pain to speak on behalf of those who are, such as physicians, spokespersons for Amnesty International, or lawyers. There is no obvious mechanism to directly communicate the pointed centre of the experience of violation. Yet, its translation, especially by others, themselves having to construct a language to capture what cannot be captured, raises questions of authenticity. It is as if the experiences being described are so unimaginable that they communicate an aura of unreality. "To have pain is to have certainty; to hear about pain is to have doubts."[13]

So, from the perspective of law, victims' voices are not usually enough. They cannot present the politics of the offence as the law conceives of politics. The personal as political is not the politics of the larger universe of planning, organization, and implementation. In a distressing way, their testimony is largely irrelevant. The tribunal hears it, because it is the humane thing to do. If there are issues of compensation, of course, then taking the measure of pain is legally significant. But, in the larger questions of liability, the law needs more.

[iii]

But what other voices are there? It has become an accepted pedagogical strategy for those who teach about the Holocaust that they should teach it through the eyes of the perpetrators. There is too much cognitive distance between the personal experiences of any survivor and the political organization of the "Final Solution" to allow the former to efficiently inform inquiry into the latter. For Holocaust teachers and for lawyers litigating Holocaust denial, they are aided by – indeed require – the considerable documentary evidence left by the servants of the Nazi state, committed as they were to punctilious documentation. In the absence of the perpetrators, or even in their presence, the words of the planners, presented mostly through the expert testimony of scholars who have mined the archives, loom very large in the projects of both teaching and prosecution.

In general, the particularity of the event, its location in time and space, and its animus, is better presented from the perspective of the violator than from that of the violated. Not only does the testimony of the accused confirm what the victims, with great difficulty, are trying to express. It also reveals more of the why, when, and where, of the reasons and the justifications, of its politics. That is so, not simply because the accused can recount more detail but because we believe them. If they confess to inflicting abuse, to torture, and to murder, they do so "against interest." We do not expect defendants to testify in this way. So while false confessions happen because there are instances where they are coerced by threats or induced by promises (and this is a real concern in South Africa where owning up to committing crimes for political reasons can lead to freedom), if there is some confidence in the process, acknowledging the truth of allegations has powerful truth-confirming effects. Even when there are elements of denial and justificatory clarification, searching cross-examination often shakes credibility. In brief, confession is more readily accepted than denial, which is often heard with great skepticism. And in instances where the defendant declines to testify, that declination itself frequently is viewed as incriminating.

Thus the law needs to hear from the perpetrators, or at least, at a minimum, confront them. So, too, does the political record that is amenable to revisionism, whether it takes the form of Holocaust denial or intelligence agency disinformation. And so too do the victims, most of all where the repression has been deliberately carried out in a manner designed to leave no record.

It was good there was a trial but for us [the Mothers of the Disappeared in Argentina] it was a parody of a trial. They never put the military in the dock. The people came to give evidence and the accused were never present. The defense lawyers came in their place. Any common person accused of something is required to be present ... Videla, Massera and the others only went to hear their sentences. In the courtroom they always referred to the accused as General someone, Admiral so and so, and the victims were always called 'terrorists' and 'subversives'.[14]

Perhaps more than anyone, the victims remain most dependent on their tormentors, the only people effectively situated to confirm the truth of their violation, or the violation of their family and friends. Whether it is from the mothers of the disappeared in Argentina or Chile or South Africa, there is a common request: tell us what happened to our children. Only the perpetrators know for sure; and the victims want to hear the answer directly, from those who can tell. Even if they lie, those who can tell hold a power of revelation not given to an army of victims.

2   AMNESTY AGAINST MEMORY

Now [having been pardoned] everything is history. and eventually the Argentine people will realize that the military acted in a correct way.[15]

[i]

Amnesty is, literally, forgetfulness. We can grasp its etymology more easily by reflecting on amnesia. It is referred to as a "legal forgetting" that includes something more than waiving the penalty. As a legal practice, it is an act of oblivion that results in a general pardon of the offences of subjects against a government. The very offences are to be forgotten. Nothing will be registered on the record. Historically, in England, monarchs at the time of their coronation, as an act of grace, would give amnesty. Amnesty is thus associated with power. Only a great power could transform the past. It is also connected with military victory. Amnesty clauses have been inserted into peace treaties, perhaps as acts of magnanimity, but also as negotiated terms of surrender.

The definition of amnesty and its history has some resonance with contemporary concerns. It is given more by new regimes than by old. The offences forgotten were committed in the past and have much to do with the old regime. It is also sometimes negotiated as a condition of succession. Beyond that, however, there is something wrong with the definition in contemporary discourse. The offences for which amnesty is now sought are those that have been committed by a government against its own subjects, whereas, traditionally, amnesty was granted to subjects for crimes against the state. Law always has difficulty with the concept of "state crime," and thus it reads that it is the "subjects" who are an amnesty's designated beneficiaries. It is a legal sleight of hand that contributes to a formal amnesia.

So there is not simply a directive to forget about the crime as well as the punishment but there is a distorting distinction between victims and perpetrators that confuses elementary truths. There are also statecraft reasons for the form that amnesty normally takes. Governments have an interest in not radically impugning antecedent governments. They might thereby bring into question the solidity of their own foundations; they might also establish discomforting precedents. Better, then, to be a successor, even if of a different stripe, than a usurper, however initially popular.

"Legal forgetting" is an arcane phrase, but it is more than merely formal. The efforts to establish amnesty constitutes a form of politics: the continuation of war by linguistic deconstruction. It is certainly fought as a means to save perpetrators of violence from imprisonment, but it is also about a struggle for the future's characterization of the past. This is reflected in the quotation that begins this section. The general, having been pardoned, is comforted that he now only awaits the verdict of history. In this sense, there is more at stake than a politics of amnesia. The offenders believe there is the possibility for a revisionist memory constructed on the foundation of amnesty. Therefore, there is understandable reluctance by the injured to support pleas for forgetting: if amnesty is amnesia, then the past is a lie, its victims dishonoured, and the future endangered.

[ii]

What makes amnesty possible is politics. I do not mean politics exclusively in the sense of strategic necessity or diplomatic wisdom, but rather in the disconnection of politics from crime. This is an old theme. In the past, amnesties were primarily exercised towards associations of political criminals and were sometimes granted absolutely. However, there were often exemptions from amnesty for highly placed political criminals. The earliest recorded amnesty of Thrasybulus in Athens excluded the "30 tyrants"; the amnesty on the restoration of Charles II did not include those responsible for the execution of his father, and the one proclaimed by Napoleon in 1815 exempted Talleyrand and thirteen other eminent persons. It was a feature of past amnesties to make peace with one's political enemies, but also, sometimes, to seek retribution for those deemed especially guilty and responsible.

Whatever the guilt of past leaders punished for their political opposition, we do not normally regard them, retrospectively, as criminals. Talleyrand, for example, may have had his troubles with Napoleon, but the historical record does not characterize his politics as criminal. Moreover, as a strictly legal matter, the law has had ways to treat political offenders differently. They are not typically regarded as criminals. Extradition treaties, for example, usually exclude from their ambit "political offences." International law rules also recognize a unique character to politically motivated criminal acts. Sometimes, it is a relatively simple matter to recognize a political offence, because the state labels it as such. Treason and sedition are paradigmatic examples of such offences. Therefore, it is unlikely that a person charged with treason could be extradited to the requesting state. In fact, even where the charge is not nominally political, extradition sometimes has been refused.[16] One reason for the different treatment of political offences in extradition law is that they are more "contextual" than other offences and that they thereby do not necessarily reveal a criminal personality. The person thus seeking refuge does not notionally present a danger. The IRA member may constitute a threat to the British government, but the US has no criminal justice reasons for extradition. And, finally, there is concern that political offences offend the principle of justice because of the suspicion that they are criminalized for reasons of politics and not reasons of law.

The reach of the political offences doctrine should not be overestimated. The jurisprudence on political offences is notoriously restrictive in giving effect to a broad liberal interpretation of their meaning. Exceptions have been legislated to deal with aeroplane hijacking and offences committed against politically protected persons. Accused people have been extradited for bombing defence installations, but they are now rarely charged with treason or sedition. The state's effort is to paint them as ordinary criminals; so they are likely to be charged with more conventional crimes. There is a long history of this in Northern Ireland. Nevertheless, there is something that might be called "relative" political offences – that is, actions which violate ordinary criminal law but are intimately connected to political events and purposes. Acts resulting from a political motive are exemplars of the definition.

Usually, courts are inclined to limit the judicial force of political motives to acts undertaken in the context of recognized patterns of political violence such as civil wars or insurrections. Perhaps the analogy to war works best; war legalizes what is normally illegal, like murder. So, perpetrators of political offences prefer to talk about being at war, even if self-defined and self-declared. They were doing battle with cancerous growths within the body politic, with Communism or some other dangerous movement. In Argentina, the military viewed itself as engaged in World War III with left-wing terrorism. In South Africa, the accused proclaim before the Truth and Reconciliation Commission that they were taught that they were engaged in a life-and-death struggle in which the very existence of the state was in question and that the murders and disappearances were essential elements in their cause. In Rwanda, there is even talk of preventive genocide: if the Hutus had not struck first, they would have been consumed by Tutsis who were planning their extinction.

The analogy with war, however, is instructive only to a point. It is, first off, the constructed version offered up by the state and is often misapplied, especially from the vantage point of the helpless unarmed victims. That is one reason why many in Argentina object to the phrase "dirty war."[17] The conflict was too one-sided.

Even war has its war crimes. These have become central components in the development of twentieth-century international law. Somehow, the more violent and indiscriminate the wars of the twentieth century have become, the more the effort to formally define the impermissible (perhaps thereby making the wide range of violence not included all the more acceptable). There are rules about the obligations towards civilians, about the treatment of captured soldiers, and about the constitution of crimes against peace and against humanity. The more rules there are, the more intense the efforts to give them effect and the stronger the consequent pressure to limit their reach. The argument is reminiscent of Nuremberg; it recites the enormity of the crimes and of the need to acknowledge responsibility and to deter by punishment their re-enactment. On the other side, it is victor's justice, it is *ex post facto*, it fails to acknowledge a certain moral equivalence between victor and vanquished; above all, it is just politics.

The losers who declaim "victor's justice" have some history on their side. Lenin characterized politics as the continuation of war by other means, thus reversing the Clausewitz dictum. Max Weber's widely referred-to definition of politics focuses on the inextricable connections between politics and violence. He identifies the state by specific reference to its monopoly over the legitimate employment of violence.[18] Weber here has in mind that politicians employ violence not only against foreign enemies but also against the citizenry, albeit, ostensibly for its own collective good. Presumably, the Weberian politician, if a person of integrity, acknowledges silently treating with the devil. In his play *Dirty Hands*, Sartre has the Communist leader Hoerderer declare, "I have dirty hands right up to the elbows. I've plunged them in filth and blood. Do you think I can govern innocently?"[19] The historical measure rarely has been couched in terms of guilt or innocence quite so starkly. Politics requires the doing of bad things, but the historical test is whether one does the bad things well, or at least well enough to ensure victory or success, not whether the bad things possess a transhistorical evil. Because historical truths cannot be known in the moment, the Argentine general who expects history to judge him right demands that no other kind of judgment be rendered, especially one not suited to the hard tasks of politics. It is amnesty that offers the best hope for history.

There is another argument for amnesty that deals not so much with the historical record but with the scope of the oppression. Because the bad things done were done by so many and were alleged to be so awful, prosecution is an impossibility. Here, there is a kind of convergence between those seeking prosecution and those seeking amnesty. In South Africa, the claim is that apartheid itself was a crime against humanity. By that very token, it is hard to know whom not to prosecute. In post-war Germany, the allied powers initiated a program of "denazification" that would have required the purging of anyone at all associated with the Nazi Party. It was soon clear that Germany would be rendered ungovernable if denazification became a serious enterprise. Abetted by the hostility between Russia and the West, the program became a dead letter. In Argentina, the army and human rights groups agreed that most acts undertaken during the repression could be judged abhorrent, but each drew a different conclusion: rights groups insisted that this justified prosecution; the armed forces argued that it could only be dealt with by amnesty.[20] The dilemma is clear: the more widespread the oppression, the more brutal its application; the greater the numbers involved, the stronger the forces demanding amnesty as a matter of necessity.

Insofar as the argument for amnesty wins out, the historical judgment being sought is not primarily moral. What the Argentine general expects is that history will judge the repression a success not as a moral enterprise but as a political and economic one. Its model is likely closer to that of post-Pinochet Chile, where the forces of the repression seem able to claim a retrospective victory in the performance of the Chilean economy. Pinochet has won. His followers boldly assert the relationship between the coup, the repression, and economic success and, further, that the economic success is somehow expected to erase from memory the filth and blood.

3 LAW AGAINST POLITICS

> Humanitarian law is luminous. It's one of the great achievements of the 20th century. The body of conventions, the Hague agreements, and so on have been incredible. The only things lacking have been enforcement provisions.[21]

[i]

First, why the luminosity of humanitarian law? Weschler is certainly right to note this as a feature of the twentieth century. It constitutes, at least at the level of aspirations, a different measure of politics. Most simply put, the ends can no longer justify the means; certainly the human casualties of political violence, and certainly many others, never thought so. It has been a hard lesson for politics, which has resisted so long the intrusion of legal modes of accounting into its sphere. I suspect that the Holocaust has had the most effect in limiting the resistance to accountability. In particular, the practice of genocide has undermined the case for distinguishing historical from ethical judgment. The Nuremberg Tribunals stand as evidence to that.

The intrusion of humanitarian standards of judgment into politics is also associated with the democratization of contemporary political life. Increasingly, the incorporation of more and more people into politics, even if only peripherally, has also entailed the spread of "conventional" moral discourse. Perhaps that is why Max Weber, in his "Politics as a Vocation" (which was, after all, about the rise of democratic politics), was so committed to reminding his audience of the central place of violence in politics.

Weber was adamant on the inappropriateness of everyday ethical concerns as bases for political judgment. "Instead of being concerned about what the politician is interested in, the future and the responsibility towards the future, this ethic is concerned about politically sterile questions of past guilt, which are not to be settled politically. To act in this way ... overlooks the unavoidable falsification of the whole problem, through very material interests; namely, the victor's interest in the greatest possible moral and material gain; the hopes of the defeated to trade in advantage through confessions of guilt."[22] Weber characterized the problem as one of holding the future hostage to the past. Certainly, this has some application to the relationship between law and politics. Law is retrospective. It aims to arrive at judgments about the past. In its ideal typical forms, it is not consequentialist. A good judge is concerned not with a judgment's potential to better the future but with its capacity to be right about the past. To think consequentially is too speculative.

Of course, specialists in the application of law, when justifying their agendas, take refuge in conventional beliefs about the connections between law and the future: societies will be condemned to repeat that which goes unpunished; or, victims will engage in vigilante justice thereby setting off a cycle of revenge. From the perspectives of politicians, these kinds of considerations seem paramount; ultimately, they choose to engage the law. But legal processes are difficult to control. They take on a life of their own and often intrude uncomfortably into political life, especially if they retain substantial elements of autonomy. Perhaps that is why judicial processes designed to deal with the crimes of previous regimes are limited in time. There will be hearings, but they cannot drag on indefinitely. It is as if there is to be a mourning period, after which the work of everyday life will begin anew.

[ii]

Weber's perspective on the political effects of moral judgments is likely widely shared by political actors holding public office. Certainly, there is little evidence that politicians were genuinely interested in pursuing Nazi war criminals who managed to locate in their countries. Whatever actions have been taken are mostly the product of political pressures brought by victim groups. Ironically, seeking redress for crimes against humanity has not so much resulted from the efforts of leaders ostensibly situated to speak for large collectivities but rather from the work of people labelled as speaking for "special interests." It reflects the mischaracterization of these crimes as crimes against humanity. In a world divided by ethnicity, race, class, and gender, humanity is without representation.

It has been characteristic of the debates about ethical considerations in politics to pit political realism against softer impulses. To some extent this divide has been viewed as gendered, with men seeming to inhabit the world of hard-headed politics, while women have been attracted to more "humanitarian" issues. Weber correctly, I believe, reflected a dominant gendered view of justice politics in his own description of the problems connecting personal ethics to political action. "Instead of searching like old women for the 'guilty one' after the war – everyone with a manly and controlled attitude would tell the enemy, 'We lost the war. You have won it. That is now all over. Now let us discuss what conclusions must be drawn according to the *objective* interests that come into play and what is the main thing in view of the responsibility towards the *future* which above all burdens the victor.'"[23] Leaving aside Weber's normative aspersions directed against women, there nevertheless is some empirical resonance with the contemporary role that women have played in seeking an accounting for past political crimes. In Argentina, but also in Chile, the Philippines, and Bosnia, women have been very visible in the movements for justice. In Argentina especially, the opposition to oppression has become associated with the campaigns of the *Madres de Plaza de Mayo*. There, on the restoration of democracy, the new political leadership sought ways to put behind it the political ramifications of the memories of the Junta. The *Madres* (or Mothers), in opposition to the government, insisted on a permanent exclusion of the military from politics and linked that exclusion with a radical transformation of Argentine society. As well, they vocally and visibly denounced efforts to arrive at an accommodation with the military that did not include prosecution by civilian courts. Above all, they were the firmest voices resisting the demands for amnesty. Perhaps not surprisingly, President Alfonsin made it clear that he saw no role for the kind of politics being advocated by the Mothers in a new constitutional regime.[24] From a legal perspective, constitutional law could not be built upon the foundations of criminal prosecutions. If the women did not understand this, it was because they were too divorced from political realities.

The connection between gender and justice, while largely contingent in the forms it takes in particular settings, seems to exhibit some more fundamental affinities. Certainly the focus on mothers is an old theme.

...You mothers, from whom all men take their breath
A war is yours to give or not to give
I beg you mothers
Let your children live
Let them owe you their birth but not their death
I beg you mothers
Let your children live[25]

Brecht's viewpoint attributes to women a political power rarely given in more conventional political discourse. If it is more than mere rhetoric; by now requiring mothers to withhold their offspring, it turns on its head the Nazi efforts to have German women reproduce the master race for the state. A version of this connection between mother and state resonates as well in the maternal expressions of loss articulated by women in Argentina. "We gave them (their *desparace-dos* children) birth, by taking them they have left a hole in our bodies."[26] This initial sense of loss then became transformed from an expression of individual maternal deprivation into a collective politics. "[W]e want to associate to witness, to denounce every violation. Because you know at the beginning we wanted only our children. But, as time passed, we got a different comprehension of what was going on in the world."[27]

How much of this politics is a form of gendered essentialism, a product of the understandings that uniquely or predominantly women bring to politics, is not made clear in these examples. But, it is reported that in contrast to the women, the experiences of the fathers in Argentina reflected a turning inward, a withdrawal from engagement, a spiralling downwards into "major narcissistic depressive states" associated with consequent high morbidity and death rates.[28] Furthermore, there is some evidence that fathers were more likely to deny the possibility of the worst interpretations of what might have happened to their children. Yet, even if that were not so, it is the women more than the men whom we associate with the political demands for an accounting of what happened with the children.

It is thus apparent that there were significant female voices in this politics of resistance, and perhaps even that these voices display a certain hegemony in the public representation of justice. What they articulate is an intimate connection between the public and private.

Those who have disappeared are sons and daughters, not comrades and guerrillas. Indeed, there is an identifiable struggle with the forces of the past in characterizing the victims. Some of the manifestations of this are especially gruesome. The daughter of Beatriz de Rubenstein disappeared in Argentina in 1977. After the return to civilian rule, Mrs Rubinstein received a parcel of human bones in 1984. Accompanying the parcel was the following:

Dear Madam,
As a culmination to your endless search for your daughter Patricia, we have decided to send you what's left of her, which, without any doubt, will satisfy your anxiety to meet her again earlier than was foreseen by God.

   This decision was taken as a result of a long investigation into your daughter's activities with the armed guerrillas and, just in case you don't know, we will give you a synthesis of the crimes that she committed, together with her husband.
– TREASON
– AIDING AND ABETTING THE ACTIVITIES OF THE ENEMY
– COLLABORATING WITH THE MONTONERO MURDERERS
As a consequence of all the above we condemned her to death. May God, our Father, have mercy on her soul.
                  Legion Condor – Squadron 33 – Mar Del Plata[29]

   Sometimes, of course, the killers get it wrong. Many people tortured and murdered were chosen by error. Or, it simply did not matter: random terror was as effective in undermining resistance as focusing on selected targets. There are many such stories that have emerged from Latin America. What is striking about the testimony of mothers, in Latin America and in South Africa before the Truth Commission, is their resistance to giving up control of the definition of their children. It is as if some are committed to retain a pre-political ownership of the public understanding of their dead, or their involvement with the process of justice engages a different conception of politics, at once more personal and yet more universal. The broader universe of listeners more readily grasps what it means to lose a child than what it means for the guerrillas to lose a comrade.

   There is a derivative tension between the relatives of the missing and the political movements whose work became the vocation of the children. Just as the oppressors want to label the victims as guerrillas, so too does the opposition. For the antagonists in the past struggle, there is a conjunction of interests in retaining and promoting a public and conventional political understanding of the murders. They may differ in the value they attach to the resistance fighters: heroes for one, villains for the other. They nevertheless see each other as true antagonists sharing the same ring.

Those who speak from somewhere on the sidelines, who enter from a more private sphere, recite a more difficult story for politics to incorporate. At every moment they are at risk of losing their public place. They may grasp at humanitarian law to provide some anchor, but they will mostly find that politics has ensured that it, too, is adrift.

IV AMNESTY IN THE SERVICE OF MEMORY

> We will show that we, at all times, believed that we were acting in the course and scope of our duties and within the scope of our authority.[30]

The absence of those responsible for gross human rights abuses from the inquiry into political violence and murders in Chile was a source of some frustration. There, the Truth and Reconciliation Commission was directed to compile a case-by-case documentation of the killings and disappearances. The aim of this process was to provide the victims some moral vindication. In the end, the report filed by the Commission verified many of the worst fears but did not provide the names of those responsible, believing that to be the proper function of a court rather than an investigatory tribunal. However, the return to democracy had included an acceptance of a 1978 amnesty law that Pinochet had enacted, effectively precluding prosecutions. Whatever the Commission might therefore have accomplished, there remained a large gap in the record and considerable anguish for the victims who wanted more concrete confrontation. Later, the courts began to interpret that amnesty law more liberally, as entailing a ban on punishment, but not on trial. In addition, President Alwyn initiated a process to assess violations for human rights abuses not covered by Pinochet's amnesty law.

Certainly, reflection on the Chilean experience seems to have been at work in the development of the South African amnesty provisions. In Chile, amnesty was first interpreted to prevent even the naming of the perpetrators of human rights violations. In South Africa, by contrast, it was felt that it was important that amnesty not have this effect and, in fact, could be harnessed to help discover truth. The South African amnesty law thus requires, as a condition of amnesty, the admission of responsibility for serious crimes.

What must be admitted to? First, because gross violations of human rights are central, the focus has been on amnesty applications for the most horrific of crimes. These have included kidnapping, conspiracy to kidnap, torture, conspiracy to murder, murder, the desecration of human remains, aggravated assault, and other serious offences. Second, the crimes for which amnesty can be given must have been committed from a political motive. In this, it re-enacts the contradictory relationships between crime and politics. If it is politics, then it is not crime.

Critics of the process who have been concerned that the crime of apartheid is going to go unpunished have a case. Apartheid was more than the sum of the criminal acts committed in its service. So, if we so define it as a gross violation of human rights, which it certainly was, it nevertheless is true that the individuation of the process that amnesty entails, by focusing on specific acts and in the absence of applications from senior government personnel, will make it difficult to provide a comprehensive picture of apartheid as a system of oppression.

The critics, mostly African National Congress (ANC) members, have another argument. The amnesty law does not distinguish between the promoters and resistors of apartheid. So all criminal acts committed from a political motive, regardless of the moral quality of the motive, are subject to the application of the law. ANC cadres are thus placed in the same position as security agents of the state. They have to apply for amnesty if their crimes are to be forgotten. Again, the "even-handed" application of the law of amnesty, like the individuation previously noted, contributes to blurring the history of apartheid.

Survivors and victim families have a third identifiable position. It is for them, and not the state, to forgive. This position has some affinities not only with perfectly understandable frustrations but, as well, with practices in many customary African legal systems. There, the dominant mode of disposition was direct reparation to the injured family. In fact, the family played a much more central role in the legal system than is characteristic of Western legal processes. So, the intrusion of the state, standing in the place of the victims in the amnesty hearings, if it is to retain victim legitimacy, requires efforts at more than perfunctory inclusion of their interests.

It is easy enough to grasp the political/strategic reasons for including this variant on amnesty in the truth and reconciliation efforts. By its formal even-handedness, it makes it somewhat easier for the forces that promoted apartheid to enter the new era on a footing of formal equality. It confirms that apartheid was all politics, explaining why criminal law will not be applied. It may also have reflected a strategic ANC goal to connect Inkatha with the National government. Not surprisingly, Inkatha was particularly loath to associate with amnesty. Also, from an ANC perspective, the process of offering proof of political direction must logically lead to revelations about the highest levels of the old regime. Finally, because of the formal neutrality built into the law, there is a view that disconnecting law from politics will contribute to establishing the legal system as an objective and neutral arbiter of political life. All this is characteristic of South Africa's constructed vision of liberal democracy. Mr Tutu, as Chair of the Commission, at one point threatened to resign if the ANC directed its members who might be at risk from prosecution to refuse to apply for amnesty. In this way, as well, by visibly insisting on compliance by all sides, the transformation to democracy may be more effectively institutionalized.

How much memory will amnesty elicit? It should be clear that amnesty is an uncertain high stakes game. We have no experience with the current effort to put amnesty in the service of the truth that reconciliation seems to require. Nevertheless, some conclusions can be tendered. First, there is always the need to be wary of confessions induced by promise of reward. Sometimes, labelling of the dead as active political enemies is contested. At other times, there is ambiguity about the politics of the crimes, about the clarity of the orders, and the extent of "gratuitous" perpetration of violence. Second, victims have followed the amnesty hearings, expecting particular revelations that will confirm their own understanding of events. Because too few perpetrators will apply – there is considerable peer pressure and threats to not do so – and because confessions will label victims as politically deserving of their fate, though not necessarily morally deserving, this will generate considerable anguish amongst survivors and families over the definition of the disappeared. Third, those who have used force to combat apartheid will likely find their own engagement with the Commission's work tarnished by the Commission's apparent neutrality, whether or not they are found criminal in the proceedings. Fourth, if the process fails to yield applications and confessions from more strategically placed servants of the apartheid state and, consequently, too few successful prosecutions, it will contribute to a general disenchantment with justice.

These are speculative conclusions. They have been arrived at not simply from reflecting on the current events in South Africa but by thinking more generally about the elusiveness of truth and the ability to arrive at some reasonable approximations through law. From the perspective that informs the starting point of the paper, given the barriers to bearing witness, the amnesty process, by "legitimizing" political violence, offers disconcerting political justifications for inflicting pain and death and allows only that the truths that are revealed will be registered in the souls but not on the bodies of the guilty. That may be alright for God; maybe even for the state; also perhaps for reconciliation; but likely not sufficient for the victims. But then it is not clear that either politics or law could ever really make whole again "these broken people."

POSTSCRIPT

Since the above essay was originally written, an extensive record of testimony has been made available. As well, South Africans were regularly exposed to radio and other presentations of public hearings. Perpetrators were named, confessions were heard, and the processes followed seem to have been reasonably fair to both perpetrators and victims. By comparison with many other efforts to expose past horrors, South Africa's Truth and Reconciliation Commission is likely to represent a modest success. Certainly, apartheid has now been sufficiently connected to criminality that most of its past supporters have been rendered either mute or apologetic. As a political matter, that is a significant accomplishment. And it may be enough to remove the question of doing justice from the political agenda unless victims and their supporters are able to force some public focus on how incomplete the accounting has been. Whether all of this constitutes a substantial step towards reconciliation seems less certain. That is a question not of justice as law understands it but of the distribution of justice, on which only politics can deliver.

NOTES

1 Nadezhda Mandelstam as quoted in Susan Jacoby, *Wild Justice:The Evolution of Revenge*, New York: Harper and Row, 1983: 357–8.
2 Marcelo Suarez-Orozco, "A Grammar of Terror: Psychocultural Responses to State Terrorism in Dirty War and Post-Dirty War Argentina," in Carolyn Nordstrom and JoAnn Martin (eds), *The Paths to Domination, Resistance and Terror*, Berkeley: California University Press, 1992: 249.
3 Beverely Allen, *Rape Warfare: The Hidden Genocide in Bosnia-Herzogovina and Croatia*, Minneapolis: University of Minnesota Press, 1996: 94–5.
4 See the discussion in Jacoby, *Wild Justice*.
5 Toni Pickard, "Lament on the Rhetoric of Pain," *Newsletter of the Conference on Critical Legal Studies*, November 1989: 41–3.
6 Suarez-Orozco, "A Grammar of Terror," 243.
7 *SAPA-AP*, Johannesburg, 10 November 1996.
8 Hannah Arendt, *Eichmann in Jerusalem: A Report on the Banality of Evil*, New York: Penguin Books, 1977: epilogue.

9 Albie Sachs has used the term "soft vengeance" to characterize the building of a multiracial democracy in South Africa.

10 Elaine Scarry, *The Body in Pain: The Making and Unmaking of the World,* New York: Oxford University Press, 1985: 27–8.

11 Ibid.

12 Ibid., 4.

13 Ibid., 13.

14 Carmen de Guide quoted in Jo Fisher, *Mothers of the Disappeared,* Boston: South End Press, 1989: 141.

15 Anonymous Argentine general quoted by Antonius C.G.M. Robben, "The Politics of Truth and Emotion among Victims and Perpetrators of Violence," in Carolyn Nordstrom and Antonius C.G.M. Robben (eds), *Fieldwork Under Fire,* Berkeley: University of California Press, 1996: 98.

16 In *Re Castioni,* no. 1, Q.B.D., 1891: 149, a British court rejected the extradition to Switzerland of Castioni who had assassinated a state official in the course of a political disturbance, arguing that crimes otherwise extraditable become political offences if they were incidental to and informed part of a political disturbance.

17 See the discussion in Suarez-Orozco, "A Grammar of Terror"; and Fisher, *Mothers of the Disappeared.*

18 Max Weber, "Politics as a Vocation," in Hans Gerth and C. Wright Mills (eds), *From Max Weber: Essays in Sociology,* New York: Oxford University Press, 1946: 77–128.

19 Quoted in Michael Walzer, "Political Action: The Problem of Dirty Hands," *Philosophy and Public Affairs,* vol. 2, no. 2, Winter 1973: 161.

20 Carlos Santiago Nino, *Radical Evil on Trial,* New Haven: Yale University Press, 1996: 116.

21 Lawrence Weschler, "Lawrence Weschler: Long Thoughts," Interview by Harvey Blume, *The Boston Book Review,* vol. 3, no. 9, October 1996.

22 Weber, "Politics as a Vocation," 118.

23 Ibid., Weber's own emphasis in the text.

24 Fisher, *Mothers of the Disappeared,* 142.

25 Bertold Brecht, "To My Countrymen," in *Poems 1913–1956,* John Willett (ed.), London: Methuen, 1987.

26 A mother quoted in Suarez-Orozco, "A Grammar of Terror," 242.

27 Renee Epelbaum quoted by Jean Bethke Elshtain, "The Mothers of the Disappeared: Passion, Protest and Maternal Action," in Donna Bassin, Margaret Honey, and Meryle Mahrer Kaplan (eds), *Representations of Motherhood,* Yale University Press, New Haven, 1994: 89.

28 Suarez-Orozco, "A Grammar of Terror," 243.

29 Fisher, *Mothers of the Disappeared,* 140.

30 South African security police commander and five of his subordinates in their application for amnesty before the Amnesty section of the Truth and Reconciliation Commission.

The Rise and Fall of New Social Movement Theory?

LAURIE E. ADKIN

"I'm nostalgic for a country which doesn't yet exist on a map."[1]

INTRODUCTION

Since the mid-1980s, contending perspectives have called into question the modernist assumptions underpinning post-Marxist new social movement theory (NSMT). The latter was itself an attempt to surpass the reductionism, economism, and evolutionism found in Marxist theory, while retaining the emancipatory impetus of Marxism and other radical critiques of the hegemonic order. From the perspective of post-Marxist NSMT, two things have been at stake all along: one, reformulation of a historical theory of emancipation and, two, the search for new collective actors or historical movements that could be the "carriers" of an emancipatory project. For some writers, NSMT has been about identifying *the* new social movement that will be the historical successor to the labour movement in Marxist theory. From the mid-1970s to the mid-1980s, many viewed the ecology movements as favoured candidates for this role because of the counter-hegemonic, societal-level discourse of such movements. This was the view of French sociologist Alain Touraine's group in the late 1970s,[2] and also that of the German sociologist, Klaus Eder.[3] In his 1989 book, *Choisir l'audace*, Alain Lipietz expressed his view that, "in present-day Europe this convergence [of new left and social movements] should not be round a specific socio-economic class, but within political ecology; not because this approach is manifested in very effective groups in particular countries, but because it provides a framework broad enough to tackle the complex problems faced by humanity at the present time."[4]

However, the emergence of radical post-structuralist critiques of modern social and political thought, as well as the apparent decline of the mass mobilizations and cultural ferment associated with NSMs from the 1960s to the early 1980s, have posed serious challenges to the claims and objectives of NSMT. Some critiques have implied that NSMT was the expression of a particular historical moment which has now been overtaken by the changes associated with neoliberalism or with postmodernism. They proclaim "the end of new social movements." Thus, like development theory, NSMT confronts a critical conjuncture in which it must redesign itself or be replaced by new interpretations of social reality and change.

In this essay I examine both the 1970s *prophesy* of the new social movement and the 1990s claim that NSMT is nothing but *nostalgia* for the political projects of the modern era. I suggest that both of these interpretations operate within grand historical narratives: a stages theory of history unfolding according to a particular structural telos. Moreover, the postmodern preoccupation with difference, identity, and fragmentation has led some to reject both the desirability and the possibility of reconceptualizing collective action. While this rejection is, in my view, mistaken, post-structuralist criticisms in general require NSMT to confront its limitations as a theory of counter-hegemonic strategy. I argue for an approach to the problem of collective action for social change that is rooted in situated knowledges and embodied subjects; speaks to actual communities; avoids the traps of moral relativism, reductionism, or universalism; and emphasizes the dialectical relationship of structural conditions and social agency. If what we wish to understand is the possibility for various social projects to succeed, the last consideration entails an argument for the importance of analysing the discourses of social actors, because, ultimately, they – while making meaning of experience – determine the course of history. To illustrate the limitations of general claims regarding the historical rise and fall of emancipatory social projects and their collective subjects, I provide a brief sketch of the different obstacles to and successes of political ecology as a societal discourse in the cases of Canada and France. These cases may more usefully be explained as the outcomes of specific dynamics among structuring traditions and institutions, the configuration of social forces, and discursive practices.

FROM PROPHESY TO DECLINE

Elements of a critique of modernization viewed as more radical than the critique made by Marxism of capitalism have been identified in the values, goals, and practices of the students' protest movements of the

1960s and early 1970s, as well as in the 1970s environmental, peace, feminist, gay and lesbian rights, and black and third-world liberation movements. By the late 1970s, various theorists had observed that these protest movements were critical of the limits and contradictions of liberal democracy, hierarchies and authoritarian practices in general, the subordination of women, sexual repression, racism, the domination of nature, neo-colonialism, militarism, technocracy, the imperative of "economic growth," "materialism," and living to work. Marcuse, for example, saw in the linking of personal liberation to political liberation the future hope for a rebellion of the instincts and the mind against the dominant rationality. Moreover, it had become apparent (following the uprisings of 1968–69) that union organizations and social-democratic and Communist parties were *bouleversés* by these events. They were, in various ways, threatened and opposed, or trying to catch up, but never *in the lead*. Groups of workers who joined the radical protests or initiated extra-legal actions did so without "official" support.

Comparativists working largely within liberal, behaviouralist, and American political culture traditions began to talk about "new social cleavages." The most influential of these approaches is Inglehart's schema of dichotomous materialist/post-materialist values.[5] For the liberals, "quality of life" issues meant that the days of class ideology were numbered. For Marxists, the same phenomena called either for the defence or the retheorization of historical materialist theory – most notably, the central and privileged role of the industrial proletariat as the carrier of the emancipatory project. The Marxist explanations of the NSMs were largely structuralist (structural changes giving rise to new social strata and to interests not directly related to capital-wage labour relations), although, of course, they had a different *telos* than the positivist assumptions of the "post-materialist" theorists.[6] By the early 1980s, the challenges that feminism posed to Marxism had spearheaded the irreversible decentering of class as a category of analysis and opened wide the doors to radical post-structuralism.

Meanwhile, the apparent exhaustion of the "long boom" of the post-war years was theorized by the French School of Regulation as the crisis of the intensive regime of accumulation called Fordism. It was not long before the emergence of the "new social movements" was explained by reference to the structural contradictions, and experiences of alienation and domination, inherent to Fordism. The discourses of the social movements themselves, and in particular their emphasis on the *similarities* between Eastern and Western models of development (industrialism, productivism, domination of nature, patriarchy, militarism, alienation of labour, and anti-democratic aspects), enlarged the whole frame within which social theorists had been viewing the meanings of social and cultural conflicts in Western societies.[7] So, bringing together post-structuralism, the crisis of Marxism, the historical-materialist referents provided by the School of Regulation, and the analyses of the discourses of the NSMs, European social theorists in particular began to conceptualize the new social movements as radical critics of modernization.

A landmark in this paradigm shift was the work of the group led by Alain Touraine.[8] Their analyses of the workers' movement, the students' movement, and the anti-nuclear movement led them to argue that a transition was occurring: to a "post-industrial society" in which the central conflict is no longer between industrial workers and capitalists, but between citizens and technocrats. The "stakes" of this struggle are not merely control of the *means* of production and over the *appropriation* of its product; the stakes are the *telos* of production. And this struggle brings citizens of industrialized societies into conflict with those elites and institutions that dominate decision-making – whose rationale, means of coercion, prestige, etc. allow them to determine the direction of societal development.

For Touraine et al., the French anti-nuclear movement expressed the elements of this emerging social conflict, its terrain, and its stakes. Its militants identified the enemy as the technocratic state, committed to a productivist, instrumental logic and prepared to control information by any means and to use repression to defend its interests. They questioned the necessity – the reason – of each decision to which the technocratic apparatus commits the society; these were reconstructed as *choices among alternatives* and reinterpreted as struggles for the control of *historicity*. Because elements within the anti-nuclear movement articulated these critiques of the anti-democratic and technocratic nature of the state to the productivist, capitalist logic of the economy and of social relations, Touraine's group viewed this movement as the harbinger of the social movement of the new historical era. What the labour movement had been to industrial capitalism in the nineteenth and early twentieth centuries, the anti-nuclear movement could become to a system of domination rooted in the control of information and technocratic decision-making.[9] This was the *prophétie antinucléaire*.

In neo-Gramscian terms, the problem became a new theorization of counter-hegemonic struggle.[10] The project of creating "working class" identity and consciousness, which would form the core of a new historical bloc, was replaced by a project to identify the themes or principles that might articulate to one another all of these contestatory movements. Their struggles encompassed many more relationships of oppression than those of wage-labour, and the "enemy," therefore, had to be grasped as multiple forms of domination. However, the assumption that these multiple subject positions and struggles *had to be articulated to unifying principles, values, or themes* expressed the continuing desire to fulfil the prophesy of the new social movement – the prophesy of emancipation. The belief in the desirability and possibility of such a project underlies the work of such theorists as Claus Offe, Klaus Eder, André Gorz, Alain Lipietz, Ernesto Laclau, and Chantal Mouffe.[11] The social project was conceptualized in various ways: as a new historical era (Touraine), a new historical compromise (Lipietz),[12] a new paradigm of social conflict (Offe), a new agenda (Gorz), a new politics of class (Eder), or a new socialist strategy in the form of radical democratization (Laclau and Mouffe).

The post-industrial society theory of Touraine, among others (including liberal theorists like Inglehart), suggested that history is a succession of stages, or an evolution of changing universes of discourse that parallel the societal types (defined by Touraine as commercial, industrial, and post-industrial, or, in his terminology, "the programmed society"). On this continuum, the old social movement (the workers' movement) ceases to represent or to engage the fundamental stakes of social conflict, and a replacement emerges. This argument rests upon a particular characterization of the workers' movement as limited to a struggle for control over the means of production and the allocation of surplus-value.[13] This characterization both downplays the extent of socialism's moral critique of capitalism and socialism's utopian elements, and posits a radical disjunction between the workers' movements and the new social movements. The latter arise with "programmed society" and are associated with a discourse about *happiness*, "that is, a global image of the organization of social life on the basis of the needs expressed by the most diverse individuals and groups."[14] The workers' movement is generally treated by Touraine as a fixed and unchanging relic of the old order, rather than as a movement capable of transformation. This view is clearly expressed in *La Prophétie anti-nucléaire*, in such statements as: "There exists only one social movement, for each class, in a type of society. This was the labour movement in industrial society. Who will occupy its place in the post-industrial, programmed society now forming?"[15]

In the conclusions to their analysis of the French anti-nuclear movement, Touraine's group expressed reservations about the capacity of this movement to transform itself into the historical social movement of the post-industrial era, but reasserted its conviction that the movement revealed "the existence and the nature of this new social movement."[16] In essence, the anti-nuclear movement contained within it both the elements of the conflicts of the earlier, industrial era, and those of the emerging, "programmed" society, representing, therefore, a period of transition and its contradictions.[17] We are thus left with the clear impression that the new social movement – though only weakly defined by the end of the 1970s – is only a matter of time. Its discursive forms will correspond to the key social contradictions (the new "stakes") of the post-industrial era. This claim is in fact repeated in Touraine's later work, despite his concern to refute the association of his approach with "historicism" and "evolutionism."[18] The importance of identifying the "central" social conflict of each societal era, which provides the essential meaning of the struggles of various social actors, is also defended by Touraine in his later reflections on social theory.[19]

The influence of European NSMT was by the mid-1980s undermined by new critiques of modern social theory and by the apparent decline of its objects of analysis. By the end of the decade, the echo of the prophesy was growing faint. Disappointed hopes, seemingly irresolvable conflicts over strategies of change (e.g., movement versus party orientations), and the consequences of neoliberal restructuring for the "social opportunity structures" of NSM actors, have given rise to what might be called an "end of social movements literature."[20] Some authors emphasize the "reabsorption" of movement activists back into the traditional political parties.[21] Others have theorized the 1960s–1980s movements as the most recent cycle of reaction against waves of modernization.[22] Claus Offe proposed a stages model of "the institutional self-transformation of movement politics," based mainly on observations of the German Greens.[23] Offe's analysis has since been corroborated by developments in the party's strategy and by other observers close to Dïe Grunen.[24] Touraine attributes the "weakness and defeat" of the 1960s-1970s movements in France to their co-optation by Marxist ideological tendencies, which "suffocated" their originality and divided them between radical political and cultural-reformist orientations.[25]

Equally as important as such analyses are the perceptions of movement activists themselves. What they spoke of from the mid–1980s to the mid–1990s was the *disarticulation* of the solidarities that had seemed to be coalescing in the late 1970s and early 1980s. In France, alliances had been developing among the radical left political groupings, political ecologists, the anti-nuclear movement, the anti-racism movement, feminists, the socialist-allied trade union confederation (CFDT), and the Socialist Party (PS). In Canada there was an upsurge of coalition-building efforts in the early 1980s. By the mid–1980s, however, the sense of belonging to a mass movement (whose values/

referents might have been identified as socialist, or whose collective subject was "le peuple de la gauche") was dissipating. The collapse of social democracy and the ascendant *pensée unique* of neoliberalism had put unions on the defensive, deepened – in some cases – antagonisms between industrial workers and ecologists, caused set-backs for other social movements, and utterly discredited the left parties.

Earlier victories seemed insecure. In France, the temporary shutdown of Superphénix was achieved, but the fast-breeder reactor was later reopened for "research" purposes.[26] A moratorium on atomic bomb testing in the South Pacific was belatedly implemented by Mitterrand, but reversed by Chirac. In Canada, environmental regulation promised by legislation passed in the 1980s had not even been enforced, for the most part, before it was threatened by reversals (e.g., the "voluntary compliance agreements") in the 1990s.[27] Women's movements have made few gains since the 1980s in terms of economic equality, or stopping violence, and have faced ongoing threats to reproductive freedom as well as a strong anti-feminist backlash. Racism against visible minorities, immigrants, and refugees grew throughout the 1980s, fuelled by far-right discourse and "normalized" by the discourses of the traditional political parties. The new authoritarian-populist parties that took the field in the 1980s (the Front National in France, the Reform Party in Canada)[28] pushed the political centre further to the right on such issues as immigration, economic policy, and policing.

Choices that existed at the end of the 1970s (e.g., regarding energy strategies) have been foreclosed. For example, about 75 per cent of France's electricity is now generated by nuclear reactors.[29] In Canada, the Free Trade Agreement (FTA) with the United States (1988) ruled out a regulatory approach to the conservation of non-renewable energy resources. By the end of the decade, alternative social movements appeared to be less and less able to mobilize support around particular issues, let alone to effect a political convergence.

A particularly brutal blow to the prophesy of a new social movement came in October 1992, with the deaths of Petra Kelly and Gert Bastian of the German Greens. Like the suicide of Eleanor Marx at the end of the last century, Petra Kelly's death seemed to express the anguish of failure, and of isolation in every sense – from her times, from her party, and from the dominant views of realism, necessity, and possibility. In newspaper reports she was described as "a lonely Green dreamer," intransigent, "emotional," "passionate." The woman who said that the alternative to the impossible was the unthinkable, the woman whose values and work had symbolized the vision and the tasks of the Greens, had died, it was said, of despair. *"The eclipse of green politics* and the multiple disillusions of the post-communist era," the newspapers said, "was more than Bastian and Kelly could bear."[30]

POSTMODERNISM AND NEW SOCIAL
MOVEMENT THEORY: NSMT "REVISIONISM"

In such a climate of demoralization on the part of social movement activists everywhere in the West, many experienced nostalgia for the brief moment of massive popular mobilizations and of convergence among different movements – for a time of empowerment and of shared hopes and vision. This mood of nostalgia, and experience of atomization or demobilization, coincided with the growing influence of new challenges to NSMT. On one hand, rational choice theory gained prominence in the social sciences; on the other hand, various "postmodern" perspectives began to penetrate social and political thought.

In *Return of the Actor* (1988), a translation of a 1984 work, and *Critique de la modernité* (1992), Touraine identifies two main challenges to social movement theory. One set groups together significantly differing approaches, including the work of Althusser, Foucault, and Marcuse, authors who – in Touraine's view – effectively deny the possibility of social actors/collective action by replacing the concept "society" with the image of a totalitarian system of domination. The other main challenge is identified as rational choice theory, which Touraine prefers to call liberalism. In this view, there is no society, but only individuals: conceived of primarily as consumers and utility maximizers; motivated by interests, but bereft of self-reflexivity and critical capacities. Touraine summarizes these approaches as "that of the system without actors and that of the actor with no system."[31] The acceptance of either amounts to the erasure of the concept of society, of the social, or of sociological thought itself, and Touraine is therefore concerned to refute their claims, while making the case for rescuing sociology by placing at its centre social actors and social movements. With regard to postmodernism, he does this mainly through a reinterpretation of modernity. He insists that, in all the attention which has been devoted to the nature and consequences of rationalism, postmodern theorists have forgotten how modernity "produces the Subject, who is neither [merely] the individual nor the Self," but "the labour through which an individual transforms himself/herself into an actor, that is to say, an agent capable of transforming his or her situation instead of reproducing it by his/her actions ... The clear response that this book makes [to the interpretations of neoliberalism and postmodernism] is that reason and the Subject, which can indeed become strangers or hostile to one another, can also unite and that the agent of this union is the social movement, that is, the transformation of the personal and cultural defence of the Subject into collective action directed against the power which submits reason to its interests." [32]

In the essay "Beyond Social Movements?" Touraine reiterates his definition of a social movement as "collective action, operation of society on itself, and organized around a central social conflict, opposing those who direct the self-production and transformation of society and those who are subjected to its effects." [33] By 1992, however, Touraine argues that the most important manifestations of this central social conflict are taking the form not of ecological struggles but of consumer resistance to the technocratic determination of health, education, and information systems (also referred to as the "cultural industries," whose dominance is a characteristic of post-industrial societies). In his view, the "logic of power and accumulation" stands opposed to "a logic of individual liberty" or to attempts on the part of individuals to protect their autonomy and needs from the pressures of commodification and rationalization. What connects these struggles, he argues, is the liberal-democratic ideal of the rights of the individual "over against encroaching political power."

Touraine's *glissade* from market logic to political power in the above formulation implies that a new social movement will arise from the recognition that the former is simultaneously the latter, exercised in the interests of a "ruling category." This analysis seems very close to Marxism, with the exception that Touraine conceives the collective identity of the "directed category" (that opposed to the ruling logic) not in class terms but in popular-democratic terms (individuals protecting different interests threatened by the ruling system). Indeed, in *Critique de la modernité*, Touraine acknowledges the influence of Marxism on his concepts of historicity and social movements, while insisting on the new content that he has given to "post-industrial society," its social classes, and its central social conflict. [34] He positions his work as the successor to Marxism and other modes of modern thought that have theorized the central conflicts of their respective historical eras. In *Critique de la modernité* he also reasserts that if various (other) theorists today fail to comprehend the central conflict and social actors of their times, it is because this is a period of transition in which the old contends with the new, and the social movement of the future is present only in confusing forms. [35]

Although in this work Touraine poses the question of whether the idea or the project of the new social movement is still valid, his response only partially acknowledges the challenges facing NSMT. In particular, his defence of the Subject does not fully address the argument that the "postmodern" fragmentation of identities rules out the future possibility of a historical social movement representing *the* "directed" or subordinate "category" of the social order. Rather than explaining *how*, Touraine simply asserts that the multiplicity of social conflicts can in some way be reduced to a "central" meaning, which he now rather vaguely defines as a struggle for individual liberty in the face of the spreading technocratic domination of all spheres of life. Moreover, his refutation of "post-structuralist" or "postmodern" views is achieved by a serious conflation of these into a particular caricature, which leaves out the more radical and critical elements.

Finally, Touraine defends a conception of human nature that privileges the individual desire for autonomy – for liberty – and explains resistance as a natural human response to domination of any kind.[36] Modern society, for Touraine, is characterized by a desire for happiness, and personal happiness is inseparable from the happiness of others and from "solidarity with their search for happiness, and compassion for their suffering."[37] These highly abstract claims do not allow us, however, to know what conceptions of happiness are being referred to, or to which subjects (historically, culturally, and otherwise situated) they correspond. Nor do they translate automatically into *strategies for movement-building* among different subjects.[38]

The same problems arise in his recent writings, in which his theorization of the Subject falls somewhere between liberal individualism and – as Charles Turner observes[39] – "a form of existentialism." In *Pourrons-nous vivre ensemble?* Touraine argues that while the social movements of the past (including those of the 1970s, linked to Marxism) advanced a project of radical societal reconstruction and a collective identity (subject), today's "societal movements"[40] defend the individual Subject "against the power of markets and against that of fundamentalisms based on communalism and nationalism."[41] Neither an overarching political ideology nor a strategy of matching a social movement to a political party is any longer tenable in highly self-reflexive societies that are "constantly transformed by ... their capacity to produce themselves and to change themselves."[42] Thus, "from now on, in the most industrialized societies, there can be no societal movement other than the collective actions that are directly aimed at the affirmation and defence of the rights of the Subject – of his freedom and equality. In this sense, one can say that societal movements have become moral movements, whereas in the past they were religious, political, or economic."[43] Yet, while Touraine predicts the inevitable emergence of a societal movement manifested by struggles (in health, education, and information sectors) in defence of the Subject against a "technocratic and commodifying logic,"[44] he says little about the importance of their succeeding or failing to *recognize one another* as struggles sharing such common adversaries. The "explanation" of their (common) meaning does not provide a strategy of collective action; it does not identify the bases for solidarity among these diverse struggles, explain why such linkages might be important, or how we might expect the "organic intellectuals" of such movement-building to be formed.[45] The picture of late modern politics sketched by Touraine resembles in important respects the idea of "identity politics" found in both liberal and post-modern thought. Yet his concern to theorize a "central conflict" that gives meaning to various struggles reaffirms his desire to refute the idea that this plethora of demands reflects purely autonomous and unrelated interests. If this interpretive project of demonstrating common goals or adversaries is what constitutes (or gives rise to) a societal movement, then we are still back where we started – in search of a non-reductionist counter-hegemonic political discourse.

The opposition that Touraine repeatedly constructs between "technocratic and commodifying logic" and the individual Subject, said to give rise to various forms of collective action, ultimately reproduces a reductionist logic. What is essential to this Subject is the desire for freedom and equality vis-à-vis globalized market liberalism; the gender, race, ethnicity, or sexuality of a subject is quite irrelevant to explaining this fundamental (universal) conflict. This unitary, universal subject – little differentiated from the liberal view of the universal man – poses a continual dilemma for Touraine, who on one hand requires his presence, and on the other hand claims to accept the need to deconstruct such universal categories. The opposition (central conflict) itself – mirroring the "fundamental contradiction" of Marxist theory – necessarily creates a hierarchy of struggles, in order of universal/historical importance, a hierarchy expressed in his categories: societal movement, historical movement, cultural movement. Citizens' struggles against the corporate-technocratic control of health, for example, express the central conflict and the emerging *societal* movement; the 1995 strikes in France against the diminution of the social security system constitute a *historical* movement, with primarily defensive aims and lacking both a clear analysis of what is at stake and an alternative vision[46]; the ecology and women's movements are *cultural* movements, defined as those "centered upon the affirmation of cultural rights more than on the conflict with an adversary, who can remain defined in a vague manner."[47] Touraine's theory suggests that historical and cultural movements are either secondary to the central conflict or need to be transformed in such a way as to realize their true meaning. Again, we are still a long way from the recognition of multiple and inter-determining subjectivities that characterizes post-structuralist understandings of contemporary social conflict and identities.

The second opposition constructed by Touraine – that between the individual Subject and all forms of religious fundamentalism or ethnic nationalism – appears to be an attempt to account for what is left out of the "struggles against the technocratic and commodifying logic" category. Individual (or group) struggles against oppressive communalism may also be interpreted as struggles for individual freedom and equality and, hence, as expressions of a "double-faced" societal movement. But, here again, we have a conception of an individual Subject defined largely in enlightenment terms, undifferentiated by gender, race, class or other positions. While patriarchal domination, for example, is an integral aspect of religious fundamentalism and ethnic nationalism, such axes of conflict are collapsed (indeed, disappear, in his treatment) into the opposition of individual to collectivity. Despite Touraine's representation of his recent work as a radical rupture with classical sociology and enlightenment thought,[48] these oppositions – linked by the device of the individual Subject and its "double-faced" struggle for freedom and equality[49] – replicate the reductionist categories of Marxism and liberalism, respectively. They do not move us substantially beyond the schema of his earlier work.

Not surprisingly, gender as an analytical category is nowhere present in his work, and the relationship between the "central conflict" (now "two-faced") and such relationships as patriarchy or racism are not specified. Thus, while he refers on occasion to the importance of the women's movement, he continues to view it as a form of identity politics – as a "cultural movement"[50] – rather than to conceive of *gender* as a subject position, or to grasp the significance of the interpretation of women's struggles for equality or autonomy as democratic struggles.[51]

With the interpretation of diverse struggles as struggles for freedom and equality (i.e., democratic struggles), Touraine moves quite close to radical democratization theory, but stops short of adopting a poststructuralist understanding of subjectivity. His revised version of the enlightenment subject ultimately resembles liberal individualism and does not permit us to theorize collective subjects, social relations, or political discourse. Remarkably, Touraine does not turn – in his defence of the actor and of the need for an emancipatory theory of social conflict and collective action – to radical democratic or postmodern feminist thought. Anna Yeatman, for example, has argued:

It is important to emphasize that if postmodernism means we have to abandon universalistic, general theories, and, instead, to explore the multivocal worlds of different societies and cultures, this is not the same thing as abandoning the political-ethical project of working out the conditions for a universal pragmatics of individualized agency. The very orientation of postmodernism to the agentic quality and features of our sociocultural worlds underlines the significance of this political-ethical project.

It is at this point that feminists, as others who are committed to developing the democratic implications of postmodernism, need to firmly distinguish their position from those who take postmodernism to imply an anomic relativism ... [Postmodernist relativism] is indeed an intellectual deregulation which permits dominant groups to maintain their privileges while evading normative debate over them in relation to principles of equity, justice, and democracy.[52]

Interestingly, in deciding to "opt for the challenges of a postmodern feminist theorizing, where the value commitment is to developing a post-patriarchal, democratic culture of individualized agency," Yeatman asserts: "I have not abandoned sociology: sociology has abandoned feminism."[53]

What do radical post-structuralist, radical democratization, and feminist theorists have to contribute to a retheorization of collective action that might enable us, on one hand, to avoid the tendencies towards reductionism and evolutionism that characterize even "revisionist" NSMT while, on the other, to reject the moral relativism or "anti-political" nature of some postmodern thought? In the work of such writers as Chantal Mouffe, Donna Haraway, and Himani Bannerji, among others, we find an intersectional analysis of subject positions and social conflicts that escapes both reductionism and relativism. We also find a conception of "situated knowledges," which is opposed to universal knowledge claims. Let us therefore take a second look at the implications of postmodernism for NSMT and the possibilities for building counter-hegemonic social movements.

ENVISAGING POSTMODERN COLLECTIVE ACTION

While by the 1980s new social movement theorists like Touraine were arguing that a new emancipatory social project had become historically *possible* (as well as desirable), for at least some postmodernists, it had become historically *impossible* (and of questionable legitimacy). The main challenges posed by postmodernist perspectives for NSMT (as a variation on the theme of the modern, emancipatory project) may be summarized as follows. First, they imply that such a project has no moral, rational, scientific, or other foundations (i.e., that universal characterizations of human nature or instincts, and scientific claims regarding historical laws of development have been shown to be particular in various ways, invalid, exclusionary, etc.). This may be viewed as a problem of the *legitimacy* of the project. Second, postmodern theories imply that such a project is no longer *possible*, because the fragmented nature of contemporary society and culture make impossible a construction of collective subjects based on universal identities.

Such "postmodern" perspectives were expressed by militants of the anti-nuclear movement and of Les Verts interviewed in France in 1991[54]:

"It is no longer possible to construct a social project."

"In my opinion, [a transformative project] is not tied to a particular economic model. I believe that it is related, instead, to a change of consciousness."

"Myself, I don't really have a precise social project. Simply, I want a society without nuclear power."

"I believe that we are in the process of posing in a very different manner the problem of the social project, of the taking of power, of the party necessary for the taking of power ... We must no longer put the question of the evolution of society in terms of taking power, and we must no longer present global visions of society. We have to put forward what we want, and fight for it, but we must not try to make everyone else share the same goals."

The view that *le projet social* is no longer possible – or that it is to be mistrusted as inherently "totalizing" (Lyotard's "terror of structuring"), i.e., rejecting of differences and of pluralism – became popular in the 1980s.[55] A "relativist" postmodern view[56] argued – on the basis of its analysis of late capitalism (i.e., globalization, decentering of the state as the locus of politics or of power, growth of an information-based society but under centralized control, the dissolution of modern discourses, etc.) – that this era's corresponding form of politics is particularist identities; societal discourses or projects are *passé*. Such views are echoed by Touraine in his 1997-98 writings (which nevertheless attempt to rescue some notion of counter-hegemonic social movements).

Responses to "relativist," "pessimistic," or "merely deconstructive" postmodern approaches have been made elsewhere.[57] Here, I am specifically concerned to identify possible strategies for establishing equivalences among diverse counter-hegemonic struggles that do not reduce all of these to a single meaning or essence, deny their autonomy, or create a hierarchy of subject positions. A social movement, by definition, must have a *collective identity*, as well as a political discourse that interprets the stakes of social conflict and identifies the adversary. This means that it adopts *normative stances* regarding the desirable directions of social development that inform the movement's vision of a better world and its concrete proposals for the reform of economic, social, and political institutions. Is it possible to advance ethical views of "the good life," as well as judgements regarding just and unjust practices or relationships, while avoiding the kind of claims to truth and universality that have in the past served to exclude the knowledges of various Others? A number of approaches to the study of social movements and social change have advanced arguments regarding the possibility and desirability of such a project. Together, they offer important elements of a postmodern vision of counter-hegemonic collective action. Analysis of the discourses of social and political actors reveals, moreover, the ways in which they are attempting to construct pluralist societal projects, and thus new forms of "postmodern" politics.

If there is to be a linking of diverse social struggles, it must take a pluralist, non-reductionist form *internally*, while identifying the enemy (or enemies) of progressive social change. How can we conceptualize this? The starting point is a philosophy of the good life that acknowledges its subjectivity, i.e., is not – as Donna Haraway puts it[58] – a "god trick," a voice coming from nowhere and accountable to no-one, but the self-acknowledged ethical stance of an embodied subject. As I have observed elsewhere,[59] deprivation, pain, desire, and happiness are experienced both physically and spiritually – by individuals, but inseparably from social situations. Among the most crucial resources for counter-hegemonic politics are all the ways in which individuals do not or cannot "fit" into the systems that are optimal for the interests of ruling elites. Another way of expressing this idea is that our stresses and strains indicate the limits of our abilities to physically and psychologically "evolve" in pace with the rapid acceleration of processes of commodification. The experience of these strains may help to explain the wide appeal of Donna Haraway's metaphor of the cyborg – used to describe the human-machines of the modern era and the non-fixability of nature/culture boundaries[60] – and of her argument that in seeking possibilities for a "livable world," we need to "work through, not the marginal position or some kind of point of resistance that's outside domination, but many kinds of not fitting."[61] This embodied subject, moreover, is not one-dimensional; it lives multiple subjectivities. It is from these bases that we can claim knowledge about what constitutes a "good life," a meaningful life, or happiness, without claiming to know what these represent for everybody (universally) and at all times (trans-historically). Yet, while such situated knowledges are particular, or partial, they are not merely individual, because many experiences are broadly shared by socially and/or spatially defined groups. For example, Eder, Gorz, and others argue that a particular "life world" is common to the new middle class, and that it is because of the threatened degradation or destruction of this life world that this class is the bearer of counter-cultural critiques of modernization. Moreover, different experiences (e.g., gendered or raced) can be shown to be related in ways that have mutual stakes in social change. In response to the question "How can a collective subject for a counter-hegemonic social project be constructed?" there is no answer but "through dialogue with others." The intervention of organic intellectuals in the realm of social and political discourse interprets the meanings of experiences.[62] Women made women's movements by sharing experiences, learning that they were not alone, talking about the kinds of lives they were living, and about the kinds of lives they were dreaming. They have also learned – through interaction and dialogue – about the ways in which women's experiences radically differ, yet are related, and inter-determining.

A key element of the philosophy of the good life common to the various NSMs is the opposition of communicative reasoning and inter-subjectivity to forms of rationality based on domination, objectification, arbitrariness, exclusion, and the privileging of particular minority interests (i.e., those of elites) in such a way as to negate the knowledges, experiences, needs, and desires of others. This conception of relationships based on mutual respect, communication, and inter-subjectivity applies to efforts to eliminate domination not only from human relationships but also from human-nature relationships. In aboriginal peoples' spirituality, which finds echoes in some variants of ecological thought, these values have a temporal dimension as well. Present generations are believed to be responsible to future generations for their relationship with the Earth. Non-exploitative and reciprocally respectful relationships are important elements of the discourse of new middle-class actors within the NSMs, as Klaus Eder, among others, observes. Indeed, such relationships might be more accurately characterized as a *precondition* for attaining the equality, autonomy, solidarity, and ecological (human-nature) needs that are associated with a good life.

A further precondition for the possibility of the good life is the democratization of social and political life. Democratic discourse interprets the meaning of diverse struggles as struggles for equality, understood as freedom from unwarranted discrimination; for autonomy, understood as respect for difference, or freedom from unwarranted assumptions of sameness in relation to some pseudo-universal norm; and for deepened and broadened participation in decision-making at all levels of society. Chantal Mouffe refers to such claims as elements of a discourse of radical and pluralist democracy/democratization. It permits the creation of equivalences among, e.g., anti-racist, anti-sexist, and anti-capitalist struggles, in such a way that a) none is privileged vis-à-vis the others; b) all become more democratic and more radical (i.e., are transformed) by the recognition that the interests of one subject must not (and ultimately cannot?) be fulfilled at the expense of the others. This democratic and pluralist discourse corresponds, moreover, to the experiential reality of multiple subjectivity (for individual subjects).

"Identity politics," applauded by some as a manifestation of a liberating pluralism, remains a negative freedom in the classical liberal sense – freedom from direct interventions by or associations with "other" subjects. Yet in reality such boundaries are not only illusory but serve to obscure relationships of power. To put this another way: What is at issue is not merely "difference" but hierarchies, privileges, inequalities, and power relationships. We see this within (or among) the women's movement(s), as we saw it earlier within a white, male-dominated left.[63] In Canada, we also see this distinction in relations between aboriginal and non-aboriginal peoples. What is at stake is not a "recognition of native difference" (i.e., pluralism) but the ending of a neo-colonial relationship and its replacement with arrangements that mean the loss of privileges and power for the white, middle-class population. Meaningful equality requires acknowledging that domination has been the foundation of the status quo. For these reasons, a "politics of difference" will not take us very far as a counter-hegemonic strategy.

In opposition to moral relativism or apolitical postmodernism, it is important to observe that in the universe of discourse, there are no positions of neutrality. As Gramsci put it: "Given that whatever one does one is always playing somebody's game, the important thing is to seek in every way to play one's own game with success."[64] To relinquish the task of making connections is to abdicate the terrain of power struggles to those who are actively constructing social meanings and articulating historical-popular blocs, i.e., seeking to play their own games with success (e.g., articulating patriarchal identities to conceptions of racial purity and homogeneity, homophobia, and xenophobic nationalism). It is evident, unless one assumes that all actors can play their own games without impinging on the freedom and autonomy of any other actors, that society is characterized by conflicts of interest and inequalities of power. Here I am reminded of an exchange with an anti-nuclear militant in Paris in December 1990. He had been asserting that – as a leading critic of state nuclear policy – his strategy was purely "deconstructive." "It is necessary to discredit the authorities as much as possible, whether it is the State, the EDF [Électricité de France], [or] the agency that is charged with regulating and monitoring radioactivity ... The essential battle is already that of information – by a game of strategy, to discredit the authority that is supposed to give information. And that is how we are trying to establish what should be, that is, transparency, democracy ..."[65] When I asked him how undermining confidence in the elites would be translated into support for democratic ecologists, he admitted that people who had lost confidence in the traditional parties could just as well go to Le Pen and that for this possibility "we have yet to come up with a solution." Certainly, for a north-African immigrant, a Jew, or a woman resisting patriarchy, such an answer is not acceptable and offers little reason to identify with ecologism.

Clearly, some of us feel our needs and desires are more negated by the predominant social relationships than others. We cannot, therefore, adopt a "relativist" position *either* in relation to so-called "external" forces/discourses that we might identify as racist, capitalist, patriarchal, homophobic, and productivist, *or* in relations *among* the subaltern subject positions; nor do we wish to just substitute ourselves for God (in the god-trick), adopting the kind of universalist discourse that has served dominant groups so well. In epistemological terms, we cannot buy the notion of so-called "objective" knowledge or universal norms that turn out to be patriarchal, androcentric, and eurocentric.

By linking diverse struggles against oppression to one another, we seek to escape the binary oppositions of modern social projects (in which all differences are homogenized, or subsumed, to the identities of the two main protagonists). This was an inherently flawed and limited conception of emancipation. It presents less radical challenges to the nature of power than the radical democratic project, which is able to conceptualize power as multiple forms of oppression. Without a new paradigm of social conflict, progressive social actors have limited choices:

a) to continue to play on terrain demarcated by the old left-right paradigm, which is less and less able to make sense of the world or to oppose domination (a problem faced by political ecology movements everywhere);

b) to advance political discourses that exclude certain subject positions in order to privilege others (often in the name of pluralism, or a "politics of difference");

c) to submit to fragmentation and atomization in the face of the growing insecurity and impoverishment of their life-worlds; "no social
project" is no answer to "there is no alternative" (to liberal-pro-
ductivism, patriarchy, and racism).

WHAT WILL A RADICAL DEMOCRATIC SOCIETAL MOVEMENT LOOK LIKE?

What will be the collective identity of a radical democratic societal
movement? There is no *general* (cross-cultural) answer to this question.[66] Its organizational forms in social, political, and spatial terms
(local, regional, national) cannot be read from static pictures of social
structures and social forces. Its impetus and the location of its leading
organic intellectuals cannot be derived from general laws of historical
development. In each case, what is determining are the dynamics
among historical traditions and institutions, social forces (their
resources, opportunity structures, and collective identities), discursive
practices, and fortuitous events. These may be reconstructed by histo-
rians, and the possibilities may be anticipated by social theorists, but
envisaging the future is itself an intervention – a discursive practice –
that influences the outcomes of social struggles. The point is that
counter-hegemonic movements are the products of complex articulations of interests which are themselves constructed politically. Thus,
the opposition of a widely shared conception of the "good life,"
encompassing conditions for happiness and democratic relationships,
to interests and institutions that obstruct or deny its realization will be
located in a *multiplicity* of sites. It will not be identified with *one* identity, or subject position, which is, by virtue of its supposed "centrality," hegemonic, but will take its meaning from the nature and the
inclusiveness of the relationships *among* these subjects and their struggles. In this sense, the counter-hegemonic movement may be found
everywhere that specific conflicts are reinterpreted as struggles for a
"livable" world and for democratic relationships.

The problem of naming has been complicated by the way in which
the meanings of labels may be subverted. Claims to representation of
homogenous collective subjects have been radically challenged, as we
have seen in regard to "the women's movement" in Canada (challenges
to white middle-class feminists from women of colour, aboriginal
women, working class women, lesbians), or in relation to the "workers' movement" (from the subjects of the NSMs). "Socialism" has been
hyphenated, extended, stretched like saran wrap over all the leftovers,
but before it could persuade subjects like ecologists, feminists, or
blacks of its inclusiveness of their struggles, its symbolic value was

severely deflated by its association with the failures of state socialism in the East and of social democracy in the West. Political or social ecology holds potential as a societal discourse, but its relationship to democratization (and to a collective subject) is highly contingent upon specific articulatory practices.[67] Inversely, radical democratic theory cannot tell us how humans are – or ought to be – imbedded in nature; for this we need a philosophy of human needs and rights in relation to nature. Thus, while radical democratization theory suggests that the collective identity of counter-hegemonic politics may be a deepened and broadened conception of *citizenship*, this identity does not speak directly to our relationship – *as humans* – to nature.

AFTER THE FALL

Post-Marxist NSMT and relativist postmodern positions – though profoundly opposed – are both prone to make overly general claims about the possibilities for social change couched within evolutionary historical narratives. The most compelling post Marxist interpretation of the "central conflict" of our era does not allow us to identify a privileged collective subject. The new social movement of the 21st century does not have a fixed collective identity (e.g., the anti-nuclear movement, the Green movement/party, the alternative health movement). At best, we might conceptualize the new social movement as participatory citizenship seeking to defend, deepen, and broaden the meaning of democracy in opposition to profoundly anti-democratic relationships that prevent the realization of a good life for heterogeneous majorities everywhere. Such struggles, however, will take unique forms in each context (local, regional, national, or global).

On the other hand, the argument that collective resistance to the destructive consequences of modernization and rationalization, to patriarchy, and to racism is no longer possible – or, at least, that existing forms of resistance are incapable of recognizing commonalities that are potentially empowering – can only proceed from a decision to ignore existing social movements and their discourses. Contrary to the earlier NSMT proclamation of a new historical era (in which the old social movement is replaced by a new one corresponding to radically different social conflicts) and to the denial by some postmodernists of the very possibility of radical politics, the analysis of oppositional politics in Canada and France illustrates that the conditions for the construction of "postmodern" emancipatory social projects – and the nature of their leading intellectuals – vary significantly and also *change*, as "universes of discourse" are transformed by the dynamics to which I have referred above.

COUNTER-HEGEMONIC POLITICS
IN ONTARIO

In Ontario, mobilization against the authoritarian, neoliberal regime of the Harris Government, elected in 1995, is characterized by attempts to link together a plurality of social antagonisms via democratic and radical ecological discourse. This kind of social-movement building is relatively unprecedented in the post-war history of Ontario. It arises from a specific conjuncture of factors. In the late 1970s and early 1980s, there was a lot of coalition-building activity in Canada, involving a plethora of so-called "single-issue" movements. Environmentalists succeeded during the 1980s in pushing governments to introduce new regulations for industry, but the discourse of the movement remained broadly social-democratic.[68] The kinds of alliances formed between environmentalists and other movements at this time – particularly the unions – were primarily at an elite-organizational level and of a tactical nature. That is, they did not bring about significant transformations of the identities of the subjects of the different movements. (Their radical democratic and counter-hegemonic potential was correspondingly limited.)

Since the late 1980s, a number of changes have combined to alter the discourses of all of the actors. One, the social opportunity structures for dissent have deteriorated, underpinning a *demobilization* problem. Two, neoliberal corporate discourse has been working a split in the environment movement: counter-cultural critiques of modernization versus a professionalization of environmentalists (or the greening of capitalism). This appears to have succeeded in deradicalizing key elements of the environmental movement (e.g., NGOs such as Pollution Probe and Energy Probe). I refer to this as a *deradicalization* problem. Three, a succession of events – coalition building against the FTA and the North American Free Trade Agreement (NAFTA), the (social-democratic) New Democratic Party (NDP) Government's performance in office (1990-95), and the election of the radical-right Conservative Government in 1995 – *reradicalized* certain sectors of the labour movement – in particular, public sector unions and the Canadian Auto Workers (CAW) – at a moment when the work of eco-socialist and feminist activists within the CAW had succeeded in making important linkages between socialist, ecological, and democratic critiques of the dominant rationality of societal development. Green economics and values, for example, are penetrating CAW national union strategic thinking.[69] Labour activists have discovered the potential of arguments about "sustainable development" and citizenship/democratic rights to cement coalitions at the local level, (as we have seen, for example, in the hemp campaign in southwestern Ontario led by the Windsor Regional Environmental Council (WREC) and in the Greenwork Alliance initiative in Brampton).[70] In the wake of the election of the Harris Government, a network of Social Justice and Ecological coalitions has formed in Ontario, in which union activists as well as members of other social movements participate. They are concerned not only with the neoliberal agenda in Ontario but also with the Multilateral Agreement on Investment.

This kind of social-movement building is defined not by the reduction of each struggle to a single meaning, but by the search for the connections among them. Democratic discourse provides these links, while social-ecological thought provides a radical critique of (and alternatives to) the hegemonic model of development that speaks in different ways to each subject. The formation of new solidarities is transformative for each subject's understanding of the meaning of its struggle. For example, the CAW activists contribute an eco-socialist perspective that counters the individualist (human nature) discourse of many in the citizens' groups and the environmental movement. The environmentalists challenge productivism, causing the union representatives to consider alternatives for security of subsistence. They are increasingly prepared to do this because the writing is on the wall with regard to what the hegemonic model of development has to offer auto workers (or most folks) in terms of security of subsistence. The predominantly white and male industrial workers who are the organic intellectuals of the CAW's socialist discourse are having to examine their own relationships to other subjects within these coalitions (e.g., women, racial and ethnic minorities, gays and lesbians, the unemployed).[71] The National Action Committee on the Status of Women (NAC) and women in the CAW were principal organizers of the national Bread and Roses March in June 1996 and of the Days of Action in Ontario in 1996. These developments suggest a shift from tactical and instrumental "umbrella-type" coalitions among labour and other social movement organizations to a form of social-movement building that is transformative for all of its subjects' identities. Democratic, ecological discourse is making it possible for CAW activists to gain entry to, and to win influence within, social justice and sustainable development coalitions, as subjects defining the stakes of societal conflict and offering an alternative model of development, rather than as subjects identified with a sectional, or corporative interest.

With the transition from "social unionism" to "movement unionism," the CAW has entered an intensified phase of political struggle and has assumed a key leadership role, both in Ontario and nationally. In doing so, the leadership has gambled that broad social mobilization (which it will help to create) will prevent the union's isolation. The social-movement-building project assumed by the leadership contains inherent tensions: it involves the rearticulation of interests and identities in new ways; none of the elements can remain unchanged, their differences left intact, their interpretations of the nature of the struggle left untouched. To link the women's movement, anti-racist struggles, youth, and the unemployed (in other words, a host of interrelated subject positions) in opposition to a multifaceted hegemonic order is an enormously complex task. It requires a philosophy of human needs and of the good life sufficiently pluralistic to speak to different experiences of subordination and to allow the coexistence of different visions. Socialist discourse will not suffice for these purposes, although its analysis of capitalism will be an essential element of a more inclusive counter-hegemonic discourse. The socialist militants of the CAW are therefore moving into partially unknown terrain, where interaction with other radical discourses will require not only that they lead but that they rethink the nature of power, "the enemy," and their own positions in relation to other subjects.

The CAW's transition to movement unionism in the 1990s was impelled by the vacuum left by the collapse of social democracy as an option and made possible by the growing acceptance at all ranks of the union (not just the national leadership) that there is no "going back" to the social-democratic relationship between unions, employers, and the state via the election of a social-democratic party. This new phase raises, however, some very interesting and important questions. First, to what extent can a union organization assume this kind of political leadership without being imploded by internal tensions or isolated in its external environment? Second, does the need to act simultaneously within civil society and within the State call for the formation of a political party (whose *raison d'être* is both the representation and the discursive articulation of the movement)? In the Ontario case, we seem to be witnessing the emergence of a societal movement without a Modern Prince.[72]

COUNTER-HEGEMONIC POLITICS IN FRANCE

In France, in contrast, the democratic, ecological, counter-hegemonic societal discourse has been represented *politically* by Les Verts. However, in this case, the party lacks a societal movement. That is, the kind of movement-building among *social actors* that I described briefly in the case of Ontario has not developed to the same extent in France. The anti-nuclear, environmental, students, and women's organizations, the movements in support of the unemployed and the *sans papiers*, and the trade union confederations pursue their various struggles with little sense of mutual support or shared objectives. Broad-based mobilizations occurred in 1995 in opposition to the terms of European monetary union, identifying both the elite (capitalist and bureaucratic) nature of the project and the undemocratic imposition of the Maastricht economic criteria by the French government.[73] Yet these mobilizations, led mainly by the labour confederations – notably the Confédération Générale du Travail (CGT) and Force Ouvrière (FO), which have shown little interest in the counter-cultural critiques of productivism, or other important elements of radical ecology – made little reference either to an alternative, ecologically sustainable model of development or to gender equality, among other possible discursive linkages. Historically rooted suspicions and conflicts – as between workers' organizations and environmentalists, or between feminists and leftist political movements – underpin a strong orientation towards autonomous organizing. Likewise, the alternative social movements' fear of *récupération* by the parties of the left – following the rupture of 1968 (with the PCF) and the subsequent disillusionment with the Mitterrand (PS) governments of the 1980s – leads to an insistence on autonomy in regard to Les Verts.[74]

The party has relatively weak links with social movement organizations in the sense of formal affiliations or declarations of electoral support. This is not to say that Les Verts have not made concerted efforts to support diverse social movements, including the defence of the *sans papiers*, the call to grant voting rights in local elections to foreigners resident in France, the Pacte civil de solidarité (PACS),[75] the gender parity legislation passed in January 2000,[76] the campaigns of environmental and anti-nuclear organizations, and the demands of the organizations of the unemployed. The exclusion of the unemployed, the insecurity of the partially employed, and the fact that the majority of part-time workers in France are women, have been linked in the discourse of Les Verts to an economic program demanding (among other reforms) the statutory reduction of work time accompanied by measures to prevent employers from increasing the part-time, low-paid work force.[77] Despite the integration of such demands into the program and structures of the party (e.g., the establishment of national commissions responsible for forming policies in respect to these diverse struggles), the establishment of a "social-electoral base" in the old model of the workers' party/mass organizations of the working class has not happened. This is due both to the desire of social actors for autonomy vis-à-vis political parties and to the generally weak social and cultural presence of certain of these movements in France (in particular, the environmental and women's movements). Some social actors have been particularly skeptical of the Greens' move to the left since 1994, a direction that was opposed by many grassroots environmentalists who preferred the earlier "neither left nor right but out in front" positioning of Les Verts.[78] It is also important to remember that Les Verts are not alone in the political field and are, indeed, late-comers in the competition for intellectual leadership of a counter-hegemonic bloc. The Socialists and Communists continue to occupy much of the space of the "left" with regard to both identity and electoral politics. Moreover, both of these parties seek to integrate aspects of Les Verts' program and to "recuperate" as their own struggles such as those for employment and a decent wage, gender equality, and environmental protection.[79]

Specific circumstances notwithstanding,[80] the relationship of the Greens to social actors is not unique. Arguably, it reflects the contemporary crisis of both the left's conception of a "societal project" and of the post-Second World War model of party politics. On the one hand, the idea of a unified mass movement, shaped and guided by the ideology of its political leaders, has been radically undermined by the diversification of political struggles and identities and by the associated decline of socialism as a hegemonic discourse. On the other hand, these diverse social actors are no longer "obedient" to the hierarchical (transmission) model of politics or to the constraints of parliamentary politics. Parties and "bases" are no longer articulated in the old sense. In these respects, both Les Verts and the new coalitions forming in Ontario confront a postmodern terrain of politics that calls for a new conceptualization of counter-hegemonic strategy and change.

CONCLUSIONS

The theorization of historical stages, be they "post-industrial" or "postmodern," led NSM theorists, on the one hand, to reconceptualize an emancipatory social project, and some postmodern thinkers, on the other hand, to proclaim the historical impossibility of such a project. The former view emphasized discontinuity with the "industrial era" and the decline of its radical collective subject (the working class), while casting about for its successor. The latter view has tended to assess pessimistically the prospects for opposing the globalization of an accelerated neoliberal model of development.

The discourses and social agency of counter-hegemonic movements in the French and Canadian cases – though only superficially sketched here – contradict such general claims about the fossilization of trade unions or the historical role of new middle strata as carriers of counter-cultural critiques of modernization.[81] They demonstrate why the collective identity of the new social movement cannot be deduced from a universal theory of historical transition – why its name is not waiting to be revealed like the innermost core of a Russian doll. Moreover, theories proclaiming the "end of social movements," or the impossibility of collective action in the postmodern era, privilege a static structural analysis while neglecting the dynamic relationships between agency and structure that explain social change. Instead, the prophets of both the rise and the fall of NSMs have made universal claims based on specific experiences (e.g., the French anti-nuclear movement, the German Greens) or trends (e.g., towards atomization in social existence) that may be reversed, subverted, or redirected.

At the same time, attempts to revise NSMT seem to have been influenced more by the "anti-political" postmodern critique of social theory and its suspicion of the very concepts of society and collective subjects, than by the "radical" postmodernism that offers a non-reductionist way of reconceptualizing counter-hegemonic collective action. The latter impetus indeed underlies Touraine's recent attempts to retheorize the new social movement. However, the oppositions he constructs (the double-facing struggles of the individual Subject vis-à-vis market logic and neo-communalism) do not resolve the problems of reductionism inherent in the earlier version of NSMT. The conceptualization of the Subject as an individual who acts rationally in defence of certain (universal) needs and desires (liberty and equality, and giving rise to "moral movements") is advanced as an alternative to a conception of a collective subject/identity that is largely equated with the idea of class and socialist discourse (and political-economic movements). This Subject – so closely resembling the liberal individual subject – remains essentially unitary. Collective action is the outcome of "a process of mutual recognition between the isolated Subject and other individuals who consider themselves Subjects."[82] Yet this conception – lacking a recognition of multiple subject positions – dissolves *social* relations and *political* subjects. Ultimately, rather than a theory *for* collective action that asks how the commonalities among diverse struggles may be articulated to one another – or why they should be – this is a theory about the historical meaning of diverse forms of collective action.

Touraine is correct (though hardly original) in arguing that we can no longer envisage a hegemonic project along the old lines of a reductionist collective identity superimposed upon multiple subjects. Simultaneously, the model of the class party with its (subordinate) mass organizations must be discarded. However, a counter-hegemonic politics also requires alternatives to identity politics, liberal individualism, and the social-democratic "catch-all" party (with its logic of "product diversification" for the purposes of "vote maximization").The Green parties of Europe are experiments in creating such a new model of "postmodern" politics. With greater or lesser success, they have attempted not to construct a unitary collective identity but rather to identify the affinities among multiple struggles and subject positions. The "ideology" that corresponds to such a vision of progressive politics is radically democratic, pluralist, and ecological.

Finally, the mobilizations that have occurred in Canada and France suggest that large segments of the populations in both countries are struggling towards some kind of post-social-democratic project of social change and that democratic and ecological discourses are potentially important linking elements in their strategies of collective action. For these actors, social-movement building is neither a prophesy nor mere nostalgia, but the only game in town.

NOTES

1 Eduardo Galeano, *Days and Nights of Love and War*, New York: Monthly Review Press, 1983: 139.
2 Alain Touraine, Z. Hegedus, F. Dubet, *La Prophétie anti-nucléaire,* Paris: Éditions du Seuil, 1980.
3 Klaus Eder, *The New Politics of Class (Social Movements and Cultural Dynamics in Advanced Societies),* London, Newbury Park, New Delhi: Sage Publications, 1993.
4 Alain Lipietz, *Towards a New Economic Order (Postfordism, Ecology and Democracy),* New York: Oxford University Press, 1992: 62–3; translated by Malcolm Slater from *Choisir l'audace,* Paris: Éditions la Découverte, 1988.
5 Ronald Inglehart, *The Silent Revolution*, Princeton University Press, 1977.
6 The objective of the Marxist accounts of the "new politics" was to identify these movements' social bases in class terms, and the possibilities for alliances with the working class.
7 After 1989, the frame enlarged even more, as it was obliged to encompass both the roles of NSM actors in the crisis of state socialism and the ways in which these regime collapses and their aftermaths confirmed the NSMs' critiques.
8 Alain Touraine, *The Voice and the Eye: An Analysis of Social Movements,* translated by Alan Duff, Cambridge: Cambridge University Press, 1981; Touraine et al., *La Prophétie anti-nucléaire*; Alain Touraine,

M. Wievorka, and F. Dubet, *Le Mouvement ouvrier*, Paris: Fayard, 1984; Alain Touraine, F. Dubet, and Z. Hegedus, *Lutte étudiante*, Paris: Éditions du Seuil, 1978.

9   This is summed up by Klaus Eder in these terms: "Attacks on modern culture based on its rationalism have always been commonplace. But something has changed. The protest has gained a political dimension that disturbs the institutional reproduction of modern societies through its attacks on the model of social development particular to advanced Western industrial societies. There is a general tendency leading to a central conflict in the modern world much more pervasive than that of the nineteenth century." *The New Politics of Class*, 119.

10   Laurie E. Adkin, "Ecology and Social Change: Towards a New Societal Paradigm," in Colin Leys and Marguerite Mendell (eds), *Culture and Social Change*, Montreal and New York: Black Rose Books, 1992.

11   Claus Offe, "New Social Movements: Challenging the Boundaries of Institutional Politics," *Social Research*, no. 52, 1985; Eder, *The New Politics of Class*; André Gorz, "Political ecology: Expertocracy versus Self-limitation," *New Left Review*, no. 202, November-December, 1993; André Gorz, "The New Agenda," *New Left Review*, no. 184, November-December, 1990; André Gorz, *Critique of Economic Reason*, trans. G. Handyside and Chris Turner, London; New York: Verso, 1989; Lipietz, *Towards a New Economic Order*; E. Laclau and C. Mouffe, *Hegemony and Socialist Strategy: Towards a Radical Democratic Politics*, London: Verso Books, 1985; Chantal Mouffe, *The Return of the Political*, London; New York: Verso, 1993; Chantal Mouffe, "Hegemony and New Political Subjects: Toward a New Concept of Democracy," in C. Nelson and L. Grossberg (eds), *Marxism and the Interpretation of Culture*, University of Illinois Press, 1988; Chantal Mouffe, "Radical Democracy or Liberal Democracy?" *Socialist Review*, vol. 20, no. 2, April–June, 1990.

12   For Alain Lipietz, the linkages between the successor "alternative compromise" and earlier emancipatory projects are evident: "as a new model presented as 'progress', the alternative compromise is heir to eighteenth-century liberalism and nineteenth-century radicalism, and to socialism and Communism. More fundamentally, its initial social base will have to encompass oppressed, reviled and exploited people who are in revolt against alienation: women, workers affected by industrial restructuring or deskilling technologies, unemployed and casual workers, young people of various ethnic groups in cities, small farmers burdened by debt or outside 'the system', and so on. In this way, it is the heir to the movements of emancipation. And in this sense (the historical sense), the alternative compromise is a 'new Left'." *Towards a New Economic Order*, 62.

13   One example of this characterization is Touraine's claim that the labour movements' challenges to the dominant "cultural model" of industrial

society were "limited to the level of labor organization," in *Return of the Actor: Social Theory in Postindustrial Society,* Minneapolis: University of Minnesota Press, 1988: 111 (translation of *Le Retour de l'acteur: Essai de sociologie,* by Myrna Godzich, Paris: Librairie Arthème Fayard, 1984).

14 Ibid.

15 Touraine et al., *La Prophétie anti-nucléaire,* 12. All the translations from *La Prophétie anti-nucléaire*; Alain Touraine, *Critique de la modernité,* Paris: Librairie Arthème Fayard, 1992; and Alain Touraine, *Pourrons-nous vivre ensemble? (Égaux et différents),* Paris: Librairie Arthème Fayard, 1997 – are mine, except where noted otherwise.

16 Ibid., 307.

17 Ibid., 335.

18 Touraine, *Return of the Actor,* 31, 42, 83; Touraine, *Critique de la modernité,* 414 et passim.

19 In *Return of the Actor,* 157, for example, Touraine states: "Most observers do not think that a social movement as central as the workers' movement was to industrial society is likely to emerge in the future. For my part, I maintain that the reference to a central conflict is of the essence in any society endowed with historicity." See also Touraine, *Pourrons-nous vivre ensemble?,* 117.

20 In *The New Politics of Class,* 113 and fn. 27, Eder uses this phrase, although in reference to earlier literature dealing with the decline of the 1960s social movements. See A. Oberschall, "The Decline of the 1960s Social Movements," in L. Kriesberg (ed.), *Research in Social Movements, Conflicts, and Change,* vol. 1, Greenwich, CT: JAI Press, 1978.

21 Sidney Tarrow, "The Phantom at the Opera: Political Parties and Social Movements of the 1960s and 1970s in Italy," in R. Dalton and M. Kuechler (eds), *Challenging the Political Order,* Cambridge: Polity Press, 1990; Mario Diani, "The Italian Ecology Movement: from Radicalism to Moderation," in Wolfgang Rudig (ed.), *Green Politics One,* Carbondale and Edwardsville: Southern Illinois University Press, 1990.

22 Karl-Werner Brand, "Cyclical Aspects of New Social Movements: Waves of Cultural Criticism and Mobilization Cycles of New Middle-class Radicalism," in R. Dalton and M. Kuechler (eds), *Challenging the Political Order,* Cambridge: Polity Press, 1990.

23 Claus Offe, "Reflections on the Institutional Self-transformation of Movement Politics: a Tentative Stage Model," in R. Dalton and M. Kuechler (eds), *Challenging the Political Order,* Cambridge: Polity Press, 1990.

24 Helmut Wiesenthal, *Realism in Green Politics: Social Movements and Ecological Reform in Germany,* New York: St. Martin's Press, 1993.

25 Touraine, *Pourrons-nous vivre ensemble?,* 122–3.

26 In 1998 the Socialist government headed by Lionel Jospin decided that Superphénix should be definitively shut down, but simultaneously offered to workers in the nuclear sector the compromise of reopening the Phénix nuclear facility for research purposes.

27 There is some discussion of the new environmental deregulation in my book, Laurie E. Adkin, *The Politics of Sustainable Development: Citizens, Unions, and the Corporations*, Montreal and New York: Black Rose Books, 1997. Under the Conservative Government of Ontario, elected in June 1995, environmental deregulation threatens to have far-reaching and in some cases irreversible consequences.

28 The Front National began to make electoral breakthroughs in 1984. The Reform Party of Canada, characterized variously by different authors as right-wing libertarian, populist, neoliberal, and neo-conservative, was formed in 1987, and, by the early 1990s, had attracted the votes of one-fifth of the electorate outside of Québec. Steve Patten, "Preston Manning's Populism: Constructing the Common Sense of the Common People," in *Studies in Political Economy*, no. 50, Summer, 1996; Trevor Harrison, *Of Passionate Intensity: Right-wing Populism and the Reform Party of Canada*, Toronto: University of Toronto Press, 1995.

29 The anti-nuclear movement in France, reduced to scattered nuclei of isolated militants by the mid–1980s, is finding new grounds for mobilization around the issue of the disposal of radioactive waste. The government's renewed efforts to secure sites for waste burial has raised concern that the French state is about to undertake the construction of a second generation of nuclear reactors. (The Messmer generation of reactors is reaching the end of its predicted lifespan.)

30 Mart Hertsgaard, "Who Killed Petra Kelly?" *Vanity Fair*, January 1993; John Vidal, "Greens' Petra Kelly – Death of a Dream," *The Guardian*, November 1992; David Gow, Jean Stead, Walter Schwarz, and John Vidal, "Death of a Lonely Green Dreamer," *Guardian Weekly*, 1 November 1992: 24.

31 Touraine, *Critique de la modernité*, 407.

32 Ibid., 429–30.

33 Alain Touraine, "Beyond Social Movements?" in *Theory, Culture, and Society*, no. 9, 1992: 125.

34 Ibid., 127; Touraine, *Critique de la modernité*, 423–4.

35 Touraine, *Critique de la modernité*, 414–5.

36 Ibid., 424–5, 429–30.

37 Ibid., 422.

38 Touraine now places extraordinary emphasis on the individual desire for "individuation," seen to be in conflict with forms of neo-communalism. Alain Touraine, "Can We Live Together, Equal and Different?" in *European Journal of Social Theory*, vol. 1, no. 2, November, 1998: 169–71.

He appears to view this privileging of liberal-individualist values not as a particularly French or "enlightenment" standpoint but as a universally paramount "will and effort of each of us to be *different* and to create his or her own particular life," ibid., 170. This, he says, is what makes his personal situation similar to that of a Moroccan or Malian immigrant living in Paris (ibid., 172)!

39 Charles Turner, "Touraine's Concept of Modernity," in *European Journal of Social Theory*, vol. 1, no. 2, November, 1998: 193.

40 Touraine introduces this term to distinguish his conception of a social movement from the tendency to call any type of collective action a social movement. For Touraine, a social movement "calls into question a form of social domination, at once particular and general, and appeals to values and to general orientations of the society which it shares with its adversary in order to deprive it of legitimacy." *Pourrons-nous vivre ensemble?*, 118.

41 In this work there is a new focus on the threats that various kinds of collective identity (Islamic or Christian fundamentalism, ethnic nationalism, racist movements) pose to individual freedom. Touraine argues that "cultural movements," the most important of which (in our era) are feminism and ecology, may also evolve in "neo-communal" directions. Ibid., 121-3, 135-7.

42 Ibid., 122.

43 Ibid.

44 Ibid., 142.

45 Touraine suggests that the interpretation of the meaning of various forms of collective action is the task of intellectuals (the sociologists?) who are sufficiently "unencumbered by thè discourses of the past" (Marxism?) to comprehend what they represent. *Critique de la modernité*, 414–5. These are "the orators and writers on the margin of the movement who ... suggest the meaning of the collective action, namely that which makes it a movement." *Pourrons-nous vivre ensemble?*, 123, see also 145.

46 Ibid., 138; Alain Touraine et al., *Le Grand refus: Réflections sur la grève de décembre 1995*. Paris: Fayard, 1996: passim.

47 Touraine, *Pourrons-nous vivre ensemble?*, 133.

48 Touraine, "Can We Live Together?"; Alain Touraine, "A Reply," in *European Journal of Social Theory*, vol. 1, no. 2, November 1998.

49 Touraine, "Can We Live Together?" 169.

50 In *Return of the Actor,* Touraine defines the women's movement not as a social movement but as a cultural movement. The latter are "particularly important at the beginning of a new historical period when political actors are not yet representative of new social movements or claims, and when the transformation of the cultural field calls forth fundamental debates about knowledge, economic investment, and mores," 70. Klaus

Eder shares Touraine's view of the women's movement as a "cultural" movement in *The New Politics of Class*, 101, and also argues that neither gender nor race can provide the collective identity of a new social class or new social movement (ibid., 182).

51 In his recent work, Touraine (*Pourrons-nous vivre ensemble?*; "Can We Live Together?") adopts an understanding of contemporary democratic struggles that has been influential in feminist thought for some time, namely, that feminist struggles are about both autonomy (the rejection of phallocentrism) and equality (resistance to unwarranted discrimination and male privilege). In his "reply" to critics, Touraine ("A Reply") refers to the women's movement as exemplary of "the combination of equal opportunities and cultural differences through the idea of the subject," 206. "By rejecting the identification of mankind with men and the consequent subordination of 'irrational' women to 'rational' men, [the women's movement] forced everyone to recognize that the most abstract expression of mankind is the duality of men and women who have the same rights but are different from each other," ibid., 206. However, while accepting (inconsistently) the feminist post-structuralist critique of the universal man, he does not incorporate the ideas of the radical decentering of the subject – of subject positions – or of radical democratization theory. Instead, he adopts autonomy/freedom and equality as two categories of struggle corresponding to the two principal realms in which – in late modernity – the individual Subject is engaged: instrumental involvement in the economic sphere, and meaning-oriented involvement in the cultural (or identity) sphere. In his view, the two spheres have become delinked by processes of globalization – a tendency he calls "demodernization" ("Can we Live Together?").

52 Anna Yeatman, "A Feminist Theory of Social Differentiation," in Linda J. Nicholson (ed.), *Feminism/Postmodernism*, New York and London: Routledge, 1990: 291–3.

53 Ibid., 294.

54 These are translated excerpts from interviews with two anti-nuclear militants and two Green Party militants, Paris, 18 June 1991.

55 Georges Benko argues: "The neo-liberalism that triumphed in economics and politics during the 1980s and cultural postmodernism are in fact parallel products of the disintegration of leftism ... The clearest example in France of this transition from leftist criticism to the postmodernist criticism of leftism, and even to the negation of the social domain, is that of Jean Baudrillard." "Introduction: Modernity, Postmodernity, and the Social Sciences," in Georges Benko and Ulf Strohmayer (eds), *Space and Social Theory: Interpreting Modernity and Postmodernity*. Oxford, UK: Blackwell Pubs., 1997: 15–16.

56 Some go further, characterizing postmodernists Lyotard and Baudrillard, for example, as "anti-political" or "anti-humanist" thinkers. Warren Montag characterizes Baudrillard as "an out-spoken anti-Marxist and defender of classical liberalism" who "celebrates a silent world, a world that has rid itself of every hint of conflict or contradiction" and in which "revolt is no longer possible," in Warren Montag, "What Is at Stake in the Debate on Postmodernism?" in E. Ann Kaplan (ed.), *Postmodernism and its Discontents*, London; New York: Verso, 1988: 96, 101. Hal Foster distinguishes between a "postmodernism of resistance and a postmodernism of reaction," in Hal Foster, "Postmodernism: A Preface," in Hal Foster (ed.), *The Anti-Aesthetic: Essays on Postmodern Culture*, Port Townsend, WA.: The Bay Press, 1983. Ann Kaplan differentiates a "utopian" postmodernism from "commercial" or "co-opted" postmodernism. In defining the former, Kaplan says: "... in its 'utopian' form, postmodernism is partly a product of feminism (i.e., feminism, deconstruction and Lacanian psychoanalysis have together brought about a significant cultural break we could call postmodern) ... [and] involves a movement of culture and texts beyond oppressive binary categories," associated with the work of such authors as Derrida, Cixous, Kristeva, and Barthes (E. Ann Kaplan, "Introduction," in E. Ann Kaplan (ed.), *Postmodernism and its Discontents*, London; New York: Verso, 1988). The collection *Feminism/Postmodernism*, edited by Linda J. Nicholson, New York and London: Routledge, 1990, provides an excellent introduction to the connections between feminist theories and postmodernism. The second (nihilistic) view of postmodernism (associated with Baudrillard), however, attributes an omnipotent, "blanketing" nature to late capitalism, new technologies, marketing, and consumerism, which are seen to have "created a new, unidimensional universe from which there is no escape and inside which no critical position is possible," Kaplan, "Introduction," 4.

57 The collection *Social Postmodernism (Beyond Identity Politics)*, edited by Nicholson and Seidman, Cambridge, UK: Cambridge University Press, 1995, "defends a postmodern perspective anchored in the politics of the new social movements" (preface). Honi Fern Haber develops a critique of Lyotard which argues that: "In insisting on the universalization of difference, postmodern politics forecloses on the possibility of community and subjects necessary to oppositional resistance," Honi Fern Haber, *Beyond Postmodern Politics (Lyotard, Rorty, Foucault)*, New York and London: Routledge, 1994: 3.

58 Donna Haraway, "Situated Knowledges: The Science Question in Feminism and the Privilege of Partial Perspective," in Donna J. Haraway (ed.), *Simians, Cyborgs, and Women: The Reinvention of Nature.* New York: Routledge, 1991.

59 Laurie E. Adkin, "Ecological Politics in Canada: Elements of a Strategy of Collective Action," in Roger Keil, David V. J. Bell, Peter Penz, and Lisa Fawcett (eds), *Political Ecology: Global and Local*, London and New York: Routledge, 1998.

60 Donna Haraway, "A Manifesto for Cyborgs: Science, Technology, and Socialist Feminism in the 1980s," *Socialist Review*, vol. 15, no. 80, 1985.

61 David Harvey and Donna Haraway, "Nature, Politics, and Possibilities: A Debate and Discussion with David Harvey and Donna Haraway," in *Environment and Planning D: Society and Space*, no.13, 1995: 515.

62 I do not mean to create here an image of a vanguard of intellectuals which drafts its manifesto and then tries to attract a mass following, or *d'y faire entrer tout le monde* – a conception of radical politics to which some socialists still adhere. By "organic intellectuals" I have in mind activists occupying many different subject positions and located in diverse organizational milieux. The point is that it is only through dialogues and interaction based on identifying commonalities and relationships, as well as differences, that all actors are transformed, and that unifying themes or principles of counter-hegemonic politics are "cemented."

63 Himani Bannerji, among others, has made the point forcefully with regard to the women's movement that the "politics of difference" ends up being a useful means for white, middle-class women to avoid acknowledging their raced and classed subject positions in relation to other women. H. Bannerji, "But Who Speaks for Us? Experience and Agency in Conventional Feminist Paradigms," in Himani Bannerji et al. (eds), *Unsettling Relations: The University As a Site of Feminist Struggles*, Toronto: Women's Press, 1991; H. Bannerji, *Thinking Through (Essays on Feminism, Marxism, and Anti-Racism)*, Toronto: Women's Press, 1995.

64 Antonio Gramsci, *Selections from the Prison Notebooks of Antonio Gramsci,* Quintin Hoare and Geoffrey Nowell Smith, eds and trans., New York: International Publishers, 1971: 154.

65 My translation (identity of interviewee withheld).

66 It may be significant that some of the major experiments in social-movement building since the 1980s have identified themselves simply as "solidarity" movements. An opposition movement in Bulgaria in November 1996 called itself simply "Together."

67 I address these questions in Adkin, "Ecological Politics in Canada"; "Democracy, Ecology, Political Economy: Reflections on Starting Points," in Fred P. Gale and R. Michael M'Gonigle (eds), *Nature, Production, Power: Towards an Ecological Political Economy*. Cheltenham, Glos.: Edward Elgar, 2000.

68 Laurie E. Adkin, "Counter-hegemony and Environmental Politics in Canada," in William Carroll (ed.), *Organizing Dissent: Contemporary*

Social Movements in Theory and Practice. Toronto: Garamond Press, 1992.

69 By contrast, in the 1970s and 1980s, radical ecological perspectives were expressed mainly by activist-intellectuals based in the environmental movement and the universities.

70 Laurie E. Adkin, *The Politics of Sustainable Development: Citizens, Unions, and the Corporations,* Montreal, London and New York: Black Rose Books, 1998; Roger Keil, "Green Work Alliance: The Political Economy of Social Ecology," in *Studies in Political Economy*, no. 44, Summer, 1994.

71 The CAW's adoption of policies to ban overtime and reduce work time has tested the solidarity of comparatively well-paid auto workers with the unemployed.

72 The reference is to Gramsci's coded term for the political party of the revolutionary movement. It is important to note that his conception of the political party differed substantially from Lenin's vanguard party, instead emphasizing the functions of organic intellectuals of the hegemonic project. Notably, some in the CAW are calling for a "new political alternative" and have in mind the creation of a "red-green alliance" to supercede the NDP.

73 In a collection which seeks to interpret the meaning of the massive strikes of 1995, Touraine characterized these events as "the shadow of a movement" that seeks to modernize France while insisting on more egalitarian criteria of societal development, but which needs to rid itself of backward-looking elements (*Le Grand refus*).

74 The split between the NSMs and the Socialist Party (PS) in the 1980s occurred sooner than in Ontario, but did not carry with it significant sectors of the union movement. The Confédération Française Démocratique du Travail (CFDT) "stayed" with the socialists; the Confédération Générale du Travail (CGT), while opposing the socialists, also opposed the ecologists – and stayed with the Communist Party (PCF). The final break with the "transmission" relationship between party and mass organizations appears to have come with the decision of the CGT at its 46th congress in February 1999 to become "autonomous" from the PCF. The "autonomy of the social movement" policy was exercised in October 1999 when the CGT leadership chose not to call upon its membership to fall out for a demonstration organized by the PCF (and supported by the MDC and Les Verts). The leadership explained that the CGT could not be among the organizers of the demonstration, because its demands were "eminently political." Bernard Thibault, leader of the CGT, declared that it was time for the "one hundred year old" organization to "cut the umbilical cord" with the PCF, quoted in *Le Monde hebdomadaire*, 16 October 1999:1, 9.

75 After prolonged opposition from conservatives, the PACS was adopted by the National Assembly, on 13 October 1999. This legislation gives same-sex couples the same rights as heterosexual common-law couples in the establishment of civil contracts and with regard to all other benefits to which common-law partners are entitled (*Le Monde hebdomadaire*, 23 October 1999: 10). Les Verts claim to be the first party to have supported equality rights for gays and lesbians, introduced in 1991 in the form of the Contrat d'union civile (Elisabeth Loichot et Alain Piriou, "Enfin!" in *Vert Contact*, 9–15 October 1999: 1). The party has also established a gay and lesbian national commission.

76 The "parity" act obliges political parties to register 50 per cent female candidates in elections in which there are list votes (municipal, regional, European, and senatorial in the departments which elect more than four senators), but does not impose any rules regarding the placement of women candidates on the lists. It will apply to the municipal elections in 2001. The act also permits a financial penalty to be imposed on parties which do not respect the goal of gender parity in legislative elections.

77 The Loi Aubry, named for Socialist Minister for Employment and Solidarity Martine Aubry, the first part of which was passed in 1998, establishes a statutory 35-hour work week to take effect between 1 January 2000 and 1 January 2002, depending on the type of establishment. The law allows for flexibility in the methods negotiated in each workplace to reach this target and offers financial incentives to employers to effect reductions in work time, while increasing employment. The full text of the law (*Loi no 98–461 du 13 juin 1998 d'orientation et d'incitation relative à la réduction du temps de travail*) as well as updates on its implementation may be obtained from the French Ministry of Employment and Solidarity, at the website http://www.35h.travail.gouv.fr/textes/loi/texte.htm. The reduction of working time, as well as the creation of a "third sector of ecologically and socially useful employment" are central elements of the program of Les Verts français and of their leading economic theorist, Alain Lipietz. The reduction of work time was part of the electoral accord between the Socialists and Les Verts prior to the last legislative elections. In late 1999, prior to the passage of the second law on the reduction of work time, Les Verts insisted on an amendment which will remove the exemption of employers from making contributions if they employ part-time workers. This demand – advanced by the National Collective for the Rights of Women within Les Verts – was accepted by the Socialists in October 1999. See Francine Comte, "Les Femmes marchent," *Vert Contact*, 6–12 November, 1999: 1; and coverage in *Le Monde* during this period.

78 These movements associate the left with statist and productivist orientations. The present leadership of Les Verts has been preoccupied since 1994
with making political accords with small alternative left groupings, in
order to clearly position the party on the left. By 1998 this strategy had
some success, with the entry into the party of former members of such
political formations as Alliance Rouge et Verte (AREV), Parti pour une
Alternative Communiste (PAC), Fédération pour une Gauche Alternative
(FGA). Les Verts claim that their membership has doubled since the 1997
elections due to such entryism. In this sense, they have become the "new
left" pole in French politics. In 1997 Les Verts made an electoral accord
with the PS for the legislative assembly elections, a strategic choice which
was rewarded by seven seats in the National Assembly and the post of
minister of the environment for one of the party's national spokespersons,
Dominique Voynet. The wisdom of the identification of the party with the
left, and of positioning Les Verts within the Jospin government's "majorité
plurielle," is still the subject of much debate within the ecology movement.

79 Guillaume Sainteny (1994) documents the rhetorical adoption by the
Socialist Party since the 1980s of environmental concerns (Guillaume
Sainteny, "Le Parti Socialiste face à l'écologisme," *Revue Française de
Science Politique*, vol. 44, no. 3, June 1994). During the Mitterrand presidency, a leading figure in the environmental movement, Brice Lalonde,
was recruited by Mitterrand to form a political grouping, allied with the
Socialists, called Génération Écologie. Lalonde also acted as minister of
the environment under Mitterrand. In this way, the president succeeded
in creating a deep schism in the environmental movement.

80 It should not be overlooked that Les Verts did not grow out of a convergence of social movements, like Die Grünen, but out of an electoral
entente of ecology organizations. So its problem has been to try to extend
and to create alliances with other social actors in comparatively unfertile
terrain. The "counter-cultural" currents (e.g., eco-feminism, vegetarianism, ecocentrism, communitarian values) which have been important elements of Green movements elsewhere in Europe (e.g., the UK and Germany) or parts of North America, have been relatively marginal in
France. There is some evidence that such currents are also marginal in
Les Verts and are one of the explanations for the divisions within the
broader ecology movement in France. At least four different political
ecology parties have contested French elections in recent years: Les Verts,
Le Mouvement écologiste indépendant (MEI), Génération Ecologie, and
Convergences Ecologie Solidarité. The MEI – created by former Vert
leader, Antoine Waechter – presented candidates in the 1998 regional
elections. A questionnaire survey conducted by the author of delegates to
the summer conference of Les Verts in August 1994 showed that, within
this highly educated sample, animal rights, "spirituality linked to natural

experiences," naturopathic, holistic approaches to health, and vegetarianism ranked lowest amongst a list of items considered "important to the project of Les Verts."

81 This is Eder's argument in *The New Politics of Class*. However, changes in the social opportunity structures of the new middle strata – such as the disciplining and atomizing effects of neoliberal restructuring – may erode their capacities or willingness to assume the leadership of counter-cultural movements.

82 Robert Fine, "The Fetishism of the Subject?" in *European Journal of Social Theory*, vol. 1, no. 2, November, 1998: 183.

The Social Economy in Québec: Discourses and Strategies

MARGUERITE MENDELL

In 1992, Colin Leys and I edited a collection, *Culture and Social Change*,[1] which was the result of several meetings we had organized between activists and academics in Québec and Ontario to debate the role of social movements in these two provinces. The exchanges were fascinating; the differences between these two provinces were even more profound than we had imagined, as our discussions and debates traced the history of popular movements, their relationship to the labour movement, their mobilization strategies, and their place in the political culture in both provinces. Indeed, the left in Québec – the labour movement and social movements – was largely committed to Québec sovereignty; we knew this, of course, but perhaps we did not fully appreciate the wide cultural and historical references that distinctly shaped these movements in each province. The history of popular struggle in Ontario and Québec was distinguished not only by language but by political and cultural influences. We could not address the issues without understanding, first, these distinct points of reference. This may seem obvious, but it was striking to discover how deep the differences were, despite solidarity between the groups represented at our meetings and a keen interest to share each other's experiences.

Exchanges were held at two universities, Queen's and Concordia. The discussions focused on the histories and strategies of the labour movement, the feminist movement, community organizations, the environmental movement, and church coalitions in Québec and in Ontario. We discussed the relationship between old and new movements and the impact these might have on a new socialist project at the time. The nationalist question in Québec was a powerful mobilizing force; popular groups with a long history of militancy succeeded in getting labour on their side. This relationship has yet to emerge in Ontario. I am glossing over important debates within the labour movement, which did occur in Québec and are ongoing, to come rapidly to a different point, central to the questions we were raising at the time, and which I would now like to raise again in the context of the "social economy" in Québec today.

I refer especially to our focus, in the book, on new discourses and practices within the labour movement and the old and new social movements at the time. This was particularly evident in Québec, with the establishment of a labour solidarity fund in 1983 and the creation of community economic development corporations (CDECs) by the Québec government in the mid 1980s. The Fonds de solidarité des travailleurs du Québec, established by the Fédération des travailleurs et travailleuses du Québec (FTQ) immediately assumed a strategic role in the Québec economy. In its initial phase, the active engagement of the Fonds in job creation and economic development brought it into open contact and often into conflict with local activists. It was also severely criticized by the Confédération des syndicats nationaux (CSN), the more radical labour union in Québec. However, its influence as a strategic player in Québec was already clear in the late 1980s, as the political discourse changed, reflecting the critical role now occupied by the labour movement in revitalizing the Québec economy and in creating employment. At the same time, the quickly expanding economic role of community organizations forced a new dialogue between the labour movement and the popular sector.

The Confédération des syndicats nationaux (CSN) had already begun an important dialogue with the feminist, environmental, and community movements, in ways in which the FTQ had not, as it focused on its solidarity fund and job creation strategy.[2] This dialogue marked a turning point not only in the debates it generated within the labour movement itself but in formulating new alliances and strategies that have influenced left politics in Québec since.

In 1995, the CSN also established a solidarity fund, Fondaction (Le Fonds de développement pour la coopération et l'emploi), which has been fully operational since late 1998. Unlike the Fonds de solidarité des travailleurs et travailleuses du Québec, which has invested widely in the Québec economy, the CSN fund will invest only in firms that have a clear and direct impact on job creation or the maintenance of existing jobs, firms with a commitment to participatory management and/or management training programs for workers, worker-managed firms, and firms engaged in environmental protection and/or environmental politics. Together, these are social economy enterprises, whose objectives move beyond profitability to social utility and the collective good.[3] In Québec, these two funds, in addition to a large number of new sources of investment capital, which, in many instances, also involve the FTQ, represent a critical source of risk capital for initiatives that, otherwise, have no access to capital. This alternative capital market includes social criteria in its allocation of investment capital.[4]

In *Culture and Social Change*, we wrote that the new intersections between labour and social movements required structural changes within the labour movement, both conceptually and politically. Once the labour movement no longer felt that it had to preserve its structures to prevent erosion by the surrounding culture of social movements, it could change its discourse and practices at the same time as it could influence the discourse and practices of these movements.[5] This has been occurring in Québec for almost fifteen years now, with strategic alliances between labour and community or social movements within a dominantly neoliberal policy regime that is thereby challenged and forced to accommodate and concede on many fronts. These new discursive practices between labour and social movements increased the capacity to mobilize a new politics of contestation in Québec. Since the time of our meetings and the publication of the book, these discursive practices have themselves dramatically changed.

Until 1995, the dialogue between labour and social movements represented an important advance in progressive politics, but social movements did not have an independent voice, as did labour in its capacity to negotiate with business and the state.[6] The force of the women's movement in Québec has dramatically changed this. Social movements have joined the three major actors – labour, business, and the state – to negotiate economic development strategies in Québec's new social economy.

FROM THE WOMEN'S MARCH AGAINST POVERTY TO A "PROJET PAR LA SOCIÉTÉ"

Over the past two years, a great deal of attention has turned to the so-called social economy in Québec. The qualifier is deliberate, as the most lively debates have centered on the very term itself. A brief history of the events that led to a formal recognition of what I prefer to interpret as a social project rather than a narrow sectoral one, which typically confounds the social economy with the third sector, tells a remarkable story of popular groups in Québec society today and their significant impact as new actors – previously confined to the margins of political debate and action – now joined with business, labour, and the state to negotiate new socio-economic strategies.[7] Far from an incremental addition of marginalized groups to a corporatist elite of experienced negotiators who now have to adapt their language to the customary political discourse, a new framework for negotiation is emerging, which not only includes an additional player, so to speak, but has adopted a new political language embedded in the culture of radical groups and their history of popular struggle.

In June 1995, women's organizations coordinated by the Fédération des femmes du Québec, organized a Women's March Against Poverty. Hundreds of women from all regions of Québec marched over two hundred kilometres for ten days and mobilized tremendous support throughout the province, including local, regional, and provincial governments. They arrived at the National Assembly in Québec City on 4 June and presented the government with nine demands, each and all of which were to address the level of poverty among women and children and the growing number of socially excluded and marginalized communities in the province of Québec.[8] This was the most influential event, I believe, in recent Québec history. It not only forced the government to respond but also to recognize the increasing and vital role played by the women's movement and the co-operative, associational, and community sectors in the economy.

The demand that received immediate attention from the Québec government and introduced the issue of the social economy into the political debate was for investment in social infrastructure. The argument was compelling: governments invest continuously in infrastructure – road maintenance, buildings, etc. – but ignore social infrastructure, goods and services with social utility essential to the well-being of all societies and provided largely by women, whose work is neither adequately recognized nor remunerated. This investment is more critical today; chronic unemployment, increasing poverty, and the growing humiliation of social exclusion have in turn increased the burden on women considerably, both as victims and as caregivers in a political environment that has abandoned the collective good in favour of market imperatives such as deficit reduction and the privatization of social services.

The response by the Québec government was immediate; it agreed to invest $225 million in social infrastructure over five years, but, more significantly, it opened a debate on the social economy, its definition, and the role of government. A committee – Le Comité d'orientation et de concertation sur l'économie sociale – was established to examine these issues. As well, regional committees – Comités régionaux d'économie sociale (CRES) – made up of representatives of women's groups and of regional ministries, were created to identify their specific funding needs. These groups were to recommend a definition of the social economy to the Québec government as well as identify criteria and projects that it should support.

The report by the orientation committee was presented to a conference organized by the Québec government in March 1996, to which representatives of women's groups and community organizations were invited for the first time. The government struck three subcommittees in preparation for a socio-economic summit on the economy and employment to be held in October, one of which was on the social economy. Once again, the principal mandate of this subcommittee was to define a Québec model of the social economy and the criteria for supporting projects. The October summit established a Task Force on the Social Economy for a period of two years. Its role was to select projects and develop a strategy for the social economy. Twenty-five projects were targeted for assistance by the Task Force, in sectors as varied as culture, forestry, domestic work, education, housing, transport, and manufacturing. These projects would create twenty thousand jobs in three years.

A NEW POLITICAL DIALOGUE

In retracing these recent events briefly, we are able to capture their far greater political significance. Indeed, the large and open mandate given to the orientation committee and its regional representatives, as well as the commitment of funds to designated projects, represented an immediate and important victory; even more important is the symbolic impact of this short history on Québec politics. The dialogue that had begun earlier between labour and popular movements was now extended to include the state. The emergence of the social economy as both a spatial and a socio-economic phenomenon transformed the role of its actors from struggling at the margins to full participation in a partnership model that, until now, had included only labour, business, and the state.

It is critical to note both the spatial and socio-economic aspects of the social economy; the collaboration of social movements with territorially based community organizations had already represented an important strategic change in left politics in Québec. This meant that, increasingly, efforts were directed towards the democratic revitalization of poor communities and regions directly challenging prevailing economic development models – both welfare state redistribution programs from above as well as the prevailing support for small- and medium-sized business (or supply-side economics writ small). The remarkable speed with which these achievements were integrated into strategic plans for the Québec economy not only contributed to their visibility but, more significantly, moved beyond spatial considerations linked to territory to a new political space occupied by movements for the first time, forcing the Québec government to embrace novel and more inclusive networks of governance, rather than subvert them, as in the past, or contain them, as they have done until recently. While some interpret this critically as a threat to the autonomy and militancy of popular movements, this view misses the profound impact that the presence of these actors are having on the political dialogue and decision-making process in Québec.

The demand for social infrastructure investment addressed fundamental questions of equity and democracy in a society that had, for almost twenty years, been ideologically driven to believe that markets had been prevented from operating efficiently due to a bloated and wasteful public sector, that the welfare state had nurtured a culture of dependency, and that a free market economy would replace indolence with innovation, dependency with entrepreneurship. The results need little documentation. While the literature abounds with analyses of globalization, the impotence of national governments to engage in domestic revitalization programs, and the need to abandon full employment as a realistic objective, the growing number of people who can no longer be assured a sustainable livelihood in a society incapable of providing paid employment for more than 10 per cent of its population,[9] has moved the debate beyond the roles that governments can play, to questions of social justice, citizenship, and democracy in societies governed primarily by principles of inevitability and a consensus on the impracticality of social intervention, especially regarding job creation.

The challenges are coming from social movements; the women's march marked a critical turning point in contesting the prevailing discourse by introducing a new political language. It openly addressed the ethical issues totally bypassed in policy discourse. The introduction of social infrastructure by the women's movement was, in a very real sense, destabilizing; the new vocabulary received the only appropriate response from the Québec government, which asked for help in defining the issues at stake. The inevitability thesis was turned on its head as the women's movement uncovered the real issue today, which is the absence of political will. The movement called upon the state to assume its role in public life, by implementing policies and strategies that both respond to a changing world economy and the necessary interventions to create new opportunities corresponding with these realities, but that do not compromise the basic rights to a sustainable livelihood inherent in democratic societies. This has diverted the debate away from, for example, "the end of work" to new sites of employment, to new relationships between the state and social movements, especially community organizations,and to the involvement of the private sector. It has not questioned the claim that the link between work and income has been severed by demonstrating instead that the options are not between no work and a guaranteed income but between the legitimation of all forms of employment with the appropriate state support to provide living wages for previously unpaid work and for new jobs responding to unmet needs in society.[10] The debates regarding work and guaranteed income flow from the inevitability thesis.[11]

THE INSTITUTIONALIZATION OF COLLECTIVE ACTION

The definition of the social economy that was accepted at the summit includes those enterprises engaged in the production of goods and services contributing to the collective good. It introduced, to distinguish the social economy from the private sector, the notion of a "social profit" and "social utility" as overriding objectives. While the social economy would create jobs, this is not its principle function; the promotion of democracy, citizenship (creating an active citizenry), and empowerment in the workplace and in the community underlies the social economy. Moreover, it contributes to the overall well-being of society, as it offers a greater variety of goods and services. Many of the defining characteristics of a social enterprise are familiar; they derive from the rules governing co-operatives, principally that of the priority of persons over capital. What distinguishes the defining characteristics of the new social economy is an emphasis on social engagement, on participation.[12]

Community organizations were able to occupy a strategic seat at the decision-making table in October 1996 because of their impressive track record. Throughout the 1970s and, especially, the 1980s, new intermediary organizations based in communities tackled difficult issues in innovative ways drawing upon the creative energies of community activists who now assumed new and additional responsibilities for economic revitalization of poor neighbourhoods and regions. These included community development corporations (CDCs), community futures development centres (CFDCs), community economic development corporations (CDECs), local community service organizations (CLSCs), the labour movement, and the co-operative movement.[13]

The 1980s, as Louis Favreau and Carol Saucier write, was a period of experimentation in which social movements moved from mobilization around issues that cut across territory to what David Harvey has referred to as a "politics of place," and Juan A. Tamas Carpi as an "instrument of social change."[14] Community groups began to define alternative socio-economic strategies that would mobilize community resources to provide needed goods and services by creating partnerships with other local actors. Favreau and Saucier consider this a redefinition of the social contract, this time between the community and intermediary organizations, which did indeed receive state funding, but which were largely autonomous. Community groups represented in these various new intermediary associations debated and implemented new strategies; the community sector assumed responsibility for resource allocation in its neighbourhoods; its mobilization skills and commitment to social issues were critical inputs to the collective project of economic revitalization that has become the basis for the social economy and for the support it is receiving from the Québec government.[15]

The credibility of the community sector underlies the new political position it occupies in Québec. Of course, this is within a predominantly neoliberal political environment, and its capacities are certainly limited and must not be exaggerated, but the presence of the community sector at the major negotiating table is extremely significant; it represents a break with paternalistic practices of top-down targeted program funding, as dialogue with new partners who have a demonstrated ability to engage in economic renewal in other ways is defining new strategies and new relationships within communities and between the communities and the state. That this is discussed at the national level provides a critical opportunity to coordinate work that was, until recently, territorially bound and often confused with local development.[16] That this dialogue is drawn from practice, from action, means that these experiences have to be and are taken seriously.

This has opened up many debates, the most serious of which is the anger and frustration expressed by women's organizations, which now fear that their struggle has been repackaged to resemble more palatable strategies of local economic development, rather than the support they sought for primarily non-market activity provided by women. This is a difficult and troubling issue.

THE OLD AND NEW SOCIAL ECONOMY IN QUÉBEC[17]

A great deal has been written in Québec to distinguish the new from the old social economy, which was generally associated with the co-operative movement and mutual aid societies and associations. The legacy of the co-operative movement is critical to the new social economy that has borrowed extensively from both the juridical and normative rules governing the movement. There are three principal contemporary theoretical references for the new social economy in Québec: Henri Desroches, Claude Vienney, and Jacques Defourny.[18] Their approaches vary according to the emphasis that they place on legal, structural, and normative issues. These are not conflictual: their definitions, which pertain primarily to co-operatives, are, in fact, complementary. These authors together represent the contemporary theorists of the co-operative movement. The intellectual roots originate in the sixteenth-century writings of Thomas More and run through the important influences of Robert Owen, the Rochdale Pioneers, and theorists such as Fourier, Proudhon, and Saint-Simon. The legacy is rich and has more generally been associated with utopian socialism. Today, the predominant references are primarily to Charles Gide and Leon Walras.[19]

In Québec, the contemporary theorist whose work has been most influential is Jacques Defourny; he focuses on the underlying values of the social economy and provides a normative framework.[20] The definition provided by Defourny, which is applied by the Walloon Council for the Social Economy in Belgium and has been influential throughout Europe, was adopted by the Task Force on the Social Economy in Québec. In this definition the social economy consists of:

association-based economic initiatives founded on solidarity, autonomy, and citizenship, as embodied in the following principles: a) a primary goal of service to members or the community rather than accumulating profit; b) autonomous management (as distinguished from public programs); c) democratic decision making process; and d) primacy of persons and work over capital and redistribution of profits.

The Task Force of the Social Economy in Québec added a fifth principle: participation, empowerment, and individual and collective responsibility.[21]

The history of the social economy in Québec begins with the first mutual insurance company, Société bienveillante de Québec, established in 1789.[22] Mutual aid associations emerged throughout the nineteenth century. The first credit co-operative was established by Alphonse Desjardins at the end of the nineteenth century. It responded to the credit needs of agricultural producers and was inspired by Raiffeisen (1818-88) in Germany.[23] Today, Le Mouvement Desjardins, Québec's highly successful credit-union movement, is actively engaged in supporting the social economy financially and as a partner in several projects.

The so-called second wave of the social economy in Québec occurred in the 1930s, supported largely by the Catholic Church and its anti-state and anti-socialist position. The consumer, fishing, and forestry co-operatives established in the 1930s were joined in the 1940s by co-operatives in education, housing, and hydro-electricity. The number of credit unions, agricultural co-operatives, and mutual societies grew during this time as well. This period is considered a turning point in Québec, as co-operatives in production and consumption provided a means to raise the low standard of living. Their growth levelled off in the 1950s and resumed once again in the 1960s. From 1960 to 1975, the old social economy experienced a marked decline, which coincided with the growing involvement of the state in the economy and the rise of oppositional movements based in community organizations. Citizens' committees established community clinics in Montreal and Québec City, which were later transformed into CLSCs. Similar mobilizations in rural communities fought for the survival of villages hit by plant closures and economic decline. This period marks the overlap between the old and new social economy as it has been defined by several writers and activists in Québec.

The Mouvement associatif Québécois, which emerged in this period as an independent political voice based in low income neighbourhoods, was rooted in Christian social action groups of the 1940s and 1950s. The Catholic left in Québec has played an important role in both labour and popular movements. Paradoxically, the development of the co-operative movement, the old social economy, carries another Catholic legacy, influenced by the Catholic social theorist, Frederic LePlay.[24]

During the 1970s, alternatives to co-operative production such as self-management appeared for the first time. Also, the state had become more involved in modernizing the economy of Québec from the 1950s onwards, laying the basis for what was to become known as Québec Inc., the concertation model that has characterized the economic development of Québec ever since.

The second generation of community action, 1976–82, is referred to as the golden age of activism. Groups began to struggle simultaneously for state recognition and autonomy, as they fought against the clientelist approach of publicly provided services. Social housing, daycare, women's health centres, and support groups for the poor and the unemployed established by community organizations demonstrated another way of providing services with dignity. It also marked a sociological shift from popular movements to territorially based community groups that began to explore and implement alternative economic development strategies. As stated earlier, this legacy is critical to the new social economy, which is built on the militancy of popular movements and the work of these organizations. As Martine D'Amours writes, the context for popular struggle had changed. The ideological sea change in the mid-1970s, which began to rip apart the welfare state and leave groups attacking its clientelist approach with the threat of complete abandonment, in fact, created new openings to develop autonomous community initiatives and to call for legislative changes to provide more freedom and flexibility.[25]

The history of the social economy in Québec has been extensively documented and is repeatedly in the many discussions on the evolving new social economy, especially as it now moves beyond the co-operative movement to include a variety of social enterprises and partnerships with the private and public sector – to oppose what is often a narrow association with the "third sector" – or, even, in some cases, with the informal economy. In fact, expanding the definition of the social economy has been, in my view, the most critical victory for community organizations thus far. I would even go further to suggest that the government was itself taken aback with the scope and breadth of the social economy concept as it was defined by the orientation committee. Its definition is conceptual not sectoral; it considers the social economy normatively, as a reorganization of economic life, in which the economy is re-embedded in society, to borrow from Karl Polanyi.[26] This is a radical victory as it demonstrates, through practice, not only the feasibility of "another way of doing" (agir autrement) but that efficiency and cost-effectiveness are not exclusive to private sector enterprises as prevailing dogma has it. Moreover, it has even forced a closer and more honest look at the private sector, which is replete with state assistance, and non-market arrangements and transactions costs, which escape the polemics about free markets.

In Québec, alternatives are emerging from the margins, contradicting prevailing views and the limited options and strategies they offer. The social economy is an important challenge. It has altered the political agenda in Québec; the dogma of inevitability has been severely shaken by the creative and imaginative ways in which community organizations have captured this new political space.

FROM DIALOGUE TO INSTITUTIONALIZATION TO DIALOGUE: THE SOCIAL ECONOMY AS PROCESS

The Task Force on the Social Economy held a year-end review to which it invited its many participants working throughout the regions of Québec. At this meeting, projects that had received support were discussed, plans for the upcoming year were debated, and the challenges ahead were raised, not the least of which was the future of the social economy (the Task Force itself has a limited, two-year existence). At this meeting, it was strikingly clear that enormous steps had been taken to broaden the definition of the social economy and thus strategically involve the private sector through partnerships in which the issue of governance remained paramount. For example, the establishment of a social economy fund – Fonds de développement de l'économie sociale – was announced. The objective is to create a twenty-three-million-dollar investment fund in one year; the government of Québec has contributed four million dollars; the remaining nineteen million dollars is expected to come from "le milieu," the community. In fact, the objective is to substantially involve the private sector, thereby obliging it to invest in the social economy. Major companies and banks have already contributed, no doubt influencing other private actors to do likewise.

Critics whose arguments are by now familiar fail to see the radical transformation process under way. Resources are being reallocated from the private to the social economy. Indeed, rates of return are expected; however, these are considerably less than rates in financial markets. Moreover, the investment horizon is much longer, shifting current investment behaviour from short-term to a longer-term perspective. This is no small feat in a predominantly short-term speculative investment environment. Most significant is the question of governance, as private sector actors are invited to participate in these initiatives in which they hold a minority decision-making role. The governing body of this fund has wide representation with social economy actors holding strategic positions.

We are witnessing what Alberto Melucci refers to as "new frameworks of sense," in which social movements of the recent past have ceased to be fixed characters but instead represent important symbolic challenges that render power visible and, thus, negotiable. Ruling groups find themselves forced to innovate and include new actors in new ways; previous distinctions between the state and civil society become blurred; the explicit role and place of the private sector becomes more fluid as well. As new public places are created, witness the many forums for discussion in Québec and the political space occupied by the social economy; the result is a pluralization of decision-making centres.[27] This then raises the controversial issue of institutionalization; there is a growing literature addressing the threats this may present to oppositional politics. This analysis brings its own risks to bear on these same actors by not recognizing the fundamental and profound effect that the institutionalization of a new social praxis grounded in solid alternative economic strategies is having on public perceptions. These perceptions legitimize what are otherwise acts of contestation from outside. They thus become the cultural form that shapes the issue for the future and the new institutional order it implies. This perspective is extremely useful in evaluating the processes under way in Québec and in assessing whether the social economy is, in fact, able to transform strategically the public agenda.

The analysis of the emergent political culture is critical and complementary to the growing literature that focuses primarily on spatial considerations – as it analyses new coordinating mechanisms emerging at national, regional and local levels – to situate an experience such as the one described here in the new context of globalization, decentralization, and the hollowing-out of the nation-state. What we are able to observe through these events in Québec is the emergence of new mechanisms that coordinate relationships between various social actors and provide new and more powerful roles for previously marginalized individuals and groups through a new cultural legitimacy ascribed to these experiences.

This is a dynamic story that continues to unfold; to dismiss it as either the formalization of an informal economy or the co-optation of progressive groups is simplistic at best and strategically irresponsible at worst. It blocks important opportunities to transform power relations in fundamental ways not only by accessing control over vital resources but by engaging in a radical cognitive project that demonstrates the viability of democratic alternatives. Indeed, the old social economy, the co-operative movement, accommodated capitalism; but the new social economy is more than a cyclical response by these traditional actors: it is redefining social relations.[28] Of course, asking these questions remains critical to the project; the process is ongoing. What does this new mixture of markets, associations, and hierarchies, to borrow from Hollingsworth and Boyer, imply?[29] As Favreau and Saucier[30] suggest, we must continue to ask whether the social economy represents an expansion of democracy or of social corporatism. Is it part of a new welfare mix of workfare/welfare? These questions remain important benchmarks to remind those involved of the objectives sought.

The role of popular education is critical as these responsibilities urgently require both analytical and practical tools. In their analysis of the social economy, the Confédération des syndicats nationaux (CSN) emphasized the importance of another way of learning or doing, "apprendre autrement." The experiences of the social economy are the product of what Anthony Giddens refers to as "knowledgeable communities" that construct their own socio-economic development strategies.[31] Sheila Rowbotham in her recent book, *Women Encounter Technology*,[32] reminds us that "women studies after all had its origin not only in the desire to extend what was studied but to transform the power relationship in how knowledge was constructed."[33] And, as she writes elsewhere, there are now new possibilities for poor women to organize around issues of production.[34]

In many regions and localities of Québec, the new capacities of communities and movements to extend their democratic practice into the organization of local economies constitute these new possibilities. The principal challenge, at the moment, is to bridge these fragmented experiences and present them as viable and democratic alternatives. This is occurring; the number of conferences organized throughout the province in a very short period of time is extraordinary; the annual review of the social economy convened by the Task Force provided a critical occasion to evaluate and to plan ahead; the labour movement continues to hold meetings and conferences both within the unions and with larger public participation. The role of dialogue has never been more important; protest discourses become integrated into the language of politics, creating Melucci's new frameworks of sense.[35] Still, there is a call for more learning opportunities: to consolidate a social project that originated within popular movements and to equip activists to move from experimentation to intervention with tools adapted to their reality and objectives.[36]

Ian Gough includes the capacity to make choices in his work on basic needs; Amartya Sen speaks of the necessity to recognize and nurture capabilities; Enzo Mingione, influenced by Sen, demonstrates the futility of vast income distribution programs to break what he calls malign circuits of poverty. To be able to do this, people need practical knowledge based in everyday life experience,[37] but the learning of a new social praxis has wider implications. The lessons of the social economy are being diffused through their increased visibility in Québec. As Tamas Corpi observes: "Citizens and community have in associative forms the process of production and management, as well as a field for democratic learning and experimentation, a mechanism of autonomy in the face of market alienation and the bureaucratic power of the state."[38]

In her year-end review of the work of the Task Force, Nancy Neamtan, director, addressed some of the critical struggles ahead, not the least of which are unrealistic expectations. In raising this, she also emphasized the very real achievements that had been made in economic, social, and political terms. The projects that had received support were committed to solidarity and democracy; they also represented hybrid enterprises that combined market, non-market, and non-monetary arrangements. She also insisted on the fragility of the social economy and its need for continued government support.

The divisions that had emerged between the women's movement and the social economy were addressed. Did these undermine the social economy? Were the objectives of economic democracy and solidarity conflictual? In French, the terms used to distinguish "l'économie sociale" from "l'économie solidaire" have created confusion and conflict. The solidarity economy refers primarily to non-monetary activity, as distinguished from the social economy and its place within the capitalist economy. The debate divides along two lines: those who feel that the non-monetary sector has lost out, as support has largely gone to social enterprises and those who fear that, indeed, the non-monetary sector will now receive support and become monetized, so to speak, as previously unpaid work is rewarded and becomes the site for poor-quality, low-wage employment. This debate is ongoing among Québec intellectuals; a recent publication L'Économie sociale. L'Avenir d'une illusion, reveals the depth of the critique.[39]

In my view, this debate is misplaced and, as the social economy develops, will be detrimental if it is not resolved or nuanced. If the social economy – including its actors, its dialogue, and the role it has played and continues to play in transforming the political landscape in Québec – is interpreted instead as a process of negotiation, the analysis changes from one that seeks a quick fix to one that recognizes the institutional gains that are being made as this process continues. An appeal has been launched by intellectuals and activists to do just this, to recognize the political space being occupied by intermediary organizations in Québec and the barriers they have broken by insisting that their role is not to manage poverty but to transform poor communities.[40] This involves resources, imagination, the ongoing commitment of the public sector, and institutionalization.

Favreau and Saucier contrast the 1980–90 period of experimentation with a process of institutionalization that began after 1990, in which new relationships and discursive practices have emerged between community organizations, the state, business, and labour. The old social economy actors – the co-operative movement (in particular, Le Mouvement Desjardins) – are playing a vital role. The labour movement and its investment funds have made investment capital available and, in so doing, are participating in decision-making bodies. The Fonds de solidarité, for example, has turned over the management of its SOLIDES fund to CDECS. This is a complete break with its earlier ways of deciding everything at head office in Montreal. Also, alternative investment funds created within communities are now forming partnerships with intermediary organizations, providing yet another source of capital with somewhat more flexible investment criteria. To this we now add the new Fonds de développement de l'économie sociale. And so, the community sector has essentially established an alternative capital market, complete with diversified funds.[41] The Québec government recently passed legislation to create solidarity co-operatives to include not only producers and/or consumers but citizens involved in these co-operatives. It also passed legislation permitting its investment agency, le Société de développement industriel (SDI) to provide loan guarantees for non-profit enterprises for the first time, including, therefore, community enterprises. This is an important step.

A recent document, in which the Québec government announced its full commitment to job creation, included a passage on the social economy that reveals the changing interpretation from its early sectoral version to a normative one. In this document, the government affirms the capacity of the social economy to generate economic initiatives based on solidarity and concertation at both the local and regional levels. It also expresses its commitment to fulfilling social needs. This is a long way from the former association of community economic development with local business development, from a social economy rooted in the co-operative movement, or from the new social economy's confused association with the third sector.

In the appeal launched by Québec intellectuals for a social and solidaristic economy, they insist that the social economy alone cannot be a "projet de société" – a social project; rather, it is part of such a project. It cannot be relied upon to create jobs; this is not its role. Instead, as the European Federation of Unions (Confédération Européenne des Syndicats) and many organizations representing the social economy in Europe recently wrote in a common declaration, the importance of dialogue is critical to recognize and make more public the exemplary role of the social economy in extending economic democracy and worker participation.[42] Québec, where this is occurring, is experiencing a radical transformation of political culture, which, as Polanyi wrote in 1932, may save democracy. For Polanyi, the crisis of the 1920s and 1930s was predicated on the fundamental incompatibility between democracy and economically driven policy. We have been living with this contradiction (the incompatibility between a policy entirely driven by economic imperatives and democracy, which is based on a different set of principles in which economic activity is embedded) for almost thirty years. It has fallen to civil society to reclaim democracy; this is the greatest challenge facing social activists today. The catastrophic record of these last thirty years and the unyielding commitment to failed doctrine has opened up unimagined spaces for a social praxis grounded in democracy.

NOTES

1 Colin Leys and Marguerite Mendell (eds), *Culture and Social Change: Social Movements in Ontario and Québec*, Montreal: Black Rose Books, 1992.

2 Only recently has the FTQ diversified its solidarity fund to include a new source of investment capital with lower rates of return, less stringent eligibility criteria, and investments within the $5,000 to $50,000 range. These instruments, SOLIDES, represent the first effort by the FTQ to work more closely with the community sector; as in most cases, these SOLIDES are managed within communities by intermediary associations such as the CDECs. This is a complicated story that includes some skepticism; even the more open SOLIDES suffer from criteria that are often too rigid and limiting. Still, it is an important step by the FTQ to diversify its highly successful fund and a salutary attempt to provide community organizations with investment capital. The eligibility requirements will, no doubt, be modified, to respond more adequately to the environments in which they are located. For more detail on these funds, see Benoit Levesque, Marguerite Mendell, and Solange van Kemenade, "Profil socio-économique des fonds de développement local et régional au Québec," report prepared for the Federal Office of Regional Development (Québec) [FORD(Q)] in collaboration with PROFONDS, groupe interuniversitaire de recherche sur les fonds de développement régional et local (Montreal, 1996).

3 Within five weeks after the legislation to create Fondaction was passed in Québec, the fund had accumulated $7.6 million. Both Fondaction and the Fonds de Solidarité offer significant fiscal advantages, which were reduced somewhat in the 1996 federal budget, but continue to attract many individual investors. This represents an important example of a facilitating environment that, in important ways, shifts decisions regarding economic development and employment from the state to the labour movement. It reduces the amount of capital available to conventional capital markets considerably. The Fonds de solidarité has accumulated approximately $2 billion; Fondaction, approximately $50 million.

4 Levesque, Mendell, and van Kemenade, "Profil socio-économique des fonds de développement local et régional au Québec."

5 Colin Leys and Marguerite Mendell, "Introduction," in Leys and Mendell (eds), *Culture and Social Change*.

6 In 1995, the CSN published a document on "l'économie solidaire" that
   addressed the increasing importance of the community sector in the provision of social services in contrast to the growing number of precarious
   jobs emerging in this sector. Although this early document remained too
   closely associated with a sectoral view of the social economy, it opened
   the door to an important, still-ongoing dialogue within the labour movement. This early work was largely influenced by the work of Jean-Louis
   Laville and others in France on "l'économie solidaire"; Jean-Louis Laville
   (ed.), *Les Services de proximité en Europe: pour une économie solidaire*,
   Paris: Syros/Alternatives, 1992; Jean-Louis Laville (ed.), *L'Économie
   solidaire. Une Perspective internationale*, Paris: Desclee de Brouwer,
   1994.

7 For more than thirty years, beginning with the Quiet Revolution, the
   Québec government has been heavily engaged in industrial strategy. The
   nationalization of Hydro Québec marked an important turning point in
   Québec economic development. It was followed by the creation of the
   Caisse de dépot et placement, the public-sector pension fund. Both these
   public enterprises have also significantly altered the place of the Québec
   economy internationally, with extensive investments outside Québec. The
   Québec model of concertation that evolved through the 1970s has distinguished Québec from other regions in Canada. The collaboration
   between labour, business, and the state was the basis for Québec's
   "grappes industriels," or what became known as Québec Inc. The overriding nationalist project is certainly a key factor; the drive to build a
   dynamic economy in Québec had the support of the major actors in
   society.

8 The nine demands consisted of: a social infrastructure program with jobs
   primarily for women; a pay equity law; an increase to $8.15 in the mini-
   mum wage, to bring it above the poverty line; application of labour standards to all persons participating in employability programs; an automat-
   ic deduction at source of spousal support payments; the availability of at
   least 1,500 low-cost housing units per year; access to training programs
   and services with appropriate financial support; for immigrant women,
   the retroactive application of a reduction from ten to three years of spon-
   sorship by their husbands; a freeze on tuitions and an increase in student
   bursaries. Martine D'Amours, *L'Économie sociale au Québec. Cadre
   théorique, histoire, réalités et défis*, Montreal: Institut de formation en
   développement économique communautaire (IFDEC), 1997.

9 The unemployment rate in Québec for 1996 was 11.3 per cent, more
   than 40 per cent in certain regions of the province, and more than 14 per
   cent in the city of Montreal. In Montreal, the unemployment rate in certain low-income districts is more than 20 per cent and much higher for
   women and youths.

10 The initial demands by the womens' organizations were very clear. This
was neither about "employability" or workfare programs; nor was it
about the transfer of public sector jobs into the social economy. Their
demands were for the legitimation and remuneration of ongoing unpaid
work by women and for new jobs. The report presented to the Québec
government by the orientation committee, *Entre l'espoir et le doute*
(*Between Hope and Doubt*) made this very clear (Comité d'orientation et
de concertation sur l'économie sociale, *Entre l'espoir et le doute*, 1996).
This was a sticking point as the initial outlay by the Québec government
came from existing budgets. The call was for new money to come from
both the private and public sectors and for the creation of new jobs.

11 *The End of Work* by Jeremy Rifkin has popularized this thesis (Jeremy
Rifkin, *The End of Work. The Decline of the Global Labour Force and
the Dawn of the Post-Market Era*, New York: G.P. Putnam Sons, 1995).
However, his argument has detractors; among them, the latest Human
Development Report, which puts the issue of political will up front. This
is a serious challenge to the inevitability argument. The HDR goes so far
as to argue for a commitment to full employment. The opposition to the
end of work thesis has been weak at best. Instead of the changing nature
of work and the validation of different types of employment, the dual
society of the future – a highly paid and small population of strategic
analysts (to borrow Robert Reich's term) and the "rest" – low-paid service workers – is the vision of the future. Rifkin's suggestion that this can
be resolved through the redistribution of income appears radical to those
unwilling to re-engage the state. The fatalism and inevitability, however,
is generally accepted. And so the counter-evidence of productive initiatives emerging in localities and communities is compelling. The emphasis
must, however, be placed on socio-economic initiatives that far exceed
the third-sector vision of Rifkin and others. Andre Gorz, a long-time
critic of the Revenu minimal d'insertion (RMI) in France, has joined with
those who support guaranteed income and a growing service economy
based in communities. The experience of the social economy in Québec has
moved considerably beyond what might be a miserabiliste view of the
world. The work of Gorz, Rifkin, and others reinforces a dualization
already well under way and must be forcefully resisted (Andre Gorz, "Le
Travail perd sa centralité dans la vie des gens," *Entretien. Alternatives
économiques*, no. 157, March 1998: 62–5; Andre Gorz, *Misère du présent.
Richesse du possible*, Paris: Éditions Galilée, 1997; Rifkin, The End of Work).

12 Comité d'orientation et de concertation sur l'économie sociale, *Entre
l'espoir et le doute*; Benoit Levesque and Bill Ninacs, "The Social
Economy and Local Strategies for Employment," in *Local Strategies for
Employment and the Social Economy*, Montreal: OECD/IFDEC, 1997:
123–36; D'Amours, *L'Économie sociale au Québec*.

13 CDCs had been established by community groups in different regions in Québec; there are currently seventeen CDCs. CDECs were created by the Québec government in the early 1980s and were the first community-based organizations with a clear economic mandate of job creation and enterprise development. The first three CDECs consolidated the work of community organizations in three low-income neighborhoods in Montreal. The CDEC in Pointe St. Charles has received the most attention, as it had already embarked on an economic development strategy that was the basis for government support for this model of local economic intervention. There are currently seven CDECs in Montreal and one in Québec City. The CFDCs were established by the federal government in fifty-five low-income regions in Québec; their mandate is similar to the CDECs in rural areas; the CLSCs grew out of the community clinics of the 1960s and 1970s to become unique, state-supported community service organizations throughout the province of Québec. If we add to this the labour movement, with its increasing involvement in local issues, and the co-operative movement, in particular, the coopératives de développement régional (CDRs), the number of intermediary institutions in Québec that had already begun to challenge prevailing economic development strategies by harmonizing social and economic objectives in their localities is surely significant.

14 Louis Favreau and Carol Saucier, "Économie sociale et développement économique communautaire – de nouvelles reponses à la crise de l'emploi?" *Économie et solidarités*, vol. 28, no. 1, 1996: 5–19; David Harvey, *The Condition of Postmodernity*, Oxford: Basil Blackwell, 1989; J.A. Tamas Carpi, "The Prospects for the Social Economy in a Changing World," *Annals of Public and Cooperative Economics*, CIRIEC International, vol. 68, no. 2, 1997: 247–80.

15 This is, of course, the "social capital" that is regularly invoked now as the missing link to economic development. Inspired by James Coleman and popularized by Robert Putnam, it is receiving great attention by policy makers everywhere. In Canada, the federal government organized meetings to bring together leading experts on this issue, in the US, President Clinton held a rally in Philadelphia during the summer of 1996 to revive the American community spirit. Moral incantation is confused with economic analysis, producing a cacophony of voices on the subject. References move from the industrial districts in Italy to church bazaars in rural America! That being said, the legacy of community organizations in Québec was the critical platform on which to build new economic initiatives grounded in community culture. Indeed, solidarity was the most important resource in these alternative economic initiatives.

16 CDECs in Montreal, for example, have formed an inter-CDEC that meets regularly to coordinate their work and develop common strategies. This

was a long time coming because CDECs felt compelled to work alone for fear of losing their gains and state support. It is only recently that these organizations have themselves shifted from a mindset attached to previous paternalistic relations with the Québec government. This is one example among many.

17 The following section is a summary of several excellent articles and monographs that have recently been published in Québec for a variety of different audiences, from the OECD to the Institut de formation en développement économique communautaire (IFDEC) to scholarly journals. The IFDEC document was intended for practitioners as part of a widespread public education program for those engaged in the social economy; D'Amours, *L'Économie sociale au Québec*; Benoit Levesque and Marie-Claire Malo, "L'Économie sociale au Québec: une notion méconnue, une réalité économique importante," in Jacques Defourny and Jose L. Monzon Campos (eds), *The Third Sector. Cooperatives, Mutual and Nonprofit Organisations*, Brussels: De Boeck-Wesmael, 1992; Benoit Levesque and Louis Favreau, *Développement économique communautaire. Économie sociale et intervention*, Québec: Presses de l'université du Québec, 1996; Levesque and Ninacs, "The Social Economy and Local Strategies for Employment"; and Benoit Levesque and Eric Forgues, "L'Économie sociale en question," Interview (Association d'économie politique, 1996) among others. Until this recent avalanche of literature (I cite only a select few), the reference for the social economy in Québec was Levesque and Malo. Fortunately, this was translated into English as well, as, to date, there is little else.

18 Jacques Defourny, "L'Émergence du secteur d'économie sociale en Wallonie," *Coopération et développement*, vol. 23, no. 1, 1991: 151–75; Henri Desroche, *Pour un traité d'économie sociale*, Paris: CIEM, 1984; Claude Vienney, *L'Économie sociale*, Paris: La Découverte, 1994.

19 Eric Bidet, *L'Économie sociale,* Le Monde-Éditions, 1997. The École de Nimes, which emerged in France at the end of the nineteenth century and established consumer co-operatives, was inspired by the Rochdale Pioneers. Charles Gide theorized these experiences and formed a school of social economy in opposition to neoclassical economics. For Gide, the co-operative movement was transformative. The term "social economy" had, in fact, first appeared in 1830 in France in the Nouveau traité d'économie sociale (Charles Dunoyer). However, it was the work of Charles Gide and the universal fair, organized in 1900 in France, that introduced a new theoretical framework to contest the principal assumptions underlying economics by demonstrating that economies can be otherwise organized. Leon Walras, considered the founder of neoclassical theory, is rarely associated with his important work, Études d'économie sociale, in which he recognizes the role of associations and the need for

state intervention in the economy (Bidet, ibid., 26–34; Christian DeBlock and Jean-Jacques Gislain. "L'Économie sociale en perspective: émergence et dérive d'un projet de société," in Benoit Levesque, Andre Joyal, and Omer Chouinard, *L'Autre Économie. Une économie alternative?* Québec: Presses de l'université de Québec. 1989: 55–89; Pierre Dockes, *La Société n'est pas un pique-nique. Leon Walras et l'économie sociale*, Paris: Économica, 1996).

20 Jacques Defourny, "The Origins, Forms and Roles of a Third Sector," in J. Defourny and Jose Monzon Campos (eds), *The Third Sector. Cooperative, Mutual and Nonprofit Organisations*, Brussels: De Boeck-Wesmael, 1992: 27–57.

21 Levesque and Ninacs, "The Social Economy and Local Strategies for Employment," 125.

22 D'Amours, *L'Économie sociale au Québec*, 37.

23 The two important influences in the credit-union movement are both German. Raiffeisen established a rural mutual credit movement (credit unions); de Delitzsch (1808-83) established people's banks in urban areas. The first theoretician on the subject of mutual credit was Proudhon (Vienney, *L'Économie sociale*, 57-60; Bidet, *L'Économie sociale*, 23-5).

24 The influence of Le Play on the co-operative movement in Québec has caused some debate and concern over the legacy of the new social economy. Alphonse Desjardins was a member of the Société canadienne d'économie social de Montréal, established in 1888 to promote the social corporatist views of Le Play, which included collaboration between employers and workers and adherence to the social doctrine of the Church. Detractors of today's social economy in Québec point to this heritage to challenge the progressive politics claimed by its supporters. These attacks have been dismissed, but they do point to the interesting legacy of the social economy, which has both socialist and social-Catholic roots. While the role of the Church in Québec is not denied, this is a misreading since it ignores the active and militant Catholic left, which continues to play a vital role.

25 D'Amours, *L'Économie sociale au Québec*.

26 Karl Polanyi, *The Great Transformation*, Boston: Beacon Press, 1944.

27 Alberto Melucci, "Social Movements and the Democratization of Everyday Life," in John Keane (ed.), *Civil Society and the State: New European Perspectives,* London, New York: Verso, 1988: 245–60. In 1996 alone, there were numerous conferences and public meetings on the social economy throughout Québec, bringing together academics, community activists, the labour movement, and members of the Québec government especially concerned with employment and regional issues. For example, in June 1996, IFDEC (Institut de formation en développement

économique communautaire) organized a large conference on community economic development in Montreal; in September, there were at least three conferences, a forum on the social economy in Québec City, an Estates General on local economic development, and a forum on social solidarity organized by Solidarité populaire Québec, among others. This does not include the many small meetings organized by popular education groups in Québec, such as the Centre St-Pierre and the Centre de Formation Populaire (Jacques Boucher and Yvan Comeau, "L'Économie sociale est-elle un projet de développement credible?" *Économie et solidarités*, vol. 28, no. 2, 1996: 1–11). In 1997, these included study sessions and a two-day-long meeting organized by the Fédération des femmes du Québec to assess the events since their march in 1995. Numerous articles appeared during this time. Today, this effervescence of dialogue and debate has resulted in the publication of an appeal signed by a variety of social actors to consolidate their work and promote further development of the social economy by recognizing its potential and addressing emergent conflicts creatively, so as not to lose the important gains being made.

28 It is suggested that the growth of the social economy (most generally associated with the co-operative movement) is counter-cyclical. For example, in the period 1974–84, as overall employment creation fell in most industrialized countries, it grew in the co-operative sector. In contrast to this period, however, something else is occurring today: we are no longer speaking about the co-operative sector alone but rather about the emergence of new forms of economic organization, developed with the collaboration of the co-operative movement among a variety of associative movements and organizations (Tamas Carpi, "The Prospects for the Social Economy in a Changing World").

29 Robert Boyer and J. Rogers Hollingsworth, "From National Embeddedness to Spatial Institutional Nestedness," in Robert Boyer and J. Rogers Hollingsworth (eds), *Contemporary Capitalism. The Embeddedness of Institutions,* Cambridge: Cambridge University Press, 1997: 439.

30 Favreau and Saucier, "Économie sociale et développement économique communautaire."

31 Ash Amin, "Beyond Associative Democracy," *New Political Economy*, no. 1, 1996.

32 Sheila Rowbotham, *Women Encounter Information Technology: Changing Patterns Of Employment In The Third World*, London and New York: Routledge, 1995.

33 V. Bahl, "Reflections on the Recent Work of Sheila Rowbotham: Women's Movements and Building Bridges," in *Monthly Review*, vol. 48, no. 6, November 1996: 40.

34 *Dignity and Daily Bread: New Forms of Economic Organizing among Poor Women in the Third World and the First*, Sheila Rowbotham and Swasti Mitter (eds), London: Routledge, 1994

35 Klaus Eder, "The Institutionalization of Social Movements. Towards a New Theoretical Problematic in Social Movement Analysis?" Unpublished paper, European University Institute, Florence, 1993; Melucci, "Social Movements and the Democratization of Everyday Life"; Eder, 1996; Melucci, 1988.

36 Marie-Andrée Coutu, "L'État des besoins actuels de recherche et de formation des organismes populaires et communautaires," Paper presented to "Colloque université et monde communautaire. Le partenariat de recherche et de formation entre les organismes communautaires et l'université est-il possible?" December 1997. In an article written in 1932 for the *Osterreichische Volkswirt* (Vienna), Karl Polanyi writes: "But new knowledge does not ensure a knowledgable and educated public! It can contribute to the cultural development of the masses only to the degree that it lends meaning to work, life and the everyday existence of the masses." (translation by Kari Polanyi-Levitt) Polanyi wrote a great deal on the necessity to ground education in daily life. The important role being played by popular education groups in Québec, as well as by the unions and community organizations, now needs the increased participation of the research community to provide more tools as these groups now face increasing responsibilities and opportunities. On Polanyi and education, see Marguerite Mendell, "Karl Polanyi and Socialist Education," in Kenneth McRobbie (ed.), *Humanity, Society and Commitment. On Karl Polanyi*, Montreal: Black Rose Books, 1994.

37 Len Doyal and Ian Gough, *The Theory of Human Need*, London : Macmillan, 1991; Enzo Mingione, "Urban Poverty in the Advanced Industrial World: Concepts, Analysis and Debates," in Enzo Mingione (ed.), *Urban Poverty and the Underclass*, Oxford: Basil Blackwell, 1996: 3–41; Amartya Sen, *Inequality Reexamined*, Cambridge: Harvard University Press, 1995.

38 Tamas Carpi, "The Prospects for the Social Economy in a Changing World," 265.

39 Louis Boivin and Mark Fortier, *L'Économie sociale. L'Avenir d'une illusion,* Montreal: Fides, 1998.

40 *Le Devoir*, "Appel en faveur d'une économie sociale et solidaire," 20 April l998: A9; and 21 April 1998: A7.

41 In a recent study, over 230 new investment funds that may be referred to as risk capital were identified. Of these, over two thirds are invested in the social economy. Benoit Levesque, Marguerite Mendell, and Solange van Kemenade, "Les Fonds de développement: un instrument indispensabale pour le développement régional local et communautaire," in Serge

Cote, Marc Urbain Proulx, and Juan-Luis Klein (eds), *Et les régions qui perdent?*, Rimouski: GRIDEQ, 1995; Levesque, Mendell, and Van Kemenade, "Profil socio-économique des fonds de développement local et régional au Québec."

42 Confédération Européenne des Syndicats and Organisations de l'Économie Sociale, "Déclaration commune," Brussels, November 1997.

New Theoretical Challenges: Political Theory and the Theory of Politics

Introduction

Alongside global changes in economy and politics, theoretical debates about how to understand and respond to those changes continue. In part four, the articles grapple with how to theorize about politics and the political, about ethics, and even about theory itself.

In "Politics in Isolation? Recent Developments in Political Theory," Anne Phillips problematizes the "return to the political" that characterizes much contemporary political thought. This "return" arises from critiques of economic determinism (which limited the political to a function of the economic) and liberal theory (which equated political liberalism with economic liberalism), both of which had served to limit the sense of significance of the political field as such. While renewed interest in the realm of politics has happily served to revitalize political theory, Phillips suggests, it has also come at the price of a diminished interest in theorizing the interrelationship of politics with society and economics. Thus politics is given attention, but at the same time it is abstracted from the realms of the social or economic. This only serves to limit our understanding of the ability of politics to effect larger social change. Phillips extends, as examples of this, theoretical approaches to equality and democracy that emphasize institutional reform.

In "An Ethical Politics of Our Times: Moral Selves or Solidarity," Banu Helvacioglu investigates the question of what constitutes progressive politics in our time. Helvacioglu makes use of Zygmunt Bauman's theoretical insights in her argument that this historical conjuncture is characterized by a composite of political modalities.

Liberal theory's focus on individual rights and rationality fails to provide an adequate ethical ground for addressing the necessarily contradictory demands of these different modalities. Helvacioglu argues, instead, for the development of an aporetic ethical stand, simultaneously both individual and universal. The emergence of such an ethical position would require attention to both the universal and to the specific. It would need to ground its understanding of political agency at both levels, not, as is so often the case with liberal thought, only at the most abstract. It would require maintaining the tension that is inevitable in an aporetic situation.

The theme of "the return of the political" and of the role of reason and agency also emerge in Radhika Desai's article, "Fetishizing Phantoms: Carl Schmitt, Chantal Mouffe, and 'The Political.'" Desai takes issue with the decision of some post-structuralist political theorists, Chantal Mouffe in particular, to adapt the ideas and insights of Carl Schmitt to their radical democratic political project. This adaptation sees in Schmitt's concept of "the political" a useful complement to a post-structural critique of liberal theory's emphasis on reason and a theoretical grounding for its recognition of the inevitability of social conflict. Desai rejects this formulation, however. The strong association of "the political" with "anti-reason" leads inevitably not to a deepening of democracy, as Mouffe argues, but to an endorsement of authoritarian politics, not to an extension of political debate but to the abandonment of all that makes it meaningful.

The critique of rationalism, which Desai decries in Mouffe, is one aspect of a broader critique of political theory that has been constitutive of the postmodern theoretical project. This project, according to Eleanor MacDonald, in "Incredulity and Poetic Justice: Accounting for Postmodern Accounts," questions both the relationship of theory to its objects (the issue of accounting) and the grounding of ethics in a discourse of truth (the issue of accountability). Yet, simultaneously, the postmodern theorists themselves develop their own political accounts of their times and their own normative justifications for their accounts, which, given their own presuppositions about theory as itself discursive practice, stand also as political interventions. Through brief overviews of the theoretical projects of Derrida, Lyotard, and Baudrillard, MacDonald demonstrates the ways in which each theory can be read as an account of the present and a response to it. MacDonald also argues that as an account, and as a response, postmodern theory is limited, contradictory, and problematic. Ultimately, it would seem, the theoretical projects are prophylactic; they offer, at best, immunization against the risk that one might put faith in an unproblematic referentiality or justice. According to MacDonald, in limiting themselves to this strategic post, they implicitly leave unanswered the need to move outside of postmodern theory in order to understand and effect change.

The questions raised here are, in many ways, timeless. They are also, it would seem, timely – the debates about how to make the world more just, about the place of the individual within it, about how we come to understand social order and disorder. The authors in this section, while differing on many points, hold in common the belief that contemporary political theory needs to sharpen its focus and to develop new and better theoretical responses to the ethical and political demands of our times.

Politics in Isolation?
Recent Developments in
Political Theory

ANNE PHILLIPS

Throughout his career as a political analyst, Colin Leys has covered an exceptionally wide terrain, ranging geographically from East Africa to Britain to Canada, spanning the analysis of neo-colonialism[1] and of declining post-colonial power,[2] and engaging variously in what is termed political economy, political analysis, and political theory. Two ideas have persisted throughout his wide-ranging work. The first is that we cannot understand contemporary politics unless we place it within its longer-term historical formation; the second is that, while politics is "distinguishable from economic and social life, it cannot be understood as a distinct 'field' of activity, occurring in a separate realm or region of its own."[3] In *Underdevelopment in Kenya*, this meant understanding the major political alternatives in relation to what Leys described as "the basic political cleavage in Kenyan politics at independence": between the groups and social strata that bore the brunt of exploitation and those that had acquired a material interest in the continuation of the colonial economy.[4] In his introduction to *Politics in Britain*, it meant interpreting the politics of the major parties throughout the 1960s and 1970s as responses to an underlying crisis in class relations, itself related to the long-term decline in Britain's position in the world economy. While Leys's work is distinguished by careful analysis of the different strata to which parties look for their political support (and the often contradictory pressures these strata generate), it stands primarily as a testament to the importance of recognizing the interrelationships between politics, economics, and social structure.

From the standpoint of the early twenty-first century, this sometimes looks like an initiative that has failed. Today's political scientists certainly recognize the centrality of economic policy in the formation of political alternatives, but the links they make between the economic and the political are a far cry from the materialist understanding of politics that has characterized so much of Colin Leys's work. In the world of political theory, meanwhile, there has been a marked "return to the political" – precisely, it would seem, as that "distinct 'field' of activity" that Leys has worked so hard to contest. The revival of normative theory – itself, a very welcome development – has encouraged a sharper demarcation between politics, economics, and social structure, and a corresponding lack of interest in the social conditions that underpin any proposed political reform – not that contemporary political theorists revel on the wilder reaches of the imagination: most of us, indeed, have developed a rather sober sense of what counts as a realistic program; and there are few remaining traces of the heady ambitions that took democracy to imply extensive and equal participation, or equality to imply equality of outcome rather than a modest redistribution of available resources. Even in this more contained universe that accepts liberal democracy as the only serious contender and reduces debates around equality to a contest between different degrees of welfare reform, the theorization of justice or equality tends to proceed in isolation from the analysis of social and economic forces. This is the complaint recurrently made by John Dunn, who sees a division of labour that allocates the analysis of political causality to one group of workers and the "emotionally self-indulgent recycling of cherished political pieties"[5] to another. The last is hardly a fair description of the modest propositions that are derived from contemporary political thought; today's political theorists are notable, if anything, for their cautious adjustments to what already exists. That said, the "return to the political" does threaten to isolate politics from the analysis of economy or society, and it is with this warning in mind that I want to explore some recent developments in political theory.

My thoughts on this arise partly out of reflection on my own trajectory. While my first research project (a PhD thesis for which Colin Leys was external examiner) explored the role of the colonial state in blocking capitalist development, my later work moved onto the terrain of sexual equality, with an increasing emphasis on issues of democracy and representation. To begin with, the difference was more a matter of substance than methodology; even in moving from a distinctly pre-feminist analysis of colonialism to a self-consciously feminist critique of contemporary democracy,[6] I carried with me a strong sense of the social and economic conditions that frame the possibilities for political change. Yet, noting that a sexually egalitarian democracy depends on major changes in the sexual division of labour and a transformed relationship between public and private spheres seemed to leave little to say that could be useful. In common with many in this "post-socialist" era, I found myself rather despondent about the prospects for social or economic transformation, and my later work shifted towards a more exclusively political focus on the forms of representation that can incorporate women and ethnic minorities more equally into decision-making assemblies. Setting aside what now seemed deeply intractable problems in achieving either social or economic equality, I turned to what could still be done within the realm of politics instead.[7] This was not just a personal trajectory but one followed by many others.

The paper that follows is largely a reflection on this, in the light of Colin Leys's repeated insistence on the interrelationships between the economic, social, and political. There are, I think, two major developments that have contributed to the separation between politics and society or economy: the first being the historical events that have put socialism (and much of social democracy) on the defensive; the second being the theoretical crises and cul-de-sacs in formulating the relationships between economy, society, and politics. In the world of political theory, the impact of the first can be tracked through the growing demarcation between political and economic liberalism. Twenty years ago, it was still widely argued that political and economic liberalism were inextricably intertwined. Socialists saw themselves as opposed to liberalism not because they objected to freedoms of speech or association but because they saw the primacy attached to individual liberties as something that led inexorably to the defence of the free market. Anyone who proclaimed political liberalism was thereby committed to economic liberalism. Since socialists could hardly support the second, they had to take issue with the first.

Nowadays, by contrast, it is hard to find a socialist who would not also describe herself as liberal: liberal, that is, in recognizing the importance of individual freedoms, the value of human diversity, and the dangers of imposing unitary solutions. In many cases, this more confident celebration of traditionally liberal concerns has gone along with a modified defence of the market. Most of today's socialists are better described as social-democrats and look to ways of moderating the effects of market forces rather than replacing them at the source. Much of the convergence between socialist and liberal traditions has depended on a stricter demarcation between political and economic liberalism: we can all be politically liberal; this does not mean we all agree about the way the economy should be run. Where liberalism was once conceived as a more seamless web, it now appears as a tradition from which we can take elements we like, discarding others we find less congenial.

I have no objection to this development, which strikes me as more intrinsically plausible than conceiving of traditions as internally rigorous and hermetically sealed. Feminism, for example, developed in close if critical relationship with liberalism. It built on a liberal critique of dependency, but employed this to challenge liberal understandings of the relationship between public and private spheres.[8] The very notion of a tradition already implies a process of historical development, and this is hardly compatible with the imagery of the seamless web. If earlier socialists too easily assumed that political liberalism must imply economic liberalism, later socialists may be too easily assuming the opposite. There is no great wealth of literature that explicitly contests the earlier assumption; it is more that people have stopped thinking about the possible connections.

A similar phenomenon seems to characterize the second major development; while everyone has abandoned what would now be considered a simple-minded economic determinism (Colin Leys's own work has contributed significantly to this), there is remarkably little clarity over what to put in its place. In the course of the 1970s, Marxists engaged in extensive auto-critique about the precise relationship between the economic and the political; in the process, the older metaphor of an economic "base" supporting a political and ideological "superstructure" was decisively discredited. One obvious point of reference here, among others, is the influence of Althusserianism, which ran for a while with the notion of the economic as "determinant only in the last instance," but ended up dissolving distinctions between economic, political and social – leaving most of its adherents in a rather unholy mess. Meanwhile, Michel Foucault's analysis of the omnipresence of power relations made it harder than ever to sustain a hierarchy of historical causation; and the post-structuralist emphasis on the discursive construction of identities undermined earlier distinctions between "objective" and "subjective." Developments within feminism are particularly instructive here. While feminists were locked in often fierce debate throughout the 1970s over the precise cause of women"s oppression (was it male control of women's fertility, the compulsory enforcement of heterosexuality, or capitalism's need for a docile labour force?), the paradigm shift that occurred in the 1980s turned feminists away from questions of fundamental causation.[9] It was not that one grand theory of how to relate the economic, social, and political was displaced by another, it was more, here too, a matter of changing the subject.

The impact of this on political theory has been indirect but substantial. Most notably, I would argue, political theorists were released from their previous enforced dialogue with sociologists or political economists. They no longer had to justify their arguments before the tribunal of material forces. Freed from the controlling influence of social theorists (no longer able to control, for no longer so sure of their ground), political theorists were able to retrieve political theory as a distinct field of enquiry. The political then returned with a vengeance, in a period that is widely regarded as the most innovative of this century. One paradox in this is that the renewed emphasis on the specifically political has occurred in an era that endlessly reminds us of the limits of the political. Pundits repeatedly inform us that politics has lost its appeal: that politicians are now held in less esteem than real-estate agents, that a younger generation (usually meaning those under thirty-five) is profoundly anti-political, that people no longer look to politics to change the pattern of their lives.[10] These pseudo-scientific observations are not in themselves conclusive, but, when they are combined with analyses of the global forces that constrain national policy-making, they paint a rather gloomy picture. Tremendous intellectual energy now goes into defining the nature and limits of justice or the conditions for a fair and equal democracy – and all at a time when politics is said to matter less than ever.

In what follows, I make some brief comments on the remarkable (and largely unanticipated) "return to the political" in political theory. Then I move on to developments in relation to democracy and representation, where there has been a particularly striking turn towards matters of institutional and procedural change. At the level of practical politics, this is evidenced in a renewed concern with constitutional matters. In Canada, this included the introduction of a Charter of Rights and Freedoms; in Britain, the parallel politics around a Bill of Rights, now taking shape in the Human Rights Act, as well as legislation reforming the House of Lords and devolving power to a Scottish Parliament and Welsh Assembly. In both theoretical and practical politics, the turn to institutional matters is also evidenced in rising concern about the political under-representation of women and members of minority ethnic groups and in explorations of the institutional mechanisms through which this pattern could be reversed. I concentrate here on theoretical developments in the analysis of fair representation and the emerging discourse around deliberative democracy.

I

In 1960, Sheldon Wolin produced a wonderfully provocative survey of Western political thought from Plato to the (then) present-day. He analysed what he saw as "the depreciation of the politicalness of the political order"[11]: the turn from politics to a preoccupation with "society," the substitution of administration for politics, and the associated decline of citizenship as a distinct sphere of activity. Classical liberalism, he argued, was not the confident rationalism that appeared in its subsequent caricatures; on the contrary, Wolin suggested, "liberalism was a philosophy of sobriety, born in fear, nourished by disenchantment, and prone to believe that the human condition was and was likely to remain one of pain and anxiety."[12] Despite the centrality they accorded to individual rights, liberals devoted "a surprising amount of emphasis to justifying the necessity and desirability of social conformity"[13]; attaching little confidence to what could be achieved through politics per se, they looked to forces generated within society and the economy to sustain social cohesion.

Wolin went on to argue that the anti-political impulse nurtured by classical liberalism became all-pervasive throughout the nineteenth and twentieth centuries, surfacing variously in the works of the utopian socialists: Proudhon, Comte, Marx, Durkheim, the Fabians, and assorted theorists of managerialism, including Philip Selznick. A distinct sphere of political – or citizen – activity was no longer considered either desirable or necessary: at best, politics only registered a more fundamental social or economic reality; at worst, it could pervert the course of human affairs. So when Lenin, for example, looked to a world in which politics would be replaced by administration, he was far more in tune with the mood of the twentieth century than his opponents have liked to believe. By the middle of this century, Wolin argued, we had lost any sense of the uniqueness of the political order; by this stage, we could see "politics" everywhere, and could no longer distinguish the activities of the citizen from assorted activities within non-political associations or groups.

Writing at the same moment (and from a related perspective), Judith Shklar also stressed what she saw as the decline of political faith. "(T)o think of politics in broad terms," she argued, "has come to seem futile"; "the urge to construct grand designs for the political future of mankind is gone."[14] Shklar saw the 1950s as dominated by a sorry combination of conservative liberalism, Christian fatalism, and romantic despair, none of which offered any confidence in politics as a means to social improvement. If politics is conceived as "the ability to act freely in history,"[15] then politics per se was dead. "To speak of justice has become intellectually hazardous"[16]; all we can manage for the moment is a reasoned skepticism.

This last comment – almost the closing remark of the book – serves as a reminder to all of us of the dangers in historical prediction. In

1957, John Rawls was already embarked on the work for *A Theory of Justice*. Its publication in 1971 was to mark the transformation of normative political theory within the Anglo-American world.[17] Rawls revitalized an earlier contractarian tradition that had sought to define the duties and responsibilities of government through a half-historical, half-hypothetical social contract; stripping this of its contentious historical foundations, Rawls outlined a hypothetical thought experiment that was designed to reveal the basic principles of justice. The results did not present a startling challenge to the principles that already underpin most modern democracies: his first principle asserted that each should have as much civil and political liberty as is compatible with the equal liberty of all; while his second ("difference") principle asserted that inequalities in the distribution of income, wealth, or power could only be justified where they could be shown directly to benefit those who were least advantaged. This favoured a greater degree of social-democracy than was prevalent throughout the USA (and a greater degree than became prevalent in Britain under the Thatcher regime), but it added up to a recognizably liberal democracy with a moderately redistributive welfare state.

Rawls can hardly be taken to task for ignoring the role of economic relations – his second principle of justice explicitly engages with the limits of justifiable economic inequality and the role of redistributive taxation – nor can he be said to restore politics to any central role. As I note later, he derives his principles of justice through a process that leaves political contestation decisively out, but there remains an important sense in which Rawls was reclaiming politics as the "master science" that could be pursued in isolation from social or economic relations. His hypothetical agreement provided a standard against which contemporary societies could be judged, but the judgement abstracted from the historical conditions that might enable any particular society to achieve the standard. Rawls thus returned us to what can be broadly described as constitutional questions: instead of asking what material developments are at work to generate particular patterns of political life (a question one might approach through sociology or political economy), or what kind of social conditions might be necessary to underpin the concerns of justice (a question raised with particular force by feminist critics of Rawls[18]), we ask what it is that justice requires.

This return to normative political theory is, in my view, profoundly welcome – and particularly so in a period when what John Dunn calls "the inscrutable rhythms of the world economy"[19] are widely deployed to tell us we must give up on much of what we had taken for granted (not to mention any wilder dreams). Failing some benchmark against which to assess claims about justice or equality or democracy, we find ourselves making the best of what is currently available; we may then fall victim to the economic "experts," whose notions of what is possible always seem depressingly restrained. So my concern here is not to take issue with the resurgence of normative theory. The revitalization of political theory, however, has come at a price. Part of the price we have paid is a diversion of interest from economic and social relations.

II

The shift from politics conceived at the broad level of the social and economic to a more precise and narrow institutional focus is particularly marked in the theorization of democracy and representation, where the (belated) recognition of the importance of the specifically political has encouraged a sharper demarcation between economic and political affairs. There used to be a pretty standard socialist line on democracy, the main feature of which was skepticism towards "mere" political equality. If you were a socialist, you would regard civil and political equalities as an important, but rather deceptive, achievement. You would note that universal suffrage equalized us only at the moment of casting our votes, and that this formal equality was continually subverted by an unequal distribution of power that favoured those with money, education, or contacts; that elected governments had limited room for manouevre on a terrain whose boundaries were set by industry, finance, and the media; and that democracy in the public sphere was particularly deceptive if pursued in isolation from democracy in the "private" spheres of family or work. These concerns might then propel you towards questions of workplace democracy. If you were a feminist as well as a socialist, they would propel you towards the sexual divisions within the household and family, and ways of democratizing the more intimate relationships of everyday life. The key question would be how to make democracy more substantial. All the answers would involve transformations in social and economic life.

Certain strands of contemporary democratic theory continue broadly within this framework: most notably, the work that is being done on associative or associational democracy,[20] which builds on a tradition of workplace democracy and looks to the extension of democratic relationships through a multiplicity of associations in civil society. Much of the work, however, even among those who would regard themselves as radical critics of contemporary democracy, has shifted direction. Iris Young's work on *Justice and the Politics of Difference*, for example, focuses on the mechanisms of political exclusion that deny political access to a heterogeneous public composed of women, people in a racial or linguistic minority, people defined as deviant by virtue of their sexuality, and people who are disabled, working class, or poor. The alternatives she proposes as means to a more inclusive democracy include a broadly cultural challenge to the myths of homogeneity, combined with specifically political mechanisms to guarantee some element of group representation to members of oppressed and excluded groups. My own work, in *The Politics of Presence*, has focused on the failures of representation that systematically disadvantage women and people from ethnic minorities. The solutions, again, operate almost exclusively through political mechanisms that will ensure a fairer system of representation – the most obvious and straightforward example being the quota systems adopted by many political parties in Europe to ensure that those chosen as candidates are drawn roughly equally from both women and men. Here, as in Young's work, problems of political inequality are understood as emanating from wider structures of social and economic inequality, but the emphasis is on what can be done to challenge this through interventions at the political level. The problems derive their urgency from structures of socio-economic inequality; the solutions depend on institutional reform.

This turn to politics is also evident in the increasingly influential tradition of deliberative democracy,[21] which takes issue with the absence of politics in contemporary theories of justice as well as the absence of justice in contemporary practices of politics. John Rawls had looked to a solipsistic thought-experiment as producing the principles of justice: imagining ourselves in a state of ignorance about our own values, preferences, abilities, or wealth, we would work out the principles we regarded as acceptable no matter what kind of person we later turned out to be (see note 17). As numerous critics have noted, this abstracts from the messy business of politics. It also leaves Rawls with some difficult questions about why we should stick to the principles if we later find ourselves better off without them. In contrast to this, deliberative models of democracy depend on argument, discussion, and persuasion as the way to arrive at just decisions, putting the politics back into the process.

The kind of politics deliberative democrats have in mind, however, is a far cry from the contemporary party politics that evacuates the realm of informed debate to compete for voter support on the basis of crudely defined (often personality-driven) appeals; deliberative democracy puts a premium on refined and reflective preferences that would be "'fact-regarding' (as opposed to ignorant or doctrinaire), "future-regarding" (as opposed to myopic), and "other-regarding" (as opposed to selfish)."[22] Exponents of deliberative democracy stress the transformative effects of discussion and deliberation in deepening understanding of the available political choices and in alerting participants to the legitimacy of other people's claims. Each person's partialities will be tested out by exposure to the partialities of others, and since none of us can hope to win the argument by simple assertions of what we want or need, all of us will be encouraged towards more open-minded exploration of policies that can be acceptable to all.

One immediate – though I think mistaken – criticism is that the ideals are so far from contemporary reality as to end up in wishful thinking (the approach has been described to me by one critic as a "warmed-over Ciceronianism"). Yet accusations of utopianism would be very far from the truth. Proposals are typically tailored to complement rather than replace existing democratic procedures; and in marked contrast to earlier versions of participatory democracy that depended on unrealistically high levels of citizen participation, deliberative democracy recognizes "the burden of political action"[23] and does not require us to attend daily meetings. Proponents of deliberative democracy draw on widely perceived and articulated dissatisfactions with contemporary political life: the dominance of "sound-bite" politics; the emphasis on personality rather than policy in the selection of political leaders; the reluctance of political parties to engage in principled political debate. Their proposed reforms are often quite modest in scope. These include the use of deliberative opinion polls,[24] multi-question referenda, [25] and randomly generated but socially representative citizens' juries to formulate policy alternatives. (This last is already the subject of experimentation in local authorities in Britain). Rather more ambitiously, they include a strong agenda on civic education to promote the capacity for political choice,[26] proposals for neighbourhood forums that would enable informed citizen debate,[27] and policies for the public funding of secondary associations that would actively favour those that engaged in deliberative practice.[28] Deliberative democracy is characterized throughout by the importance it attaches to institutional and procedural design in raising the quality of democratic decisions; this can hardly be described as utopian.

The question, rather, is whether the weight attached to (achievable) procedural reform may be misplaced. Deliberative democracy often presents itself as a third way – beyond liberal and libertarian conceptions of citizenship,[29] or beyond populist democracy and negative liberalism.[30] In its different versions, it also presents itself as resolving problems of democratic legitimacy,[31] pointing a way out of the dilemmas of social choice,[32] avoiding the paradoxes of majority rule,[33] or resisting the conservatism that takes voter preference as final.[34] Yet there seems to be a discrepancy between the claims made on behalf of deliberative democracy (its capacity, that is, to resolve so many conundrums in the democratic tradition) and the relative modesty of its institutional design. One conception is that deliberative democracy relies on political mechanisms to deal with what may not be an exclusively political malaise; if so, the weaknesses are not to be attributed to any supposed utopianism, but to a misplaced confidence in politics per se. This links back to similar charges that can be levelled at those pursuing a fairer pattern of representation: if political inequalities (between, say, men and women or white and black) arise against a background of wider socio-economic inequalities, what is the basis for thinking that changing the first does anything for the second?

III

I have three points in response to this set of criticisms. My first is that the relationship between the economic, the social, and the political does not fit the old metaphor of an economic base on which rises a political or juridical superstructure; even within a broadly similar economic framework, there are considerable and important variations between countries that derive from developments at a political level. The political status of women, for example, does not seem to depend on any simple causal relationship with their status in the labour market; the countries that have achieved the greatest gender parity in politics (concentrated in Northern Europe – Norway, Sweden, Finland, Denmark) are not markedly different from other countries in their patterns of female employment. With the exception of Finland, which has long had a high proportion of women in full-time employment, they do not stand out as significantly different from, say, Britain, where female participation in the labour market is also at a very high level. And while these countries enjoy a considerably smaller "wage gap" between women and men, they share with the rest of Europe a marked under-representation of women in management and the higher professions. They also exhibit a sharply segregated employment structure that allocates to women the bulk of "caring" work in the public sector, leaving men with the majority of private sector jobs. Women nonetheless occupy one third, in some cases nearly half, of elected posts, and it is hard to explain this without focusing on specifically political struggles and interventions. Instead of regarding political variables as derivative of more fundamental structures in socio-economic life, we might then be better employed in exploring the impact of politics on social and economic relations. Reversing – perhaps too dramatically – the standard Marxist doctrine, Claus Offe and Ulrich Preuss argue that, "it is no longer the 'autonomous' development of the forces of production which gives rise to new institutions and new forms of popular government; on the contrary, democratic institutions and procedures are being discovered as liberating and 'productive' forces sui generis, considered capable, apart from their political aspects, of energizing the economic system and paving the road towards social and economic progress."[35]

I suspect that this summary goes too far in the opposite direction, but the political choices we make do matter – arguably, indeed, they matter more than ever when the prospects for social and economic change seem so remote. No-one could confidently claim this as a period of socio-economic equalization. All the indicators (except, possibly, those relating to gender) point decisively the other way. This has occurred, moreover, at a moment when the internal disarray of anything resembling a socialist project has called into question much of what used to be understood as the route to equality: people are more troubled than before about the relationship between state and market and the tensions between equality and freedom; even those who continue to describe themselves as socialists are more likely to view equality in terms of a modified equality of opportunity. Political equality, by contrast, has retained its status as a basic principle to which most citizens give their formal support, and this provides me with the second positive point in defence of specifically political interventions. Considering what is implied in it, democracy has had an extraordinary global success: how did we ever get to this position where all adults, whether male or female, white or black, rich or poor, college educated or illiterate, are deemed to have identical status, at least in the moment of casting their vote? We got to it, of course, through lengthy (and only very recently accomplished) struggles, but having arrived there, it is hard to envisage any turning back. Democracy derives its legitimacy from the roughly equal capacity for reason – or what Robert Dahl calls the "roughly equal qualification"[36] for government – but this remains an act of faith rather than something to be established through future research. What evidence would conceivably be allowed as a basis for removing the right of certain citizens to a vote? That they consistently failed to reach a certain score on intelligence tests? That they voted for crazy policies? That they supported crazy people? We can certainly imagine arguments in which these are proposed as grounds for disenfranchisement (and we don't have to look too far back in American history to find a period when literacy tests were employed to deny black citizens their right to a vote). But while democracy has proceeded slowly, and only under great duress, towards equality between the sexes and equality between black and white, democratization operates with a powerful ratchet effect that blocks later reversals. Political equality may sound a rather minimal expression of the commitment to human equality, but it does have this powerful feature: once granted, it is hard to take back.

One consequence of this greater democratization is that equality now figures, in some guise or another, in the justification for virtually every belief. Amartya Sen has argued that "equality of something" is now the universal starting point for all contemporary theory, with disagreements revolving around what is to be equalized rather than the value of equality per se.[37] In a similar vein, David Miller has noted that even those conservatives who write books with titles like *Against Equality* are careful to clarify that they are not against equality in voting or equality of opportunity or equality before the law; and that the principle of equality is increasingly presented as the starting point in the defence of contemporary liberalism.[38] The presumption in favour of equality is now so well established that it is impossible to generate a plausible social theory without some version of this presumption. This provides us with an important leverage in otherwise unfavourable conditions.

Political equality is the least contested version of human equality. That being so, it makes sense to press as far as one can on its further and fuller implications: to start, for example, from the relatively uncontested baseline that recognizes our equal right to vote and explore further implications of this in terms of equal access to representative assemblies. Fairer representation will not, of itself, resolve all the problems of inequality, nor will equal access to deliberative assemblies guarantee that we arrive at decisions acceptable to all. Given, however, the scope that remains for pursuing a more ambitious understanding of political equality, it makes sense to concentrate on what can be achieved through political means. This is a self-consciously pragmatic argument, but still has a great deal of force.

There is, however, a more troubling final point. I have no difficulty with those who object that political equality cannot solve all our problems; I cannot think of any candidate that would satisfy the requirement for a final and total solution and would strongly resist setting this as the ultimate test. (I don't think, to take a different example, that sexual equality will solve all our problems, but that does not weaken my conviction that a sexually egalitarian society would be a wonderful advance on current conditions.) Failing to do everything is not a problem. What *is* a problem is when the focus on one part of our dilemmas makes it more difficult to address the rest. It is frequently noted, for example, that efforts to redress the racial and gender imbalance in representative assemblies seems to sideline the continuing imbalance by class and that strategies that successfully increase ethnic minority or female representation can reduce even further the number of representatives who are working class. This is a standard objection to gender quotas from inside the British Labour Party, where critics repeatedly summon up images of power-dressing, middle-class women taking over seats from "authentically" working class men. I have little sympathy with this invocation of one oppressed group in order to disparage the claims of another (if there is one thing feminists have learnt, it is to distrust the "hierarchy of oppressions"), but still find it hard to dismiss the underlying anxiety. We are in a period when class inequalities are becoming even more apparent and yet far less seriously addressed, and I would not want to be contributing further to their erasure from the political agenda.

The more complicated point in relation to deliberative democracy is that it potentially displaces attention from substantial conflicts of interest to failures of communication; in doing so, it may also shift attention from issues of socio-economic redistribution. Consider here the strong association that has developed between deliberative democracy and the problems of multicultural citizenship, an association that threatens to reconceptualize what used to be addressed under the rubric of racism (violence, discrimination, inequality) as a "softer" problem of ignorance or prejudice. A number of theorists have presented deliberation as peculiarly appropriate to societies that are multicultural and/or contain significant ethnic minorities; in encouraging a more reflective engagement with different experiences and values, deliberation seems to offer a particularly promising avenue for promoting the mutual understanding between majority and minority groups. Where a rights-based understanding of democracy might draw up an a priori list of fundamental rights, deliberative democracy recognizes the importance of intercultural dialogue in formulating central principles; and where a votes-driven understanding of democracy might simply aggregate existing preferences (leaving those in a numerical minority with minimal political influence), a deliberative approach to democracy encourages the participants in dialogue to recognize when their initial judgements were formed out of ignorance, partiality, or prejudice. For example, people who object to what they see as "special privileges" for cultural minorities may not have realized how much "special privilege" has been extended to cultural majorities; once confronted with this additional knowledge, they may well modify their original objections. The stereotypical images through which we view people from different cultures are more likely to dissolve in a democracy that attaches weight to engaging with others. Inconsistencies of treatment become less easy to defend.

These arguments combine into a powerful case for deliberation in culturally plural societies, but the case carries greatest conviction where disagreements stem from ignorance, prejudice, or the failure to see that what one is claiming for oneself must consistently be extended to others. It has less obvious purchase where what is at issue is the redistribution of economic or social resources. And here, again, we see theorists just changing the subject. Earlier discussions of racism often dealt with stark inequalities in housing, education, or employment; discussions of multiculturalism, by contrast, typically focus on issues of cultural or religious difference. In European discussions of multicultural citizenship, the paradigmatic "problem" of multicultural societies is now the accommodation of Muslim minorities. This emphasis meshes more neatly with the emerging discourse of deliberative democracy than did the earlier "problem" of race. Muslim minorities are notoriously exposed to demonization as an incomprehensible "other," and failures in communication or recognition rank high in the "problem" they supposedly pose. A politics that promotes more sustained intercultural dialogue looks particularly appropriate to this context; it directly addresses issues of recognition. But if issues of cultural (mis)recognition then displace issues of socio-economic inequality, the turn towards deliberation has significantly redefined the field.

The questions raised here relate closely to what Nancy Fraser has formulated as a shift from redistribution to recognition: "the eclipse of a socialist imaginary centred on terms such as 'interest', 'exploitation' and 'redistribution'"; "the rise of a new political imaginary centred on notions of 'identity', 'difference', 'cultural domination', and 'recognition.'"[39] Fraser is not interested in nostalgic invocations of the first as a basis for criticizing the second, nor is she saying that injustices located in the structures of the political economy are more "fundamental" than injustices in the cultural sphere. She argues, on the contrary, that justice today requires both redistribution and recognition, but notes that the two remedies often pull in different directions. At its sharpest, this is because the goal of redistribution struggles is to put certain identities "out of business," to "eliminate" class, race, or gender as the basis on which resources are distributed. The goal of recognition struggles, by contrast, is to end demeaningly stereotypical depictions by revaluing the despised sex or race; this means according positive recognition to a devalued group specificity, thereby confirming, rather than eliminating, the identity of that group. Fraser's concern is to formulate strategies that minimize the mutual interference between these two goals. Her main conclusion is that a deconstructive cultural politics – a politics that destabilizes rather than reinforcing the categorical differences between "male" and "female" or "white" and "black" – works best to finesse the redistribution-recognition dilemma.

I share Fraser's belief that these two struggles are not logically incompatible. I also think she is right to stress that this is not a matter of the socio-economic, represented by class, versus the cultural-valua-tional, represented by race and gender; the issues raised by racial and sexual equality are simultaneously cultural and socio-economic. Sus-taining battle on both these fronts is proving particularly difficult in a period that has dislodged socio-economic equality from its status as both desirable and possible; it is far too tempting to focus exclusively on institutional reform, and in the process change the subject. My worry about recent developments in political theory is that they are doing just this; my hope is that we can restore the richer understand-ing of the interrelationship between the economic, social, and political that underpins Colin Leys's work.[40]

NOTES

1 Colin Leys, *Underdevelopment in Kenya: The Political Economy of Neo-Colonialism, 1964–1971*, Portsmouth, NH: Heinemann, 1975.

2 Colin Leys, *Politics in Britain: an Introduction*, Portsmouth, NH: Heine-mann, 1983.

3 Leys, *Politics in Britain*, 11.

4 Leys, *Underdevelopment in Kenya*, 212.

5 John Dunn, *The History of Political Theory and Other Essays*, Cam-bridge, UK: Cambridge University Press, 1996: 30. He notes, later in this book: "I have never been a Marxist. But I have not the slightest doubt of the validity of the central Marxist tenet – that it is the historical development of human productive powers and the ferocious causal force of the rhythms of the global economy which these powers have created which now dominate the life of the species to which we belong. In this respect, political movements and actors propose, and it disposes," 221.

6 The first was published as *The Enigma of Colonialism*, London: James Currey and Indiana University Press, 1987; the second as *Engendering Democracy*, Cambridge, UK: Polity Press and University of Pennsylvania State Press, 1991.

7 Anne Phillips, *The Politics of Presence*, Oxford: Oxford University Press, 1995.

8 See Susan James's argument in "The Good-Enough Citizen: Citizenship and Independence," in G. Bock and S. James (eds), *Beyond Equality and Difference*, London and New York: Routledge, 1992.

9 See Michèle Barrett and Anne Phillips, "Introduction," in *Destabilizing Theory: Contemporary Feminist Debates*, Cambridge: Polity Press, 1992.

10 In Britain, this is the repeated refrain of the think-tank DEMOS (formed out of a strange alliance between conservatives and ex-communists).

11 Sheldon Wolin, *Politics and Vision*, Boston: Little, Brown and Company, 1960: 431.

12 Ibid., 293–4.

13 Ibid., 344.

14 Judith Shklar, *After Utopia: The Decline of Political Faith*, Princeton: Princeton University Press, 1957: vii.

15 Ibid., 216.

16 Ibid., 271.

17 John Rawls, *A Theory of Justice*, Cambridge, MA: Harvard University Press, 1971.

18 For example, in Susan Moller Okin's *Justice, Gender and the Family*, New York: Basic Books, 1989.

19 Dunn, *The History of Political Theory*, 63.

20 For example, Paul Hirst, *Associative Democracy*, Cambridge: Polity Press, 1994; Joshua Cohen and Joel Rogers (eds), *Associations and Democracy*, London: Verso, 1995.

21 As developed, for example, in Bernard Manin, "On Legitimacy and Deliberation," in *Political Theory*, vol.15, no. 3, 1987; Joshua Cohen, "Deliberation and Democratic Legitimacy," in A. Hamlin and P. Pettit (eds), *The Good Polity: Normative Analysis of the State*, Oxford: Oxford University Press, 1989; Cass Sunstein, "Preferences and Politics," in *Philosophy and Public Affairs*, vol. 20, no. 1, 1991; Claus Offe and Ulrich Preuss, "Democratic Institutions and Moral Resources," in D. Held (ed.), *Political Theory Today*, Cambridge: Polity Press, 1991; Amy Gutmann, "The Disharmony of Democracy," in J. W. Chapman and I. Shapiro (eds), *Democratic Community: NOMOS XXXV*, New York: New York University Press, 1993; Iris Marion Young, "Justice and Communicative Democracy," in R. Gottlieb (ed.), *Tradition, Counter-Tradition, Politics: Dimensions of Radical Philosophy*, Philadelphia, PA: Temple University Press, 1994; David Miller, "Deliberative Democracy and Social Choice," in D. Held (ed.), *Prospects for Democracy*, Cambridge: Polity Press, 1993; Seyla Benhabib, "Deliberative Rationality and Models of Democratic Legitimacy," in *Constellations*, vol. 1, no. 1, 1994; David Miller, "Citizenship and Pluralism," in *Political Studies*, vol. 43, no. 3, 1995; and Amy Gutmann and Dennis Thompson, *Democracy and Disagreement*, Cambridge, MA: Belknap Press of Harvard University Press, 1996.

22 Offe and Preuss, "Democratic Institutions and Moral Resources," 156–7.

23 Gutmann, "The Disharmony of Democracy," 143.

24 James Fishkin, *Deliberation and Democracy: New Directions for Democratic Reform*, New Haven: Yale University Press, 1991.

25 Benjamin R. Barber, *Strong Democracy: Participatory Politics for a New Age*, Berkeley: University of California Press, 1984.

26 Gutmann, "The Disharmony of Democracy"; Gutmann and Thompson, *Democracy and Disagreement*.

27 Barber, *Strong Democracy*.

28 Joshua Cohen and Joel Rogers, "Secondary Associations and Democratic Governance," *Politics and Society*, vol. 20, no. 4, 1992.

29 Miller, "Citizenship and Pluralism."

30 Gutmann, "The Disharmony of Democracy."

31 Benhabib, "Deliberative Rationality."

32 Miller, "Deliberative Democracy."

33 Gutmann, "The Disharmony of Democracy."

34 Sunstein, "Preferences and Politics."

35 Offe and Preuss, "Democratic Institutions," 144–5.

36 Robert Dahl, *Democracy and Its Critics*, Yale University Press, 1989: 97.

37 Amartya Sen, "Equality of What?" in Amartya Sen (ed.), *Choice, Welfare and Measurement*, Oxford: Basil Blackwell, 1982.

38 David Miller, "What Kind of Equality Should the Left Pursue?" in Jane Franklin (ed.), *Equality*, London: Institute for Public Policy Research, 1997.

39 Nancy Fraser, "From Redistribution to Recognition? Dilemmas of Justice in a 'Post-Socialist' Age," in *New Left Review*, no. 212, 1995.

40 I have subsequently developed my thoughts on these issues, in *Which Equalities Matter?*, Cambridge: Polity Press, 1999.

An Ethical Politics of Our Times: Moral Selves or Solidarity?

BANU HELVACIOGLU

Since the 1980s there has been an ongoing controversy on what constitutes critical thinking and political action. Following the collapse of the Soviet Union, developments such as the rise of ethnic and religious nationalisms, the violent reconfiguration of cultural and geographical boundaries, the increasing salience of neoliberal policies, and the growing influence of identity politics around the world intensified this debate by challenging conventional frameworks used in political studies. The theoretical renaissance brought by postmodern, poststructuralist, postmarxist, and feminist analyses guides us in different directions to reflect critically on the formations, since about the eighteenth century, of the modern, colonial, European, liberal political orders. From the purview of these analyses, what is at stake in the current conjuncture of world disorder is the disintegration of modern culture, society and the ideological foundations of the nation-state. Marxist analyses, on the other hand, continue focusing on the restructuring of capitalism in a global context and offer critical reflections on the pervasive influence of capitalism on social relations. On the question of what constitutes progressive politics in our times, the proposals range from class struggle, through the politics of coalition and solidarity between different social movements, to the politics of particularism, isolationism, and the contingency of political action.

Regardless of the framework, there are two recurring issues in problematizing the notion of the political. First, as a methodological problem, there is the dichotomy between the particularity and locality of political developments and the general, historical trends which define the present conjuncture of world disorder. Second, although the notion of political agency is analyzed at a theoretical level, it is rarely problematized in conjunction with concrete political developments. This paper aims to address these issues by examining the intricate relationship between morality, ethics, and politics at both a global and a singular level simultaneously. It defines the present conjuncture of world disorder as an aporetic condition which contains "pre-ethical," modern, and postmodern moral codes.

The major argument of this is that the liberal notion of the individual as the prime agent for political action fails to address contradictory moral/ethical impulses that this aporetic condition poses. In the first part, the paper contextualizes the present phase of moral revivalism within the frameworks of Luhmann's conception of morality and Bauman's conception of the paradoxical constitution of modern morality. In the second part, it focuses on the morality of neoliberalism by scrutinizing the liberal notions of individual rationality and individual rights in two interrelated contexts: the political economy of neoliberalism and the contradictory role of the nation-states in preserving law and order. In conclusion, it offers a loose framework for an ethical political stand that aims to problematize the contradictory imperatives between recognizing the particularity of political events, the singularity of the worth of a human being, and the need for solidarity with those caught in destitution, in deprivation, and in different webs of physical violence.

I CONTEXTUALIZING MORALITY, ETHICS, AND POLITICS

When the term ethics is used synonymously with morality and with the study of moral philosophy, it addresses the question of how human beings ought to live. Enriched by philosophical, theoretical, and theological perspectives, ethics and morality deal with two interrelated issues: the constants of human nature (such as reason, rationality, love, hedonistic pleasure, natural feelings, care for others, vulnerability, responsibility, selves, selfish ego, knowing subject, self-determination, care of self, self-sacrifice and self-interest) and the collective social values and prescriptions regulating rights and wrongs, dos and don'ts, good and evil, virtue and vice. Since the times of early civilizations in Mesopotamia, ethics and morality have been used in regulating what is now considered as the political realm. Under the rule of Hammurabi in Babylon (1728–1646 BC), and later in Egypt, a set of ethical/moral conventions, rules and obligations were developed to regulate social interactions in conjunction with codes dealing with business, bureaucracy and family law.[1] Similarly in ancient Greece, underlying the question of ethics was a philosophical reflection on the basic features of Greek society and politics.[2] At the outset, then, the symbiotic relationship between ethics and morality has both a social and a political character.

In the current political and theoretical conjuncture there are different conceptions of the relationship between ethics, morality, and politics.[3] For the purpose of clarity, it will be helpful first to explain what type of ethics is being explored in this paper and why. Niklas Luhmann defines ethics as "a theoretical reflection of morality" and argues that since the spread of printing, "the ethics wave returns in the eighties of every century with astrological regularity." He further notes something pathological about these waves, in that morality becomes an issue "only when things become dangerous."[4]

In his framework, the first wave of ethics can be traced to the 1580s in the form of a theory of morality independent of theology. The key factor in this periodization is the conflict between the will of God and an exploration of the conditions of a secular human social order embodied in natural feelings. In the 1680s the split between the morality of theologians for a divine providence and the morality of a social order became more astute. In the 1780s the ethics wave returned in three different trends, namely Kant's transcendentalism, Bentham's utilitarianism, and that of Marquis de Sade. What is common to the eighteenth-century wave is that ethics became a new form of moral reflection grounded in rationality. Luhmann does not explain the political context of the return of ethics prior to the nineteenth century. Yet he notes that in the 1880s, the ethical waves of Nietzsche and neo-Kantians took place in the context of nationalism, imperialism, colonialism, and socialism.[5]

According to Luhmann, the ethics wave of this century emerged in response to the disintegration of modern society. His main argument is that morality, conceived as "a special form of communication which carries with it indications of approval and disapproval," can no longer serve the purpose of social integration, nor can it "allot people their place in the society."[6] Luhmann also views "moral communication [as being] close to conflict and thus located close to violence."[7] The type of ethics he develops, aims "to thematise morality as a distinction," "to warn against morality," and "to limit the application of morality."[8] In his framework ethics is not devoid of moral values but is critical of moralizing judgements. He argues that "if ethics is to be and remain a theoretical reflection of morality ... then it must bind itself to the code of morality, that is, submit itself to the binary schematism of good and bad, it must itself desire the good not the bad." In so doing, however, "the researcher on ethics does not have to write an ethics which submits itself to a moral judgement." [9]

To reiterate Luhmann's argument about the disintegration of a modern society in a global context, since the 1980s "the pathological development" of our times has been the revival of diverse historical trends that are provisionally identified with Western modernity. Among these revivalist movements at the political level, there are searches for origins of human civilization in Athens, Mesopotamia, Jerusalem, and Medine; the politicization of theological perspectives of Judaism, Christianity, and Islam; and the revival of the seventeenth-century split between divine providence and secular human order in the formation of national identities, of the seventeenth- and eighteenth-century classical liberal notions of individual rationality in a free-market setting, and of colonial, post-colonial, nationalist, and imperialist discourses on politics in general. Accordingly the political realm in general has become a contested terrain for competing moral claims and codes of social/political conduct.

a) Paradoxical Constitution of Modern Morality

Given the rich ahistorical pastiche of moral revivalism, the first task of ethical politics is to problematize morality in a historical context. Following Luhmann's framework, Bauman conceptualizes modern morality in the context of eighteenth-century understanding of ethics grounded in rationality.[10] He traces the origins of ethics and morality to the search for order, rule, law, legislation, universality, and foundationalism in modernity. According to Bauman, modern morality emerged in a context where "modern developments forced men and women into the condition of individuals, who found their lives fragmented, split into many loosely related aims and functions, each to be pursued in a different context and according to a different pragmatics ... Morality, rather than being a 'natural trait' of human life [was] something that need[ed] to be designed and injected into human conduct ... the void left by the moral supervision of the Church [was] filled with rational rules."[11]

Bauman analyses the distinguishing aspect of morality in general and modern morality in particular with reference to the notion of aporia. Aporia is a Greek word for a contradiction that cannot be overcome. Since the invention of politics, morality, and ethics, the condition of aporia has been disguised in a search for the reconciliation of logically contradictory objectives and aspirations. Rowe argues that Greek ethics always contained the contradiction between a fundamentally individualistic ethos and the demands for co-operative behaviour.[12] In Midgley's account, both in ancient Greek thinking and in Hobbes's framework, ethics is a device of egoistic prudence that originated from the social contract. From an Hobbesian point of view, while the "pre-ethical" existence was a state of nature characterized by "a war of every man against every man," the age of ethics emerged as the political requirement for a survival in social order.[13] Bauman supports these claims and examines the paradoxical ways in which modern morality contributed to creating a political order.

In the initial phase of modern developments, the radical solution for the aporetic situation was to introduce the notions of universality and foundation. The principle of universality compelled individuals to recognize certain prescriptions as right and thus to accept them as obligatory. The principle of foundation was laid through the coercive powers of the state that rendered obedience to rules and through the popular belief that the rules are well-justified. According to Bauman the contradictory principle in this configuration of order by means of universality and foundation is that modern morality tried to rule over chaos, disorder, and fragmentation by creating an illusion: a promise that contradictions will be resolved in the future.

It is upon this promise that modern ethics was introduced as "a code of law that prescribes the correct behaviour 'universally,' that is for all people at all times; one that sets apart good from evil once for all and for everybody."[14] To highlight the contradictory role of modern ethics, Bauman distinguishes between these universal moral imperatives and the singularity of moral selves. He argues that, although ethics and morality "grow of the same soil, moral selves do not "discover," their ethical foundations but ... build them up while they build themselves."[15] In this understanding while modern ethics/morality has a foundational character, moral selves are defined by contingency. Related to this distinction, modernity as the age of ethics legislated moral selves and prevented their full growth.

I will elaborate on Bauman's conception of moral selves later in detail. For the time being it suffices to note that the moral imperatives of the modern political order were legislated in the name of individual rationality and that state laws were presumed to be founded on reason. Looking back to the promise of modernity in today's global conjuncture of disorder, Bauman argues that universal values under modern etatization of social space spawned massive oppression and "the greatest crimes against humanity (and by humanity) have been perpetuated in the name of reason, of better order and greater happiness."[16] The present conjuncture is defined by the dissolution of the promise of modern political order, which, in moral terms, creates the dichotomy between defending universal values and "postmodern privatisation of social spacing." The latter refers to three specific developments.

First, in the context of political economy, Bauman notes that the freer is the global flow of capital and merchandise, the more fragmented are the sovereign units. The nation-states become weaker and narrower in their grip over their respective territories. Second, in the political context of international relations, it denotes the end of the "secure" bipolar configuration of the world between the NATO and Warsaw Pact line. This implies the absence of a supranational policing force to adjudicate local and regional power struggles within and between nation-states. Related to this development, third, the nation-states fail to perform their past role of producing and supplying identities. This specifically refers to the erosion of the ideological role of states in bringing nations together with reference to particular symbols of citizenship, individual rights, or historically specific cultural representations of a uniform nationhood. In this conjuncture, postmodern privatization of social spacing denotes the increasing salience of identity politics at a global level. The evident failure of supranational and national institutions to effectively perform their role of centralized policing paves the way for communal autonomy and "neo-tribal self-assertion" of particular ethnic, national, and religious groups.

In noting the violent configuration of identity politics in this international conjuncture, Bauman argues that the power struggle and perpetual tug of war are revealed as the sole reliable grounds of an orderly habitat.[17] What he refers to as the "logic of dark ages" in this particular context of violence can also be regarded as a return to a "pre-ethical" stage, which in the Hobbesian framework is characterized by lawlessness, wars, and chaos in the contestation for sovereignty among numerous power holders. In addition to the violent configuration of power struggle between different "communal," "neo-tribal" groups in asserting their identities, postmodern privatization also raises a moral dilemma. According to Bauman, while the universal values of modern morality expect individuals to confirm to the laws and order set by the state, postmodern morality gives way to the dictum that every order is good. In this respect, postmodern privatization of social space refers to a condition of dispersion and "disocclusion" where the divide between right and wrong is no longer determined. Insofar as the morality of identity politics is concerned the violent dispersion of ethnic, national, and religious moral claims makes it also difficult to determine the divide between the victims and the victimizers.

b) Contradictory Imperatives of Ethical Politics

In reviewing the moral progress of modernity in our times, Bauman notes how the victims of the past – Serbs during the Croat genocide in

the 1940s, Vietnamese during the Vietnam war, Jews during the Holocaust – commit cruelty when the opportunity arises.[18] Recalling the
Gulf War in 1990, which was presented as a war between democracy
and fascism, between Kuwait as victim and Iraq as the victimizer, making moral and political choices on international violence is extremely
difficult, if not impossible. From a historical point of view, Bauman
rightly argues that "no victory over inhumanity seems to have the
world safer for humanity," yet "moral shocks, however devastating
they might have seemed at the time, gradually lose their grip – until
they are forgotten. All their long history notwithstanding, moral choices seem always to start from square one."[19]

The political significance of Bauman's analysis is that he proposes a
thorough critique of both politically promoted parochialism of modern
moral codes that pretend to be universal and the "everything goes
approach" that has come to be identified with postmodern morality. In
his words, as long as the choice is merely between these two medicines,
"the chance of health must be meagre and remote."[20] This critical
stand on both modern and postmodern morality has two implications.
First, Bauman's framework helps us to scrutinize the relationship
between moral codes and the modern constitution of reason and individual rationality. Second, having refused to choose between modern
and postmodern moral codes, he focuses on the notion of moral self as
the prime agent of political change.

As to the former implication, his main premise is that "morality is
incurably aporetic, the majority of moral choices are made between
contradictory impulses."[21] In his conceptualization, moral phenomena
are inherently "non-rational, not regular, repetitive, monotonous and
predictable."[22] Hence they cannot be exhausted by any universal moral
code of dos and don'ts. By the same token this claim does not give a
free reign to an unproblematic contingency of accepting all competing
moral claims promoted by identity politics. If we accept the premise
that all moral phenomena are aporetic, then an ethical stand in our
times is not redeemed from contradictory imperatives. In listing the
ethical issues in the present conjuncture, Bauman calls for a balance
between personal self-assertion and peaceful co-operation as well as
synchronization of individual conduct and collective welfare.[23] The
crucial element in maintaining this balance is Bauman's notion of
moral self.

In his framework, there is no self before moral self. This implies two
things. First, in becoming a person we all carry in us a moral responsibility for another person, which is the act of self-constitution. In the
relation between self and the other, this moral responsibility precedes
all engagement, including knowing, evaluating, and acting together

with the other person. To put it simply, before I engage in any political, social, personal relationship, I utter to myself that I am a person because I care for the other, I am responsible for the other, and I need to curb some constitutive elements that make me an individual. Second, putting the moral self before oneself implies the limitations of the liberal notion of individual rationality. Bauman argues that morality in general, individual morality in particular, and moral self in and of itself are bound to be irrational. In this respect the moral self is a mystery contrary to reason. In his words, "Reason cannot help the moral self without depriving the self of what makes the self moral: that unfounded, non-rational, un-arguable, no-excuses-given and non-calculable urge to stretch towards the other, to caress, to be for, to live for, happen what may."[24]

In Bauman's formulation, the moral self escapes logic, reason, and rationality because in stretching to caress, to be responsible for, to live for, and to make things happen for the other, it follows its own resilient autonomy. This resilient autonomy is received as a scandal by modern morality, which tames, cages, and cultivates moral self with a list of rights-directed prescriptions and with manuals about dos and don'ts. In this particular context, the postmodern condition of dispersion and "disocclusion" provides acting individuals with a possibility of using their moral selves for the task of learning and applying an unambiguous ethical principle suitable for the occasion.[25]

Bauman's call for a return to moral selves suggests that an ethical stand critical of both modern and postmodern morality is inherently aporetic. On the one hand, it is singular, that is to say an ethical stand has to be cognizant of the particularities of the political issue at hand as well as the singularity of the moral responsibility that one has towards the other. In this respect, Bauman's conception of an ethical stand defies any universality and a general moral code of conduct. On the other hand, as a safeguard against the postmodern morality of approving the diversity of all moral claims and code of conduct, Bauman returns to the key contradictory imperatives of ethics since ancient Greece. His ethical stand of moral selves carries within itself the contradictions between personal self-assertion, individual moral conduct, and concern for collective, co-operative, peaceful conduct. The latter concern for collective welfare is both singular and universal at the same time. It is singular to the extent that it is guided by the peculiarities and mysteries of the moral responsibility one carries within oneself. It is universal because it carries the moral imperatives of caring and being in solidarity with others. On all accounts, the singular and universal responsibilities that constitute moral selves escape reason and rationality to the extent that Bauman's critical ethical stand are not founded on the premise of the resolution of such problems as the violent configuration of the world, the increasing salience of ethnic, national, and religious groups, or the free flow of capital and merchandise in the context of the globalization of capitalism.

II THE POLITICS OF NEOLIBERAL MORALITY: THREE FOR THE PRICE OF ONE

To elaborate on the political significance of Bauman's critical analysis of modern and postmodern morality in the present conjuncture, it is important to recall that Bauman's conception of morality is founded on a particular conception, that is, the eighteenth-century understanding of morality grounded in reason and rationality. The predominant elements of modern morality are founded on the liberal notion of individual rationality, the foundational character of the nation-state to maintain order, and a firm metaphysical belief in the resolution of contradictions. By this criterion, postmodern morality is characterized by the dispersion of moral claims, the individual inability to distinguish right from wrong, and a growing challenge to the foundational character of nation-states. Bauman's narrow conception of modern morality raises a number of questions about the extent to which the existing dispersion, in particular moral codes, can be considered as postmodern.

The politicization of religion, particularly in light of the increasing salience of Islam in the international arena and the re-emergence of religious-nationalist movements in Bosnia, India, China, Israel, Turkey, former Soviet Republics, and elsewhere, suggests that the moral codes of the present need to be problematized in conjunction with these developments. The state-centered morality founded on reason and rationality and the sixteenth-century understanding of morality founded on the split between individual will and the will of theologians are two currently contesting moral codes in politics. More specifically, in the above mentioned cases, the power struggle contains both the secular will to reason and to nationhood and the communal will to an Islamic, Hindu, or Zionist order. On the specific question of order and chaos, the politicization of religion, ethnicity, and nationhood is determined by a firm metaphysical belief in the resolution of contradictions and a search for a lawful society. It is upon this fundamental belief that religious claims for salvation, the assertion of ethnic identities independent of nation-states, and the revival of territorial claims by nationalist groups are justified. In this respect, it will be useful to broaden the conception of modern morality to include two specific codes, one from the sixteenth century and the other from the eighteenth century.

This broadened conception of modern morality has two political implications. First, as Marx astutely remarked, European morality of individual rationality assumes that "in his most immediate reality ... man is a secular being."[26] As was the case on the "Jewish question," this secular construction, however, was enriched by Christian morals, which have been an integral element in definitions of nationhood as well as in regulating the political/social order.[27] Depending on the specificities of the political conjuncture, Christian morals have been politicized during the rise of fascism in Europe (by both fascists and anti-fascists), by the military regimes and their opponents in the 1970s in Latin America, and by the rise of Christian fundamentalism during the Ronald Reagan presidency in the USA. Second, these historical reminders also aim to alert readers to the modern dimensions in the politicization of Islam since the early 1980s. This process is a product of modern formation of nation-states in Muslim countries. Political Islam in its call for a return to *shariat* (the rule of Islam) carries in itself the foundational character of statism and nationalism. Regardless of its anti-modern, anti-Western discourse, political Islam articulates the will of Allah with the capitalist will to make profit.[28] In the Turkic Republics of the former Soviet Union and in eastern Europe, Islamic capital has become a significant force in foreign trade and investment. Insofar as its nationalist and international market oriented operations are concerned, there is nothing postmodern about the rise of Islamic identity in global politics.

In the international conjuncture, political Islam filled the void left by the Cold War threat of Communism. In this respect, as was the case with Cold War politics, strategic concerns of NATO members define the contradictory imperatives of the sale of arms to Iran, Afghanistan, Algeria, and other "dangerous" zones since the early 1980s. In this context too, then, the international conjuncture strikes us as "predictably ordered" and contingent on national interests as it historically has been.

In critically examining the specific conception of modern morality grounded on reason and rationality, it is also necessary to reconsider the search for order and the volatility of the political realm from the point of view of the seventeenth- and eighteenth-century liberal thinking. From Hobbes and Locke to utilitarian thinking, the notions of order and law were investigated in conjunction with the need for a social contract. Without going into the details of liberal thought, it suffices to note that, in a competitive free-market setting where there is no social contract, one individual is the enemy of another in an egoistic state of war. Two centuries of experience taught adherents of liberalism to never leave the free market in its "pre-ethical" state of egoistic prudence. Hence, the state was given the role to maintain civil law, the defence of the national territory, and the assurance of judicially defined rules regarding the exchange of property, accumulation of wealth and socially "acceptable" levels of poverty, destitution, and exploitation. As will be explained later in detail when examining the liberal emphasis on individual rights and rationality and the contradictory role of states, it is necessary to distinguish the formation of a "pre-ethical" mode within the context of the globalization of capitalism.

With this hindsight, if we revisit the current conjuncture of global disorder, the dissolution of modern morality gives way to three modalities in politics. There is the persistence of modern morality characterized by searches for order, rule, and law, which are regulated by both the will to reason and rationality and the will to a religious order. There is the so-called postmodern morality characterized by the privatization of social space and the individual inability to take a universal moral stand on political developments. Third, in places where liberalism and capitalism have been introduced from above, there are particular moral conducts reminiscent of the "pre-ethical" chaos. The globalization of neoliberal policies since the late 1980s cuts across these three moral modalities; political order under neoliberalism contains modern, pre-ethical, and postmodern moral codes.

a) Modern Morality in Neoliberalism

Susan Strange defines the main trends in the globalization of neoliberalism with reference to the growth of a) "the conference business and of travel and transnational communication," b) "the proportion of production of goods and services controlled by foreign based firms," c) "the reduction of direct controls and taxes on capital mobility," as well as d) "the increased mobility of factors of production," including capital, technology, and energy, d) "the liberalisation of long-standing regulatory restrictions within national financial markets," and e) "the introduction of new technologies in the process of financial intermediation."[29] To highlight the three moral modalities in this schema, it is important to recall Bauman's claim about the aporetic condition of moral phenomenon. In this respect the first contradictory nature of neoliberalism is that, even though it is founded on the premise of reducing the scope of state involvement in markets, it has come to be globalized by direct state involvement at the political level. Stephen Gill notes that market monetarism in New Zealand was introduced in the 1980s under a social democratic government. The "shock therapy" introduced in Poland and Russia since the late 1980s was "based on experiments carried out in Latin America in the 1970s and 1980s."

The EC's 1992 Single Market Program "has elements of Jacques Delor's vision of a new form of European democracy combined with Anglo-American laissez-faire."[30] The growing influence of the neoliberal agenda manifests itself elsewhere in the formation of NAFTA and in the GATT summit in Uruguay in 1994, which just like the cases cited above, are characterized by the paradoxical combination of the triumph of transnational capital and the preservation of political economic order through state policies.[31]

What is modern about this process is the intensification of both commodity and financial exchange at a global level. Furthermore this global exchange, at the political level, is regulated by the triangular relationship between transnational firms, nation-states and international financial institutions such as the World Bank, the IMF, and the European Bank for Reconstruction and Development.[32] Third, just like in the nineteenth century when capitalism started to infiltrate into the social realm, this phase of the globalization is characterized by social unrest and political resistance.[33] What is particularly modern about this social/political resistance is that it contains such elements as the political mobilization of labour, the ideological preservation of national values as a means of opposition to globalization, and a strong state-centered discourse against the transnational capital. As to the Third World, where political opposition has historically been repressed, the globalization of neoliberal agenda, among other things, has brought the "super-exploitation of female labor in the Maquiladoras in Mexico and the persistent use of child labour in the Colombian coal mines."[34]

When it comes to the morality of the globalization of capitalism, there are two distinctly modern aspects to neoliberalism. First, having founded on the eighteenth-century conception of morality, neoliberalism further deepens the classical liberal notions of a universal understanding of individual rights and rationality. In this understanding, the self-worth of an individual is defined in accordance with both state legislation and the ideological requirements of the free-market economy.[35] A century ago, Marx defined this modern morality as follows: "[t]he real human being is the private individual of the present-day state-constitution."[36] At the political level, what defines the real human being as a private individual is the state that "abolishes, in its own way, distinctions of birth, social rank, education, occupation, when it declares [them as] non-political distinctions, that every member of the nation is an equal participant in national sovereignty."[37] Related to that second, in spite of the challenges of transnational capital to the sovereignty of nation-states, the present social/political "order" at global, regional, and local levels is still maintained through state legislation.

To illustrate the modern morality of the relationship between the state and individual rights, we need to pay attention to particular political modes through which neoliberal policies are implemented. In Europe, the bastion of the post-Second World War social democracy, the real worth of a "European" is specifically designed in the Maastricht Treaty. According to the Treaty, union citizenship has become mandatory for nationals of the member states who possess the right to live and work in member states and are guaranteed all the social benefits of the host country.[38] Here, the individual right to work implies the free movement of labour and the individual freedom to sell one's labour as a commodity in the markets. In this particular context, to be European denotes the free movement of only those who are considered citizens of the European Union. By this definition non-Europeans are those who are codified as immigrants – blacks, Muslims, Bosnian refugees, etc. – whose worth is not recognized by the Charter of European Citizenship. On the issue of compliance with neoliberal requirements of economic efficiency, competitiveness, and cutbacks in social spending, different political criteria are used. Sometimes neoliberalism is morally justified in the name of national interest. For example, in Britain the Labour Party has been offering its supply side politics of export-led growth and neo-corporatism in the name of making "British market participants" winners.[39] In France, opposition to a single currency in the European Union is justified by means of national interest. In both cases those who take a critical stand on national interests and/or of government policies are politically codified as "angry demonstrators," "workers," "human rights activists," and so on.

In North America, the politics of the morality of neoliberalism is regulated by the same modern principle of defining the private individual in accordance with the legal inscription of citizenship rights and the compliance with national interests defined by specific government policies.[40] If Europe and North America are considered as the natural habitat of liberal democracy, morality of neoliberal politics is enriched by culturally specific symbols for social cohesion and varying degrees of heightened individual self-interest. In spite of innumerably different articulations of these symbols and cultural constructs, the common element in the morality of modern politics is that in maintaining social cohesion, the liberal notion of individual rights is tailored in conjunction with the political economy of capitalism in such a way that the value of a human being is always measured in hierarchical ranks. In this context, the "private individual" worthy of social and political attention has always been the one who works, who has a job, a career; in other words, a future.[41] The notion of the unemployed is a specific moral code by which rational individuals are ranked. It sounds as if rational, self-interested, self-motivated individuals ought to be employed in a waged job and accumulate wealth. Failing these obligations, they are demoted to something else than an individual, say an unemployed or a "deserving" poor, which, in the liberal hierarchy of human worth, is a degree higher than dependants on welfare programs, but certainly lower than a "good" middle-class citizen working for a wage.

In today's (neo)liberal constructions, a private individual not only possesses the "natural traits" of employment and ownership of private property, but is also self-motivated, competitive, efficient and, for the "right reasons," looks down on such analogous beings as the "unemployed," the "lazy welfare recipients," "single mothers on welfare," "drug addicts," "criminals," and so forth. In both political and moral terms the liberal notion of individual is embedded in a multitude of hierarchical oppositions such as citizen/non-citizen, worker/unemployed, worker/lazy welfare recipient, individual/drug addict, etc. Neoliberalism rebuilds its economic platform on the bases of these moral hierarchical ordering of the singular worth of a human being. These hierarchical distinctions also determine the political priorities of maintaining order and law.

b) Pre-ethical, Postmodern Privatization

In contrast with the modern articulations of (neo)liberal morality, the trend towards privatization in economy, politics, and social norms also denotes the emergence of new moral constructions of the worth of a private individual. As a result of the paradoxical effects of neoliberalism, the nation-states have, on the one hand, tightened their political grip over the society, but, on the other, have been subjected to challenges posed by the globalization of neoliberal trends. Susan Strange argues that the "necessity of the state as a public good ... the very idea of the social contract ... was conceived together with the economic necessity of civic co-operation between state and society." In drawing attention to the increasing power of "market forces" since the post-war period, she argues that transnational private enterprises in finance, industry, trade, communications, and organized networks of crime are now more powerful than states to whom ultimate political authority over society and economy is supposed to belong. In particular the state is less effective on "security against violence, stable money for trade and investment, a clear system of law and the means to enforce it, and a sufficiency of public goods like drains, water supplies, infrastructures for transport and communications."[42] To this list of specific areas in which state power has been in a steady decline, we can add Bauman's argument about the "postmodern privatisation of social spacing," notably the absence of a supranational force to adjudicate the contestation for power among "communal," "neo-tribal," ethnic, religious, and nationalist groups and a reliance on physical force and wars in maintaining order.

In this conjuncture of the declining power of states, particular policies of neoliberalism contribute to the formation of a pre-ethical existence. With reference to the declining power of states in exercising their centralized policing role against violence Susan Strange draws attention to the peculiarities of organized crime. She argues that organized criminal gangs, which are associated with mafia and drug trading, operate in a similar way to transnational corporations. In terms of their financial operations, "the most important tax havens and off-shore centres are situated at the cross-roads of the principal routes of the illegal narcotics trade." Referring to Panama and Bahamas for the cocaine trade in the USA, to Hong Kong for heroin trade from South East Asia to the West, and to Switzerland, Liechtenstein, and Gibraltar as "shelters [for] illegal proceeds of heroin produced and exported by traffickers from Turkey and other Middle East countries," she notes the formation of a "some kind of anarchical international society of mafias."[43]

She notes three contributing factors to the emergence of this global phenomenon. As a result of the liberalization of financial regulations, mafia and drug traders have "become such good customers of tax heavens and even respectable banks that no one has much interest in distinguishing their dirty money from the rest." Second, mobile technology in refining heroin and cocaine from the raw material and easy access to high-tech communications make it easier for the transnational gangs to evade state laws. Third, the limitations in national laws in collaborating with Interpol and Europol create conducive conditions for illegal transnational operations in drug trade.[44] She argues that criminal gangs emerge when state authority is weakened and the government has lost or failed to obtain the consent of the governed.[45]

In two particular cases, Russia and Turkey, the political realm is akin to a pre-ethical stage of lawlessness. Both Turkey and Russia entered the neoliberal phase of globalization through the financial regulations of the IMF, but the state in both places failed to regulate mafia activities. Moreover, in both cases there is enough evidence of the collaboration between the military, the intelligence agents, mafia, drug traffickers, and the judicial system. Both Turkey and Russia are considered potential members of the EU, despite questionable records on individual rights. In reviewing the constitutional requirements of individual rights, the existence of mafia within state apparatuses does not become either a moral or a political issue in the neoliberal understanding of democracy. By the same logic of neoliberal democracy, individual rationality in Russia and Turkey is celebrated to the extent that it is compatible with the drive towards privatization. But privatization in these countries implies not only the transfer of state assets to private enterprise and the growing share of transnational corporations in production but also the privatization of crime and the collapse of the social contract.

From where I write, I observe the truism of cutthroat competition in a society where the state fails to oblige itself to the basic requirements of a social contract, either in terms of minimum welfare provisions or maintaining law. Individual competition in this context implies shooting incidents among rival mafia groups as well as strangling each other for a meagre income of taxi drivers, prostitutes, or passersby. The effects of the international society of mafia are felt in similar ways outside of these two cases. Pre-ethical moral code needs to be distinguished from postmodern indifference because the role of the state jurisdiction in preserving consent of the ruled differs drastically from one case to another. In these private times, Russia and Turkey (among others) are reminders of the collapse of the nation-state to fulfil the modern requirements of social, economic and political order. As such they are reminders of a lawless chaos in today's global conjuncture of disorder. In places where neoliberalism is brought from above without the social contract and the historical struggle for individual rights, the morality of politics oscillates between cutthroat competition, violence in every day life, individual indifference to the singular worth of the "private individual," heightened individualism in the preservation of self-interest, and a strong communal belonging with the moral codes of the state, military, mafia, and religious and nationalist groups.

CONCLUSION

If ethics is a critical reflection of morality, then the imperatives of an ethical political stand in this conjuncture are to be aporetic. This aporetic stand ought to be singular and universal at the same time. Singularity of an ethical approach to politics recognizes that the responsibility to care for strangers is contrary to reason and rationality and hence cannot be morally coded in a blueprint of rights and wrongs, dos and don'ts. Yet, if ethics is at the same time a theoretical reflection of the morality of politics, it can, at least in theory, identify recurring general trends in world politics. In this respect, neoliberalism, with its insistence on individual rights and rationality, fails to recognize the singular worth of human beings. This being the case, it continues to preserve a rights-based view of morality devoid of self-responsibility to oneself and to others. To reiterate Bauman's conception of moral selves in this conjuncture, the contradictory imperative of ethical politics is to be in solidarity with those caught in wars, destitution, and deprivation without making a universal moral claim about this being the correct course of action. What is right is being regulated by the morality of liberal and neoliberal discourses and what is left is to be investigated not in writing but in the resilient autonomy of moral selves who, in spite of their self-interest, continue the tradition of solidarity in action.

NOTES

1 Larue A. Gerald, "Ancient Ethics," in Peter Singer (ed.), *A Companion to Ethics,* Oxford: Blackwell, 1993: 32–5.

2 Christopher Rowe argues that "the rise of Greek ethics can be seen in large part as a reflection of the overlaying of a fundamentally individualistic ethos with the demands for co-operative behaviour implied by the political institutions of the city state." Christopher Rowe, "Ethics in Ancient Greece," in Singer, *A Companion to Ethics,* 126.

3 Theoretical debates on morality and ethics provide us with a rich medley ranging from Aristotelian, Hobbesian, (neo-)Kantian ethics to the ethics of feminism, which is different from ethical feminism, postmodern ethics, which is different from modern and postmodern morality, and an ethics of the deconstruction of Western philosophy, which is not the same as repudiating, opposing, or going beyond the ontological premises of Western philosophy.

4 Luhmann Niklas, "Paradigm Lost: On the Ethical Reflection of Morality," *Thesis Eleven*, no. 29, 1991: 83–4.

5 Ibid., 82–4.

6 Ibid., 84, 90.

7 Ibid., 86.

8 Ibid., 85–91.

9 Ibid., 88, 90.

10 Unless otherwise noted, Bauman uses the notions of ethics and morality interchangeably.

11 By 'modern developments" Bauman specifically refers to the rise of capitalism and the separation of the private realm (household economy, civil society, religion, and church) from the public, political realm. Zygmunt Bauman, *Postmodern Ethics*, Oxford: Blackwell, 1993: 6.

12 Rowe, "Ethics in Ancient Greece."

13 M. Midgley, "The Origin of Ethics," in Singer, *A Companion to Ethics,* 4.

14 Zygmunt Bauman, "Morality without Ethics," *Theory, Culture and Society*, vol. 11, no. 4, 1994: 2

15 Ibid., 9.

16 Bauman, *Postmodern Ethics*, 238.

17 Ibid., 230.

18 Ibid., 229.

19 Ibid., 228–9.

20 Ibid., 239.

21 Ibid., 11.

22 Ibid., 11.

23 Ibid., 4.

24 Ibid., 247.

25 Bauman, "Morality without Ethics," 25–32.

26 Derek Sayer, *Readings from Karl Marx*, London: Routledge, 1989: 123.

27 For the pervasive influence of Christian morals in the secular, national formation of Europe, see Gerard Delanty, *Inventing Europe: Idea, Identity, Reality*, London: MacMillan, 1995: 28, 47, 70. The most informative source for investigating the Christian influence on the secular conceptions of nationhood is European literature. In 1912 James Joyce constructs, the self-definition of a young man as follows: "Steven Dedalus is my name, Ireland is my nation. Clongowes is my dwelling place and heaven my expectation." James Joyce, *A Portrait of the Artist as a Young Man*, NY: Bantam Books, 1992: 10.

28 For an explanation of the modern character of the politicization of Islam in Turkey see my "Allahu Ekber, We are Turks: Yearning for a Different Homecoming at the Periphery of Europe," *Third World Quarterly*, vol. 17, no. 3, 1996.

29 Susan Strange, "The Limits of Politics," *Government and Opposition*, vol. 30, no. 3, Summer 1995: 293–6. For an elaboration of these points see Susan Strange, *The Retreat of the State: The diffusion of Power in the World Economy*, Cambridge: Cambridge University Press, 1996.

30 Stephen Gill, "Knowledge, Politics and Neo-Liberal Political Economy," in R. Stubbs and G.R.L Underhill (eds), *Political Economy and the Changing Global Order*, London: MacMillan, 1995: 79, 82.

31 For an analysis of the 1994 GATT summit in the context of the paradoxical relationship between state legislation and the globalization of information as commodity, see John Frow, "Information as Gift and Commodity," *New Left Review*, no. 219, 1996.

32 The European Bank for Reconstruction and Development is on par with the IMF and World Bank in terms of its international, interregional financial operations, except to note that, unlike the latter two, the EBRD gives loans "to those governments committed to constitutional reforms and to

the principles of free market economics." Gill, "Knowledge, Politics and Neo-Liberal Political Economy," 83.

33 For an analysis of social movements against NAFTA see Andre Drainville, "Resisting Integration in the America's: Internationalism in One Country," paper presented at the International Studies Association Conference in San Diego, April 1996.

34 Gill, "Knowledge, Politics and Neo-Liberal Political Economy," 82.

35 Unless otherwise noted, in this section I use the notion of individual rights in the intertwined context of individuals as members of nation-states and individuals as rational, competitive, self-interested participants in the free market.

36 In Sayer, *Readings from Karl Marx*, 122.

37 Ibid., 122–3.

38 With the ratification of the Maastricht Treaty, the twin notions of European Economic Union and Citizens of the Union are codified as one. Cris Shore and Annabel Black, "Citizens' Europe and the Construction of European Identity," in Victoria A. Goddard et al. (eds), *The Anthropology of Europe: Identities and Boundaries in Conflict,* Oxford: Berg, 1994.

39 Noel Thompson, "Supply Side Socialism: The Political Economy of New Labour," *New Left Review*, no. 216, 1996: 45.

40 For particular examples check your local newspaper or TV station to find out specific interpellations of "lazy welfare recipients," "babies born to mothers with AIDS," "drug addicts," "angry protesters," and the like.

41 The pervasive influence of this particular moral interpellation of a worthy individual can be found outside of Europe and North America. Clarice Lispector, in portraying the self-definition of a young worker in Brazil, captures the liberal morality of self-hood as follows: "Olimpico de Jesus was a metal worker and Macebea failed to notice that he never once referred to himself as a *worker* but always as a *metallurgist*. Macebea was delighted with his professional standing just as she was proud of being a typist even if she did earn less than the minimum salary. She and Olimpico had social status. 'Metallurgist and typist' were categories of some distinction." Clarice Lispector, *The Hour of the Star*, Manchester: Carcanet, 1986: 45.

42 Strange, *The Retreat of the State*, xii, 4, 5.

43 Ibid., 113, 117.

44 Susan Strange, "The Limits of Politics," 306–7.

45 Strange, *The Retreat of the State*, 116.

Fetishizing Phantoms:
Carl Schmitt, Chantal Mouffe,
and "The Political"[1]

RADHIKA DESAI

... what fray was here? ...
O anything, of nothing first create!
O heavy lightness! Serious vanity!
Mis-shapen chaos of well-seeming forms!
Feather of lead, bright smoke, cold fire,
sick health!

        – Romeo

With no meagre relish in the disconcertation of the prosaic, certain left and democratic post-structuralist political theorists have turned to the revolutionary conservative and "Crown Jurist" of the Nazi regime, Carl Schmitt. He allegedly offers "hard and valuable lessons" about the nature of politics: "Schmitt can legitimately be regarded as the Hobbes of the twentieth century and his ideas are inescapable as surely as his personal politics were repellant."[2] Shorn of its fascist detritus, Schmitt's "realist" concept of "the political" is to serve the emancipationist purposes he resolutely opposed. Eager to deflect criticism, aware of the potential for controversy, new Schmittians genuflect contortedly to invoke Schmitt. In perhaps the most elaborate deployment of the political in a theorization of a radical and plural democracy, Chantal Mouffe proposes to "think with Schmitt, against Schmitt, and use his insights in order to strengthen liberal democracy against his critiques."[3]

Liberal and left responses[4] focus on conceptual difficulties in Schmitt's critiques of liberalism and democracy and the consonance between his theory and politics. However, new Schmittians' insistence on the "realism" of the political with which they would fill an alleged gap in left political theory invites a more thoroughgoing response. In this essay I argue first that the political that underlay Schmitt's conservative and fascist politics behind the baroque facade of his diversionary and none too consistent or accurate polemics was the true root of his objection to liberalism and of his denaturing of democracy. However it is not a "realism" – eschewing moralism and sentimentality in theorising a harsh arena of politics – but a phantom of a hysterical anxiety for order – rationally ungrounded and discursively uncontestable power. Like Nietzsche's irrationalism on which it was modelled, the political is a philosophically and historically spurious absolutisation of the uncertainties, contingencies, and perplexities of politics into an "other" of reason. This irrationalism, modernization, and radicalization of conservatism into the fascist politics of order yielded a "decisionist" theory of law and sovereignty that was "nothing but an arcanum for the maintenance of power."[5] Lukacs had argued long ago that the philosophical descent into irrationalism buttressed political reaction in our century.[6] When, among the various paths post-structuralism has traced back to this irrationalism, the new Schmittian enterprise has an added iterative plausibility from the too-long unquestioned and always pernicious tradition (dating back to Weber's Nietzscheanism) of an irrational "realist" political, it now seems necessary to recall this nexus.

The current invitation to learn from Schmitt (not *about*, as Stephen Holmes discerningly pointed out[7]) carries no emancipatory potential, certainly none to radicalise democracy or buttress it with its "realism" but, necessarily perhaps, one to denature it. My second aim is to show how Schmitt's authoritarianism is carried into Mouffe's "radical and plural democracy" because she fails to see its fateful link to the irrationalism she would import into her post-structuralist democracy. Her choreography of a strenuously precise tango of pluralism between the ideal of democracy and the reality of the political is actually democracy's macabre dance of death.

SITUATING CARL SCHMITT

Carl Schmitt's ideas cannot be understood outside the context of Weimar Germany's complex crisis "fueled not by *insurgent* popular forces against the established order but by *re*surgent ultra conservatives bent on bracing it"[8] against socialism and proximately against liberal democracy, which kept the door open to socialism. Armed with the political Schmitt thought and fought at the juridical centre of this enterprise.

Initially a traditional Catholic conservative critic of bourgeois culture, Schmitt reacted to the crisis of Weimar democracy with a Nietzschean "modernist anti-modernism"[9] forsaking any impossible restoration of pre-modern orders, deepening and hardening the irrationalism of anti-Enlightenment conservatism into a new politics of order. Friedrich Nietzsche had brilliantly and dramatically set the pattern of marshalling and adapting the cultural resources of Europe's pre-bourgeois, pre-industrial elite (whose social power "had yielded little ground during the heyday of liberalism"[10]) not only against bourgeois culture and modern society but also – in his oppositions between rationalism and art and, later on, "life," liberalism and aristocracy, "ultimate" and "super" men, and in his mystified identification of domination with creativity – against reason as such. Schmitt and other, less sophisticated conservative revolutionaries, such as Spengler, Juenger, and Moeller van den Bruck,[11] elaborated these oppositions into the climate of opinion on which fascism fed: irrationalist and volkishly authoritarian. While the customary distinction between traditional and revolutionary conservatives[12] is frequently useful, Schmitt's intellectual and political career suggests that traditional conservatives determined to retain political purchase on the fast-changing context of the crisis became revolutionary conservatives.

While socialism tended less to be understood or criticised than simply vilified (as also befitted its social moorings!), liberalism was a substantial target. Following another Catholic counter-revolutionary Donoso Cortes, Schmitt believed rationalist bourgeois liberalism was doomed by its indecisiveness and could not juridically or politically answer the requirements of the preservation of capitalist order when it seemed that "the maintenance of capitalist economic relations and political democracy [were] so antithetical ... that the abandonment and undermining of the Republic were self-evident necessities for the dominant classes."[13] Liberalism was a rationalist denial of politics, a critique of politics, not a theory. Preoccupied with the "everyday" and the "normal," it reduced politics to a mundane calculus of self-interest (economics) or altruism (ethics). Its efforts to tame and domesticate politics by "hindering and controlling the state's and government's power"[14] yielded only "an entire system of demilitarised and depoliticised concepts" that vainly attempted to annihilate the political as "the domain of conquering power and repression."[15] Its characteristic institutional innovation, parliament, was an eternal debating club embodying indecisiveness because "the truth could not be found in an unrestrained clash of opinion" among the "particles of reason that are strewn unequally among human beings gather themselves."[16] A Nietzschean Manicheanism pervaded his declaration of bourgeois rationalist liberalism's bankruptcy. As rationalism was ranged against irrationalism and vitalism, liberalism was opposed to absolutism, Jewry and bourgeoisie (not to mention the working class) to aristocracy, democracy to elitism, free trade to imperialism, reform to order, business to militarism. Invariably the "critique" of the former term was actually a reification of the latter.

Schmitt rethought democracy itself into an authoritarianism tailored to emasculate the power of a public swelled by the entry of the now-enfranchised masses. *Opposed* to liberalism, democracy was merely the "dominant concept of legitimacy"[17] of the time, an attempt to establish an identity between rulers and the ruled, not rationally but by mythically evoking unity and loyalty around themes of nationality. "The democratic plebiscitary procedure of acclamation" was a necessary concession to maintaining legitimacy through the *appearance* of democracy: "the people can only say yes or no, it cannot counsel, deliberate or discuss. It cannot govern or administer, nor can it posit norms; it can only sanction by its 'yes' the draft norms presented to it. Nor, above all, can it put a question, but only answer by 'yes' or 'no' a question put to it."[18] To claim that Schmitt was not volkish is to ignore that his "democracy" is actually an ersatz volkism.

Contrary to the arguments of contemporary epigones, Schmitt's Nazi career, far from being an aberration or a tragic deviation from his intellectual convictions,[19] is seamlessly defined by these convictions. One of Weimar Germany's most eminent jurists, Carl Schmitt's most productive phase covered the denouement of the republic and the early years of the Nazi regime. His alleged "defense" of the Weimar constitution until 1933 actually accentuated its centralising and authoritarian aspects, thereby contributing to the *Machtergreifung*. Although a "March violet," joining the Nazi party only *after* the Enabling Act of March 1933, Schmitt "[f]iercely ambitious and committed to anti-liberal, anti-democratic philosophy, [had] no need, personally or theoretically ... to do anything but join the 'revolution.'"[20] For the next several years, under the patronage of Hermann Goering, he sought influence in the Nazi regime. He drafted the notorious *Reichsstatthaltergesetz* at the behest of the Nazis in April of the same year, earning the appellation "Crown Jurist" of National Socialism, was appointed to the Prussian State assembly, participated in the reorganization of German legal education, and went on to write about forty articles that supported various Nazi legal initiatives, many of them peppered with an intellectual devaluation of Jewish scholars and Judaism. During that period, he also received the "highest honour" of his academic life, a chair at the Friedrich-Wilhelms University in Berlin. If after 1936 he fell out of favour with the regime, like Heidegger, it was not he who broke with the Nazis but, "[t]he party had broken from him, and the movement."[21] Schmitt had "outlived his usefulness. In December 1936, *Deutsche Brief* celebrated his dismissal ... 'The Moor has done his duty, the Moor can go.'"[22]

THE BAROQUE FACADE OF
SCHMITT'S REALISM

Mouffe and other new Schmittians approach Schmitt with a readerly naïveté surprising among post-structuralists. Schmitt's style of presentation is not exegetical but polemical: not building up his *own* argument but primarily aimed at establishing distance from competing views – liberal, pluralist, romantic and so on – by any means at hand, including arguments irrelevant to the construction of his own view, whose inconsistencies are thus conveniently masked and dissimulated by the baroque facade of his polemics.

Schmitt appropriates an antique value to his "realism" through the threadbare premise that "[o]ne could test all theories of state and political ideas according to their anthropology and thereby classify these as to whether they ... presuppose man to be by nature evil or by nature good"[23]: realist (and conservative) political thinkers from Hobbes onwards who "presuppose[d] man to be evil ... a dangerous and dynamic being" were "genuinely political."[24] Also laying claim to historical insight, Schmitt argued that rationalist liberals failed to understand that: "All significant concepts of the modern theory of the state are secularised theological concepts not only because of their historical development – in which they were transferred from theology to the theory of the state, whereby, for example, the omnipotent God became the omnipotent lawgiver – but also because of their systematic structure, the recognition of which is necessary for a sociological consideration of these concepts."[25] With the advent of secularization in the sixteenth century and the loss of an all-embracing, theistically grounded worldview, Europe had searched for a rationally constructed neutral sphere (successively metaphysics, humanism, economics, and now technology),[26] but in vain: "the political is the total, and as a result we know that any decision about whether something is *unpolitical* is always a *political* decision, irrespective of who decides and what reasons are advanced."[27] The political had erupted in Europe in an organic development of the twentieth century reversing the neutralisations and depoliticisations characteristic of modern times.[28]

Finally Schmitt appeared to draw his ideas from a perceptive reading of the then-mounting political tensions. Crises revealed things starkly and it was now surely clear, he argued in 1928, that with the advent of democracy, "state and society penetrate each other" creating a situation in which "everything is at least potentially political"[29] and the state is weakened. The political now demanded to be defined in terms of "its own ultimate distinctions, to which all action with a specifically political meaning can be traced."[30]

His theorization of the specificity and autonomy of the political appeared forcefully clear. Like independent criteria of other autonomous spheres of life – the distinction between beautiful and ugly in aesthetics, good and evil in ethics, and profitable and unprofitable in business – "[t]he specific political distinction to which political actions and motives can be reduced is that between friend and enemy."[31] While they may arise in other spheres – economics, religion, etc. – antagonisms become political by becoming friend-enemy groupings. The enemy is not simply a competitor nor a private adversary. No matter how hated, "The political enemy need not be morally evil or aesthetically ugly; he need not appear as an economic competitor, and it may even be advantageous to engage with him in business transactions. But he is nevertheless, the other, the stranger ..."[32] The political is ultimately defined by the possibility of violence: "The friend, enemy and combat concepts receive their real meaning precisely because they refer to the real possibility of physical killing."[33]

Although the political "may yield pluralistic consequences" for the state and sovereignty, they must be avoided. English pluralists who denied "the sovereignty of the political entity [the state] by stressing time and again that the individual lives in numerous different social entities and associations,"[34] left the decisive question unanswered: "[W]hich social entity (if I am permitted to use the imprecise liberal concept of 'social') decides in the extreme case and determines the decisive friend- and-enemy grouping? Neither a church nor a labour union nor an alliance of both could have forbidden or prevented a war which the German Reich might have wanted to wage under Bismarck ... The political entity is by its very nature the decisive entity ..."[35] Not only does "the concept of the state presuppose ... the concept of the political," the former is *defined* by its mastery over the latter: it is not possible that "within the same political entity, instead of the decisive friend-enemy grouping, a pluralism could take its place without destroying the entity and the political itself."[36] The essence of the state lay in brooking no opposition, in externalising the enemy so that, ideally, all politics becomes essentially foreign affairs.

In Schmitt's analytic, the political is an autonomous realm with its own criteria and expert practitioners – those who could grasp the harsh and violent facts of politics and make the potentially cruel decisions it often necessitated. Its association with war, combat, and rule – and Schmitt's vivid disdain for liberals and the bourgeois (not to mention the socialists and the working class) – bespeaks the feudalised modernity of Schmitt's enterprise in the *Gleichzeitigkeit der ungleichzeitigen*.

Stephen Holmes's witty demonstration that for Schmitt liberalism was essentially a sissy theory baulking at the harsh realities of politics[37] must be taken further: there are no sissies without bullies. The more obvious intellectual swagger in Schmitt's rhetoric is easy enough to dispel. The notion that human beings are inherently conflictual rather than co-operative may have a certain cachet, but little intrinsic validity. If "[i]n the Expressionistic style of the day, Carl Schmitt constructs a dramatic concept of the political, in the light of which everything normally understood by the word must seem banal,"[38] Giovanni Sartori criticises Schmitt for exploring only "politics-as-war" rather than peace-like politics – co-operation, brokering and successful hegemony – which Schmitt dismisses as only "taming" and non- or anti-politics. While "Schmitt was after *the category* of the political ... he has actually deployed *one of its modalities*."[39] But this is arguably conceding too much.

Crude and ahistorical ("political") theology masquerades as history in Schmitt's argument about the structural derivation of "modern secular" concepts from their "theological" counterparts – e.g., the modern work ethic as a secularization of asceticism, or the modern idea of progress as a secularization of the notion of salvation. In an illicit form of reasoning with which the right has habitually inflated and devalued the currency of discourse, an immanent critique of reason's incomplete victory over religion[40] is deployed as a bland assertion of fact or necessity that is trans- and a-historical, misconstruing the issue of the relation of ideas to history. Despite Schmitt's stated conviction that "without a concept of secularization we cannot understand our history of the last centuries,"[41] Hans Blumenberg points out that "What is remarkable, methodologically, about Carl Schmitt's political theology, is that he finds any value at all in this secularization nexus since ... it would have been more natural, in view of the intention of this 'political theology,' for him to establish the reverse relation of derivation by interpreting the apparent theological derivation of political concepts as a consequence of the absolute quality of political realities."[42] This absurd inconsistency is compounded by the historically (and, one might add, theologically) crude notion that theism in feudal society precluded opposition (rather than aided its violent suppression) and thereby, the political.

Schmitt's claim to acuity in understanding Weimar's crisis is also belied by his ahistorical categories. Since he was exclusively concerned with essences and anti-theses – i.e., with concepts, rather than historical realities – no understanding of the crisis, however acute, underwrote the political. In contrast to the analyses of other contemporary observers (e.g., Otto Kirchheimer's[43]), Schmitt's understanding of Weimar politics is schematic and aimed principally "to liberate an unrationalised potential for existential decision"[44] and authoritarianism.

Schmitt's conceptual and essentialist mode of argument, upon which his famously clear criterional argument relies, also dissolves upon scrutiny. Are art, business, or ethics governed by the simple oppositions between terms whose meanings are clear once and for all rather than complex situational judgements about beauty, profitability, or moral worth, which often change the criteria themselves? Any intellectual of the early twentieth century of modernism who believed that judgements in art merely distinguished between "beautiful" and ugly" was clearly a philistine; that business judgements in the age of corporate concentration were made on some simple notion of profitability, was equally clearly naive; and that good and evil were simple oppositions, was a scarcely credible Catholic.

THE IRRATIONALIST FOUNDATION OF "THE POLITICAL"

A form of intellectual bullying, Schmitt's polemics demonstrate little other than the credulity of his followers. Moreover, claims to historical accuracy, philosophical and experiential acuity, or criterional clarity, invariably formulated with brutal and fatuous panache, are structurally incidental to the conceptual architecture of the political. Built upon philosophical irrationalism, a fundamental opposition between the political, an irrationalist "real," and the rational, the political is defined by its radical normlessness, whose most visible indication is the reification of war into the epitome of normlessness. "War, the readiness of combatants to die, the physical killing of human beings who belong to the side of the enemy – all this has no normative meaning, but an existential meaning only ... there exists no rational purpose, no norm no matter how true, no program no matter how exemplary, no social ideal no matter how beautiful, no legitimacy nor legality which could justify men in killing each other for this reason."[45]

While the appearance of an uncharacteristic pacifism may be disarming, Schmitt's real aim is to portray war and violence as being wholly beyond reason. But no matter how horrifying the violence of modern wars, how unspeakable the suffering it inflicts, how unjustified its usual occasion, how murderously inept its conduct, how frequent the contravention of the rules and norms that are intended to govern it, and how few their number and weak their enforcement, existential othering of war from reasons, rationalism, norms, and human purposes, rather than a critique of their limitation, perversion, and inversion in war, can only be an unrestrained glorification of war above a despised finitude of humanity and its reason.

Schmitt's existentialist irrationalism drew upon the Nietzschean critique of an Enlightenment reason that ignored its own perspectivism: the very attempt to comprehend reality rationally also constituted it as a rationally comprehensible reality. Ordinarily necessary for and indeed effective in survival, such knowledge vainly imposed orderly conceptions on an actually chaotic reality, and left out "the formless unformulable world of the chaos of sensations – *another* kind of phenomenal world, a kind 'unknowable' for us."[46] The opposition of the political to reason mimicked the Nietzschean opposition between "life" and "intellect" ("Every rational interpretation falsifies the immediacy of life"[47]). Its juridical and political deployment as an existentialist fetish for "exceptions" is clearest in his engagement with the preeminent liberal constitutionalist of the time, Hans Kelsen. By analogy with its laws of nature, the desired legal structure of Enlightenment rationalism "repudiated every form of the exceptional case."[48] But "[p]recisely a philosophy of concrete life must not withdraw from the exception and the extreme case": "The exception can be more important than the rule, not because of a romantic irony for the paradox, but because the seriousness of an insight goes deeper than the clear generalisations inferred from what ordinarily repeats itself. The exception is more interesting than the rule. The rule proves nothing; the exception proves everything: it confirms not only the rule but also its existence, which derives only from the exception."[49] Schmitt argued that it was impossible to "understand the legal order in *exclusively rationalist terms*."[50] Each legal decision entailed an irreducible "extralegal dimension" of adjudication beyond legal norms which represented "a type of vital substrate," an element of "pure life" that stands forever opposed to, and indeed, over the formalism of law as such.[51] In jurisprudence,

[the] decision becomes instantly independent of argumentative substantiation and receives an autonomous value. The entire theoretical and practical meaning of this is revealed in the theory of the faulty act of state. A legal validity is attributed to a wrong and faulty decision. The wrong decision contains a constitutive element precisely because of its falseness ... That constitutive, specific element of a decision is, from the perspective of the content of the underlying norm, new and alien. Looked at normatively, the decision emanates from nothingness ... A point of ascription first determines what a norm is and what normative rightness is.[52]

The essence of politics in any putatively rule-bound context, say administrative or judicial, lies precisely in that element of any such action that cannot be subsumed under rules – the indeterminate, unanticipated, and unpredictable must be decided upon outside norms.

SOVEREIGNTY OF IRRATIONALISM: DECISIONISM

Schmitt's authoritarian state and decisionist sovereignty followed relentlessly from his irrationalist "political" and owed nothing to the oversights of pluralists: having once portrayed a "reality" of conflict and violence, the possibility of even a minimum of social order can only be realised in a boundlessly authoritarian and centralised state.

Although only the "state of exception," calling the very existence and survival of a given state into question, rather than any old danger or threat facing the state, demands transcendent (theological or "political," it hardly matters) decision ("Sovereign is he who decides on the state of the exception"[53]), the distinction is practically meaningless since the state of the exception is both the object and the product of sovereign decision. Not only does the sovereign decide on the course of action in an exceptional situation, by suspending the law to preserve the state, but he is also "sovereign who definitely decides whether [a] normal situation exists."[54] Apologists of Schmitt, who argue that Schmitt was not totalitarian,[55] succeed only by reifying totalitarianism into something far more systematic and premeditated than it historically was. No more than decisionism was either necessary or convenient for the Nazis.

In Schmitt's formulation, politics is a centralised and sovereign taking of decisions (not constantly deferring them to rationality, as liberals are wont to do). Just as Nietzsche, in order to prevent a slide into uncomprehending passivity, was forced to postulate a way of grasping the rationally unknowable "true reality" without rational mediation in artistic creation and judgement, so Schmitt argued that decisions as a way of mastering the political are not justifiable but pure existential acts: "a pure decision not based on reason and discussion and not justifying itself ... an absolute decision created out of nothingness."[56] Schmitt strove to place this irrationalism within modern juristic and political theory as "a specifically juristic element – the decision in absolute purity"[57] against constitutionalist sovereignty of law.

Schmitt argued that the essence of sovereignty becomes clear when the "systematic structural kinship between theological and juristic concepts"[58] is recognised: "The exception [sic; or does Schmitt mean decision?] in jurisprudence is analogous to the miracle in theology. Only by being aware of this analogy can we appreciate the manner in which the philosophical ideas of the state developed in the last centuries."[59] But, by lodging modern philosophical irrationalism at the core of his theory of state and sovereignty, Schmitt departed radically from modern conceptions of the state. Schmitt's declared aim to become the Hobbes of the twentieth century meant, principally, correcting Hobbes's rationalism. For Schmitt, Hobbes erred in positing a private realm, civil society, which imposed limitations on the exercise of untrammelled state power, and more so in subjecting the Leviathan to purposes and reasons, which could then be disputed or changed. "Hobbes was satisfied in keeping in check the instincts of disorder by just as much sovereign terror as is needed for the purpose. Schmitt's Leviathan is inimical to the mention of purposes, as this would entail a calculus of proportions: no more terror than necessary. But ... [this] ... would be setting rational bounds to that which is essentially boundless, wholly other, and beyond comprehension."[60]

Schmitt's irrationalist radicalization of conservatism was not without determinate historical consequences: recruited by Reich Chancellor Papen to defend his 1932 decision to remove the Prussian state government and impose martial law, Schmitt successfully gave the Weimar constitution a controversial interpretation: the "guardianship" of the Weimar constitution rested not with the courts, parliaments, or governments but in the Reich president. It also favoured the granting of exceptional powers to the president and in general freed fascist acts after 1933 from the necessity of justification.

"THE POLITICAL": REALISM OR PHANTOM?

Insofar as the political is not a religion (and, arguably, this possibility must be given the benefit of the doubt) but claims logical and philosophical validity, it stands or falls with the Nietzschean philosophical irrationalism that lies at its core. The critique of the general post-structuralist resort to Nietzschean conservative philosophers, by Jurgen Habermas and Peter Dews, among others, has demonstrated that the latter were caught in the performative contradiction of attempting to demonstrate reason's debility by rational means. How could Nietzsche speak of an ultimate reality if he has argued that for us reality is only revealed through our partial perspectivist knowledge of it?[61] Analogously, when Schmitt posits the political, a "true" reality of violence, irreconcilable difference, and war, he fails not only to show how it can be possible to rationally posit a "political" reality that is by definition not apprehensible to reason but also to indicate its character.

On the epistemological-practical axis of this irrationalism, just as Nietzsche's taste and aesthetic judgement, "the Yes and No of the palate," did not constitute a form of knowledge free of the limitations of rationality (Nietzsche did not "recognize as a moment of reason the critical capacity for assessing value that was sharpened through dealing with modern art ... at least procedurally connected with objectifying knowledge and moral insight in the process of providing argumentative grounds"[62]), the purely existential sovereign decision as a way of apprehending and mastering the political runs into a contradiction that Samuel Weber identifies in a key passage from *Political Theology*:

What characterises an exception is principally unlimited authority, which means the suspension of the entire existing order. In such a situation it is clear that the state remains, whereas law recedes. Because the exception is different from anarchy and chaos, order in the juristic sense still prevails even if it is not of the ordinary kind.

The existence of the state is undoubted proof of its superiority over the legal norm. The decision frees itself from all normative ties and becomes in a true sense absolute. The state suspends the law *on the basis of its right of self-preservation, as one would say.*[63]

As the last sentence quoted above reveals, Schmitt's decisionism is not beyond norms and justification. The decision *is* justified, involving an appeal to a norm – the state's right to self preservation – however Schmitt may rhetorically diminish it as "a way of speaking" rather than a "norm." The decision "constitutes itself in and as a *break with* ... an interruption or suspension *of* ... *a norm*." The validity of the decision, even in Schmitt's own discourse, can, furthermore, only be judged "*after the fact* as it were, which is to say, from a point of view that is once again situated *within* a system of norms,"[64] only on the basis of its effectiveness in re-establishing a certain order. Thus "the non-legal or a legal status of the sovereign and exceptional decision is justifiable and indeed identifiable only insofar as it provides the conditions for the reappropriation of the exception by the norm."[65]

Like all attempts to deal with the limitations of reason by positing "true" chaotic and/or horrifying realities and extrarational ways of apprehending them, the political is a phantom concept. It has a certain iterative plausibility since an opposition between rationality and politics is all too frequently evoked more or less casually to give an impression of profundity of understanding. Take Claude Lefort: rationalism's "inability between the wars to understand the drama that was unfolding in the world, and in particular its inability to understand the depths from which the collective identifications and death wishes sprang" requires a recognition of the political.[66] Needless to say the interwar drama was comprehensible to many (socialist and communists among them) who would have been surprised to be told by Lefort that they were not rationalists. When accepted by prominent liberals such as

Max Weber who vainly attempted to draw different political implications from it, this opposition nevertheless gained in currency.

Weber's identification of politics with conflict was also owed to Nietzsche. The politics of his time, which meant for Weber the manipulation of mass passion and faith, intensified politics' fundamental association with violence and conflict and exceeded the possibilities contained within rationalist liberal social contractarian models of politics. Weber's endorsement of the will to power of a great charismatic individual "setting objectives for society out of his own unmotivated convictions"[67] and his more general hope that politics will be tempered with an understanding of science and a self-limiting "ethics of responsibility" on the part of its practitioners was, if not authoritarian, at least insufferably elitist. Weber equated politics with conflict and irrationalism, Mommsen argues, because he adopted "in its entirety the traditional doctrine of 'reasons of state' [and described] the constitutional state as the typical modern form of power dominance *but without much attention to its rational basis.*"[68] This was a contradiction within Weber's liberalism and must be criticised as such.

The opposition between politics and reason must ultimately be traced back to the false idea that the incursion of reason into politics is somehow peculiarly modern, and that it pitted itself against a normless and irrational absolutism. However necessary for Enlightenment reason's heroic self-image, this opposition must be scrutinised. Samuel Weber has argued that Walter Benjamin employed Schmitt's "normless" sovereignty (rooted neither in a transcendent deity nor in "any profound fusion of historical and moral concepts, [which] was unknown to the pre-rationalist West"[69]) in his analysis of seventeenth-century German Baroque drama (the *Trauerspiel*). Benjamin, however, demonstrated rather the radical impossibility of any such sovereignty, precisely the impossibility of decision in a world where universal principles, including "the principle of the interruption of principle *qua* decision – can no longer be counted on."[70] Instead of the *drama* of decision, the *Trauerspiel* then reflected a vain *"theatricality"*[71] where "plot is replaced by plotting" and it is the intriguer who is in his element and "the sovereignty of the tyrant is replaced by the mastery of the plotter."[72]

In Benjamin's hands this conception of absolutism was a heuristic device in a forceful cultural critique of Germany's period of petty absolutisms. Freed from the dictates of theology, and as yet untamed by democracy as the constraining influence of popularly generated norms on power, which once again reinstated the possibility of meaningful (i.e., dramatic) history, this "normless sovereignty" worked as a caricature of an interregnum. In fact, of course, in no society is power absolute and entirely free from norms and rationality of some sort, however limited. It constitutes a requirement both in the functioning of the apparatus of power itself, securing its self-understanding, as well as its legitimation amongst the people at large.

All societies, whether democratic or otherwise, have norms, traditional and "modern,"[73] which place limits on the legitimate exercise of political authority and the purposes to which this exercise is directed. These traditions are, in however muted forms, the vectoral sum of the political struggles over sets of norms and rationalities that have gone into a society's constitution and evolution, which are in turn vulnerable to further rational and normative contestation. The medieval monarch was not free to rule as he pleased, but was bound by customs, norms, and purposes that governed the lives of the people, in particular those whose voices were backed by power. The actions of the absolute monarchs of the sixteenth- and seventeenth-century Europe, also, were not a paradise of the ungrounded whim of the sovereign: the proclamation of the positive theory of law in this period ("Law is nothing other than the command of the sovereign in the exercise of his power"[74]) was accompanied, in Bodin's own writings, by the counterweight of "the complex of conceptions designated divine or natural law"[75]; for, while the exercise of brutal force against the peasantry was part of its rationale as the "carapace of a threatened nobility," this very rationale necessitated that "[n]o Absolutist state could ever dispose at will of the liberty or landed property of the nobility itself, or of the bourgeoisie ... Absolutism ultimately operated within the bounds of the class whose interests it secured."[76] The period of absolutism was not so much one of normlessness in the exercise of power but one of maximum distance between the norms of those who so brutally exercised it and those of the mass of those over whom it ruled, a distance secured by purposive (not "normless") violence and *dissimulated by an alleged normlessness*.

Schmitt was not wrong in seeing bourgeois (i.e., liberal-democratic) politics distinctively constituted as a politics of reason, as a resistance to power, based on an *opposition* of reason and power. But it may be too much to say that the bourgeois revolution, which initiated the long national marches to modern democracies as a critique of the absolutist state, was "intended to change domination as such," invoking "more than just an exchange of the basis of legitimation while domination was maintained in principle,"[77] as if domination was ever normless (rather than unpopular and violent). There *is* an element of self-consciousness about the role of rational-critical debate in the public sphere generating public norms and the insistence that "the exercise of power is to be demoted to a mere executor of such norms."[78] In formally institutionalising processes whereby *popular* norms would now subject those of the rulers, their limited and oppressive rationalities could no longer be shielded, by a distant God or an alleged normlessness, from rational and popular questioning.

THE PHANTASY OF RADICAL AND PLURAL DEMOCRACY

In the name of pluralism, without which "the logic of popular sovereignty can[not] avoid descending into tyranny,"[79] Mouffe accords Schmitt's concept of the political the central place in her radical democracy. Although she refers to several of its incidental attributes, the central attraction of the political for Mouffe is its recognition that antagonism has a "constitutive role" in social life: "some modes of life and some values are by definition incompatible with others and that it is this very exclusion which constitutes them."[80] Any rationalist democratic political theory would, in aiming to eradicate conflict, be insufficiently pluralist and "blind to the specificity of the political in its dimension of conflict/decision,"[81] a "dangerous liberal illusion." "Politics cannot be reduced to rationality, precisely because it indicates the *limits* of rationality."[82] Although apparently connected with the poststructuralist identification of reason, including rational adjudication of claims of rival groups with closure and domination, Mouffe's anti-liberalism and anti-rationalism are axiomatic rather than consequentialist: contrary to Mouffe, Schmitt rejected liberal democracy not because he believed that rational deliberation would yield an absolute truth and reconcile political differences but precisely because parliamentary discussion is thought only by vulgar liberals to achieve truth whereas in fact the "specific relationship to truth" involved here was "renouncing a definite result."[83] (On this Schmitt is surely right, making liberal democracy and rationalism attractive to any poststructuralism wary of closure!).

In order to gear Schmitt's ideas for democratic service, Mouffe must dispose of their authoritarian incubus. This is, however, impossible. It is precisely in the irrationalism of the political – imported intact into radical and plural democracy – that authoritarianism inheres. Not surprisingly, on both pluralism and democracy, Mouffe's disagreements with Schmitt are more apparent than real. As a pluralist she dismisses Schmitt's unified sovereign and argues that Schmitt is wrong when he claims that democracy requires homogeneity over pluralism. ("What renders his conception questionable and potentially totalitarian is that he presents this homogeneity as being substantial in nature, leaving no room for pluralism."[84]) However, having accepted the political, she too must also affirm that "total" pluralism is political nonsense in the interests of some semblance of political order: there cannot be "[a]ntagonistic principles of legitimacy ... without the political reality of the state automatically disappearing."[85] Democratic pluralism will need an overarching public power and enabling legal and political structures to ensure it.[86] Without some underlying "democratic" homogeneity, there can be no democracy. A democratic homogeneity "constituted by agreement on a certain number of political principles ... would provide the common substance required for democratic citizenship."[87] The state, which embodies this homogeneity cannot be neutral, it must be *political*, a partisan of plural and radical democracy, *fostering* democratic communities and *excluding* anti-democratic ones.

In shifting democracy from a rational to a extrarational 'political' foundation, Mouffe also endorses Schmitt's ersatz volkism as democracy. Liberal democracy as a set of procedures cannot give shape to a political will. "For Schmitt, such a conception is contradictory, since he believes that in democracy such a will has to be pregiven at the outset and cannot be the product of discussion. The people must be able to express its [!] political unity directly and without mediation. It is on these grounds that he criticises the idea of the 'social contract' since, he says, either unanimity is pregiven or it is not pregiven; where it does not exist, a contract will not bring it into being and where it does exist, there is no point in a contract."[88] And since rational-deliberative means cannot create consensus,[89] democracy must simply be entrenched in society by creating unreflective "identifications" with it as widely as possible. "[A] hegemony of democratic values ... requires a multiplication of democratic practices, institutionalising them into ever more diverse social relations, so that a multiplicity of subject positions can be formed through a democratic matrix. It is in this way – *and not by trying to provide it with a rational foundation* – that we will be able not only to defend democracy but also to deepen it."[90] Democracy's form, rules, and values become a sort of protomythical substrate, within which its denizens operate but which they do not subject to ethical or rational choice. Since struggle and antagonism give vitality to political life, a Nietzschean agonism among rival principles of conceptions of liberty and equality which "can never be perfectly reconciled, but ... [whose tension] ... is precisely what constitutes ... the principal value of liberal democracy"[91] must tame the dangerous potential of the political within an overarching mythic democratic consensus and double as its continuing affirmation and entrenchment. Without recourse to disciplinarian and disabling reason, "which would imply a structure, the structure would imply a framework, the framework is common and shared world view," agonism – "the root of all freedom [*Freisinnigkeit*] of antiquity – would give the forces of instinct and nature [the political] a measured discharge, not annihilation and denial."[92] "Rival" conceptions of democracy would joust for power on the basis of the extent of identification each has managed to achieve for itself in society while being able to act decisively to exclude anti-democratic enemies.

Like Schmitt, Mouffe cannot formulate her idea of a political order, however democratic, without resort to a mystic homogeneity, in her case, a "democratic" one. The consequent agonism is telling of the impoverished choice that Mouffe's radical and plural democracy affords. More importantly, perhaps, in her vision the state, a partisan of democracy, must act decisively to *exclude* anti-democratic tendencies. But if the acceptance of democracy is ungrounded in rational-discursive norms, how is such action to be justified? What is to prevent the state acting against *more* radical versions of democracy – say socialist or feminist?

So much for pluralism. What about democracy? Mouffe argues that "Schmitt's main target is not democracy but liberalism, whose pluralism he violently opposes."[93] While Schmitt sought to extinguish pluralism, did he endorse democracy? For Schmitt democracy was an ersatz volkism: a pre-given identity of the rulers and the ruled. Mouffe's disdain for Schmitt's "pre-modern" conception of value homogeneity (which, in any case, is only a caricature of pre-modern societies in which worldviews did in fact compete and which witnessed rebellions and oppositional movements) barely masks the fact that in her own radical and plural democracy she would banish rational deliberation from any role in determining the more fundamental questions about the basis of the political order, even if she would admit it into less important issues. But how is the demarcation made? Should the contours of a democratic order be any less the subject of rational critique and reformulation than other issues? Indeed, it could be argued that liberal democracy retains a radical potential only insofar as it is able to evolve in its basic structures in response to political demands.

Indeed, it appears that the chief defect of Mouffe's Schmittian democracy, for all her commitment to pluralism, diversity, and the coexistence of different worldviews, lies in a histrionic *intolerance* for dissent, difference, and uncertainty that she shares with Schmitt and that is the hallmark of the politics of order of the modern age. The "[p]ublic willingness to censure and criticize government [that] depends on the underlying confidence that such attacks will not cause the indispensable law-enforcing powers of society utterly to collapse."[94] The lack of such confidence, indeed a "primal anxiety" about it, is the cue for authoritarianism.[95]

NOTES

1 The burden of this essay's argument is that the idea of "the political" is without sense – empirically and historically, logically and politically. Both as it occurs in Schmitt and elsewhere, it has been employed only in the service of authoritarianism and reaction. The essay also argues that it cannot be otherwise. Given this, the scare quotes will be used sparingly, lest they give the wrong impression that there might be some other concept of the political that is viable and legitimate.

2 Paul Hirst, *Representative Democracy and Its Limits*, London: Polity Press, 1990: 10–11.

3 Chantal Mouffe, *The Return of the Political,* London: Verso, 1993: 2.

4 See, for example, Bill Schuerman, "Modernist Anti-modernism: Carl Schmitt's Concept of the Political," *Philosophy and Social Criticism*, vol. 19, no. 2, 1993; "The Rule of Law under Seige," *History of Political Thought*, vol. 14, no. 2, Summer 1993; "Is Parliamentarism in Crisis?" *Theory and Society*, no. 24, February 1995; Mark Neocleous, "Friend or Enemy: Reading Carl Schmitt Politically," *Radical Philosophy*, no. 79, September-October 1996; and Stephen Holmes, *The Anatomy of Anti-Liberalism,* Cambridge, MA: Harvard University Press, 1993: especially chapter 2.

5 Franz Neumann, *The Rule of Law,* Leamington Spa, UK, and Dover, NH: Berg, 1986: 285.

6 Georg Lukacs, *The Destruction of Reason,* London: Merlin Press, 1980, trans. Peter Palmer.

7 Holmes, *The Anatomy of Anti-Liberalism*, 37.

8 Arno Mayer, *The Persistence of the Old Regime: Europe to the Great War*, New York: Pantheon Books, 1981: 301.

9 Schuerman, "Modernist Anti-modernism."

10 Mayer, *The Persistence of the Old Regime*, 278.

11 Richard Wolin, "The Revolutionary Conservative Habitus and the Aesthetics of Horror," *Political Theory*, vol. 20, no. 3, August 1992: 426.

12 See for example, ibid., and Jerry Z. Muller, "Carl Schmitt, Hans Freyer and the Radical Conservative Critique of the Liberal Democracy in the Weimar Republic," *History of Political Thought*, vol. 12, no. 4, Winter 1991.

13 David Abraham, *The Collapse of the Weimar Republic. Political Economy and Crisis*, Princeton, NJ: Princeton University Press, 1981: 287,

quoted in Geoff Eley, *From Unification to Nazism,* Boston: Allen and Unwin, 1986: 273.

14 Carl Schmitt, *The Concept of the Political*, Rutgers University Press, New Brunswick, NJ, 1976, translation, introduction, and notes by George Schwab with Leo Strauss's "Comments on Carl's Schmitt's *Der Begriff des Politischen,*" 70. Originally published in German in 1927. This is a translation of the 1932 edition.

15 Schmitt, *The Concept of the Political*, 71.

16 Carl Schmitt, *The Crisis of Parliamentary Democracies*, Cambridge, MA: MIT Press, 1985, translated with an introduction by Ellen Kennedy, 35.

17 Ibid., 30.

18 Cited in Otto Kirchheimer, "Constitutional Reaction in 1932," in *Politics, Law and Social Change*, New York, Columbia University Press, 1969: 78.

19 As argued by Joseph Bendersky, *Carl Schmitt: Theorist for the Reich,* Princeton, NJ: Princeton University Press, 1983. There is another major (and apologetic) biography in English: George Schwab, *The Challenge of the Exception: An Introduction to the Political Ideas of Carl Schmitt between 1921 and 1936*, Berlin: Duncker and Humblot, 1970. Manfred Weigandt, "A Biographical Sketch of Schmitt," *Cardozo Law Review*, Vol. 16, no. 5, March 1995, is a more reliable overview that also considers Paul Noack, *Carl Schmitt: Eine Biographie,* Berlin: Propyläen Verlag, 1993. Relevant chapters of Ian Ward, *Law, Philosophy and National Socialism*, Berne: Peter Lang, 1992, discuss the connection between Schmitt's ideas and his politics in detail.

20 Ward, *Law, Philosophy and National Socialism,* 156.

21 Ibid., 94.

22 Ibid., 161.

23 Schmitt, *The Concept of the Political*, 58.

24 Ibid., 61. The contentious inclusion of Lenin in this lineage had later echoes in Samuel Huntington's politics of order.

25 Carl Schmitt, *Political Theology: Four Chapters on the Concept of Sovereignty*, Cambridge, MA: MIT Press, 1985 (originally published in German in 1922, revised 1934), trans. George Schwab, 37.

26 See Schmitt's "The Age of Neutralizations and Depoliticisations," a lecture delivered in 1929. *Telos*, no. 96, Summer 1993, trans. Matthias Konzett and John P. McCormick.

27 Schmitt, *Political Theology*, 2.

28 Ibid.

29 Schmitt, *The Concept of the Political*, 22.

30 Ibid.

31 Ibid., 26.

32 Ibid., 26–7.

33 Ibid., 33.

34 Ibid., 40–1.

35 Ibid., 43–4.

36 Ibid., 45.

37 Holmes, *The Anatomy of Anti-Liberalism*.

38 Jurgen Habermas, "Sovereignty and the *Fuhrerdemokratie*," *Times Literary Supplement*, 26 September 1986: 1053.

39 Giovanni Sartori, "The Essence of the Political in Carl Schmitt," *Journal of Theoretical Politics*, vol. 1, no. 1, January 1989: 73.

40 Karl Lowith.

41 Schmitt, *Political Theology*, op.cit., 2.

42 Hans Blumenberg, *The Legitimacy of the Modern Age*, Cambridge, MA: MIT Press, 1983, trans. by Robert M. Wallace, 92.

43 Otto Kirchheimer, "Weimar – und was dann?" *Politik und Verfassung*, Frankfurt, 1964, cited in Alfons Soellner, "Beyond Carl Schmitt," *Telos*, no. 71, Spring 1987.

44 Ulrich Preuss, "The Critique of German Liberalism," *Telos*, no. 71, Spring 1987: 103.

45 Schmitt, *The Concept of the Political*, 49.

46 Friedrich Nietzsche, *The Will to Power*, New York : Random House, 1968, trans. of *Wille zur Macht* by Walter Kaufmann and R.J. Hollingdale (ed.), with commentary by Walter Kaufmann, 307, quoted in Peter Dews, *Logics of Disintegration*, London: Verso, 1988: 179.

47 Schmitt, *Political Theology*, 71.

48 Ibid., 49.

49 Ibid., 15.

50 Wolin, "The Revolutionary Conservative Habitus," 431.

51 Ibid., 431.

52 Schmitt, *Political Theology*, 31–2.

53 Ibid., 5.

54 Ibid., 13.

55 Schwab, *The Challenge of the Exception*, 143–8.

56 Schmitt, *Political Theology*, 66.

57 Ibid., 13.

58 Carl Schmitt, *Politische Theologie II*, Berlin: Duncker and Humblot, 1970: 101n, quoted in Blumenberg, *The Legitimacy of the Modern Age*, p. 94.

59 Schmitt, *Political Theology*, 37.

60 Gerschon Weiler, *From Absolutism to Totalitarianism*, Durango, Colo.: Hollowbrook Publishing, 1994: 47.

61 Dews, *Logics of Disintegration*, 179-80.

62 Jurgen Habermas, *The Philosophical Discourse of Modernity*, Cambridge, MA: MIT Press, 1987, trans. by Fredrick Lawrence, 96.

63 Schmitt, *Political Theology*, 12.

64 Samuel Weber, "Taking Exception to Decision: Walter Benjamin and Carl Schmitt," *Diacritics*, Fall–Winter, 1992: 10.

65 Ibid., 10.

66 Claude Lefort, *Democracy and Political Theory*, Minneapolis: University of Minnesota Press, 1988: 4.

67 Wolfgang Mommsen, "Max Weber's Political Sociology and His Philosophy of World History", *International Social Science Journal*, vol. 17, no. 1, 1965: 36.

68 Ibid., 41. Emphasis added.

69 Walter Benjamin, *The Origin of German Tragic Drama*, London: NLB, 1977: 88.

70 Weber, "Taking Exception to Decision," 16.

71 Ibid., 15. Emphasis added.

72 Ibid., 16.

73 Jayant Lele, "The *Bhakti* Movement in India: A Critical Introduction," *Journal of Asian and African Studies*, vol, 15, no. 1-2, 1980.

74 Jean Bodin, *Les Six livres de la République*, Paris, 1578: 114, as cited in Perry Anderson, *Lineages of the Absolutist State*, London: Verso, 1979: 50.

75 Anderson, *Lineages of the Absolutist State*, 50.

76 Ibid., 16, 49–51. The same tensions also existed in Machiavelli and Hobbes.

77 Habermas, *The Structural Transformation of the Public Sphere*, Cambridge, MA: MIT Press, 1989: 28.

78 Ibid., 81.

79 Mouffe, *The Return of the Political*, 105.

80 Ibid., 127.

81 Ibid., 2 and 127. Mouffe criticises the political theorist Joseph Raz for this, see Joseph Raz, *The Morality of Freedom*, Oxford: Clarendon Press and New York: Oxford University Press, 1986.

82 Ibid., 115.

83 Schmitt, *The Crisis of Parliamentary Democracies*, 35. Schmitt could not say otherwise. the political (which liberalism could attempt to but never succeed in negating) rested on a recognition that there *were* no universally valid norms that governed politics; his conservative, anti-liberal bias for order involved precisely a decisionist resolution of this problem.

84 Mouffe, *The Return of the Political*, 129.

85 Ibid., 131.

86 Ibid., 99.

87 Ibid., 129.

88 Ibid., 128.

89 Of course, like most post-structuralists, Mouffe cannot banish rationality entirely:

> It is agreed today that we need to broaden the concept of rationality to make room for the "reasonable" and the "plausible" and to recognize the existence of multiple forms of rationality. Such ideas are crucial to the concept of a radical democracy in which judgement plays a fundamental role that must be conceptualised appropriately so as to avoid the false dilemmas between, on the one hand, the existence of some universal criterion and, on the other, the rule of arbitrariness. That a question remains unanswerable by science or that it does not attain the status of a truth that can be demonstrated does not mean that a reasonable opinion cannot be formed about it or that it cannot be an opportunity for a rational choice. (Ibid., 14.)

Of course, Mouffe would be hard put to find anyone with a consistent belief that political practice can be based on "scientific certainty," if there be such a thing. The real questions are first, is it possible to have *any* rationality that does not oppose general criteria to arbitrariness? And second, if forms of rationality can, and, in her scheme, are expected to, play a role in the practice of politics, why are they banished from the arena of the basis of the democratic order?

90 Ibid., 18. Emphasis added.

91 Ibid., 110.

92 Nietzsche, quoted in Tracy Strong, *Friedrich Nietzsche and the Politics of Transfiguration*, Berkeley: University of California Press, 1975: 150.

93 Mouffe, *The Return of the Political*, 109.

94 Holmes, *The Anatomy of Anti-Liberalism*, 270n30.

95 Ibid.

Incredulity and Poetic Justice: Accounting for Postmodern Accounts

ELEANOR MACDONALD

Postmodernism, states Lyotard, is incredulity toward metanarratives. And, under the rubric of postmodern definitions and exegesis, we find not only this loss of faith but a critique of theory more generally – of theoretical approaches to historical and social structure, of the theoretical grounding of ethics in truth, and of the relationship of theory to its objects. In light of this postmodern critique of theory, what are we to make of the fact that postmodern theorists go on theorizing? Does all this theorizing about the apparent impossibility of theory indicate a deliberate self-contradiction, a flouting of the theoretical demand for coherency and consistency? Does it then become a way to mark the failure of postmodern theory as theory? Or does it betoken some new success in eluding old theoretical prescriptions in favour of some more appropriate relationship of theory to its objects?

More specifically I seek to examine the issue of what can be learned from the numerous postmodern writings that self-reflexively theorize about postmodern theory itself and that, in so doing, situate postmodern theory in the present, as symptom of, corollary of, and indicative of the present – those writings that, further, evidently remark on that relationship in unmistakably ethical tones. One is left wondering how to describe, let alone analyze, the kind of account that postmodern theory makes; or to ask, in this theoretical strategy of ambivalence, paradox, and self-contradiction, on what do such accounts rest. In short, what sort of accountability is operative in postmodern accounts?

The ambivalences of postmodern theory take on special import when we look at the political and strategic aspects of their commentaries on the present. If these theorists are, as they appear to be in some portion of their work, engaged social theorists, then what kind of role does their theory play not only in accounting for the present but in making some kind of intervention into it? To what degree, to play on words here (in typically postmodern fashion) are they accountable to the present? (I am thinking here, for example, of Derrida's controversial commentaries on such things as South African politics, European unification, and nuclear war, Baudrillard's even more controversial commentaries on the Gulf War, on the contrast between American and European cultures, on sexual politics, of Lyotard's commentary on the growth of technology, and so forth.)

This interrogation of the "accountability of postmodern accounts" is significant within the ongoing debate about the relationship of postmodern theory to progressive social theory. Despite many trenchant left-wing critiques of postmodern approaches, it is fair to say that many on the left have found, in postmodern theory, some ability to address gaps or problems with theoretical models whose scope or explanatory frameworks have seemed too narrow or limited. There is, in the turn to postmodernism, a hope that it holds some means for looking at what historical materialism and political economy traditionally have not: questions around space, difference, recognition of the Other; and the appeal of complexity in theory that moves away from analyses based on class (strictly) or economics (overly).

POSTMODERN THEORETICAL ACCOUNTS OF THE PRESENT

To give some sense of the range of critical approaches and sensibilities within the broad framework of postmodern theory, it is helpful to examine the work of several theorists. To this end, I have chosen three authors: Jacques Derrida, Jean-Francois Lyotard, and Jean Baudrillard. The brief overview provided focuses on the way in which each "gives an account" of the present, and on the kind of "account" that each gives. In this, the question of what constitutes an "account" is necessarily raised, and with it the question of "accountability."

It is necessary, prior to moving into an account of these theorists, to state certain caveats, principally about who receives the label of "postmodern" theorist. In part, my approach defines the category in terms of the argument that I set out to make: defining postmodern theory is itself a certain way of making accounts. More broadly speaking, these theorists, despite their differences from each other, and despite the changing agenda of their projects, have in common a critique of nominalist approaches to language, of rationalist approaches to ethics, and of the dissemblance of power in Enlightenment appeals to truth, reason, and historical progress as intrinsic to the theoretical project.

Derrida

Derrida's work is often accused of being among the most abstract of the postmodern theorists. His study of language is the source of much of its abstract expression. In Derrida's theory, language masks what it actually is. The referential appearance of language – the appearance that words refer directly to things – disguises the arbitrary relationship between words and things. The connection that "actually exists" is one Derrida describes as "différance" – a neologism coined by Derrida to describe how meaning is never a property of language or of objects, but is rather the result of constant deferral or differentiation of meaning. Meaning is always in process, and never actually occurs, despite its appearance as inherent in the event or object.[1]

In much of his work, Derrida demonstrates the impact of this deconstructive approach on major texts of philosophy and literature – in part, showing how arbitrary the distinction is, for example, between the two, between what is rhetoric and what is philosophy, between what is considered fiction or non-fiction. He undoes the dominant interpretations of various philosophers by demonstrating the ambivalence of hinged terms, the arbitrary nature of tropes and metaphors, and the contradictory stories that can be spun out of different interpretations of a footnote or a translation.[2]

Because of this quality of his work, deconstruction has often been taken as purely abstract – as a set of elaborate word games, bearing no relationship, particularly, to politics, to questions of context, to questions of the present. He has been read as a nihilist and a relativist – eschewing questions of the truth, in order to celebrate such notions as "undecidability," "supplementarity" and so forth. But there is another, profoundly political, aspect to the deconstructive project, to raising questions about what gets decided as "truth" or "knowledge," or how something like "identity" is formed and established.

In his article "No Apocalypse/Not Now" Derrida develops these questions in relation to the issue of nuclear war and the nuclear arms race.[3] In a convoluted and fascinating set of speculative arguments, Derrida describes how the "experts" on nuclear war cannot claim expertise – since nuclear war is something that, as he says, "has no referent." It is a great "undecidable" in language, because unlike most words or "signifiers," it does not have a known or knowable "referent." The referent – in this case all-out nuclear war – is non-existent, or its existence is purely at the level of the language that develops in reference to it.

Derrida then elaborates the implications of this, and other similar statements, (that nuclear war would be fought purely in the "name of the name," that it would be "remainderless," that what would be destroyed would be language and writing) in suggesting that because what is going to be lost, in a nuclear war, is all of human history, and because there are no "objective" experts, that the claims of "experts" in technology and science and the military must be exposed as "just another fiction." And because there are no experts on fiction, or rhetoric – because the undecidability of fiction is more obvious – the prospect of nuclear war – its lack of referent, as it were – creates "experts" out of all of us – something that we should claim and act upon.

One reading of this article, then, would be directly political, and would situate the deconstructive project as itself a democratic political project. Derrida sees nuclear war as the opportunity for increased democratic control over technology and science. As Derrida puts it, "nowhere has the dissociation between the place where competence is exercised and the place where the stakes are located ever seemed more rigorous, more dangerous, more catastrophic."[4] And yet, while this is the place where the stakes *seem* higher, it is this seeming that allows us to take the "essence of knowledge and techne itself, as socialization and de-socialization"[5] seriously. In other words, to embark on the project of deconstruction.

So, another relevant aspect of this is that Derrida also sees "nuclear reference" as what makes the understanding of "deconstruction" possible. Because, in understanding nuclear war, we can see language unhinged from its objects, we can see the play of rhetoric and language games, we can understand the limits of rationality, etc.

If we are bound and determined to speak in terms of reference, nuclear war is the only possible referent of any discourse and any experience that would share their condition with that of literature. If, according to a structuring hypothesis, a fantasy or phantasm, nuclear war is equivalent to the total destruction of the archive, if not of the human habitat, it becomes the absolute referent, the horizon and condition of all the others ... The only referent that is absolutely real is thus of the scope or a dimension of an absolute nuclear catastrophe that would irreversibly destroy the entire archive and all symbolic capacity ... This is the only absolute trace – effaceable, ineffaceable.[6]

To the democratic implications he locates in nuclear discourse, Derrida adds a historical dimension. The insight of deconstruction into the impossibility of reference is made possible by the threat of the nuclear destruction of all meaning, of all reference, of all archives.

"The hypothesis of this total destruction watches over deconstruction, it guides its footsteps; it becomes possible to recognize, in the light, so to speak, of that hypothesis, of that fantasy, of phantasm, the characteristic structures and historicity of the discourses, strategies, texts, or institutions to be deconstructed. That is why deconstruction, at least what is being advanced today in its name, belongs to the nuclear age."[7]

This political aspect of Derrida's work, the informing of his work and ideas by political questions, is also to be found in his book, *The Other Heading: Memories, Responses and Responsibilities*.[8] In this work, Derrida grapples with the issue of "identity" and its implications in the context of European unification.

Hope, fear and trembling are commensurate with the signs that are coming to us from everywhere in Europe, where, precisely in the name of identity, be it cultural or not, the worst violences, those that we recognize all too well without yet having thought them through, the crimes of xenophobia, racism, anti-Semitism, religious or nationalist fanaticism, are being unleashed, mixed up, mixed up with each other, but also, and there is nothing fortuitous in this, mixed in with the breath, with the respiration, with the very "spirit" of the promise.[9]

Derrida structures the long essay around the "cap" – meaning, variously, the "heading," the head or the extremity of the extreme, the aim or the end, the last, the final moment, or last legs, the "telos" of an "oriented, calculated, deliberate, voluntary movement, the directions of the 'captain.'"[10] In this choice of words, Derrida also makes use of the related "capital": in French, playing on both "la capitale" or the capital city of a country, and "le capital" or capital in capitalism.

The Other heading can imply a number of things – a change in direction or destination, a change in goals, an acknowledgment that there is an "Other."

Indeed it can mean to recall that there is another heading, the heading being not only ours but the other, not only that which we identify, calculate, and decide upon, but the *heading of the other*, before which we must respond, and which we must *remember, of which* we must *remind ourselves*, the heading of the other being perhaps the first condition of an identity or dandification that is not an ego-centrism destructive of oneself and the other.

But beyond our heading, it is necessary to recall ourselves not only to the *other heading*, and especially to the *heading of the other*, but also perhaps to the *other of the heading*, that is to say, to a relation of identity with the other, that no longer obeys the form, the sign, or the logic of the heading, nor even of the *anti-heading* – of beheading, of decapitation.[11]

Again, without being able to do full justice here to his argument, Derrida tries to show how the understanding of the creation of a new Europe raises questions of identity and difference that, if we maintain the traditional understanding of the name and of language's relation to its objects, inevitably limit the kind of political relations that could take place (and that would also likely lead to the kind of violence that takes place in the "name of the name").

We are speaking here with names (event, decision, responsibility, ethics, politics – Europe!) of "things" that can only exceed (and must exceed) the order of theoretical determination, of knowledge, certainty, judgement, and of statements in the form of "this is that," in other words, more generally and essentially, the order of the present or of presentation. Each time they are reduced to what they must exceed, error, recklessness, the unthought, and irresponsibility are given the so very presentable face of good conscience.[12]

To summarize, Derrida's work unambivalently demands of us that to think ethically is to think deconstructively. To engage meaningfully in the world, it is necessary to take apart the meanings that have been given to us – to discover their ambiguities and uncertainties, to allow for new meanings to emerge. Ironically, this new kind of "account" of the world is one that is made both increasingly necessary and increasingly possible by such current circumstances as the threat of nuclear war or the possibility of European unification. In each case, the event can only be understood by an account that destabilizes the meanings that these events superficially appear to have and that, as a result, provides for a different kind of "accounting," a progressive and democratic one.

Lyotard

In Lyotard's book, *The Postmodern Condition: A Report on Knowledge*,[13] throughout his discussion of the implications of technology on the reception and legitimation of knowledge, his thought is more directly linked to the idea of the "postmodern" present than Derrida's. In subsequent writings, Lyotard continued to work out the implications of technology and science for human thought. The periodization of the earlier work, the use of the label "postmodern," he confesses to have been an attempt to draw attention to something, but in a way that he regrets, because it makes it appear that the current "postmodern" condition is somehow divorced from, or unique in respect to, the problems of modernity.[14] Rather than focusing on the "postmodern" per se, his concern was with the ongoing question of legitimacy and the prospect of human emancipation in light of technological development and change. As with Derrida, accounting for these changes also requires new ways of making accounts.

My last observation concerns the question born of the spectacular introduction of what are called the new technologies into the production, diffusion, distribution and consumption of cultural commodities ... In my view, the noteworthy result of this is not, as Baudrillard thinks, the constitution of an immense network of simulacra. It seems to me that what is really disturbing is much more the importance assumed by the concept of the bit, the unit of information. When we're dealing with bits, there's no longer any question of free forms given here and now to sensibility and the imagination. On the contrary, they are units of information conceived by computer engineering and definable at all linguistic levels – lexical, syntactic, rhetorical and the rest. They are assembled into systems following a set of possibilities (a "menu") under the control of a programmer. So that the question posed by the new technologies to the idea of rewriting as expressed here could be: it being admitted that working through is above all the business of free imagination and that it demands the deployment of time between "not yet", "no longer" and "now", what can the use of the new technologies preserve or conserve of that? How can it still withdraw from the law of the concept, of recognition and prediction? For the moment, I shall content myself with the following reply: rewriting means resisting the writing of that supposed postmodernity.[15]

The Postmodern Condition concluded with a cry to "wage a war on totality," to be "witnesses to the unpresentable," to "activate the differences and save the honour of the name."[16] In this earlier work, Lyotard gave the name of "the postmodern" to this project – to what would be committed to the unpresentable, to what would resist the "nostalgia of the whole and the one." His work points to the loss of overarching systems that constitute a complete explanation, provide certainty and security, establish identity, and explain cause and effect. His fear was that even where this fact may have been recognized, as in the field of modern aesthetic practices, a "nostalgia for the absolute" still remains. According to the ethical imperative that informs his work, this nostalgia must be resisted; it boils down to a nostalgia for fascism, for the imposition of unity.

This concern continues in his critique of contemporary technology, in its effects in transforming human life, indeed forcing certain changes upon us, without any correlative basis for making the ethical judgments that would be requisite to these changes.

It is clear that with techno-science in its current state, it is a power to "put in series" that is at work on planet Earth, and that the human race is its vehicle much more than its beneficiary. The human race even has to "dehumanize" itself, in the sense that it is still a bio-cultural species, so as to rise to the new complexity, so as to become tele-graphic. The ethical problems raised by techno-science are there to prove that the question has already been raised ... More knowledge and power, yes – but why, no.[17]

In *The Differend: Phrases in Dispute*, Lyotard assesses the implications of this collapse of unity in knowledge.[18] According to Lyotard the "differend" is the recognition, with no attempt at a forced reconciliation, of the incommensurability of phrases. It appears in his work as the "ethical response," the alternative to modernity and technology's "scanning" of the world, the subjection of all things to the rigour of scientific pursuit. In his introduction to *The Differend*, he defines "the differend" and sets out the context of the present – a collapse of Western metaphysics – and the ethical stakes he sees as introduced in his argument. What characterizes this "just" thinking" is recognition of:

the "differend", the undecidable, the incommensurable, "a case of conflict, between (at least) two parties, that cannot be equitably resolved for lack of a rule of judgment applicable to both arguments. One side's legitimacy does not imply the other's lack of legitimacy. However, applying a single rule of judgment to both in order to settle their differend as though it were merely a litigation would wrong (at least) one of them (and both of them if neither side admits the rule).[19]

And the context in which the differend emerges as philosophical problem is summarized as:

"The linguistic turn" of Western philosophy ... and correlatively, the decline of universalist discourses (the metaphysical doctrines of modern times: narratives of progress, of socialism, of abundance, of knowledge). The weariness with regard to "theory" ... The time has come to philosophize.[20]

Lyotard further establishes what this alternative philosophy involves. He uses an essay of Freud's to distinguish between the effects of repetition, remembrance, and working through. As in psychoanalysis, it is "working through" that is required in order to achieve emancipation. Without the work of psychoanalytic theory, the analysand is stuck in repetition, or a remembrance that is doomed to repeat itself. Without philosophy, and without philosophy employing the technique of suspending the ills of the past, humanity is likely to continue to suffer from its overdependence on and faith in science, technological knowledge, and the concept.

Freud calls this attitude "free association". All it is is a way of linking one sentence with another without regard for the logical, ethical or aesthetic value of the link. You will ask me what relation this practice can have with rewriting modernity. I recall that in working through, the only guiding thread at one's disposal consists in sentiment or, better, in listening to a sentiment. A fragment of a sentence, a scrap of information, a word, come along. They are immediately linked with another "unit". No reasoning, no argument, no mediation. By proceeding in this way, one slowly approaches a scene, the scene of something. One describes it. One does not know what it is. One is sure only that it refers to some past, both furthest and nearest past, both one's own past and others' past. This lost time is not represented like in a picture, it is not even presented. It is what presents the elements of a picture, an impossible picture. Rewriting means registering these elements.[21]

This approach to reality is marked by a similar ethic to that of Derrida's. The practitioner/philosopher relinquishes modern attempts to master time, or to attain knowledge, in favour of a kind of thought that portrays the subject more accurately, more painfully, as one who is inherently divided and alone.[22] As with Derrida, the possibility for this more truthful and more just approach is increased by current technologies at the same time as it is made more essential. Both strive for a justice that is not analytic so much as it is poetic, an address to contemporary loss.

[By] contrast [to aesthetic pleasure] the patient's discourse or the analyst's listening is work, working through, "free" in its means but called by an end. This end is of course not knowledge, but the approach to a "truth" or a "real" which is ungraspable ... analytic work "motivated by an intolerable suffering which places the subject in a state of separation from itself.

Rewriting, as I mean it here, obviously concerns the anamnesis of the Thing. Not only that Thing that starts off a supposedly "individual" singularity, but of the Thing that haunts the "language", the tradition and the material with, against, and in which one writes. In this way rewriting comes under a problematic of the sublime as much as, and today more than, more obviously than, a problematic of the beautiful.[23]

Lyotard frames the political problem at the same time as an ethical and as an aesthetic one: what kind of freedom is possible, what kind of differences can be allowed to exist, and what kind of thinking or approach will permit them to be realized? If this can be realized, then it is only in an exercise of philosophy that continually questions itself and its legacy and that requires a conscious recovery of what is repressed or lost. And these questions necessarily and only fully emerge in the context of a technologically dynamic modernity in which all old habits of thought are being undercut and in which there is a constant danger of permitting the demands of scientific and technological change to run ethically unchecked, to put a stop to philosophy itself.

Baudrillard

Baudrillard's work reads as the most extreme of the "postmodern" accounts. Like Derrida, his work contains a critique of the dissembling quality of language. And like Lyotard, his work also focuses on the effects of technology in the present, although with rather different conclusions. Like both theorists, his analysis implies not only that the "present" has provoked our contemporary understanding of language, of knowledge, or of – in Baudrillard's case – value and, perhaps, the sign/the image and reality but also that the critiques proposed by these theorists demand a qualitatively different relationship between theory and its object, reality.

Baudrillard's "accounts" of the present often "shock" in their descriptive force. For example:

The Boy in the Bubble is a prefigurement of the future – of that total asepsis, that total extirpation of germs, which is the biological form of transparency. He epitomizes the kind of vacuum-sealed existence hitherto reserved for bacteria and particles in laboratories but not destined for us as, more and more, we are vacuum-pressed like records, vacuum-packed like deep-frozen foods and vacuum-enclosed for death as victims of fanatical therapeutic measures. That we think and reflect in a vacuum is demonstrated by the ubiquitousness of artificial intelligence.[24]

In any case we will suffer from this forced extroversion of all interiority, from this forced introjection of all exteriority which is implied by the categorical imperative of communication. Perhaps in this case one should apply metaphors drawn from pathology. If hysteria was the pathology of the exacerbated staging of the subject – of the theatrical and operational conversion of the body – and if paranoia was the pathology of organization – of the structuring of a rigid and jealous world – then today we have entered into a new form of schizophrenia – with the emergence of an immanent promiscuity and the perpetual interconnection of all information and communication networks. No more hysteria, or projective paranoia as such, but a state of terror which is characteristic of the schizophrenic, an over-proximity of all things, a foul promiscuity of all things which beleaguer and penetrate him, meeting with no resistance, and no halo, no aura, not even the aura of his own body protects him. In spite of himself the schizophrenic is open to everything and lives in the most extreme confusion. He is the obscene victim of the world's obscenity. The schizophrenic is not, as generally claimed, characterized by his loss of touch with reality, but by the absolute proximity to and total instantaneousness with things, this overexposure to the transparency of the world.[25]

Baudrillard's early critique of Marxism focused on a criticism of the centrality of exchange value in Marxist theory (and its concomitant substitution for use value). For Baudrillard, sign-value had already replaced the commodity (exchange-value) in terms of its function in society. Yet just as Marx's critique of the commodity betrays a kind of nostalgia for the "reality" of use-value, so did Baudrillard's theoretical substitution of sign-value suggest the possibility of a critical return to "the real," even if only through a convoluted recognition of the impact of the sign in producing its referent.[26]

In subsequent self-critique, Baudrillard reflected on his commentary on the development of "value" and introduced a new concept into the schema, that of "fractal value":

... let me introduce a new particle into the microphysics of simulacra. For after the natural, commodity, and structural stages of value comes the fractal stage. The first of these stages had a natural referent, and value developed on the basis of a natural use of the world. The second was founded on a general equivalence, and value developed by reference to a logic of the commodity. The third is governed by a code, and value develops here by reference to a set of models. At the fourth, the fractal (or viral, or radiant) stage of value, there is no point of reference at all, and value radiates in all directions, occupying all insterstices, without reference to anything whatsoever, by virtue of pure continuity. At the fractal stage there is no longer any equivalence, whether natural or general. Properly speaking there is now no law of value, merely a sort of epidemic of value, a sort of general metastasis of value, a haphazard proliferation and dispersal of value.[27]

It is clear that Baudrillard offers a quasi-historical account of this development, one in which the changes in value are related to a proliferation of technologies in which everything is indeterminate, circulation is incessant, and meanings proliferate to the point of meaninglessness.

At the same time, this is not an account that is designed to reproduce, or even to analyze, these circumstances. Baudrillard's critique of sign value was based, like Derrida's, on a critique of "denotation" that saw the denotative function of language as inherently ideological in its supporting the notion that there is "something outside the sign" – that the referent exists in some pure form to which language, if properly used, can attach itself.

Both this critique of sign value and the further introduction of the concept of fractal value raise fundamental questions for the role of any kind of theoretical account of reality. If the attempt in language to reflect and match reality is both presumptuous and artificial, if, moreover, the effects of thought remaining trapped within this artificial logic also has the effect of limiting one to what exists, then the only means to get beyond what exists, or the best kind of intervention one can make, is to seek to go beyond what exists in language – to deliberately, consciously, attempt to explode and expose the relationship between language and reality. In doing so, one hopefully escapes some of the detrimental effects of the language's dissemblance (appearance of referentiality); one also may (but only may; there are no guarantees) produce alternative effects (ones which the system is currently unable to incorporate or master).

Instead of attempting to achieve critical distance, Baudrillard attempts to achieve something like critical proximity – a collapse of objectivity, an aesthetic venture, an exaggeration of the effects of reality:

Once again, what is the point of saying that the world is ecstatic, that it is ironic, that the world is objective? It is those things, that's that. What is the point of saying that it is not? It is so anyway. What is the point of not saying it at all. What theory can do is to defy the world to be more: more objective, more ironic, more seductive, more real or more unreal, what else? It has meaning only in terms of this exorcism. The distance theory takes is not that of retreat, but that of exorcism. It thus takes on the power of a fatal sign, even more inexorable than reality, and which can perhaps protect us from this inexorable reality, this objectivity, from this brilliance of the world, whose indifference would enrage us if we were lucid.

Let us be Stoics: if the world is fatal, let us be more fatal than it. If it is indifferent, let us be more indifferent. We must conquer the world and seduce it through an indifference that is at least equal to the world's.[28]

This project of Baudrillard's, to change the world through deliberately changing our account of it, can perhaps be used to excuse some of his more outrageous statements – that the Gulf War did not exist (one of the better known), that we are all transsexuals, that the possibility for experiencing real catastrophe no longer exists, and so forth. They are not accounts in the proper sense, but are instead intended as political interventions, designed, like Derrida's and Lyotard's, to change what we take an account to be.

CRITIQUE: ACCOUNTING FOR
THE ACCOUNTS

There is ample evidence in each of these theorists' work that they consider their own theoretical work to be in response to and an account of the present. As such, each also presents an alternative to the historical materialist project of accounting for the present, and in some cases, for the presence of postmodern theory within it.[29] Postmodern theory, it would seem from the accounts, arises as an effect of material and social circumstances to which postmodern theory also offers itself as the ethical and political response.

Yet, as specific accounts of the present, Derrida, Lyotard, and Baudrillard's presentations tend to frustrate in their generalizations. While many have gestured to postmodern theory vaguely as a body of theory that is able to accommodate questions of difference and specificity, the accounts offer no prescription that allows one, for example, to sort out the nuances of how to research the subject in a way that does not impose unity or efface difference. There is no analysis of power that puts power in the hands of actors, or on a particular side of the equation. The analyses of language, thought, and appearance provided by each, in turn, suggest that we are likely caught in an endless and circular response to the dilemma.

So while situating themselves in the present, these theories, I think, work principally as commentary on the nature of theory itself and on the nature of the relationship between theory and context. They successfully raise the question of what it means to give an account, and in doing so, raise some frustrating and significant questions about what it means to be accountable. In fact, it is the intended ethical demands in their thought, provoking or motivating their approach to giving an account, that stand to criticize any other kind of accounting – any that would, for example, seek knowledge of reality in order to alter it.

According to these theorists, one cannot attempt to use an account as an understanding; any account is, in and of itself, an intervention. An account is itself a hope for "poetic justice," for insight into the impossibility of actual justice. The problem is that these theories appear to be limited to this – at the politics of giving account; of deconstruction for Derrida, of anamnestic "rewriting" for Lyotard, of poetic seduction or exorcism for Baudrillard. They circumscribe the possibilities for thought as intervention at the same time as they are sensitive to the need for theory as strategy.

And yet the theorists appear, as well, to contradict themselves, or at least to display an ambivalence in this approach. They do so in the very offering of analyses that locate thought in a describable present, one that, by virtue of technological change and concomitant changes in human relations, has made postmodern theory both possible and necessary as intervention. For Derrida, the increased possibility of deconstruction is a result of an analysis of the present in which certain factors (such as the growth of nuclear technology and the possibility of European unification and subsequent loss of political boundaries) increase the general mistrust of language's apparent transparency. Lyotard's enjoinment to rewriting as an ethical accounting is directly connected to his analysis of the historical loss of "meta-narratives" and to capitalism's encroachment on thought, alongside the growth of micro-technologies and their materialization of thought as computer bit. And Baudrillard's account of fractal value and the dispersal of all chains and orderings of value is premised on social and historical change as well, on the proliferation of communications technologies especially.

Ultimately, I think the source of this ambivalence is directly linked to the ethical problem of representation – of accounting (responsibly) for accounting (correctly). What the postmodern theorists are clear about is that all accounts are political. Their work raises the question of the politics of representation, of what it means to do what we necessarily do (represent the world), and of the ethical and strategic concerns that must arise when we do so. The ethical and strategic concerns that they raise are, too, ones with which historical materialist approaches need to be continually aware: concerns about the subject and what kinds of theoretical assumptions are made about unitary, solitary subjects; concerns about language and the effects of language in defining the objects of our thought; and concerns about power and our misapprehension of the forms in which power exists and the tyranny of many possible exercises of it.

The ambivalence itself, it seems, is strategic. The theoretical approaches are prophylactic in nature. Derrida's deconstruction, Lyotard's philosophy, or Baudrillard's exaggeration – each is a theoretical immunization against the greater risk: that one might believe in the ready possibility of reference, of justice, or of truth.

The unanswered questions remain and must remain unanswerable within the confines of the postmodern approach. Can postmodern poetic justice be translated into the terms of real justice, as measure or as impetus? And if not, what must this mean but the need, always implicit in postmodern thought, to move outside of postmodern theory in our efforts to understand and change the present?

NOTES

1 See Jacques Derrida, *Of Grammatology*, trans. by Gayatri Chakravorty Spivak, Baltimore: Johns Hopkins University Press, 1976.

2 See, for example, Derrida's book *Specters of Marx*, which reads Marx alongside Shakespeare, blurring the distinction of social science and literature. Jacques Derrida, *Specters of Marx: The State of the Debt, the Work of Mourning and the New International*, trans. Peggy Kamuf, New York and London: Routledge, 1994: 92.

3 Jacques Derrida, "No Apocalypse/Not Now (full speed ahead, seven missiles, seven missives)," *diacritics*, Summer 1994: 26.

4 Ibid., 22.

5 Ibid.

6 Ibid., 28.

7 Ibid.

8 Jacques Derrida, *The Other Heading: Reflections on Today's Europe*, trans. by Pascale-Anne Brault and Michael B. Naas, Bloomington and Indianapolis: Indiana University Press, 1992.

9 Ibid., 6.

10 Ibid., 14.

11 Ibid., 15.

12 Ibid., 81.

13 Jean-Francois Lyotard, *The Postmodern Condition: A Report on Knowledge*, trans. by Geoff Bennington and Brian Massumi, Minneapolis: University of Minnesota Press, 1982.

14 "I have myself used the term 'postmodern.' It was a slightly provocative way of placing (or displacing) into the limelight the debate about knowledge. Postmodernity is not a new age but the rewriting of some of the features claimed by modernity, and first of all modernity's claim to ground its legitimacy on the project of liberating humanity as a whole through science and technology." Jean Francois Lyotard, *The Inhuman*, trans. by Geoffrey Bennington and Rachel Bowlby, Stanford: Stanford University Press, 1991: 34.

15 Ibid., 34–5.

16 Lyotard, *The Postmodern Condition*, 82.

17 Ibid., 53.

18 Jean-Francois Lyotard, *The Differend: Phrases in Dispute*, trans. by Georges Van Den Abbeele, Minneapolis: University of Minnesota Press, 1988.

19 Ibid., xi.

20 Ibid., xii.

21 Lyotard, *The Inhuman*, 31.

22 "... the imagination gives the mind 'a lot to think', a lot more than does the conceptual work of the understanding. You see that this thesis is

related to the question of time I posed at the beginning – the aesthetic grasp of forms is only possible if one gives up all pretension to master time through a conceptual synthesis" (Ibid., 32).

23 Ibid., 33.

24 Jean Baudrillard, *The Transparency of Evil: Essays on Extreme Phenomena,* trans. by James Benedict, London and New York: Verso, 1993: 61.

25 Jean Baudrillard, *The Ecstasy of Communication*, trans. by Bernard and Caroline Schutz, edited by Sylvere Lotringer, Brooklyn, New York: Autonomedia, 1988: 26–7.

26 The temptation to criticize the signifier in the name of the signified (referent), to make of the "real" the ideal alternative to the formal play of signs, is congruent with what we have analyzed as the idealism of use value. The salvation of use value from the system of exchange value, without realizing that use value is a satellite system in solidarity with that of exchange value, is precisely the idealism and transcendental humanism of contents that we discover again in the attempt to rescue the signified (referent) from the terrorism of the signifier. The velleity of emancipating and liberating the "real" leaves intact the entire ideology of signification – just as the ideology of political economy is preserved *in toto* in the ideal autonomization of use value (in Jean Baudrillard, *For a Critique of the Political Economy of the Sign,* trans. by Charles Levin, St. Louis: Telos Press, 1981: 160).

27 Baudrillard, *The Transparency of Evil*, 5.

28 Baudrillard, "Why Theory?" in *Ecstacy of Communication*, 100–1.

29 See, for example, David Harvey, *The Condition of Postmodernity,* Oxford: Basil Blackwell, 1989; or Fredric Jameson, *Postmodernism, or the Cultural Logic of Late Capitalism*, Durham: Duke University Press, 1991.

Afterword

ABIGAIL B. BAKAN AND
ELEANOR MACDONALD

The articles in this volume speak persuasively of our contemporary need for a consistently critically engaged intellectual practice. Around us, in our investigations of countries like Britain or continents like Africa, in state policies, social movements, and the practices of international institutions, we witness complex and rapidly changing economic, political, cultural, and social practices and institutions. Whether we are considering the role of the state or the possibilities of democracy, the impact of globalization or the problematics of theoretical inquiry, we are humbled by the analytical challenges that face all our investigations. There are no easy formulas or simplistic solutions to the complicated and profound questions that our times present. At the same time, we are also struck at every turn by the necessity for that investigation. Our times are marked by environmental devastation and dramatic increases in poverty, inequality, and violent conflict. Critical political inquiry demands that we seek out the explanations and find workable solutions to these crises.

The preceding articles, inspired in no small part by the work of Colin Leys and intended as a tribute to his scholarship, are a contribution to this kind of critical undertaking. Through rigorous debate and conscientious attention to detail, we hope to provide an understanding of this world that brings into focus the changes that are necessary and the means through which that change is possible.

Abigail B. Bakan
Eleanor MacDonald
Editors

About the Authors

LAURIE ADKIN is associate professor in the Political Science Department and the Canadian Studies Programme at the University of Alberta in Edmonton, Canada. She is the author of "The Greening of a Red Union," in Franz Hartmann and Graham Todd (eds), *Space, Place and Nature: The Landscape of Canadian Political Economy*, University of Toronto Press, 1998; *The Politics of Sustainable Development: Citizens, Unions, and the Corporations*, Montreal and New York: Black Rose Books, 1997; "Ecological politics in Canada: Elements of a Strategy of Collective Action," in David V. J. Bell, L. Fawcett, R. Keil, and P. Penz (eds), *Political Ecology: Global and Local*, New York and London: Routledge, 1998; and "Ecology and Social Change: Towards a New Societal Paradigm," in Colin Leys and Marguerite Mendell (eds), *Culture and Social Change*, Montreal and New York: Black Rose Books, 1992.

ABIGAIL B. BAKAN is professor of Political Studies at Queen's University, Canada. Her publications include "Foreign Domestic Worker Policy in Canada and the Social Boundaries of Modern Citizenship," with Daiva Stasiulis, *Science and Society*, vol. 58, no. 1, Spring 1994; *Ideology and Class Conflict in Jamaica: the Politics of Rebellion* Montreal and Kingston: McGill-Queen's University Press, 1990; *Not One of the Family: Foreign Domestic Workers in Canada*, edited with Daiva Stasiulis, Toronto: University of Toronto Press, 1997; and *Imperial Power and Regional Trade: The Caribbean Basin Initiative*, co-edited with David Cox and Colin Leys, Waterloo, Ont.: published for the Canadian Corporation for Studies in Religion by Wilfrid Laurier University Press, 1993.

BRUCE BERMAN is professor of Political Studies at Queen's University, Canada, and is the author of "Only a Glancing Blow: Penrose on Artificial Intelligence," *Science and Culture*, no. 16, 1993; *Control & Crisis in Colonial Kenya: The Dialectic of Domination*, London: J. Currey, 1990; and, with John Lonsdale, *Unhappy Valley: Conflict in Kenya and Africa*, Athens, Ohio: Ohio University Press/James Currey, 1992. He has edited several volumes, including *African Capitalists in African Development*, with Colin Leys, Boulder, CO: Lynne Rienner Publishers, 1994; and *Africa and Eastern Europe: Crises and Transformations*, with Piotr Dutkiewicz, Kingston, Ont.: Queen's University, Centre for International Relations, 1993.

MANFRED BIENEFELD is professor at the School of Public Administration, Carleton University, Canada. He is the author of "The New World Order: Echoes of a New Imperialism," *Third World Quarterly*, vol. 15, no. 1, Spring, 1994; "Financial Deregulation: Disarming the Nation State," in Jane Jenson et al. (eds), *Production, Space, Identity: Political Economy Faces the 21st Century*, with Jane Jenson and Rianne Mahon, Toronto: Canadian Scholars' Press, 1993; and "Karl Polanyi and the Contradictions of the 1980s," in M. Mendell and D. Salee (eds), *The Legacy of Karl Polanyi*, New York: St. Martin's Press, 1991. He co-edited *Production, Space, Identity: Political Economy Faces the 21st Century*, with Jane Jenson and Rianne Mahon, Toronto: Canadian Scholars' Press, 1993.

ALEX CALLINICOS is professor of Politics at the University of York, UK. His publications include *Theories and Narratives: Reflections on the Philosophy of History*, Cambridge, UK: Polity Press, 1995; *Socialists and Trade Unions*, London: Bookmarks, 1995; *Imperialism*, London: Bookmarks, 1994; *Race and Class*, London: Bookmarks, 1993; and *Revenge of History Marxism and the East European Revolutions*, Cambridge, UK: Polity Press, 1991. He edited *Between Apartheid and Capitalism*, London: Bookmarks, 1992.

BONNIE CAMPBELL is professor of Political Science at the Université du Québec à Montréal and is the author of "Débats actuels sur la reconceptualisation de l'État par les organismes de financement multilatéraux et l'USAID," *Politique africaine: numéro thématique Besoin d'État*, no. 61, mars 1996; "L'Ajustement en Afrique à la lecture de l'expérience de la Côte d'Ivoire," *Canadian Journal of African Stud-*

ies/Revue canadienne des études africaines, vol. 29, no. 2, 1995. She has edited several volumes, including *Structural Adjustment in Africa*, with John Loxley, London: Macmillan Press, 1989; and *Political Dimensions of the International Debt Crisis*, London: Macmillan, 1989.

MICHAEL CHEGE is associate professor of Political Science and Director of the Center for African Studies at the University of Florida in Gainesville. His publications include "The Social Science Area Studies Controversy from the Continental African Standpoint," *Africa Today*, no. 44, April/June 1997; "Paradigms of Doom and the Development Management Crisis in Kenya," *Journal of Development Studies*, vol. 33, no. 4, April 1997; "Between Africa's Extremes," *Journal of Democracy*, no. 6, January 1995; "Sub-Saharan Africa: Underdevelopment's Last Stand," in Barbara Stallings (ed.), *Global Change, Regional Response: The New International Context of Development*, Cambridge: Cambridge University Press, 1995; and "Remembering Africa," *Foreign Affairs*, vol. 71, no. 1, 1992.

RADHIKA DESAI is associate professor with the Department of Political Science at the University of Victoria, Canada, and is the author of *Intellectuals and Socialism: "Social Democrats" and the British Labour Party*, London: Lawrence and Wishart, 1994; "Second Hand Dealers in Ideas: Think-Tanks and Thatcherite Hegemony," *New Left Review*, no. 203, January–February 1993; and "The New Right and Fundamentalism," in *Women: A Cultural Critique*, vol. 1, no. 1, April 1990.

LAUREN DOBELL is the author of *Diplomacy by All Means: Campaigning for Namibia, 1960–1991*, Basel: Schlettwein Publishing, 1998; and "Silence in Context: Truth and/or Reconciliation in Namibia," *JSAS*, vol. 23, no. 2, 1997.

PHIL GOLDMAN is assistant professor of Political Studies at Queen's University, Canada. He is the author of *Dimensions of Criminal Law*, with Toni Pickard, Toronto: Emond Montgomery, 1992; "Zundel and His Victims," *The Lizzard*, Canadian Law Society newsletter, 1987; and "Law, Ideology and Social Causality," *Queen's Law Journal*, no. 12, 1987.

BANU HELVACIOGLU is assistant professor of Political Science at Bilkent University in Ankara, Turkey, and is the author of "Allahu Ekber, We Are Turks: Yearning for a Different Homecoming at the

Periphery of Europe," *Third World Quarterly*, vol. 17, no. 3, 1996; "Once upon a Space, There Were Sieve-like Times: Historical Geographical Materialism; Evvel mekan icinde kalbur zamanlar icinde: Tarihi-cografi materyalizm," *Toplum ve Bilim/Science and Society*, 1994; and "The Thrills and Chills of Postmodernism: The Western Intellectual Vertigo," *Studies in Political Economy*, no. 38, Summer 1992.

ROBERT D. JESSOP is professor of Sociology at the University of Lancaster, UK. His publications include *State Theory: Putting the Capitalist State in Its Place*, Cambridge, UK: Polity Press, 1990; *Thatcherism : A Tale of Two Nations*, Cambridge, UK: Polity Press, 1988; and *Political Economy of Post-war Britain*, London: Basil Blackwell, 1988.

COLIN LEYS is professor emeritus at Queen's University, Canada. He is the author of *The End of Parliamentary Socialism: From New Left to New Labour*, with Leo Panitch, London: Verso, 1997; "The British Labour Party's Transition from Socialism to Capitalism," *The Socialist Register 1996*, London: Merlin Press, 1996; *The Rise and Fall of Development Theory*, London: James Currey, 1996; "The World, Society and the Individual," *Southern Africa Report* (SAR), vol. 11, no. 3, April, 1996; "A Radical Agenda for Britain," *New Left Review*, no. 212, July–August 1995; *Namibia's Liberation Struggle: The Two-Edged Sword*, with John Saul, London: J. Currey, 1995; "Confronting the African Tragedy," in *New Left Review*, no. 204, March–April, 1994; "Still a Question of Hegemony," *New Left Review*, no. 181, 1990; *Politics in Britain: From Labourism to Thatcherism*, London: Verso, 1989; "Thatcherism and British Manufacturing: A Question of Hegemony," *New Left Review*, no. 151, 1985; *Politics in Britain: An Introduction*, London: Hutchinson, 1983; and *Underdevelopment in Kenya*, Los Angeles and Berkeley: University of California Press, 1975. He has edited several volumes, including *African Capitalists in African Development*, with Bruce Berman, Boulder, CO: Lynne Rienner Publishers, 1994; and *Culture and Social Change: Social Movements in Quebec and Ontario*, with Marguerite Mendell, Montreal: Black Rose Books, 1992.

ELEANOR MACDONALD is associate professor of Political Studies at Queen's University, Canada. She is the author of "Vectors of Identity: Determination, Association and Intervention," in *Studies in Political Economy*, Fall 1998; "Critical Identities: Rethinking Feminism Through Transgender Politics," in *Atlantis: A Women's Studies Journal*, special issue on "Feminisms and Sexualities," Fall 1998; "The

Conceptual Practices of Power: A Feminist Sociology of Knowledge," *Canadian Journal of Political-Science/Revue Canadienne de Science Politique*, vol. 24, no. 2, June 1991; "The Trouble with Subjects: Feminism, Marxism and the Questions of Poststructuralism," *Studies in Political Economy*, vol. 35, Summer 1991.

MARGUERITE MENDELL is associate professor and vice-principal of the School of Community and Public Affairs at Concordia University, Canada. She is the author of "New Social Partnerships: Crisis Management or a New Social Contract?" in Vered Amit-Talai and Henri Lustiger-Thaler (eds), *Urban Fields: Subject, Locality and Practice*, Markham, Ont.: McLelland Stewart, 1994. She has edited several books, including *Culture and Social Change: Social Movements in Quebec and Ontario*, with Colin Leys, Montreal: Black Rose Books, 1992; and *The Legacy of Karl Polanyi: Market, State, and Society at the End of the Twentieth Century*, with Daniel Salée, New York: St. Martin's Press, 1991.

LEO PANITCH is professor of Political Science at York University, Canada, and is the author of "Globalisation and the State," in R. Miliband and Leo Panitch (eds), *Between Globalism and Nationalism, Socialist Register 1994*, London: Merlin Press, 1994; *The Assault on Trade Union Freedoms: From Wage Controls to Social Contract*, with Donald Swartz, revised and updated edition, Toronto: Garamond Press, 1993. He has edited several volumes, including *A Different Kind of State?: Popular Power and Democratic Administration*, with Gregory Albo and David Langille, Toronto: Oxford University Press, 1993; and *The Canadian State: Political Economy and Political Power*, Toronto and Buffalo: University of Toronto Press, 1986.

ANNE PHILLIPS is professor at the Gender Institute, London School of Economics and Political Science. She is the author of *Which Equalities Matter?*, Cambridge, UK: Polity Press,1999; *The Politics of Presence*, Oxford and New York: Clarendon Press, 1995; *Democracy and Difference*, Cambridge, UK: Polity Press, 1993; *Engendering Democracy*, Cambridge, UK: Polity Press, 1991; *The Enigma of Colonialism: British Policy in West Africa*, London: J. Currey, 1989. Her edited volumes include *Destabilizing Theory: Contemporary Feminist Debates*, with Michèle Barrett, Cambridge: Polity Press, 1992.

JOHN SAUL is professor of Political Science at York University, Canada, and is the author, with Colin Leys, of *Namibia's Liberation Struggle: The Two-edged Sword*, London: J. Currey, 1995; *Recolonization and Resistance: Southern Africa in the 1990s,* Toronto, Ont.: Between the Lines Press, 1993; *Socialist Ideology and the Struggle for Southern Africa,* Trenton, NJ: Africa World Press, 1990.